The Unforgettable Queens of Islam

In this landmark study, Shahla Haeri offers the extraordinary biographies of several Muslim women rulers and leaders who reached the apex of the political system of their times. Their stories illuminate the complex and challenging imperatives of dynastic succession, electoral competition, and the stunning success they achieved in medieval Yemen and India, and modern Pakistan and Indonesia. The written history of Islam and the Muslim world is overwhelmingly masculine, having largely ignored women and their contributions until well into the twentieth century. Religious and legal justifications have been systematically invoked to justify Muslim women's banishment from politics and public domains. Yet this patriarchal domination has not gone without serious challenges by women – sporadic and exceptional though their participation in the battle of succession has been. *The Unforgettable Queens of Islam* highlights the lives and legacies of a number of charismatic women engaged in fierce battles of succession, and their stories offer striking insights into the workings of political power in the Muslim world.

Shahla Haeri is Associate Professor of Anthropology and a former director of the Women's Studies Program at Boston University. She is the author of the pioneering ethnographic book *Law of Desire: Temporary Marriage in Shi'i Iran* (1989, 2014) on the unique Shi'a practice of temporary marriage in Iran and *No Shame for the Sun: Lives of Professional Pakistani Women* (2002). She is the producer and director of a video documentary on Iranian women presidential contenders entitled *Mrs. President: Women and Political Leadership in Iran* (2002). Haeri is the recipient of many grants and postdoctoral fellowships.

The Unforgettable Queens of Islam

Succession, Authority, Gender

Shahla Haeri

Boston University

CAMBRIDGE
UNIVERSITY PRESS

University Printing House, Cambridge CB2 8BS, United Kingdom

One Liberty Plaza, 20th Floor, New York, NY 10006, USA

477 Williamstown Road, Port Melbourne, VIC 3207, Australia

314–321, 3rd Floor, Plot 3, Splendor Forum, Jasola District Centre, New Delhi – 110025, India

79 Anson Road, #06–04/06, Singapore 079906

Cambridge University Press is part of the University of Cambridge.

It furthers the University's mission by disseminating knowledge in the pursuit of education, learning, and research at the highest international levels of excellence.

www.cambridge.org
Information on this title: www.cambridge.org/9781107123038
DOI: 10.1017/9781316389300

First published 2020

Printed in the United Kingdom by TJ International Ltd. Padstow Cornwall

A catalogue record for this publication is available from the British Library.

Library of Congress Cataloging-in-Publication Data
Names: Haeri, Shahla, author.
Title: The unforgettable queens of Islam / Shahla Haeri, Boston University.
Description: New York : Cambridge University Press, 2020. | Includes bibliographical references and index.
Identifiers: LCCN 2019041200 (print) | LCCN 2019041201 (ebook) | ISBN 9781107123038 (hardback) | ISBN 9781316389300 (ebook)
Subjects: LCSH: Queens – Islamic countries. | Islamic countries – Kings and rulers. | Islamic countries – History.
Classification: LCC DS35.64 .H34 2020 (print) | LCC DS35.64 (ebook) | DDC 920.720917/67–dc23
LC record available at https://lccn.loc.gov/2019041200
LC ebook record available at https://lccn.loc.gov/2019041201

ISBN 978-1-107-12303-8 Hardback
ISBN 978-1-107-55489-4 Paperback

به هیچ مبحث و دیباچه ای قضا ننوشت

برای مرد کمال و برای زن نقصان

Nowhere in the Preface has judgment been written

That man is perfect and woman deficient

Parvin Etesami, 1907–1941

For

Pouné & Parya

Yashar & Laili

Q-mars & Daniel

&

Reza

Contents

Figures

Preface

> From your world, I like three things: perfume, women, and prayer.
>
> Prophet Muhammad

The news was brief: Iranian women contesting the presidential election of 2001. The news was as shocking as it was novel. Who would have thought that of all the places in the world, the twenty-first century would be ushered in by women standing for election in the Islamic Republic of Iran! This was news like no other coming out of Iran at the time. Here in Boston I expected to read the headlines in the *New York Times*, watch it on CNN, and hear it on National Public Radio. Alas, the American media and press hardly took notice. If it had been a case of "[dis]honor killing," I thought, media coverage would have been probably extensive. But not professional, middle-class, veiled Muslim women challenging the presidential election in Iran, and eager to assume political authority. The *New York Times* included but a passing reference in the last paragraph of a short article to "two women" among the forty or so male contenders, noting that all of them were rejected by the Guardian Council (MacFarquhar 2001).[1] Little was said about Iranian women presidential contenders, and few people heard about them. The news of who these women were was apparently not deemed "fit to print," nor did it fit the dominant Orientalist and colonial narrative of "Muslim women": veiled, victimized, oppressed, and passive, languishing in walled-in "harems." Ironically, nothing was said about them in other Muslim countries either, nor did they get much news coverage in Iran! By the time I went to Iran for my annual summer visit, much to my astonishment, I discovered that not two but forty-seven educated, middle-class, professional women from all over the country had actually filed their application with the Interior Ministry, determined to stand for the presidential election.

For well over a decade, I have been fascinated by the unprecedented and paradoxical emergence of large numbers of Muslim women as

---

[1] www.nytimes.com/2001/05/05/world/iran-s-president-seeks-new-term-vowing-more-political-change.html.

political agents. From their impressive mobilization and participation in the Iranian revolution of 1979 and the presidential election of 2009 to their vocal presence in North Africa and the "Arab Spring,"[2] to the Voice of Concerned Mothers in Indonesia, women are joining their voices and energetically mobilizing their resources to participate in the public domain in ever-increasing numbers. Brief though the Arab Spring seems to have been, it has already engendered a more vocal gender reflexivity and rekindled political awakening in the region. Increasingly educated and well informed, women have shed the age-old cloak of cultural inhibitions and have challenged the rigid patriarchal constructions of gender (in)justice, political/legal inequalities, and gender hierarchy. They come from all walks of life, backgrounds, beliefs, classes, and strata, religious or secular, and are determined to have a seat at the political table, one that has long been so jealously monopolized by men. Caught between a rock and a hard place, between the enduring Western Orientalist narratives and the lasting indigenous misogynist policies, "Muslim women" have a delicate balancing act to perform. Not wishing to feed the tired universalized colonial narrative of victimized and passive "Muslim women," nor willing to suffer the intolerant "fundamentalist" and "essentialist" discourse of "Islamists" in their own home countries, women activists and scholars of all backgrounds have shown considerable awareness of and reflexivity to local and global political dynamics. They have questioned the male domination of political authority and monopoly of sacred knowledge and have challenged men on both fronts, though more successfully in the latter. Unwilling to subordinate their piety and devotion to misogynist "orthodoxies," women scholars of Islam have pursued a two-pronged strategy. First, to retrieve from the recesses of historical neglect the names and biographies of women who contributed to religious knowledge and gained religious authority; and second, to pursue and develop a "feminist theology," based on a modern rereading of the Quranic revelations: one that is egalitarian, tolerant, and inclusive.[3] They have been equally critical of the essentialist Orientalist stereotyping of "Muslim women" as victimized, needing "saving" by colonial and Western powers (Abu-Lughod 2013). Women's political authority, however, has received less

---

[2] Attributing the adjective "spring" to the Arab uprising of 2011 has become contested. See a series of commentaries and exchanges in the Sociology of Islam list electronic posting (September 14, 2018). Retrieved from Sociology of Islam, sociology_of_islam-g@vt.edu. I continue to use "Arab Spring" because of its identification with these particular uprisings.

[3] See, for a few examples, the work of Asma Afsaruddin, Leila Ahmed, Kecia Ali, Laleh Bakhtiar, Asma Barlas, Riffat Hassan, Mervat Hatem, Aziza Al-Hibri, Ayesha Hidayatullah, Amira Sonbol, D. Spellberg, Barbara Stowasser, and Amina Wadud.

systematic attention[4]; it is highly contested and fraught with tensions and contradictions, and has faced a much tougher patriarchal challenge from within the Muslim world. Meaningful political authority and representation at the highest echelons of the state is still far out of women's reach, and not just in the Muslim world. But the rough political terrains have not stopped women from mobilizing and organizing in the Muslim world, and beyond.

My interest was initially sparked by the election of Benazir Bhutto in Pakistan in 1988, the first democratically elected woman prime minister in the Muslim world, and was further piqued by Mrs. Shahid Salis, the tightly veiled, highly educated, and articulate woman who told me that she saw no incompatibility between being a woman and becoming the president of a country such as the Islamic Republic of Iran. She was one of the six presidential contenders whom I interviewed for my video documentary, *Mrs. President: Women and Political Leadership in Iran* (2002).[5] She underscored the legitimacy – indeed, the necessity – of her run for the presidency in Iran, first and foremost on the basis of the Quranic revelations regarding the sovereignty of the Queen of Sheba (27:20–44). "We have [in the Qur'an]," she said, "a country where a woman called Queen of Sheba was ruling. This is very important for us." She continued, "Historically, women have played fundamental roles, *naqsh-i asli*," in the lives of male religious and political leaders (19:14–54). She stressed the role mothers and wives played in the lives of Abrahamic prophets, including Muhammad, Jesus, and Moses. Mrs. Shahid Salis emphasized the indispensable financial assistance and emotional support Khadija, the Prophet's first wife, provided him, and underscored the special attention the Prophet lavished on his daughter Fatima by taking her to public places. Her remarks sounded well thought out and strategic to me. She was determined to engage in the "serious games" (Ortner 2006) of political competition in Iran. Knowledgeable about the tenor of religious discourse of the Islamic Republic of Iran, Shahid Salis supported her run for the presidency by systematically quoting Quranic verses or Prophetic hadiths – much as the current male political and religious elite do in Iran. She used similar religious/political logic to counter the patriarchal elite's justification of restricting women's access to the political domain.

Ten years later, in another Muslim society, the 2011 Nobel Peace Prize winner Tawakkol Abdel-Salam Karman[6] also legitimated her political activism by reaching back in history to trace her noble genealogy to the

---

[4] See Jalalzai (2008, 207).   [5] http://ffh.films.com/search.aspx?q=shahla+haeri.
[6] http://nobelwomensinitiative.org/meet-the-laureates/tawakkol-karman/#sthash.cNv2Dn OV.dpuf.

Queen of Sheba *and* to Queen Arwa, locally known as the "Little Queen of Sheba" (the subjects of Chapters 1 and 3, respectively). Wrapped in her colorful headscarf, Karman addressed the Nobel Committee in Sweden with eloquence:

And here I am now . . . coming from the land of Yemen, the Yemen of wisdom and ancient civilizations, the Yemen of more than five thousand years of long history, the great Kingdom of Sheba, the Yemen of the two queens, Bilqis[7] and Arwa, the Yemen which is currently experiencing the greatest and the most powerful and the largest eruption of Arab spring revolution.

She defended the values of the "Arab spring" and voiced her dream of having a peaceful, democratic country, one that would function under the rule of law.[8] Karman's call for democracy, rule of law, and orderly transfer of power in Yemen echoed that of her countrywoman Dr. Faufa Hassan al-Sharqi, a candidate for a seat in the parliament. Some twenty years earlier and in one of her campaign speeches in the capital city of San'a al-Sharqi also connected women's political activism in Yemen to the legendary Queen of Sheba and the eleventh-century Queen Arwa (Warburton 1993, 12).

Informed on their history and confident of their objectives, these women exhibited political acumen and determination in their quest to reappropriate the unforgettable queens of Islam. I intend to accompany them on this quest. I want to bring to life stories of legendary and historical women rulers from medieval to modern times, those formidable women leaders who have reached the apex of authority and power in patriarchal Muslim societies. As I embarked on this project, however, I have at times wondered why the Quranic revelations regarding the sovereignty of the Queen of Sheba, whose transcultural story has historically enjoyed transnational popularity, have not been systematically appropriated by her Muslim daughters to claim political authority and leadership – just as Mrs. Shahid Salis was doing in Iran. Why and how was the queen's bond with her worldly daughters severed, metaphorically speaking? What kind of sacred justification or secular logic has been employed to justify Muslim women's banishment from political domains? Yet this patriarchal history has not proceeded without challenges by women, sporadic and exceptional though their participation in the political "games of thrones" has been. Succession, be it to the throne in the legendary land of Saba, medieval Yemen and India, or modern Pakistan

---

[7] Bilqis is the popular name for the Queen of Sheba (see Chapter 1).

[8] www.nobelprize.org/prizes/peace/2011/karman/26163-tawakkol-karman-nobel-lecture-2 011/. Sadly, foreign intervention and frequent bombing is rapidly destroying the Yemini people and their ancient civilization.

and Indonesia, has almost always been contested, whether through dynastic ties or electoral procedures.

This book is about gendering the history of sovereignty and political authority in the Muslim world by highlighting the lives of Muslim women leaders who have contested rules of dynastic and political power to become sovereigns in their highly patriarchal societies.[9] How did women rulers achieve such feats? What sociopolitical structures, cultural mechanisms, and personal qualities enabled them to realize their objectives? In talking about women and political authority, however, I am mindful that women have always wielded power – in the sense of influencing others' behavior – but often from behind the throne. Women have, throughout history, lived with men of power and have influenced them and exerted power over them. Indeed, there are more examples of women swaying the course of a society's events through their sons, husbands, and fathers than women who have actually worn the crown.[10] My interest in this book is with women at the forefront of the political scene, women who have engaged the existing structures of power and authority and have overcome objections and obstacles to become political leaders in medieval Egypt, Yemen, and India, or in modern Pakistan, Bangladesh, and Indonesia.

The written history of Islam and the Muslim world, in all its geographical breadth and layers of cultural diversity and complexity, represent an overwhelmingly masculine history, one that has by and large ignored women and their sociocultural and political contributions – at least until well into the twentieth century. Yet while the written history has assiduously ignored women, if not actively forgotten them, the oral history of the region and its folklore have given a prominent place to its womenfolk and their ingenuity. I am referring to the enchanting stories of *The Thousand and One Nights* that bring women's intelligence and agency to life, in their kaleidoscopic complexities, colorfulness, and intrigues.

I take a long-term ethnohistorical view of Muslim women's paths to power, contextualized within a cross-cultural anthropological perspective. Presently, with Muslim women's mobilization in the public domain and their demand for political representation and leadership, a book on medieval and modern Muslim women who have actually occupied the position of queens, sultans, and prime ministers is timely – if not overdue. A major goal of this book is thus to make visible aspects of Islamic history and Muslim women's political lives and leadership unknown to a vast

---

[9] For a description of the specificities of patriarchy in the Middle East, see Joseph and Slyomovics (2001).
[10] For two excellent monographs on such women, see Peirce (2017) and Lal (2018).

number of people, including many Muslims themselves. Muslim women's paths to power depend on a multiplicity of factors, including dynastic ties and descent, marriage and political alliances, the presence or absence of competent and viable male heirs, ethnicity and race, and the dynamics of the relation between the ruling patriarch and the religious establishment. They also depend on women's own personal resourcefulness, ambition, and charisma, and on their political acumen to patronize networks of the palace and popular support. In modern times, succession and transfer of power depend principally on the constitution, public support, and the ballot box – though dynastic ties always help. Political rivalry and battles of succession, however, may be no less intense – they may even be deadly – as I discuss in Chapters 5 and 6.

Daniel Varisco finds anthropologists "guilty of writing almost exclusively for, and often against, themselves" (2018, 2), thus remaining unknown among a wider readership. I wish to avoid falling into that category. I have tried to write this book on Muslim women rulers and political leaders in such a manner that would appeal to a wider audience and find a larger readership, particularly among students and young people. Last year, I had a chance to discuss parts of this book with my advanced undergraduate and graduate students at Boston University, some of whom were from the Muslim world. They were mesmerized to learn about women leaders and rulers, and almost without exception expressed surprise that they had not heard about them before.[11] Why was it, they repeatedly commented, that the images of Muslim women they see around them – whether in their own home countries or abroad – are often so woefully misguided. I hope this book addresses some of their concerns, satisfies their inquisitive minds, and quenches their thirst for knowledge about some remarkable Muslim women who have achieved political authority and left indelible marks on the history of the Muslim world.

---

[11] The class' final project was called "Adopt a Queen." Students were required to write a research paper about a Muslim queen from any historical period and continent. A majority of them told me how much they learned doing the research and gained new understanding of challenges of authority faced by women in their societies and cultures.

Acknowledgments

I have benefited enormously from the existing – and rapidly growing – work done by scholars of Islam, Muslim, and non-Muslim. My intellectual debt to this scholarship is huge. Knowledge is not only accumulative, it is also shared. As scholars, we stand to benefit from the knowledge produced by our predecessors as well as by our contemporaries, even as we wish to differentiate our work from that of others and to underline its originality. I wish to join the many indigenous and international scholars of Islam and activists who have made it their objective to listen to the echoes of Muslim women's voices from the past and the present – to retrieve their political history, render them visible, and make stories of their lives accessible to a larger readership. A heartfelt collective thanks to all.

Several grants and fellowships helped me launch this book project and to continue working on it. A postdoctoral fellowship at the Women's Studies in Religion Program at Harvard Divinity School (2005–2006) provided me with the perfect intellectual opportunity to think through my project on Muslim women's political authority. I am grateful to Ann Braude, the director of the WSRP, and to my cohorts Gannit Ankori, Constance Furey, Rosemary Carbine, and Jia Jinhua for their stimulating comments and contributions.

A Jeffery Henderson Senior Research Fellowship in the Humanities (2008–2009) from Boston University's Humanities Foundation further enabled me to conduct research on women's political agency and authority in Iran. I am very grateful for the opportunity.

A visiting fellowship at the Center for International and Regional Studies (CIRS), Georgetown University's School of Foreign Services in Doha, Qatar (2012) provided me with a welcoming environment to work further on my research. I am thankful for the generous hospitality accorded me by Mehran Kamrava, director of the Center, and his highly qualified staff, particularly Zahra Babar, the Associate Director for Research, John Crist, Suzi Mirgani, Flora Bayoud-Whitney, Nadia Talpur, and Elizabeth Wanucha.

My deep appreciation goes to the American Institute of Pakistan Studies for a short-term lecturing and research fellowship that enabled me to go to London, Pakistan, and India (2016) to conduct archival research and to interview close friends and colleagues of Benazir Bhutto. Before leaving for London, I interviewed Ambassador Peter Galbraith in Cambridge, to whom I owe a debt of gratitude. I would also like to thank him for introducing me to Sanam Bhutto and Victoria Schofield, sister and close friend of Benazir Bhutto, respectively. I met them both in London and talked with them at length. I acknowledge their help with sincere thanks. I am particularly grateful to Sanam Bhutto, with whom I spent several hours of intensive talks over two days, going over some very emotionally wrenching issues regarding her beloved sister, Benazir. While in London, I met Ambassador Shamsul Hassan, who generously gave of his time and shared his knowledge of Benazir Bhutto, her family, and her administration – many thanks to him.

I enjoyed the warm hospitality of my friends of many years, Sharan Tabari in London, and Victoria Haeri at Oxford. They hosted me graciously in their lovely homes while I was pursuing my interviews and research. Still in London, I was delighted to meet Delia Cortese and Simonetta Calderini at the Ismaili Institute. I had read their excellent book on the Fatimid women, and further benefited from our stimulating conversations. I thank them both, and also express my appreciation to Delia Cortese for sharing with me her unpublished paper on Sitt al-Mulk.

In Pakistan, where I have gone many times since 1987, I felt right back at "home," thanks to Nadeem Akhtar's impeccable arrangements for my lodging and transportation. I sought out old friends, and had long conversations with Durre Ahmad, Senator Aitzaz Ahsan, Asma Jahangir (whose untimely death in February of 2018 I mourn deeply), Ambassador Seyyda Abida Hussein, Naheed Khan and her husband Senator Safdar Abbasi. Their willingness to share their firsthand knowledge of the times they had spent with Benazir Bhutto was invaluable and I thank them all with much gratitude. I spent much time discussing the topic of my book with Kishwar Naheed and Ayesha Siddiqa, two of the remarkable women whom I had interviewed for my book on professional Pakistani women (2002) and whose friendship I have since continued to enjoy.

Several Pakistani friends read my chapter on Benazir Bhutto and provided much-appreciated commentary, including Durre Ahmad, Raza Rumi, Beena Sarwar, Tanvir Khan, and Masood Khan. I also had several constructive discussions with Najam Adil at Boston University. I am grateful to them all.

I was delighted to return to Delhi, and once again stay with Shahla Haidar, my namesake. Her continuous hospitality I cannot praise enough. I would also like to thank Sunil Kumar from Delhi University.

I am appreciative of the Indonesian attaché, Professor Dr. Ismunandar, who kindly responded to my inquiries and put me in touch with Dr. Lily Yulianti Farid and Professor Musdah Mulia, both of whom quickly responded to my questions. Dr. Yulianti Farid corresponded with me from Australia and very kindly sent me a copy of her dissertation, followed by further email exchanges and communications; my sincere appreciation to both of them. I thank my friend Mahnaz Afkhami, who introduced me to Siti Nurjanah, who has been a constant source of support. I have referred to her for many of my frequent inquiries regarding Indonesia. She has been ever so gracious and I am very grateful to her.

I have discussed my project with many friends and colleagues, most of whom have read one or another of the chapters and provided insightful comments. My ongoing thanks go to Kaveh Safa, who did not read any of my chapters, but his ideas are present in all of them. I have benefited greatly from our frequent long conversations and arguments. I would like to gratefully acknowledge Leila Ahmed, Lois Beck, Thomas Barfield, Christopher Candland, Farhad Daftary, Mary Harvey, Robert Hefner, Mary Elaine Hegland, Maryam S. Kafi, Farzaneh Milani, Fallou Ngom, Leslie Peirce, Robin Porteous, Eliz Sanasarian, Sunil Sharma, Abdul Karim Soroush, Margaret Studier, and Elise Young for their engaging conversations and valuable comments on different chapters of my book.

In Iran, I would like to thank my friend and colleague Soheila Alirezanejad and her talented graduate students, including Elham Rahmatabadi, Nafiseh Azad, Azar Darvish, and Sahar Khakpour, who attended a talk I gave on my book in Tehran during the summer of 2018 and provided excellent comments.

Marla Dale wins my gratitude for her timely and excellent editing of an earlier draft of this manuscript. I am grateful to my assistant Nasrin Afzali, who rendered the genealogical figures creatively and assisted with the bibliography.

Last but not least, I want to thank my students past and present, who are constant sources of inspiration for me. Lydia Barski is one of my bright undergraduate students and an early reader of the stories of my queens. She was eager to read my chapters and provided highly intelligent comments. Sekar Krisnauli is another bright student of mine who conducted searches in *The Jakarta Post* and translated some short articles and passages from Bahasa to English. Salwa Tareen and Justin Montes carried out literature and library research for me. To all of them a very warm thank you.

I have been particularly fortunate to have Maria Marsh, Daniel Brown, Robert Judkins, and Atifa Jiwa as my editors and contacts at Cambridge University Press. I could not have asked for a better team of experts and professionals. I want to express a heartfelt thanks to the four anonymous readers of my proposal, who recommended its publication, and the anonymous reviewer of my manuscript, who read it in its entirety and provided highly constructive comments and suggestions, which in the end made this book better and richer.

As always, the love of my husband, Walter (Rusty) Crump, my siblings Shirin, Shokoofeh, Mohammad Reza, and Niloofar, and my nieces and nephews to whom I have dedicated this book, sustained me emotionally and gave me the energy and strength to persist and to continue.

Abbreviations

AZO	Al-Zulfikar Organization
CIMC	Congress of the Indonesian Muslim Community
Golkar	The New Order Party
JI	Jamaat-e-Islami
ISI	Inter-Service Intelligence
JUP	Jamiat Ulema-e-Islam
MPR	People's Consultative Assembly
NU	Nahdlatul Ulama
PDI-P	Indonesian Democratic Party - Struggle
PKB	National Awakening Party
PLO	Palestine Liberation Organization
PPP	United Development Party
PPP	Pakistan People Party

Glossary

'adat	custom, tradition
'afarit (sing. *'ifrit)*	demons, supernatural creatures
abangan	a nominal or syncretic Javanese Muslim
'adil	just
amir	king, leader
amir ahkur	lord of the stable
amir hajib	military chamberlain
'arsh-i 'azim	mighty throne
aya/ayah	a verse in the Qur'an
Basra	a city in southern Iraq
Bay'a	pledge of loyalty
Begum	lady, honorific term of address in South Asia
benazir	without parallel, incomparable
chamcha	henchman, crony
Chihilgani	the forty slave devotees of Sultan Iltutmish
da'wa	mission
da'i	missionary
da'i mutlaq	supreme missionary with absolute authority
dam	breath
danishmand-guneh	quasi-intellectual, learned
dalang	puppeteer, storyteller
dupatta	a long rectangular scarf, an indispensable part of Pakistani dress
durbar	royal court
fitna	civil war, chaos
fuqaha	jurists
ghaba/qaba	long traditional male garment
ghairat	jealousy (primarily male), honor
ghulam	slave
Golkar	Suharto's New Order party
hadith	sayings and deeds attributed to the Prophet Muhammad, recorded over a century and half

	after his death. Hadiths constitute the second most important source of authority in Islam
hajib	cover, veil
halus	smooth, calm, harmony
hammam	bathhouse
harem	women's quarter
hazrat	majesty (honorific)
hikmat	wisdom
howdah	a seat or covered pavilion on the back of an elephant or camel
hudhud	hoopoe
hujja	the highest rank after the imam-caliph in the Ismaʿili-Shiʿi religious and political hierarchy
ibu	mother in Bahasa
idda	the four-month period of sexual abstinence obligatory for Muslim widows
ifk	"story of the lie"
ʿifrit	demon
iqtaʿ	the assignment of lands for a fixed value
ʿishrat	pleasure
jahiliyya	ignorance, i.e., of Islam
jinn	supernatural creature
kadhatona	the inner quarter in a royal palace where women lived in Indonesia
kaghzi pirhan	dyed garment
khalq	people, masses
kham	raw, inexperienced
khatib	public speaker
khatun	lady, princes, queen consort
khudavand-i jahan	Lord of the World
khunriz	blood thirsty
khulʿ	Islamic divorce initiated by wife
khutba	religious sermon
kulah	hat
labuhan	a purifying ritual
lahv va la ʿb	indulging in one's desires
lashkar kish	military leader
Limbuk	a female figure of Indonesian mythology
mamluk	slave
mastureh	chaste, covered, veiled

mbak	respectful term for older sister
mimbar bebas	free speech forum
mukhannisan (pl.)	castrated, effeminate men
mulahideh	apostate
muqti	holder of *iqta'*
mut'a	temporary marriage
naqsh-i asli	fundamental roles
namdar	famous, world renown
naskh	cancelled
Nijahid	a Yemenite tribe
parwarish	foster
Pathan	synonymous with Pashtun, an ethnic group in Afghanistan and Pakistan
punakawan	clown/servant
qaba	long traditional male garment
qaramatih	an Isma'ili offshoot
qadi	judge
qibla	direction of Muslim prayer toward Mecca
qaum	tribe, nation
qumus	envelope
Qur'an	Muslim holy book, the scripture; the highest source of authority
qurbat	proximity, favor
Qureish	the Prophet Muhammad's tribe in Mecca
ra'iyat parvar	guardian of people
reformasi	reformist
sahar	dawn
sahih	correct, authentic
Semar	a beloved mythical male character in Indonesia
shadgan	a safe space in the royal court
Shafi'ism	one of the four schools of Sunni law
shaheed	martyr
shihna	police magistrate
sijill	official letter
sunna	tradition, a way of life, tradition of the Prophet Muhammad
sura	a chapter in the Qur'an
talaq	Islamic divorce
tankah	coin
tavakkol	trust in God, surrender
Tayyibi Isma'ilism	a branch of Isma'ilism
'urf	custom, tradition

valide sultan	mother of the sultan
wahju	divine inspiration
wali	representative, guardian
Wayang	shadow puppet play
wazir	prime minister

Introduction
Games of Succession: Patriarchy, Power, Gender

The Unforgettable Queens of Islam is a book about Muslim women rulers, women who have contested rules of dynastic succession in medieval Yemen and India and stood for election in modern Pakistan and Indonesia. How did they achieve such feats? How could young Muslim women come to occupy the exalted office of the sultan in Delhi in medieval India, or be democratically elected prime minister in modern Pakistan? Did they contravene religious laws and moral orders to become rulers in their societies? What sociopolitical structures, cultural mechanisms, and personal qualities enabled them to realize their objectives? History provides us with many cases of powerful women – Muslim and non-Muslim – who influenced men of power (or men in general) to change the course of their relations, dynastic successions, and sociopolitical events.[1] My interest in this book is with women at the forefront of the political scene – women who have engaged with the existing structures of power and authority, overcoming institutional obstacles and individual objections to become ruling queens. Following the trajectory of the political ascent of Muslim women rulers, I explore four women's paths to political power and authority. But first, I lay out the broader historical contexts and theoretical frameworks of the book by discussing the diverging interpretations of revelation and tradition, the Qur'an and the hadith, regarding women and political authority. For that I tell the Quranic story of the Queen of Sheba and her Mighty Throne (Qur'an 27:20–45) and discuss the political leadership of Mother of the Faithful, *hazrat* 'A'isha[2] in the Battle of the Camel that occasioned the pronouncement of a Prophetic hadith.

As I contemplate the life stories of Muslim women political rulers from medieval to modern times, I recall an oft-repeated hadith on the subject allegedly attributed to the Prophet of Islam: "Never will succeed

---

[1] Shahrzad, the protagonist of *The Thousand and One Nights*, is a perfect example. For a study of variations of power, see Eric Wolfe (2001, 384–385).

[2] Muslims use the honorific prefix *hazrat* (Excellency) for exalted personalities such as 'A'isha. To prevent repetition, I refrain from doing so after the first mention.

such a nation as makes a woman their ruler."[3] Where this hadith came
from, and why? Contestation over leadership and the caliphate erupted
almost immediately after the Prophet Muhammad's death. His silence
regarding an heir – or not specifically nominating one – confronted the
nascent Muslim community with the dilemma of succession: was it to be
based on descent and blood kinship or on the consensus of the political
elite? By the time the Umayyad caliphs (661–750) consolidated power,
patrilineal dynastic succession had become hereditary.[4] The military
involvement of ʿAʾisha, the "beloved of Muhammad," in the battle of
succession played a crucial role in polarizing the community's sentiments during the reigns of the third and the fourth caliphs.[5] Her dramatic loss in the Battle of the Camel (see Chapter 2), in which she led
the opposition to the fourth caliph, ʿAli, allegedly occasioned the pronouncement of the above-mentioned hadith. It was not, however, until
almost two hundred years later that this hadith was "authenticated" by
the famed scholar and hadith collector Imam Bukhari (d. 870), who
subsequently included it in his compendium of "correct" (*sahih*)
hadith – despite the fact that it was a "singleton" and "weak" (i.e. not
corroborated by other companions and associates of the Prophet).[6]
Whether this is a "forged hadith" (Brown 2018) or the Prophet of
Islam actually said it has been debated in modern times by scholars,
including Mernissi (1991), Abou El Fadl (2001), Fadel (2011), and
Ibrahim (2016), and the debate continues on the web. Twelve centuries
later and in the waning years of the twentieth century, the same hadith
was retrieved from the recesses of history to challenge the democratic
victories of Benazir Bhutto in Pakistan (see Chapter 5) and Megawati
Sukarnoputri in Indonesia (see Chapter 6).

Yet I also recall that the Prophet of Islam had received divine revelations regarding the Queen of Sheba and her astute political leadership.
The Quranic Queen of Sheba is, as I describe in Chapter 1, the sovereign
of an idyllic and peaceful community to which God has denied neither
bounty nor riches. Above all, the queen is given a Mighty Throne (ʿarsh-i
ʿazim), representing the seat of her power and authority (Qurʾan 27:23).
Note that the Qurʾan uses the same term to describe God's celestial
throne, "God: there is no God but He, the Lord of the Mighty Throne

---

[3] https://sunnah.com/bukhari/92.

[4] Rather than giving both the Islamic and Christian dates simultaneously, I have opted to
cite only the latter. Suffice it to say that the Islamic calendar, the Hijri, begins with the
migration (*hijra*) of the Prophet Muhammad from Mecca to Medina in 622 CE.

[5] Brown defines caliph as meaning "succession" or "appointed representative," though it
generally refers to those delegated with supreme political authority (2018, 211).

[6] For a critique of al-Bukhari's recording of hadiths such as the above, see Mernissi (1991).

['arsh-i 'azim]" (27:26). Might we infer such meaningful parallelism as support for the legitimacy of the queen's sovereignty?[7]

For Muslims the Qur'an is divine and Quranic revelations constitute the supreme source of authority. Hadith, the recorded words of the Prophet Muhammad – collected and recorded almost two centuries after his death in the ninth and tenth centuries – form the second highest source of authority. Muslims believe that the Prophetic hadiths are divinely inspired.[8] In the course of time, the staggering number of unverified and unauthenticated hadiths collected and attributed to the Prophet Muhammad led medieval Muslim scholars to set in place mechanisms for the verification of the Prophetic hadith. Nonetheless, Muslims are far from unanimous on many hadiths, and Sunnis and Shi'ites each have their own corpus of "authenticated" hadiths, though much of them may overlap.[9] The hadith literature, the Tradition, has been a major source of Islamic law or shari'a in many contemporary Muslim societies, often incorporating some of the local customs, 'urf and 'adat, into the legal structure.

How are we to interpret the differences between these two supreme sources of authority regarding women and political authority in Islam, one supportive and the other opposed? Juxtaposing the Quranic support for women's sovereignty – or absence of opposition to it – with that of its purported prohibition in the Prophetic hadith, I revisit the story of the Queen of Sheba, and examine the sociopolitical circumstances that occasioned the recollection of the Prophetic hadith in order to contextualize women's chances of – or impediments to – political leadership. It is in the intersections of these two supreme sources of authority *and* the sociopolitical dynamics on the ground that I locate the prospects for and challenges to women's paths to political leadership, and Muslim exegetes' opposition to or ambivalence regarding women and political authority. I ask whether the objections to women's political leadership are to be sought in the divine revelations, the prophetic hadiths, or in the pragmatics of patriarchal sociopolitical structures.

The two overlapping themes that run through women's narratives of paths to power are succession and dynastic ties – be it to the throne in medieval times or to the office of president or prime minister in modern

---

[7] Tabari, in his interpretation of the meanings of the Qur'an, argues that the scripture explains the meanings of revelations itself. See also Lawrence (2006, 87, 91) and Barlas (2006, 261–262).

[8] Al-Shafi'i, the ninth-century legal theorist, declared that Muhammad's actions were divinely inspired based on the Quranic command to obey God and his Prophet (24:52). See Stowasser (1994, chapter 9).

[9] For an informative discussion on hadith, see Brown (2018).

times. Specifically, the thread that ties the chapters together is the dynamics of the father-daughter relationship (and sometimes that of husband and wife), what I have elsewhere called the "paradox of patriarchy" (2002). Succession to high office, as argued by Ortner, is a "serious game" (2006, 129; Goody 1966). It is also a deadly game and has primarily been played among men, usually devolving from father to son – but not necessarily to the first-born son. Islamic history, however, has recorded instances in which some women have also tried their hand at the games of succession. More often than not, they were supported by their father, who was in a position to promote his daughter – for a variety of personal, political, and emotional reasons – in the absence or at the expense of his sons. I situate women rulers' rise to power within three interrelated domains: kinship and marriage, patriarchal rules of succession, and individual women's personal charisma and popular appeal. Family is the heart of human society. It is the source of support and sustenance, but also a wellspring of resentment and competition. Across cultures, kinship and family relations are riddled with irresolvable paradoxes of love and hate, competition and cooperation, devotion and betrayal. Both men and women of the elite draw their power and authority from – or meet their ruin and demise within – their families. But particularly fraught is the relationship between royal fathers and sons, who are each in a structural position to deprive or dislodge the other from power.

I hope to demonstrate that women's restricted political role in the public arenas of Muslim-majority societies is ultimately the product of a multiplicity of local and historical factors, only one of which is religion, albeit an important one. However, with the radicalization of religion in the Muslim world – indeed, in much of the modern world[10] – the backlash to women's political activism has increased in tandem with women's demands for gender justice, legal equality, and fair political representation. As modern phenomena and movements, both the "feminists" and the "fundamentalists" are vying for political authority: one for inclusion and equal gender representation, and the other for exclusion and maintaining – even sanctifying – the male-dominated status quo.[11] The precariousness of such complex, multifaceted, and ongoing contests of

---

[10] See the six volumes of the Fundamentalism Project, edited by Martin Marty and Scott Appleby (1991–2004).

[11] "Fundamentalist" backlash against women's increasing political agency is not peculiar to the Muslim world. As a record number of women from diverse ethnic and racial backgrounds gained representation in the United States' Congress in 2018 and increased their political clout, more and more state legislatures enacted laws to restrict access to contraception and criminalize abortion. The most draconian step was taken by the all-male state government of Alabama that passed a law in May of 2019 banning all abortions and threatening abortion providers with ninety-nine years' imprisonment.

gender inequality as they unfold from Algeria to Indonesia are simultaneously inspiring and foreboding, as vividly visualized in the video documentary *Feminism Inshallah: A History of Arab Feminism* (2014).[12] Riveted by the unexpected twists and turns that gender dynamics are taking in the public domain in Egypt and Tunisia, Iran and Indonesia, we are alternately exhilarated by the expressions of gender unity and harmonious chants for equality and dignity, and demoralized by the painful demonstration of patriarchal brutality bent on denying education to young girls in Pakistan and Afghanistan. Now the gentle breath of the "Arab Spring" lifts our spirits and fills us with hopes of flourishing democracies from North Africa to South Asia; now the shameful cruelty of a woman's exposed body clad in a blue bra chokes us with anger (Amaria 2011). Now the indomitable spirit of the young Malala Yousafzai's determination to highlight the need for girls' education gives us hope for future generations of young girls – and boys – in Pakistan and Afghanistan;[13] now the fierce political competition and assassination of women political leaders in the same neighborhood expose state terror and structural violence in all their poignant ugliness. While patriarchs and patriarchal regimes are changing and adapting to the demands of modern times, "patriarchy" has never been an unchanging monolith and has not worked in cultural vacuums, locally or globally. Amina Wadud defines patriarchy, based on a discussion by Elisabeth Schussler-Fiorenza, as "a hegemonic presumption of dominance and superiority" that "extend[s] humanity to women only in functional juxtaposition" to male norms. It does not mean that all men dominate all women equally (Wadud 2006, 96).

A look at the recorded history of women rulers across the Muslim world reveals that a number of women have actually governed as queens in different societies and at various junctures in history, hailing primarily from South and Southeast Asia. Their authority and leadership indicate that however compelling dominant religious ideologies might be, specific local cultures and political traditions have led to outcomes that challenge and undermine such ideologies. This should, perhaps, not come as a surprise since the farther away societies are from the center of the Arab/Islamic world, the stronger is the influence of cultural traditions

---

[12] Created by Feriel Ben Mahmoud; distributed by Women Make Movies. Color (52 minutes).

[13] Born in Pakistan in 1997, Malala Yousafzai was seriously wounded in 2012 in an attack on her school bus by a member of the Taliban. She has since recovered and lives in England. She champions the cause of girls' education and was awarded the Nobel Peace Prize in 2014, becoming the youngest person to ever receive that honor (https://en .wikipedia.org/wiki/Malala_Yousafzai). See also *I Am Malala: The Girl Who Stood Up for Education and Was Shot by the Taliban* (2013).

and local customs (*'urf* and *'adat*) that pattern people's behavior and shape their sensibilities. In other words, a society's geographic location, ethnic identity, and political economy contribute significantly to patterning of gender hierarchy, roles, and relationships.

Culture, Ethnicity, Sensibility

A detailed discussion of the diversity of the changing social attitudes and sensibilities around expressions of women's political agency and gender relations, as Islam expanded on the world horizon, is beyond the scope of this introduction. Suffice it to say that as the political structure and administrative bureaucracies became more centralized in the Islamic caliphate in Baghdad, increasingly restrictive and negative attitudes were expressed toward women's autonomy, mobility, and political leadership. Comparing the representations of female companions of the Prophet in the biographies of chroniclers from the ninth to the fourteenth century, Asma Afsaruddin clearly demonstrates the rise in patriarchal gender negativities (2010a). Barbara Stowasser (1994, 104–118) similarly highlights the increasingly unfavorable – or conflicting – depiction of the lives and legacies of the wives of the Prophet Muhammad in the works of hadith collectors and biographers. In the farther East and Southeast Asia and in Central Asia, attitudes toward women, the extent of their autonomy, independence, and relationships were markedly different. As those communities came under the control of Turco-Mongolian domination, gender boundaries tended to become more fluid, particularly among the elite, whose womenfolk exerted authority and were accorded greater autonomy. Women often shared political leadership with their husbands or were supported in leadership positions by their fathers – sometimes even by their fathers-in-law. Despite the increasing influence of "Islam, Christianity and Buddhism over the last four centuries" in Southeast Asia, women's autonomy and authority remained undiminished (Khan 2009, 168). Sher Banu A. L. Khan describes the rulership of four successive generations of mothers, daughters, and sisters in the seventeenth-century Sultanate of Aceh, whose leadership was supported by both custom, *'adat*, and Islam (2009, 168). All four queens ruled "peacefully," and it was not until the leadership of the fourth and last queen, Kamalat Syah, that pressures were brought to bear upon the state by "a fatwa purportedly produced from the Shariff of Mekah [*sic*] stating that a woman cannot rule in Islam" (Khan 2009, 167). Shaharyar Khan (2000) likewise examines the political leadership of four consecutive generations of mothers and daughters in the nineteenth and early twentieth centuries in Bhopal,

India. Qudsiyya Begum, the first of the four, seized the opportunity to succeed her assassinated husband to become the regent of her infant daughter at the age of nineteen (r. 1819–1837). Qudsiyya's daughter, Sikandar Begum (1816–1868), grew up to become the second female ruler of Bhopal, whose reign partly overlapped with that of Queen Victoria of England (d. 1876).[14] Although pious, Qudsiyya abandoned veiling, arguing that it was not a sign of piety and virtue. When faced with opposition to her leadership from her male relatives based on the alleged Prophetic hadith, she countered that the Prophet Muhammad's wife "was a great role model for women and even took part in battles" (Preckel 2011; Khan 2000, 77). Her great-granddaughter, Sultanjahan Begum, on the other hand, took to veiling again and attended the coronation of King George of England in 1911 clad in her bejeweled white *burqa*. She abdicated her throne in 1926 on behalf of her son (Khan 2000).

Sporadic and scattered though it was, the thirteenth century is recorded as the most momentous period for women's political leadership in the annals of the medieval Islamic world. Three women in three different corners of the Muslim world took the reins of power (Lane-Poole 1903, 74). Most notable among them was Razia Sultan, the only female ruler of the Delhi Mamluk Sultanate, who ruled from 1236 to 1240. She is the subject of Chapter 4. Her near-contemporary Shajarat al-Durr (The Tree of Pearl) was another high-spirited Mamluk queen, who ruled Egypt in her own right for several months in 1250 before being ordered by the "short-sighted" caliph in Baghdad to forfeit the crown and marry (discussed in Chapter 4). Last is Abish Khatun (b. 1263), the ninth sovereign of the Persian dynasty of the Atabeks, also known as the Sulghurid dynasty (Lane-Poole 1903, 74). Her formidable mother, Terken Khatun,[15] ruled as the regent of her son, Abish's brother, in the southern province of Fars in Iran, which was under the hegemony of the Ilkhanid dynasty (1256–1353; Dalkesen 2007, 174). As a child Abish was sent to Shiraz, her native city, during the troubled period of Mongol supremacy in the region. She was still very young when her mother arranged her marriage (c. 1272) to an *ilkhan*, a Mongol prince, who ruled Fars in Abish's name until his death in 1282. Abish Khatun was caught in a revolt against the *ilkhan*s and sent to jail in Tabriz (northwest Iran) in 1286–1287, and executed subsequently in 1289. Abish was only twenty-six years old (Spuler 2011, 210).

---

[14] For an interesting and informative account of Sikandar Begum's memoir on her *hajj* pilgrimage to Mecca, see Lambert-Hurley (2008).

[15] Terken/Tarkan/Turkan Khatun means "the Queen of the Turks." Khatun is a general honorific used for Turco-Mongolian queen consorts.

All three sovereign queens hailed from Turco-Mongolian back-grounds, with Shajarat al-Durr and Razia owing "their position in part to Turkish slave officers, first-generation converts from the steppe, who originated in a society where women enjoyed wider latitude" (Jackson 1999, 189). All three queens had coins minted in their names and a *khutba* (official sermon) read in their honor, two criteria indicative of their supreme position as sovereigns (Mernissi 1994; Lambton 1987, 106–107; Dalkesen 2007, 173 ff.). All three came to power, nominal though it was in the case of Abish, through dynastic ties and marriage connections.

Succession, Primogeniture, Polygyny: "Law of Fratricide"

Whatever the system of succession, force is the final arbiter.

Goody (1966, 18)

Succession is always coveted and contested, be it in medieval India or in modern Pakistan, though the means through which it is expressed and achieved vary. Much is written about dynastic and electoral forms of succession and it is not possible to cover the issues and debates in one chapter. The following is a brief discussion of general patterns of succession in Islamic medieval royal courts and contemporary Muslim societies, incorporating arguments made by Goody (1966), Fletcher (1979–1980), Peirce (1993, 2017), McIntyre (2005), Barfield (2012), and Duindam (2018).

Dynastic Succession

"No system of succession," argues Jack Goody, "is completely automatic, even setting on one side the recurrent possibility of dethronement, abdication or usurpation" (1966, 13). Sometimes succession takes place through primogeniture and the orderly transition of power from father to son, other times violently through fratricide and regicide. Sometimes royal fathers name their successor, but a cast-off son could always rebel against the chosen one – and history has recorded ample evidence of such political resentments. In Iran, for instance, it was not usually primogeniture that determined the basis for legitimacy, but "Divine Grace," which in practice "could be claimed by anyone who managed, often by force, to succeed" (Katuzian 2013, xv). Conflict and violence over succession is not haphazard, however. There is logic to the "Law of Fratricide!" A remnant of the Turco-Mongolian monarchic tradition of the grand khan (winner takes the crown), argues Joseph Fletcher, fierce political competition survived the transition of nomadic political economic culture to the settled agricultural communities in Central Asia, South Asia, and the Middle East (1979–1980, 236). Concomitantly, as the governments became centralized in these agricultural and feudal societies, the absolute domination of the grand khan was replaced by dynastic rule (Fletcher 1979–1980, 236). Under such political system, the most talented male member of a royal dynasty would usually be chosen as the principle successor, and other contenders would be disposed of by either murder or war. This principle worked so well that no other replaced it (Fletcher 1979–1980, 239):

> Far from there being any theory of primogeniture … the law of succession may well be described as a "free-for-all", in which the strongest of the sons inherited the throne, while the others – according to the Law of Fratricide – suffered death. The stakes were indeed very high and the resulting struggles correspondingly fierce, each prince being supported by those leaders and officials who thought that he would best serve their purpose. It clearly rested with the officials in power to decide which of the dead sultan's sons was to be sent the message which would bring him to the throne. (Alderson in Goody [1966, 19])

The absence of a clear principle of primogeniture in medieval Muslim societies and the presence of legalized polygyny and concubinage among the male elite exacerbated games of succession. As mechanisms for the transfer of power and succession in medieval royal courts were loosely routinized and generally based on the "Law of Fratricide," domination and authority were often preserved through the extermination of one or all other contenders to the throne. Additionally, the prevalence of concubinage and slave ownership effectively rendered legal marriage (*nikah*) redundant; apparently the limitation of legal marriage to four official wives was perceived as too restrictive for some men of power. Besides, not only would the amount of bride prices and gifts given to legal wives "drain" the sultan's treasury (Peirce 1993, 38), the legal wives' powerful relatives at the royal court or in other states could make demands on the monarch and potentially cause trouble.[16] The changing patterns of marriage practice in these royal courts also led to congregations of a growing number of "slave" women from different social, ethnic, and religious backgrounds in the royal courts that heightened competition among the mothers of potential caliphs and sultans-to-be (Peirce 2017; Cortese and Calderini 2007, 109). It also boosted the pool of viable male heirs – hence, the potential for more palace intrigue and fraternal violence.

---

[16] Thomas Barfield, personal communication, May 2018.

Such polygynous royal palaces with their legendary harems – often functioning as "shadow governments" (Gholsorkhi 1995, 144) – would also become arenas for strategic alliances and deadly rivalries among royal mothers, daughters, sisters, wives, and concubines, not to mention other palace stakeholders such as *wazir*s, eunuchs, advisors, pages, nannies, and others – all vying to have their favorite son recognized as the legitimate heir; their survival depended on his success. Mernissi has argued that polygyny is an enabler for powerful sultans and fosters despotism (1994, 98). I would add that polygyny and concubinage also tend to foster self-indulgent, pleasure-seeking, and administratively challenged princes, ultimately leaving the throne bereft of a competent and viable male heir. A case in point is Rukn al-Din Firuz Shah (d. 1236), the half-brother of Razia Sultan of India and her predecessor, as I discuss in Chapter 4. It was within such overlapping networks of dynastic ties, kinship relations, and marriage alliances that a politically savvy and charismatic princess could find a real chance to walk out of the shadows, become visible, and take charge, particularly if she had her father's support or had been married to the ruling patriarch.

As the palace was the center of administration, political intrigues were primarily concentrated in the royal court, and power and authority were dominated by the person of the sultan. Princes and princesses enjoyed privileges and possibilities that were denied other classes of people. In the feudal societies of South and Southeast Asia, for example, by inheriting land, some women of the feudal families were – and still are – potentially in a position to exercise feats of national greatness and authority. The enabling mechanism, however, is not the ownership of land per se; it is the strong and special relationship between a lineage patriarch and his daughter, as I discuss later. Local knowledge was primarily based on oral communication and gossip, rather than on written texts and scriptures. For that matter, differences of opinion and a variety of views coexisted and were tolerated. Religious institutions and individuals functioned at the pleasure of the sovereign, though the caliph or sultan paid only lip service to the former. The political elite ruled and fought over succession amongst themselves, irrespective of the wishes of the people who would be tolerating the powers-that-be so long as their livelihood, security, and welfare were safeguarded (Barfield 2012).

Electoral Succession

With the post-Enlightenment institutionalization of authority in constitutions, political competition became routinized and "democratized" –

initially exclusively among Western white males. Legitimate authority was no longer based on the arbitrary whim and authority of one person (i.e. the king, the sultan, or the caliph), at least theoretically. Rather, it was based on the abstract principles of equality, liberty, citizenship, and political participation (Eisenstadt 2000, 120), though that has not stopped autocratic men in postcolonial Muslim societies from trying to monopolize authority and become presidents for life, as we see in the cases of both Pakistan and Indonesia. Political rivalry and electoral violence may be no less intense, however, and at times may even turn deadly. The assassinations of Robert F. Kennedy in the US and Benazir Bhutto in Pakistan while they campaigned for political office are cases in point. Primogeniture would be theoretically meaningless in a modern democratic political system, though dynastic ties may give greater visibility to a contending candidate. Polygyny, on the other hand, has survived structural changes in the law of succession in Muslim societies. Legally, Muslim men are permitted to have up to four wives simultaneously, and some men of power continue to enjoy the full benefit of the law. Benazir Bhutto's father, Zulfikar Ali Bhutto of Pakistan, had three wives concurrently, the last of whom he fell madly in love with and married clandestinely. In Indonesia, Megawati's father, Sukarno, was in lockstep with his medieval imperial forefathers and married nine women, some of whom lived together and with him in the presidential palace.

Whether succession was to be an orderly transfer of power through kinship and descent, usurpation, or via electoral procedures, in practice the situations on the ground have historically made the process of the transition of power far more complicated, contentious, and at times deadly.

The Shadow Government: "Wearers of the Veil"

The king's underlings must not be allowed to assume power, for this causes the utmost harm and destroys the king's splendor and majesty. This particularly applies to women, for they are wearers of the veil and have not complete intelligence ... But when the king's wives begin to assume the part of the ruler, they base their orders on what interested parties tell them, because they are not able to see things with their own eyes in the way that men constantly look at the affairs of the outside world ... Naturally their commands are mostly the opposite of what is right, and mischief ensues; the king's dignity suffers and the people are afflicted with trouble ... In all ages nothing but disgrace, infamy, discord and corruption have resulted when kings have been dominated by their wives.   Nizam al-Mulk in Darke (1978, 179–180)

The object of the chief minister Nizam al-Mulk's irritation,[17] as expressed in the above quotation, was Tarkan Khatun, a favorite concubine/wife of Malik Shah Seljuq (r. 1072–1092). Her meddling in the court's affairs ultimately led to the toppling of none other than Nizam himself (Darke 1978, xix). His frustration had to do with the nature of gender politics in the royal court, which, as mentioned before, due to its Turkish ethnicity, afforded women greater autonomy. With all his political acumen, however, the Nizam made the ultimate mistake! He recommended "the son of another wife for the succession," thus turning himself into the enemy of the sultan's beloved wife. Nizam was soon dismissed by the king and assassinated shortly thereafter, reportedly encouraged by Malik Shah himself (Katuzian 2013, 44).

Nizam's bewilderment may have stemmed from two incompatible sentiments: his belief in women's inferiority – presumably because they wore the veil, and in women's uncanny ability to influence men of power, the patriarchs. His lamentation is ironically a pathetic acknowledgment of royal women's ability to operationalize their political agency and to shape the course of palace events. In this sense, the eleventh-century Persian *wazir* seems to have anticipated Foucault's theorization of power as "relationship" (i.e. power unbound by place, person, or position). For Foucault, "the individual is an effect of power" and a product of "regimes of power/knowledge" (Bevin 1999, 65). Saul Newman views Foucault's notion of power as "dispersed throughout the social network" (2004, 139); and for Foucault this relationship of power may "become a confrontation between two adversaries" at any moment (1982, 794). As the chief minister recognized clearly, it was the kinship system and marital ties that provided the networks of support for elite women, enabling them to exert power and exercise authority. The context would be the same for men; it is just that the honorable *wazir* considered it "natural" for men only and hence illegitimate for women. While women's authority was restricted within the existing patriarchal courts, their reach for power was extensive and unpredictable, as I will discuss shortly, challenging the assumption of a rigid separation of private and public domains. It was the fluidity of the boundaries that concerned Nizam al-Mulk the most.

Warning against women's influence and political agency, Nizam al-Mulk realized their potency – "nefarious" from his point of view – and the need to curtail it before it was realized. From this eminent *wazir*'s

---

[17] Abu Ali Hasan ibn Ali Tusi, popularly known by the honorific title Nizam al-Mulk (Order of the Kingdom), was born in 1018–1019 in Tus, Iran, and assassinated in 1092 in Nahavand, Iran. He was a Persian *wazir* of the Turkish Seljuq sultans, best remembered for his long treatise on kingship, the *Seyāsat-Nāmeh*. See Lambton (1984).

point of view, authority, domination, and force are inherent characteristics of royal authority – or sovereignty – which by definition are masculine, and from which women ought to be excluded. Adding a religious twist to his political ideology, in his advice to kings, he echoed a variation on the theme of the aforementioned alleged Prophetic hadith, "be assured that whenever a king leaves affairs to women and boys, the kingship will depart his house" (Darke 1978, 182). It is hazardous enough when princes compete with each other over the throne and lose their heads for it. It would be even more so were women, with their uncanny ability, allowed to enter the race to the throne – hence his appeal to the alleged authority of the Prophetic hadith.

In almost all cultures, be they medieval or modern, some women have used their relationships and proximity to powerful men to influence their decisions and manipulate the course of events. They have pushed to eliminate rivals, tried to maintain control of palace personnel, and enable their sons – and sometimes their brothers – to succeed to the throne. The growing scholarship on the lives of medieval women has brought to light stories of royal wives and concubines, mothers and daughters, sisters and nannies, and their huge retinues, all living in the shadow of the monarch and his equally powerful *wazir*s, advisors, eunuchs, and other palace personnel.[18] Little or no information is available on the background, ethnicity, religion, and pedigree of the female slaves/concubines who populated the harems of many caliphs, sultans, and other members of the male elite. As women were often captured during raids, one could reasonably assume that some were of high birth and from aristocratic or royal backgrounds. A glimpse into the political lives of women in these royal courts gives us an idea of the cultural context from within which a charismatic woman might emerge to seize power. In the following pages I describe briefly a few cases of powerful wives, mothers, and sisters from the royal courts of the Abbasids, Fatimids, Safavids, and Ottomans.

Behind the Throne: Mothers, Wives, Concubines, and Princesses

There are no kings without queens, even if some might not be actually called "queen" – the survival of the dynasty depends on queens, concubines, and slave girls. Far from languishing idly or waiting their turn to be called on by the king or the sultan at his pleasure, many of them honed their political skills and wielded power in the harem from behind the

---

[18] See, for example, Peirce (1993, 2017), Hambly (1999), Duncan (2000), Nashat and Beck (2003), Cortese and Calderini (2007), Walker (2011b), Booth (2015), and Lal (2018).

throne. The extent of their influence in the Seljuq Turkic royal court, as mentioned above, was lamented by Nizam al-Mulk and opposed vehemently in many manuals and guidebooks written at the time – and since. Only a fraction of these women's activities and intrigues have been recorded and come to light. But there are many more women whose feats of greatness – or craftiness – we may only hear about in the enchanting stories of *Thousand and One Nights*, or we may yet uncover through historical records and documents.

Nabia Abbott, in her book *The Two Queens of Baghdad* (1946), details the intriguing palace politicking of Khayzuran (d. 789) and her niece/daughter-in-law, Zobeideh (d. 831), the mother and wife, respectively, of the legendary Harun al-Rashid (r. 786–809). Khayzuran was a beloved slave/concubine/wife (in that order) of the Abbasid Caliph al-Mehdi (r. 775–785), who enjoyed unrestricted power within the court of her husband's caliphate and exercised influence on the caliph's decisions, including who should be his heir. When her eldest son, Musa al-Hadi (r. 785–786), succeeded his father, despite Khayzuran's preference for her younger son, he attempted to curtail his mother's influence in the royal palace. Khayzuran was offended and outraged. The relationship between mother and son became so poisonous that they reportedly plotted to eliminate each other. In the end it was the mother whose wish was realized. The young caliph was found dead by poisoning or suffocation, but exactly how and by whom remains a mystery (Abbott 1946; Tabari 1989, Vol. 30, 42–45). Khayzuran then succeeded in her original plan to have her second son, Harun al-Rashid, ascend the Abbasid throne and become the caliph. He in turn gave his mother a free hand in his court, though she did not live long enough to enjoy it, dying in 789.

Minhaj al-Din Siraj Juzjani, the thirteenth-century biographer and author of the *Tabakat-i Nasiri*, (also, Tabaqat-i Nasiri) describes the following story of the highly powerful wife and mother of two of the thirteenth-century Khawrazmi sultans. Of Turco-Mongolian ethnicity, Terkan Khatun was a daughter of a minor king of Khorasan, in northeast Iran, and wife of Sultan Takish b. Il-Arsalan of Khawrazm. Terkan Khatun was quick to punish insubordination and was strongly supported by her own tribal leaders. She was "world renowned" (*namdar*) and addressed as "Lord of the World" (*khudavand-i jahan*). Upon discovering that her husband had professed his love for a recently acquired concubine, she was reportedly so offended and enraged that she had him locked up in a hot bathhouse (*hammam*) and left him there. By the time he was rescued by his *amir*s and assistants he had lost an eye and was near death (Juzjani 1962, Vol. 1, pp. 300–301).

In another corner of the Muslim world lived Sitt al-Mulk (Lady of Power), a remarkable princess who had the "ability and the means to change dynastic history"[19] (Cortese and Calderini 2007, 124). Sitt al-Mulk was the beloved daughter of al-Aziz, the fifth Ismaili Fatimid imam-caliph,[20] who "adored her mightily and denied her nothing" (Walker 2011b, 33). She was also the older half-sister of the heir to the throne, al-Hakim. Sitt al-Mulk had the good fortune of being born (b. 970) when the power of the Fatimid dynasty in Egypt was at its height and enjoyed a lavish and commanding lifestyle. Being in a strong financial position, she sought to influence her half-brother the heir apparent with unparalleled gifts. She also patronized and maneuvered the *wazirs*, court dignitaries, and palace personnel. She even had her own private army and a personal "spy" in her brother's palace (Walker 2011b, 39).

When her beloved father died (d. 996), Sitt al-Mulk swiftly mobilized her private army to prevent her brother al-Hakim from ascending the throne. She had planned to have her cousin, with whom some say she was in love, to succeed her father (Walker 2011b, 34). The eleven-year-old al-Hakim's tutor, and later *wazir*, just as quickly prevented her from carrying out her plan. He effectively shut her out of the palace and even initially placed her under house arrest (Cortese, 2019).[21] As a punishment, al-Hakim reportedly subjected Sitt al-Mulk to a humiliating virginity test, reportedly performed by "trusted old women." He wanted to make sure that she was not pregnant and carrying a potential successor (Walker 2011b, 38).[22] Soon, however, the royal siblings reconciled and formed a strong relationship. For several years Sitt al-Mulk was her brother's closest advisor and companion. The young imam-caliph valued her opinion, so much so that he would change his mind on matters at the last moment on account of his sister's advice (Cortese and Calderini 2007, 121). But their relationship started to show signs of strain once again, primarily because of al-Hakim's erratic behavior, particularly his peculiar brand of misogyny.[23] For instance, he issued a series of increasingly bizarre decrees and edicts severely restricting women's mobility. Women were banned from going to the market, leaving home in the evening, appearing unveiled in public (Fatimid women did not generally observe veiling), going to cemeteries and even to public bathhouses. The imam-caliph went so far as to ban the manufacturing and sale of women's shoes

---

[19] See the genealogical chart in Chapter 3.
[20] An *imam* for the Shi'ite is one who is a blood descendant of 'Ali, the Prophet Muhammad's paternal cousin.
[21] Delia Cortese generously shared with me her then unpublished paper "A Patron of Men: Sitt al-Mulk and the Military at the Fatimid Court." I thank her sincerely.
[22] Unlike their brothers and fathers, many Fatimid princesses never married. Whether it was by choice or circumstance (i.e. not having a "suitable" match), is not clear.
[23] For debates regarding al-Hakim's bizarre behavior, particularly his draconian economic policies and misogynistic edicts, see Haidar (2008).

altogether. The objective was to make sure that his orders were carried out and that women stayed put (Cortese and Calderini 2007, 192). But what particularly incensed Sitt al-Mulk was her brother's inexplicable and unprecedented decision to bypass his own son and nominate a cousin as his heir and successor (Walker 1995, 247). As fate would have it, however, in one of his nightly solo treks al-Hakim simply vanished (d. 1021), leaving no trace. Few tears were shed over his disappearance (Walker 2002, 57). Like his life, the imam-caliph's death carries to this day an inexplicable aura of mystery. Speculations abound as to whether Sitt al-Mulk had a hand in her brother's mysterious disappearance, but there is no hard evidence to implicate her (Cortese, 2019 Halm 2014).[24] Sitt al-Mulk moved quickly and decisively to declare her nephew as his father's successor and the new imam-caliph. Al-Hakim's designated heir was swiftly removed and eventually eliminated (Walker 2002, 61; Cortese, 2019). Sitt al-Mulk assumed the position of regent for her sixteen-year-old nephew, whose royal name was al-Zahir and who was, incidentally, the oldest of the Fatimid imam-caliphs at the time of his coronation. "She released women from confinement and allowed the Jews and Christians to regain their earlier status and prominence in part by rebuilding their houses of worship" (Walker 2011b, 39).[25] Sitt al-Mulk stood by her royal nephew's side, assumed administrative duties, and maintained power until her own rather untimely death in 1023 due to diarrhea. So effectively had she ruled Egypt that when she died, her obituary noted that "although a woman, she had been a patron to men" (Walker 2011b, 39).

Queen consorts and royal princesses did not always get their way, try as they might. Iranian princess Pari Khan Khanum was the second daughter of Shah Tahmasb Safavid (r. 1524–1576). She was dearly loved by her father and was held in high esteem and awe at her father's court. Many prominent leaders and courtiers sought "her patronage and assistance" (Parsadust 2009; Gholsorkhi 1995).[26] Highly educated, Pari Khan Khanum expertly supervised the court's administration after her father's death and rescued the throne for her half-brother, Ismail II. He had long been kept in exile far away from the capital at the Qahqahaeh fortress in northwest Iran, fearing a rebellion against his royal father. Upon returning to the capital to claim the crown, he went on a rampage killing all his brothers, half-brothers, and nephews, whom he perceived as threats to his crown. Ismail II promptly banished Pari Khan Khanum from the palace, feeling threatened by her administrative expertise, the extent of her

[24] For an anti-Fatimid case made against Sitt al-Mulk, see Walker (2011b, 40–42).
[25] Sitt al-Mulk's mother was a Christian concubine of al-Aziz.
[26] Pari Khan Khanum is the subject of the historical novel *Equal of the Sun* by Anita Amirrezvani (2012).

influence, and her networks of support in the royal court. Barely a year and a half into his reign (r. 1576–1577), Ismail II and his ever-present male companion were found dead in his chamber, by either opium overdose or poisoning. Did Pari Khan Khanum the kingmaker have anything to do with her royal step-brother's early demise? No one knows for sure. Pari, however, met her own tragic end shortly after Ismail's death. She was suffocated at the instigation of a duplicitous *wazir* and the order of her sister-in-law, Khair un-Nisa Begum, known as Mahd Ulya (The Cradle of Nobles). She was the aristocratic wife of Mohammad Khodabandeh, Pari's older and legally blind half-brother, who reportedly made no decision without his wife's input. Mohammad had been spared by Ismail because of his disability, but subsequently assumed power, ironically at Pari's instigation. Pari had apparently calculated that her brother's poor eyesight would make him inevitably dependent on her, given her knowledge of and experience with the palace administration. But Mahd Ulya, Mohammad's wife, had the same idea and was determined to prevent any rivalry, particularly against someone with Pari's skill in the royal court. She brooked no competition and lost no time in having Pari put to death. Pari Khan Khanum died in 1578, just short of her thirtieth birthday (Parsadust 2009; Gholsorkhi 1995, 153; Soleimani 2010).

In medieval royal court, be it in Asia or Africa – and sometimes even in modern times – by far the most powerful authority behind the throne has traditionally been the queen mother. Mothers were particularly powerful in the Ottoman and Fatimid courts. With the changing patterns of marriage and concubinage, the official role of the mother of the sultan, the *valide sultan*, became firmly institutionalized, and they were charged with the education and administrative supervision of their young sons (Peirce 2017). Islamic history has a rich record of powerful women regents, though for our purposes here, I point to only two of them. From two corners of the Muslim world and in two different eras, two formidable mothers-of-the-sultan or of the imam-caliph stand out. One is Rasad, mother of the Fatimid imam-caliph al-Mustansir (d. 1094), who was an Ethiopian or Sudanese concubine/slave of his father. I discuss the extent of her power in her son's royal court in Chapter 3. Briefly, however, Rasad became the regent of her son when he ascended the throne at the age of six. She controlled the royal Fatimid court in the mid-eleventh century and fought a protracted turf battle with al-Mustansir's equally powerful *wazir*, which devastated the state's treasury.

Kosum Sultan of the seventeenth-century Ottoman royal court was another highly impressive *valide sultan*. She entered the Ottoman imperial harem in 1604 and became a concubine of the sultan in 1609. She became the regent of her twelve-year-old son in 1622, and when he died in 1640, she maintained her powerful position as the *valide sultan* and regent of Ibrahim, another son. But Ibrahim was an incompetent, pleasure-seeking young man, capable of controlling neither the state nor his sexual appetite. He was also known to have some intellectual shortcomings. Soon it became clear, particularly to his mother, that Ibrahim was incapable of managing state affairs, and so he was eliminated, reportedly at his mother's instigation. His seven-year-old son was then crowned as the new sultan, with Kosum Sultan continuing as the grand *valide sultan* of her grandson. But the new sultan's mother, Hatice, was unwilling to relinquish her newly gained powerful position to her domineering mother-in-law. The two women competed fiercely for control of the royal court and its resources, and in the end Hatice had her all-powerful and meddlesome mother-in-law assassinated (Peirce 1993).

Not all women of the elite spent their time worrying about or scheming against an actual or potential rival in the royal harems. Maria Szuppe (1999), writing on Safavid women of the elite, highlights two categories of activity other than politics that were highly prized by royal princesses, namely patronage and poetry. Patronage was not exclusive to the royal Safavid women, however. Many royal women, including mothers, wives, sisters, and daughters of kings, sultans, and caliphs, used their wealth and position to sponsor architectural monuments, mosques, *madrasas*, and charitable organizations. Such monuments have dotted many Muslim city landscapes, keeping the names of these remarkable and charitable women etched in history.

Methodological Reflections

> The imagination needed to reconstitute a society from the written clues available is even greater than that required when one goes out to a living society and analyses the permanence behind the surface ripples.
>
> MacFarlane (1977, 12)

Writing an ethnohistory of Muslim women rulers from medieval to modern times, one is immediately confronted with multiple methodological dilemmas. To begin with, taking a transhistorical approach necessitates going back and forth between different cultural traditions, political structures, and systems of succession. Not being trained as a historian or a political scientist, I have at times felt the limits of my expertise. As an anthropologist, too, I have wondered how one is to write an ethnography of women rulers and leaders who belong to ages past and are no longer living in this world. What written clues and folk narratives about medieval women rulers, for example, are available in a region where history has been written almost exclusively by men, about men, and for men? The history of Islam and the Muslim world, in all its geographical expanse and cultural diversity and complexity, is an overwhelmingly masculine history, as acknowledged by Mohsen Kadivar, an Iranian scholar of Islamic studies: "Muslim scholars (whether exegetists, hadith specialists, theologians, jurists, mystics or philosophers) have been predominantly men" (2011, 214; see also Hambly 1999, 3). Such masculine perspectives, however, are not limited to the history/story of Muslim women, whether rulers or commoners. Referencing Gavin Hambly, "the European Orientalists tradition" also "largely ignored the existence of women" (1999, 4). Women are not the only forgotten or overlooked category, however. Ordinary people, the "commoners," are also systematically overlooked. As noted by MacFarlane, the recorded history is one of the lives and legacies of the "higher classes" and the political elite (1977, 4). Until challenged by feminist discourse, historians almost invariably wrote about the political conquest and military adventures of the male elite, leaving out references to the public and the ordinary people – the followers, supporters, or detractors. That, too, is not unique to Islamic history. Either by inference or evidence, we come to learn that the opposition to – or support for – Muslim women's leadership has historically not been unanimously negative, be it in the early days of Islam, in medieval, or in modern times. The women leaders of this book, including the legendary Queen of Sheba, enjoyed the support of their people, whether it was expressed overtly and enthusiastically, as in the cases of Benazir Bhutto and Megawati, or unstated and implied, as in others. Although contested by some, I hope to demonstrate that the military leadership of 'A'isha, the beloved wife of the Prophet Muhammad at the Battle of the Camel (656), was supported by the rank and file, and at the time, her political authority did not seem unusual to those who followed her to the battleground. Neither 'A'isha herself nor her "soldier-sons" questioned her political legitimacy or the righteousness of her military objective – at least not until her defeat, as reported by the famed tenth-century chronicler Tabari (subject of Chapter 2).

Furthermore, much of this history, particularly the history of the early days of Islam, has come down to us through oral tradition and popular narratives, and we "have no direct means of learning what it was like to live life" at the time of the Prophet (Ahmed 1992, 121). To quote Andrew Shyrock, it is "[t]he history of things heard and said" and "not of what was seen or read" (1997, 95). The oral tradition of early Islam allowed for multiple readings and constructions of events, personalities, and companions of the Prophet Muhammad. As the hadith literature became reified in writing, for example, the representations of the wives of the Prophet and his female companions became progressively more one-dimensional – if not negative – and closely aligned with the evolving restrictive patriarchal worldview (Stowasser 1994; Afsaruddin 2010a). These observations apply equally to medieval Muslim women rulers and sovereigns whose activities and voices were often left out, under/unrepresented, or reconstructed to fit the patriarchal "sociomorality" and conservative sensibility of the time. Richard Bulliet (2003), writing on historical Muslim biographers' methods of inclusion and exclusion of women's education in the twelfth to the fifteenth centuries, argues that biographers wrote primarily about women who were related to them through kinship or marriage. That might be because of the prevailing beliefs and etiquette around not mentioning other men's womenfolk – or rendering them "visible" – as feminist discourse has it. Bulliet concludes that the total number of educated women not mentioned must have been much greater, and that educated and knowledgeable women continued to be underrepresented (2003, 78).

Women, for their part, seldom wrote memoirs or autobiographies until modern times, nor did they write biographies or record the social history of their time or those of their predecessors or contemporaries, save for a few exceptions.[27] It was not until the nineteenth and twentieth centuries and the rapid increase in female literacy that Muslim women, similar to women from other faiths and nationalities, took to writing their own memoirs and autobiographies, publishing newspapers and magazines, and avidly researching, unearthing, and writing about other women's accomplishments and lives (Booth 2001).[28] Their sustained efforts have led to the construction of more accurate representations of Muslim women's identities, activities, and agency (Elsadda 2001, 39), more so in the religious domain than in the political domain. Marilyn Booth (2001, 2015) writes in detail about how Egyptian women of the nineteenth and twentieth centuries moved quickly to make up for lost time. The rapid growth of scholarship by and about Muslim women has not only focused critical attention on the colonial history of the Muslim world and the distorted Western and Orientalist narratives of women, but has also challenged the revisionist doctrinal Islamist interpretation of gender hierarchy, male privilege, and legal inequality. Muslim women scholars

---

[27] The Iranian Bibi Khanum Astarabadi's (d. 1921) satirical book, *Vices of Men (Ma'ayib al-rijal*, 1858/1859), has been translated form the Persian and published by Afshaneh Najmabadi (1992), and the Lebanese/Egyptian Zaynab Fawwaz (d. 1914) wrote a monumental short biography of world famous women, *Pearls Scattered in Times and Places: Classes of Ladies of Cloistered Spaces* (c. 1894), translated from the Arabic and published by Marilyn Booth (2015).

[28] Among these women are Beth Baron, Lois Beck, Marilyn Booth, Suad Joseph, Deniz Kandiyoti, Nikkie Keddi, Farzaneh Milani, Afsaneh Najamabadi, Leslie Peirce, and Judith Tucker, to mention a few.

and feminists have questioned the patriarchal monopoly of sacred knowledge and misogynist reconstructions of Prophetic hadiths and tradition, and have offered fresh and thoughtful readings of the egalitarian message and spirit of the Qur'an.[29] While such interpretive and progressive readings of the scripture have posed a challenge to the patriarchal monopoly of sacred knowledge and tradition, it is Muslim women's collective demand for political representation and legal equality that has threatened the foundation of the "sacred" patriarchal political domination.

The ethnographic studies pursued by anthropologists and feminists in the second half of the twentieth century have likewise highlighted subtle or significant contributions made by Muslim women in the private and public domains, the arts and architecture, religion, literature, and wider culture. Muslim women's political leadership, however, has received less attention and has been almost "forgotten," as noted by Fatima Mernissi in her pioneering book *Hidden from History: Forgotten Queens of Islam* (1994). By the first decade of the twenty-first century, however, growing numbers of Muslim women have moved into the public domain and assumed leadership positions. My objective in this book is not to provide a summary of all women rulers who have come to power in the Muslim world. Rather, it is to focus on the lives and legacies of six women leaders from medieval to modern times who have sought political authority and played games of succession in their patriarchal societies. Specifically, I wish to bring to light aspects of Islamic political history and make visible lives that have long been shrouded in layers of neglect, stereotyping, myth-making, misunderstanding, or misrepresentation – including among Muslims themselves. My selection of these particular women rulers was partly by design and partly because of the circumstances surrounding their lives. The Quranic revelations regarding the Queen of Sheba and the alleged negative Prophetic hadith provide the theoretical scaffolding for the narratives of the leadership of the women sovereigns that follow. The Yemenite queen Arwa's long leadership and her unprecedented position as both a spiritual and temporal leader made her an obvious choice, as did Razia's four-year leadership and continuous popularity in South Asia. Benazir Bhutto was the first Muslim woman democratically elected prime minister, and Megawati Sukarnoputri is the first Muslim woman president. The women rulers featured in this book present images of political agency, power and authority, wisdom and caring that are not only missing in the Western media and the mounting literature on Muslim women, but also challenge the highly unequal gender hierarchy in the increasingly restrictive Muslim societies.

[29] See the Preface fn. 3

Summarizing the lives and leadership of these unforgettable queens of Islam in only one chapter each does not do justice to their achievements, nor does it allow me to be expansive in describing the triumphs and trials of their remarkable lives and leadership. Obviously, one could write a whole book – if not multiple books – about every single one of them – and many such books have been written, particularly about our modern queens. On the plus side, this book brings together the life stories of a few charismatic women rulers from medieval to modern times, giving the reader a chance to compare and contrast women's paths to power and the strategies they employed to operationalize their political agency to rule a Muslim-majority state.

Finally, this book includes historical and biographical sources on Muslim women leaders from several linguistic communities, including those of Yemen, Egypt, Pakistan, Iran, Indonesia, and India. I wish I was familiar with all these local languages in addition to Persian (my mother tongue) but, alas, that is not the case. Fortunately, many of the Arabic – and other – primary sources I have consulted for this book are already translated into English, and I do not find compelling reasons to distrust them.

Organization of the Book

This book is divided into three parts, six chapters, an introduction, and a conclusion. Each chapter begins with a synopsis of a woman ruler's "battle of succession" for political authority and power, followed by a narrative positioning her within her family and society's existing political and social structures. Each chapter explores in detail the circumstances under which women rulers achieved political authority in medieval and modern times, focusing on their personal ambitions and charisma. Women rulers' life stories are contextualized within the two interrelated themes of succession and dynastic ties, while highlighting the paths by which they achieved legitimate authority. The first two chapters frame the broader outlines of this book theoretically, within which I locate Muslim women leaders' challenges of – and to – political authority.

Part I, "Sacred Sources of Authority: The Qur'an and the Hadith," comprises Chapters 1 and 2. Chapter 1, "The Queen of Sheba and Her Mighty Throne," retells the Quranic story of the dramatic encounter between King Solomon and the Queen of Sheba. Although she is popularly known as Bilqis, the queen is left nameless in the Qur'an. It is her sovereignty that is highlighted in the holy book. In this Chapter I discuss the Quranic revelations as interwoven with their medieval patriarchal reconstructions by Muslim biographers such as the eleventh-century scholar Thaʿlabi. He considered the queen's authority suspect, presumably because in his account she inherited supernatural power from her maternal connection to the *jinn* – thus making her sovereignty a usurpation of masculine power. I argue that in the Qurʾan it is her faith that is at issue and not her sovereignty. I contend that the divine revelations have more to do with the sun-worshiping queen's subjective transformation from ignorance of Islam (*jahiliyya*) to enlightenment than with sexual politics as imagined by medieval biographers.

Chapter 2, "ʿAʾisha Bint Abu Bakr: Battle of the Camel, Battle for Succession," explores the highly contentious issue of succession after the death of the Prophet Muhammad. I discuss the role that ʿAʾisha, Mother of the Faithful, played as a military leader in the Battle of the Camel, which further polarized the fast-growing Muslim community. Her role in the civil war and her subsequent defeat in the battle of succession were – in retrospect – blamed on her gender, which allegedly occasioned the recollection of the aforementioned Prophetic hadith. ʿAʾisha is the only woman in this book who is not a ruling queen, whether legendary or historical. But she was/is a leading Muslim woman and one of the major religious and political authorities of the early days of Islam. I juxtapose the popularity of the prohibitory hadith in modern times with the relative obscurity of the revelations regarding the sovereignty of the Queen of Sheba. The legacy of ʿAʾisha's political agency has historically been held up as a warning against Muslim women's political authority and leadership. It is at the intersection of the Qurʾan and the hadith and the on-the-ground pragmatics of patriarchal power dynamics that I situate women's paths to leadership.

Part II, "Dynasty and Descent: Medieval Queens," comprises Chapters 3 and 4. Chapter 3, "Sayyida Hurra Queen Arwa of Yemen: 'The Little Queen of Sheba,'" discusses the life and leadership of the Yemenite queen. Her long reign (1067–1138) coincided with three of the Ismaʿili Fatimid imam-caliphs in Cairo, beginning with al-Mustansir (1029–1094). Highly educated, intelligent, and politically savvy, Queen Arwa played the games of political leadership and succession so successfully that not only did she survive the intense tribal competition in Yemen, she was also able to keep the Fatimid imam-caliphs in Cairo at arm's length while enjoying their full support. Queen Arwa was elevated to the status of *hujja* (the highest rank after the imam-caliph on the Ismaʿili-Shiʿi religiopolitical hierarchy) by al-Mustansir and is the only Muslim woman sovereign ever to hold both temporal and spiritual authority simultaneously. The queen's timely intervention in the battle of succession between the two Ismaʿili factions, namely the Nizaris and the Tayyibis, ensured the survival and continuity of the latter. She kept the powerful and competitive Yemenite tribal leaders in check while delivering justice and prosperity to her people who called her their "Mistress."

Chapter 4, "Razia Sultan of India: 'Queen of the World Bilqis-i Jihan,'" covers the brief but brave sovereignty of Razia Sultan, the only female sultan of the thirteenth-century Mamluk Sultanate of Delhi. Unlike Arwa, who was accidently thrust into the political limelight, Razia actively vied for power, and in that she had her father's full support. Razia brought peace and prosperity to her people, but three years into her reign, she became the subject of an ethnically and racially motivated rumor. She was alleged to have had improper relations with one of her loyal advisors, who happened to be Ethiopian. Soon after, a treacherous plan was drawn up to remove Razia from power and to enthrone one of her half-brothers.

Neither during the long reign of Queen Arwa in Yemen nor during the short sovereignty of Razia Sultan in India do we hear of any organized religious objections to their temporal authority. The Prophetic hadith, as I will discuss later, was not invoked, at least not publicly.

Part III, "Institutionalizing Succession: Contemporary Queens," comprises Chapters 5 and 6. Chapter 5, "Benazir Bhutto: A Queen 'Without Parallel,'" focuses on the life and leadership of the first Muslim woman democratically elected to the office of prime minister in Pakistan, not once but twice, despite fierce opposition from the religious establishment and the male political elite, including her own brother. Benazir Bhutto's personality and legacy, I argue fall more within the mystical tradition of legendary female "seekers" in South Asia. Her passionate desire to return home to Pakistan in 2007 – even in the face of serious threats to her life – to unite with her people after a relatively long period of separation and exile, is indicative of that spirit. And true to the mystical form, her quest ended in tragedy at the moment of reunification with her beloved Pakistan.

Chapter 6, "Megawati Sukarnoputri: 'Limbuk Becomes Queen,'" focuses on the coming to power of Megawati Sukarnoputri in Indonesia, as the first women to become president of a Muslim-majority state. A daughter of Sukarno, Indonesia's first post-independence president and a national hero, Megawati, the "housewife," left the privacy of her home to occupy the presidential palace – the most public and visible place in her country. Her steep climb unsettled powerful men such as Suharto, the general who had overthrown her father, and confounded the male elite (some of whom were her friends), who perceived her active presence in politics and the public domain to be disruptive and subversive. But, as with Limbuk, the popular mythological character who "broke out" of the seclusion of the royal harem to become vocal and visible, Megawati defied the odds. Given the lowly position of Limbuk in the mythological hierarchy and the space she occupied in the most inner section of the mythical palace, some may interpret the association between Limbuk and Megawati as derisive. On the contrary, I find the metaphorical celebration of Megawati as Limbuk an exciting perspective to pursue, given that both of them broke barriers of seclusion to become visible, vocal, and active. Megawati found her political voice and galvanized the long-oppressed Indonesian people to support her to oust the strongman President Suharto, who had, for almost three decades, succeeded in vanquishing his rivals in the game of succession.

During the governments of Prime Minister Benazir Bhutto and President Megawati the alleged Prophetic hadith was explicitly invoked by some among the religious and political elites to disqualify these two women from assuming political leadership of their respective countries. The greater currency of this hadith in the modern era may be surprising at first. But Muslim women's growing demand for political representation has seriously threatened traditional patriarchal domination, and male elites are doing everything in their power to hold back the tide.

Muslim women political leaders and sovereigns, like their male counterparts – and political leaders in general – occupy a contested position, and their policies and activities are scrutinized from many vantage points. Seldom, if ever, do sovereign leaders have universal support – or unanimous approval ratings. Leadership is a contested position and so, in writing about Arwa or Benazir, for example, I do not consider them saintly leaders or flawless and unique. But I am impressed by the trajectory of their eventful lives and their remarkable achievements, and would like to highlight aspects of their lives and legacies that have not been given as much attention as they deserve. Women rulers' governmental policies and administrative successes or failures, therefore, are not necessarily my primary concern in these chapters.

As historical or legendary queens, all the women highlighted in this book clearly benefited from their dynastic connections to their fathers – or husband, in the case of Queen Arwa – whose popularity gave them the name, fame, and visibility they needed to enter the games of succession. But their own charisma was no less important. Both Megawati Sukarnoputri and Benazir Bhutto subsequently had to compete fiercely in the complicated electoral politics of their respective societies in order to gain the people's vote and win the highest office.

The book concludes with a discussion of what I have elsewhere called "paradox of patriarchy" (Haeri 2002). Games of succession have historically been played among men, particularly between fathers and sons – and sometimes between brothers – whose dynastic ties legitimate the customary devolution of power. Yet the father-son axis potentially, and sometimes actually, is the nexus of tension and rivalry between the two men, who may in fact fear, resent, or even eliminate each other. Father-daughter relations, on the other hand, might be more personally satisfying and politically less consequential – for the father. The patriarch's preference for his daughter, however, stems not just from feelings of self-preservation but also from his recognition of his daughter's talent and political acumen. The women leaders mentioned in this book, whether medieval or modern, proved to be more capable and charismatic than their brothers or husbands; they showed talents that were keenly noted by their fathers. Viewed within this context, the patriarch's support may in fact be not so much paradoxical as pragmatic. Although dynastic ties help, as we shall see, it is women leaders' own charisma that carries the day, particularly in the modern era. Charisma, in its Weberian sense, is that innate quality of possessing "specific gifts of the body and spirit" that are perceived as mythical or "supernatural" by followers (in Keyes, 2002, 245). Charles Lindholm views charisma, above all, as "a *relationship*, a mutual mingling of the inner selves of leader and followers" or of the "lovers attracted to the beloved" (1990, 7; emphasis original). Charismatic leaders often emerge in times of socioeconomic, religious, or political crisis – as did the women rulers discussed in this book. Women's presence at the helm appealed to people who related to them not only as a member of their family, as "mothers" and "sisters," but also as more savvy and caring leaders than run-of-the-mill male politicians.

Part I

Sacred Sources of Authority: The Qur'an and the Hadith

1 Queen of Sheba and Her Mighty Throne

> Be ye not arrogant against me, but come to me in submission.
>
> Qur'an 27:31

The story of the Queen of Sheba climaxes with King Solomon's threat to conquer her paradisaical oasis and usurp her Mighty Throne. King of the world, Solomon was a "warfaring man" and "a very good conqueror who rarely rested from invading. Whenever he heard of a king in any part of the world, he would come to him, weaken him, and subdue him."[1] He would load "people, draft animals, weapons of war, everything" on carved wood, and command "the violent wind to enter under the wood and raise it up" and "the light breeze" to carry them – the distance of a month in one night to wherever he wished (Lassner 1993, 171; see also Qur'an 34:12, 38:36–39). When Solomon heard of the sovereign Queen of Sheba, much to his astonishment, he immediately set out to conquer this "last kingdom not yet under his control."[2] He did not need to take his extraordinary army of demons, 'ifrits, and shaytans, jinns[3] (genies) and humans, birds and beasts flying on the wings of the wind. He sent his spy/messenger bird, the little hoopoe (hudhud), to the queen armed with a letter and instructed the bird to wait for her reply. His message was brief: "Be ye not arrogant against me, but come to me in submission" (Qur'an 27:31); that is, submit or be destroyed.

Who was the Queen of Sheba, and why did Solomon wish to attack her paradisaical "Garden"?

---

[1] The two major primary sources used here are those of Abu Ishaq Ahmad Ibn Muhammed Ibn Ibrahim al-Tha'labi (d. 1035–1036) and Abu Ja'far Muhammad ibn Jarir al-Tabari (838–923). William M. Brinner (2002) has translated and annotated Tha'labi's book, 'Ara'is al-Majalis fi Qisas al-Anbiya (Lives of the Prophets). All references to Tha'labi in this chapter are taken from Brinner. Chapter 4 and appendix I of Jacob Lassner's book, Demonizing the Queen of Sheba (1993), which I have also consulted for this chapter, are likewise based on Tha'labi's text. Tabari is one of the most prominent medieval Muslim biographers and historians, and many scholars have translated different volumes of his monumental forty-volume Ta'rikh al-rusul wa'l muluk (The History of the Prophets and Kings). Volume three, The Children of Israel, is translated by William M. Brinner (1991); I have also consulted Ja'far Moddares Sadiqi's Persian translation of Tabari's interpretation of the stories, Tafsir-i Tabari: Qisseha (1994).

[2] Tabari in Elias (2009, 61).   [3] Haleem translates jinn as "unseen beings" (2004, 393).

The story of the encounter between King Solomon and the Queen of Sheba appears in the three Abrahamic scriptures but none identifies her by name. Only in the *Kebra Nagast*, the revered Ethiopian book of kings, is she named, as Makida (Wallis Budge 2007). The Quranic version of the story of the Queen of Sheba is part of *Sura* 27, known as *al-Naml*, meaning "the Ant." It belongs to the middle group of Meccan *sura*s (Pickthal n.d., 272) and was revealed to the Prophet nine years after he claimed prophecy (Rahnema 1974, 189–229). This *sura* is composed of ninety-four *ayah*s (verses), in which verses twenty through forty-four include the mesmerizing story of the fateful encounter between King Solomon and the Queen of Sheba.[4] The Quranic story is short, condensed, and inconclusive regarding their ultimate fate, leaving much to the imagination of generation after generation of individuals to construct and reconstruct it according to the sensibilities of their time and culture.

While she is the only queen mentioned in the Qur'an, she is not the only woman left unnamed.[5] Except for Mary, mother of Jesus, no other woman – some twenty or so – is identified by name. All these women, except for the Queen of Sheba but including Mary, are situated in relation to a man, as mothers, wives, or daughters. Only the Queen of Sheba is identified by her position: that of a sovereign queen – an independent woman with political authority. The issue of why women are not named in the Qur'an demands greater scholarly attention. But for my purposes here, and contextualizing the issue historically, I would argue that the specificity of women's names is not the point of the Quranic revelations; the enduring significance of kinship relations is. Similarly, the Queen of Sheba's name is immaterial to her position as a queen. The rationale behind it, in my view, is one that renders female sovereignty a likely story, a general principle or a rule that may be utilized by other women at other historical junctures. Indeed, this was the logic used by Mrs. Shahid Salis, one of the Iranian women presidential contenders I interviewed in 2001, mentioned in the Preface. Had the queen been given a name, her position would have become specific to that person and for that particular time.

Popularly, however, the Queen of Sheba is known as Bilqis.[6] But why Bilqis? The origin and meaning of the name is unclear, though Montgomery Watt suggests that it may be rooted in the Greek term *pallakis*, and its

---

[4] I have consulted the Qur'an in Arabic, and translations in Persian and English, including those of Arberry (1991), Pickthal (n.d.), Rahnema (1974), Yusuf Ali (1946), Zafarullah Khan (1981), and Haleem (2004), most of which can be accessed through the website http://tanzil.net/#27. See also http://quran.com/27.

[5] I am grateful to my friend Farzaneh Milani, who drew my attention to this point.

[6] Variations of the Latin spelling of the Queen of Sheba's name include Bilqis (the most common and the one adopted here), Belqis, Belqeis, Balqis, Balkis, Bilkis, Belkis, Birkiisa, and the like.

Hebrew equivalent, *pilegesh* – Arabic *bilqis* – meaning "concubine"[7] (Haeri 2015, 100–101). Bilqis is thus another identity marker based on a position, that of a concubine! "Demonizing" the Queen of Sheba, Jewish and medieval Muslim sources demoted her from the exalted position of queen to that of a concubine, a sex object – a *bilqis*. But popularly and across many cultures, she has remained the unforgettable Queen of Sheba.

Over many years and across many different cultures, religions, races, and ethnicities, infinite variations of the story of the Queen of Sheba's visit to the court of King Solomon have been told and are still being told. Back-and-forth cultural borrowings and diffusions have added layers of meanings, metaphors, and symbolism to this story, making it a truly transnational and transcultural story, infused with universal themes and cultural specificities. Yet across all cultures, one impulse remains dominant: the Herculean patriarchal effort to conquer her "Garden," appropriate her authority, banish her from the public, restrict her mobility, and control her body.

In the following pages I describe and discuss at some length the Quranic story of the encounter between the Queen of Sheba and the Prophet-King Solomon, interwoven with its imaginary – and often entertaining – reconstructions by medieval Muslim biographers and storytellers. The inconclusive, enigmatic, and abbreviated narratives in the Qur'an, as well as the silence of the scripture regarding the fate of both king and queen, have left multitudes of people from different cultures and faiths wanting to know what exactly transpired in that dramatic encounter and the exchanges – gifts, wits, and all – between King Solomon and the Queen of Sheba. Sages, scholars, Sufis, creative artists, poets, musicians, and storytellers have been intrigued by this fairy tale of a cosmic gender encounter. For most of them, sex and violence, love and marriage, take the center stage, despite their absence in the Quranic revelations. The patriarchal discourse of might and righteousness thus reproduced through the retelling of the story reaffirms the "natural" differences between the sexes, appropriates the divine word, and legitimates male domination and control, but not without ambivalence. After all, the queen's sovereignty is the subject of revelations in the Qur'an. Muslim scholars have thus had to balance the rather positive image of a thoughtful woman political leader in the Qur'an with its purported condemnation in a prophetic hadith, "Never will succeed such a nation as makes a woman their ruler," as I discuss in Chapter 2.

Much of the scholarly writing about the Queen of Sheba and King Solomon concerns a debate about which is the "true," the "earliest," or

---

[7] See also Jacob Lassner (1993, 228, fn. 11).

the "original" version of the tale.[8] What interests me is what the story tells us about women and political authority. I am interested in the queen's leadership and charisma, in her wisdom and genuine concern for her people's lives, in her sustained diplomatic effort to negotiate peace with a much stronger and uncompromising adversary. I read this story as an example of desirable leadership, regardless of gender; as one that values negotiation over domination, peace over war and destruction.

To understand the transcultural staying power of this Quranic story, we need to frame it within the context of its many patriarchal reconstructions by medieval Muslim exegetes, chroniclers, and biographers. Inasmuch as the story of the queen's sovereignty in the sacred texts has captivated creative imaginations, it has confounded the exegetes and confronted them with moral and political dilemmas regarding women and political agency, mobility, and sexuality. They have vacillated between praising the trappings of her authority – the majesty of her Mighty Throne, the unparalleled gifts she sent to Solomon – and simultaneously condemning her for her transgression against the "natural" patriarchal order, for usurping male authority, and for not being a fully human woman. The chroniclers' ambivalence toward women's political authority and their wish to differentiate it from, and subordinate it to, male authority seems to have led them to anxious exaggerations of the queen and the source of her power. Demonizing the Queen of Sheba, Jewish sources view her as "a supernatural being with seductive sexual power and an intention to kill infants in their cradle" – a Lilith (Lassner 1993, 21; Silberman 1974, 84). Muslim medieval biographers, including Tha ʿlabi and Tabari, also question her humanity and argue that the queen was human on her father's side and a *jinn* from her mother's, a *jinn* princess from whom the queen inherited hairy, donkey-like legs. But Muslim scholars have also had to balance their ambivalence and negative characterization of the queen with the positive Quranic image of her political authority. In this chapter I juxtapose the Quranic story with its patriarchal version in which the queen is defeated, her Mighty Throne appropriated, and her mobility is curtailed through concubinage/marriage.

In the following pages, I first position King Solomon and the Queen of Sheba within their kinship and genealogical parentage, pedigree, and position – historical or fictional – as reconstructed by medieval Muslim scholars and biographers, before moving on to discussing the Quranic revelations. Knowledge of the king's and the queen's purported kinship and religious and political backgrounds situates them within the

---

[8] For a few examples, see Watt (1974), Silberman (1974), Ullendorf (1974), Lassner (1993), Jeenah (2006), and Elias (2009).

patriarchal scheme of the medieval power structure, cosmology, and gender hierarchy, from which I intend to retrieve the queen's political authority and peace-building activities.

Kinship and Genealogy: Situating King Solomon and the Queen of Sheba

Solomon: Man-God

Muslims and Jews agree that Solomon, son of David, was both a mighty king of Israel and a Prophet of Islam. But they differ on some crucial details surrounding his exalted birth. Jewish and Muslim stories both maintain that King David was on the roof of his palace chasing a "golden dove" when he saw Bathsheba, wife of Uriah, bathing. Smitten by Bathsheba's flawless beauty, King David arranged for Uriah, a war hero in his army, to be killed in battle, which then freed David to marry Bathsheba (Lassner 1993, 252, n. 101). While medieval Muslim biographers tell the same story, they assert that it was Satan disguised as the golden dove who misled David to the edge of the palace roof from where he saw Bathsheba (Tabari 1991, 144–147; 1994, 152–153). In this Islamic version, while David did connive to have Bathsheba's husband killed in battle (for which he later repented and was forgiven), his action was mitigated by the fact that he did so over the course of two – or three – wars. He then dutifully abstained from consummating the relationship with Bathsheba, allowing her to complete her ʿidda, the four-month period of sexual abstinence obligatory for Muslim widows, before actually marrying her (Thaʿlabi 2002, 469; Tabari 1991, 148–149). Thus was born Solomon (Figure 1.1).

In the Quranic story, the son is not held accountable for his father's indiscretion. God showers Solomon with favors, despite some personal imprudence – large and small[9] – and lavishes incredible riches and power upon him, granting him unrivaled political authority and supernatural clout.[10] God grants Solomon the ability to understand the languages of birds and bees, to command humans, demons, and jinn, and authorizes the wind to stay in his service to facilitate rapid transit for him and his extraordinary army anytime he wishes (Qurʾan 27:16–17; 34:12; Thaʿlabi

---

[9] In the Jewish tradition he is more of an erring king than the rather blameless prophet of the Islamic version (www.bbc.co.uk/programmes/b01jhjc7). Solomon is not considered blameless in all Islamic sources, however. Some, for example, relate that his carelessness led to the momentary loss of his signet ring (Tabari 1994, 161–166; Rumi, Masnavi 4; Mottahedeh 2013, 257).

[10] Regarding Solomon's clout, see Mottahedeh (2013).

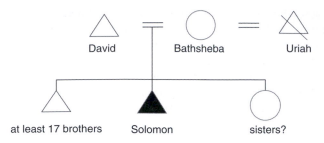

Figure 1.1 King Solomon's Genealogy

2002, 491; Tabari 1991, 154). The supernatural *jinn* live among humans, and just as humans, some are good and some are evil (Qur'an 72, 14). King Solomon's powerful army stretched out over "one hundred *parasang*s [about three miles]: twenty-five of them consisted of humans, twenty-five of *jinn*, twenty-five of wild animals, and twenty-five of birds" (Tabari 1991, 154; Lassner 1993, 69). "Solomon ordered the violent wind and it lifted all this, and ordered the gentle breeze and it transported them. God inspired him while he was journeying between heaven and earth" (Tabari 1991, 154), and reminded him further, "Lo, I have increased your rule that no creature can say anything without the wind bringing it and informing you" (Tabari 1991, 154).

Solomon's riches extended to his harem. He amassed some "one thousand houses of glass on the wooden [carpet],[11] in which there lived 300 wives and 700 concubines" (Tabari 1994, 161). While some Jewish and Muslim sources have expressed skepticism regarding the exact number of women in the king's enormous harem, others have disputed the exact ratio of wives to concubines: was it 300 wives to 700 concubines or 700 wives to 300 concubines?[12] (Tabari, 1991; Lassner 1993, 239, n. 79). Well, said Victorian author Rudyard Kipling, "in those days everybody married ever so many wives, and of course the King had to marry ever so many more just to show that he was the King" (1907, 231). Some sources tell us that Solomon had "the sexual potency of forty men, and clearly he needed it" (Lassner 1993, 86) – though apparently most of his wives were "horrid," as Kipling humorously concluded in his story "The Butterfly that Stamped." No wonder, then, muses Lassner, that "for all this prodigious lovemaking, he could produce only a single progeny." Still, powerful, perfect, and potent, Solomon was said to be "the greatest of all lovers"

---

[11] The carpet served as the troupe's vehicle (Lassner 1993, 48).
[12] See also www.bbc.co.uk/programmes/b01jhjc7.

(Lassner 1993, 86). But so much power needed to be balanced by wisdom and tempered with justice. That, too, God granted him. Accordingly, Solomon would grow up to be exceedingly intelligent and wise, and his justice and judgments universally recognized. Above all, God gifted Solomon a miraculous ring carved with "His"[13] ineffable name that "opened all doors," in Qaʾani's[14] poetic rendition (Sattari 2002, 105). The eleventh-century chronicler Muhammad ibn ʿAbd Allāh al-Kisaʾi elaborates further:

> To ensure Solomon's domain over forces natural and supernatural, Gabriel dusted off the signet ring of God's Vice Regent, which had been lying about paradise almost since time immemorial. That is, when Adam had been expelled, it flew from his finger and returned to its place of origin. (Lassner 1993, 68)

Nothing moved without Solomon's knowledge. The patriarch's power was absolute – almost divine. He was at the peak of his power and global dominance when his spy bird, the little hoopoe, informed him of the sovereign Queen of Sheba and her Mighty Throne.

The Queen of Sheba: Jinn-*Woman?*

Who was the Queen of Sheba? Was she a sovereign head of her state and the commander-in-chief of her peaceful and prosperous oasis? Was she the commander of the faithful, even if she worshiped the Sun God? Or was she an apparition, a *jinn* of sorts, of a powerful and autonomous woman – deadly and dreadful to patriarchs and patriarchy? Some say the Queen of Sheba was a virgin beauty from Ethiopia, others say from Yemen and Southern Arabia, but no one really knows. By all accounts, the queen's leadership, grace, intelligence, and wisdom held universal appeal. Little wonder, then, that the story of her sovereignty and the mystery of her relationship with Solomon – political and sexual – continues to captivate the popular imagination. Her story has inspired many renowned artists, sculptors, architects,[15] musicians,[16] filmmakers,[17] painters, and miniaturists throughout the ages in eastern and western societies – and in some

---

[13] The Muslim God is genderless.

[14] Popularly known as Qaʾani, Mirza Habibollah Shirazi (b. 1808) was a famous Persian poet of the Qajar era (1789–1925).

[15] The fifteenth-century Persian queen Gowhar Shad, who patronized several buildings and monuments in Herat, Afghanistan, had the following inscription carved on her mausoleum: "The Bilkis of the Time" (Rashid 2001, 38).

[16] See Georg Friedrich Handel's "The Arrival of the Queen of Sheba" and Carl Goldmark's opera "The Queen of Sheba," an opera in four acts, www.musicwithease.com/goldmark-queen-sheba.html.

[17] *Solomon and the Queen of Sheba* (1959) by King Vidor is a classic example; see also Conrad (2002).

African countries, most notably in Ethiopia. Popular cultures and folk imaginations have also transformed this remarkable transnational story of an intelligent and thoughtful queen to suit their own cultural sensibilities and fantasies.

As with Solomon, God bestowed on the Queen of Sheba "something of everything," including sovereignty of an idyllic oasis – a paradisaical "Garden" somewhere in Yemen or Southern Arabia, or in Axum in Ethiopia (Tha'labi 2002, 525; Lassner 1993, 77). In the Qur'an the queen is portrayed as a wise, just, and caring ruler from whom God has denied no bounty or riches. Above all, God has given the queen a magnificent Mighty Throne ('arsh-i 'azim; Qur'an 27:23). "Of all the implements that became symbols of Solomon's authority," writes Lassner, "none, including perhaps his signet ring, received such prominence in so wide a variety of cultures as did this legendary throne" (1993, 77). Tha'labi describes Queen of Sheba's throne:

The front of her throne was of gold set with red rubies and green emeralds, and its back was of silver crowned with jewels of various colors. It had four legs: one leg of red ruby, one of green sapphire, a leg of green emerald, and a leg of yellow pearl. The plates of the throne were of gold. Over it were seventy rooms, each with a locked door. The throne was eighty cubits long and rose eighty cubits in the air. (2002, 525)

With no hint of irony, however, Tha'labi then goes on to claim that it was the queen herself who ordered the throne to be made for her (2002, 525). Was it not God Almighty who had given her that magnificent and Mighty Throne, just as "He" had given the signet ring to Solomon (Qur'an 27:23)?

The queen's military arsenal and army, however, paled before that of the awesome firepower of King Solomon. Hers was entirely made up of human beings with no supernatural creatures or celestial forces to perform mighty deeds or magical tricks. But then, lest we forget, the queen's mother was a *jinn* princess with supernatural power, and the queen herself was "brought up among the jinn" (Jeenah 2004, 56; see also Lassner 1993, 171).

Significantly, while we hear nothing about the queen's parentage in the Qur'an (unlike Solomon son of David), medieval Muslim biographers and storytellers have written extensively on and repeatedly recounted her mixed parentage and genealogy. Popularly known as al-Hadhhadh, we are told that the queen's father was a "mighty king and the ruler of all the land of Yemen" (Tha'labi 2002, 523). One day, the story goes, the king was out hunting when he saw two serpents locked in combat; one was black, the other white. As the black serpent was about to overpower the white, the Yemenite king intervened and killed it. With that he broke the curse on the white snake, who happened to be none other than the king of the *jinn*[18] (Stowasser 1994, 153, n. 8; Tabari 1994, 166; Lassner 1993, 169). In gratitude the king of the *jinn* offered his daughter's hand to the king of Yemen, who was only too happy to marry the princess *jinn*, for he "disdained" to marry any of the daughters of local dignitaries, whom he found beneath his status. This "haughty" attitude of the father, Tha'labi tells us, was inherited by his daughter Bilqis (2002, 523; Sattari 2002, 127–128). Tha'labi also relates a hadith from a close companion of the Prophet of Islam that "One of the parents of Bilqis was a jinni" (2002, 523). Ibn 'Arabi, the thirteenth-century mystic philosopher, however, identifies Bilqis with "divine wisdom" because she "was both spirit and woman since her father was one of the jinns and her mother a mortal being" (Schimmel 1997, 59). In those days it was not unusual for *jinn* and humans to fall in love and that's how the King of Yemen married a *jinn* princess (Tha'labi 2002, 523; Lassner 1993, 50).

Thus was born the beautiful Bilqis (aka the Queen of Sheba) from the union of a *jinn* mother (or father) and a human father (or mother) (Figure 1.2). Whether from her mother, her father, or both, Bilqis inherited super-natural power and carried it in her veins. As an only child,[19] Bilqis grew up to learn, conceivably, magical power and transfiguration[20] from her mother, and authority and leadership from her father. Some say she was thirty years old, long past the customary age of marriage, when her father died. She then succeeded him as the Queen of Yemen.[21] In some accounts a male rival emerged to contest her authority and for a time ruled over parts of Yemen (Lassner 1993, 50–51), but he turned out to be a ruthless leader, particularly violent toward women, whom he would deflower before their husbands (van Gelder 2013, 117). Outraged at his behavior and respond-ing to the plea of the Yemenites under this tyrant's rule, Bilqis planned a daring strategy. She proposed to marry him and he accepted happily, despite his advisers' opposition. In his palace as his bride, she arranged to get him drunk, and "in a move symbolic of removing his improperly over-active genitalia, she severed his head and hung it from the palace before slipping away under cover of night" (Lassner 1993, 75–76). Applauding

[18] In some Persian versions, the white snake is the son of the king of the *jinn*, who offers his sister, Pari (meaning 'angel,' i.e. an invisible supernatural being like a *jinn*), to the King of Yemen (Tabari 1994, 167; Parvizi 1969, 162–163).

[19] In some accounts, Bilqis has an elder – or half- – brother who died in infancy (Tabari 1994, 166–170; Lassner 1993, 228, n. 15), again rendering Bilqis a substitute.

[20] The *jinn* are shape-shifters and have the ability to appear and disappear at will, collapsing time and space (Tabari 1994, 170; Lassner 1993, 169–170). For a study on the *jinn*, see El-Zain (2009).

[21] Citing several Perso-Islamic sources, Lassner writes of a version of the story in which Bilqis was to succeed her father and rule as a regent only until her nephew – or a male cousin – would come of age and take the helm of the state (1993, 228, n. 15).

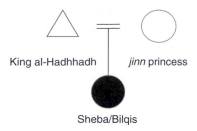

King al-Hadhhadh   *jinn* princess

Sheba/Bilqis

Figure 1.2 Queen of Sheba's Genealogy

her liberating action, the Yemenites hailed her as their savior and leader: "You are worthier than anyone of this realm" (Tha'labi 2002, 524; see also Van Gelder 2013, 118). And so Bilqis became the Queen of Sheba, establishing her rule firmly and became the unrivaled sovereign of Yemen.

Acknowledging the Queen of Sheba's strategic planning to free her people from the tyranny of a decadent and morally corrupt ruler (an ironic twist on the alleged Prophetic hadith), Tha'labi then goes on to relate a hadith from Ibn Maymunah, tracing the chain of his transmissions all the way back to caliphs 'Ali and Abu Bakr, stating that when Bilqis was mentioned in the Prophet's presence, he said, "Never will succeed such a nation as makes a woman their ruler" (2002, 524; see also Lassner 1993, 52).

Did Tha'labi – and Ibn Maymunah – have momentary lapses of memory? Did Tha'labi via Ibn Maymunah not just tell us about a heroic Queen of Sheba who saved her people from the tyranny of a violent and corrupt ruler? Did they overlook that the Prophet of Islam received revelations about the Queen of Sheba and her diplomatic attempts to save her people from certain war and destruction?

The Queen of Sheba in the Qur'an

> Lo! I found a woman ruling over them, and she has been given (abundance) of all things, and she possesses a Mighty Throne.
>
> Qur'an 27:23

According to the Qur'an, neither King Solomon nor the Queen of Sheba had any knowledge of the other. It is the little hoopoe, Solomon's spy/guide that makes them aware of one another.[22] The story begins with

---

[22] Farid ud-Din Attar, the thirteenth-century Persian Sufi poet and author of *The Conference of the Birds*, represents the hoopoe as the guide (*salek-i rah*). See the translation by Dick Davis (1984).

Solomon reviewing his extraordinary army. Not finding the hoopoe among the flock, he flies into rage, vowing to punish the bird by having its[23] feathers plucked or slaughtering it unless it has a good excuse (Qur'an 27:20–21).

Why the temper tantrum and the promise of such unusual and cruel punishment? Medieval sources have provided several reasons for the king's anger and justification for his threat of harsh punishment. The hoopoe, according to the Perso-Islamic traditions, has the ability to see water underground (Tabari 1991, 157; Rumi, *Masnavi* 1, 89–91; Paydarfard 2011). The reason for the King's rage, we are told, was that it was time for him to perform his prayer ablution and he needed water to do so (Tha'labi 2002, 521; Tabari 1991, 157–158).[24] Soon the hoopoe returns to Solomon's camp and, thank goodness, he does have a good excuse. The little bird tells its master that it has come to know of something as yet unknown to the King. The hoopoe then tells Solomon all about the Queen of Sheba and her prosperous oasis and how God has given her something of everything, including a Mighty Throne ('arsh-i 'azim) – "the tools and equipment in her dominion" (Tha'labi 2002, 525). The only problem, the hoopoe explains to an incredulous Solomon and his attending army, is that the queen and her followers worship the sun because Satan (*shaytan*) has deceived them by hiding knowledge of Allah from them (Qur'an 27:24–25). The commentators explain that the reason for the queen's wrong-headed faith was that once when she asked her advisers what her forefathers worshiped, she was told, "They worshiped the Lord of Heaven." Not being able to see the deity, she decided to bow to the sun, for in her eyes nothing was more powerful than its light.[25] As her people's sovereign, she then "obligated her people to do likewise" (Tha'labi 2002, 525).

The hoopoe ends its report by praising Allah, "Lord of the Mighty Throne," using the same term, 'arsh-i 'azim, used to describe God's celestial throne in the Qur'an (27:26). The news discombobulates the King. Had God not placed the wind at his service to inform him of all that happened in his kingdom and beyond? Not exactly! God in "His" infinite wisdom wished to humble Solomon occasionally and to let him know that there were limits to his power (Lassner 1993, 228, n. 12; Sattari 2002, 84). The news of a ruling queen was of a different order. There were plenty of queen consorts in Solomon's extraordinary harem, including the Pharaoh's daughter. But a *sun-worshiping sovereign queen* was well outside

---

[23] In some accounts of Persian folklore, the hoopoe, *hudhud* is female (Sattari 2002; Paydarfard 2011).

[24] In the Jewish version it is an excess of wine that sparks King Solomon's fury (Lassner 1993, 39–40).

[25] The sun is feminine in Arabic (*al-shams*) and Persian (*khurshid*) mythology.

of the patriarchal order and beyond the limits of his imagination. Incredulous, Solomon decided to determine the truth of the bird's eye-witness account for himself. He gave the hoopoe a letter, instructing it to take it to the queen and wait to see what answer she gave.[26] The message to the queen was ominous: "Be ye not arrogant against me, but come to me in submission" (Qur'an 27:27–31).

The queen became alarmed. Was this yet another imposter king? Had she not established her legitimate authority by beheading one already? But then she reckoned that "Any ruler who uses birds as his emissaries is indeed a great leader" and must be "a mightier sovereign than herself" (Tha'labi 2002, 526; Lassner 1993, 192). The queen knew better than to mock or ignore a powerful adversary's threat. Once again, she planned her strategy carefully.

Sitting on her royal throne, Tha'labi imagines, the queen "typically" assembled her advisers and spoke to them "from behind a veil." But then, Tha'labi stresses, "when an affair distressed her, she unveiled her face" (2002, 526). Unveiled and in control, she told her advisers about the threatening letter she had received from Solomon and asked for their advice (Qur'an 27:29–30). Acknowledging their leader's authority, they declared their willingness to fight on her behalf: "We possess force and we possess great might. The affair rests with you; we follow your command" (Qur'an 27:32–33). Mindful of the King's serious challenge to her sovereignty and her community, however, the politically savvy queen cautioned her counselors, "Kings, when they enter a city, disorder it and make the mighty ones of its inhabitants abased" – and the All-Knowing Almighty confirms, "That they will do" (Qur'an 27:34). The Queen of Sheba's act of consultation, however, gives Tha'labi pause. He dismisses the queen's advisors as submissive men, and the queen as a cunning woman. Granted, he observes, the queen was an intelligent and clever woman, but she "dominated the chief men of her people" and "exercised control and managed them at will" (Tha'labi 2002, 527). Tha'labi's sexism notwithstanding, the Queen of Sheba decided astutely to send Solomon splendid gifts (Qur'an 27:35), in hopes that the exchanging of gifts would serve as a prelude to ceasing or avoiding hostilities.

Gift Exchange and Peace-Making

What kind of gifts did the Queen of Sheba send Solomon? The Qur'an is silent on that. But medieval storytellers tell us that in addition to

---

[26] For a sixteenth-century image of Bilqis, see https://commons.wikimedia.org/wiki/File:B ilquis.jpg.

camel-loads of silver, gold, spices, and frankincense, the queen's gifts included riddles. The commentators tell us that sending gifts, engaging the king in witty exchanges, and solving riddles were not only a means by which the queen sought to avoid conflict. Having heard of Solomon's boundless intelligence,[27] the Queen of Sheba – no less intelligent herself – decided to test him and in the process determine whether he was a king or a prophet. The queen reasoned that if he accepted her gifts and looked at her emissaries with a "look of wrath" it would mean that he was only a king and no mightier than she – that his intention was political and that he desired to depose her and confiscate her mighty throne. But if he refused her gifts and appeared to be an "affable, kindly man," that would be a sign that he was a prophet of God and would not be satisfied until she submitted to him and followed his religion (Tha ʿlabi 2002, 528–529; Stowasser 1994, 64–65).

She arranged for some five hundred adolescent boys to be dressed as girls and an equal number of adolescent girls to be dressed as boys, and asked Solomon to "distinguish the maidservants from the menservants" (Tha ʿlabi 2002, 528). The King was able to identify the sex of the cross-dressed crowd only when Angel Gabriel and his hoopoe spy came to his aid – the hoopoe had watched the queen's preparations from the sky and informed the king accordingly (Tabari 1994, 173; Tha ʿlabi 2002, 529). The difference between the sexes, we are told, could be seen in the "natural" (i.e. habitual) ways young boys and girls wash their faces: "A girl would take water from the vessels with one of her hands, put it in the other, and then splash her face with it, while a boy would take it from the vessel with both his hands and splash his face with it" (Tha ʿlabi 2002, 530; Tabari 1994, 174).[28]

---

[27] In his book *The Wisest Man in the World* (1968), Benjamin Elkin writes that the Queen of Sheba did not initially believe that Solomon was the wisest man in the world and so decided to test him. She had her advisers replicate a beautiful flower from Solomon's garden 100 times. Then the queen asked Solomon to pick out his flower. Try as he might, he was unable to do so; all 100 flowers looked exactly alike and had the same fragrance. It was then that a little bee whom the king had earlier freed by letting it out the window, came to his aid and, buzzing quietly in his ear, led him to his unique flower. Without the little bee's help, the king would have failed.

[28] In another instance, the skeptical Queen asks, "Tell me about how your lord exists." Hearing this, Solomon "leapt up from his throne and fell down in worship, and [suddenly] it began to thunder. His troops ran and scattered, and the angel Gabriel came to him and said to him: 'Solomon, your Lord says to you: "What ails you?"' Solomon says: 'Gabriel, my Lord knows best what she has said.' Gabriel says: 'However your Lord commands you to return to your throne, and to send for her and for whoever is present with her of your army and hers, and to ask her and them what she asked you.'" Solomon did so, and lo and behold, neither the queen nor her army could remember anything. By then all was wiped from their memory: "God had made them forget it" (Tha ʿlabi 2002, 535; Tabari 1991, 162).

Solomon rejected the queen's gifts, professing that what God had given him far surpassed what God had given her (Qur'an 27: 36). He then accused the queen and her emissaries of being "a vainglorious people, trying to outdo each other in things of this world" because they did "not know anything else" (Tha'labi 2002, 530) – presumably meaning that they knew nothing but power and greed. Solomon sent her emissaries back with another threatening message, warning of his imminent attack and the expulsion of the queen and her people from their land, "abased and utterly humbled" (Qur'an 27:37).

Once again the commentators moved to soften the harsh language of the quick-tempered patriarch. Tha'labi has him dabbing his letter with musk and sealing it with the impression of his famous signet ring (2002, 526), "the ring from which he derived so much of his power" (Lassner 1993, 52). In the Jewish *Targum Sheni*, Solomon starts his letter with: "From me, Solomon the King, who sends greetings. Peace unto you and your nobles, Queen of Sheba! No doubt you are aware that the Lord of the Universe has made me king of the beasts of the field, the birds of the sky, and the demons, spirits, and Liliths. All the kings of the East and West, and the North and South, come to me and pay homage." He then goes on to politely but firmly demand that she come to him, pay homage, and submit (Lassner 1993, 166). Certain that Solomon is a prophet of God, the Queen of Sheba decided to embark on a journey to Jerusalem to meet with Solomon personally in hopes of averting the certain destruction of her community. But before leaving her homeland, Tha'labi tells us, the queen

[O]rders her throne to be placed in the innermost of seven rooms, arranged one within another, in the most remote of her castle. She closed the doors behind it, and set guards over it to keep it safe. She said ... "Keep my royal throne secure, and do not trust it to anyone or let anyone see it until I return."

The Queen of Sheba then embarked on her journey to Solomon's court, accompanied by 12,000 chiefs of Yemen, under each of whom were 100,000 warriors (Tha'labi 2002, 531).

In the meantime, King Solomon, who had earlier rejected the queen's gifts and accused her of vaingloriousness, now wanted to possess her Mighty Throne – the seat of her power. The King was not wanting in mighty thrones – God had given him plenty of those.[29] It is recorded that

Solomon b. David had six hundred thrones set out. The noblest humans would come and sit near him, then the noblest jinn would come and sit near the humans.

---

[29] See Mottahedeh (2013). See also Lassner (1993, 77) for descriptions of Solomon's thrones in the Jewish and Muslim sources.

Then he would call the birds, who would shade them, then he would call the wind, which would carry them. (Tabari 1991, 154–155)

Still, Solomon coveted the queen's Mighty Throne, given to her by none other than the Almighty. But why would he want to seize her throne? Tha'labi argues that when Solomon saw from afar the cloud of dust stirred up by the queen's mighty army marching toward his kingdom, he moved swiftly to appropriate the queen's throne (2002, 531). Did the King feel fearful, envious, or threatened by the Queen's formidable army? Relying on his vast army of supernatural beings, the warrior king asked his companions and minions, "Which one of you can bring me her throne before they come to me in submission?" (Qur'an 27:38). A mighty creature from among the *jinn* offered to bring it to him before he could rise from his seat. "I want it faster than that," Solomon said. (Lassner 1993, 58). One who had the knowledge of the Book,[30] a certain Assaf Barkhia, the king's *wazir*, offered to bring the queen's throne to Solomon's court in the blink of an eye – and so he did (Qur'an 27:40).[31] Knowledge is indeed power,[32] but prayers also help. Assaf's prayer was, "Our God and God of all things! One God, there is no god but You. Bring me the Throne" (Tha'labi 2002, 532; Tabari 1994, 174–175). The world-renowned Persian philosopher and mystic poet Maulana Jalal al-Din Rumi (d. 1273) makes clear, however, that this feat was made possible only because of "Assaf's breath" (*dam*), the power of his faith, rather than a magician's trick (Masnavi 4, 57).

Be that as it may, Solomon thanked God for having made it possible for him to confiscate his rival's Mighty Throne (Qur'an 27: 40). He then instructed his minions to disguise the throne in order to "see whether she is guided," that is, if she recognizes the "truth" (Qur'an 27:41). Muslim scholars and sages have argued extensively over the legality of taking the queen's throne. Clearly, they realize Solomon's action requires explanation. Some say "It was because its description amazed him ... so he wanted to see it before he saw her." Others say it was because "he wanted to show her the omnipotence of God." Still others say it was because he wanted to show "the greatness of his own power" and prove his prophethood (Tha'labi 2002, 531; Rahnema 1974, 211). But most agree "it was because Solomon knew that if she surrendered,

---

[30] A reference to Jews, Christians, and Muslims.

[31] The Qur'an does not specify a name, but according to Tabari, Assaf Barkhia was a Jewish convert and a close confidant of the king. He would go to Solomon's harem anytime he wished, and the king's wives did not observe veiling in his presence. In fact, if they needed something, they would go to him rather than the king (Tabari 1994, 163–164). See also Tottoli (2009).

[32] Long before Foucault, a Persian poem had pithily expressed the relation between knowledge and power: *tavana bovad har ke dana bovad* (she/he who has knowledge has power).

her property [as a Muslim] would be unlawful for him [to take], and he wished to seize her throne before it was thus forbidden to him" (Tha'labi 2002, 531). When the queen finally came before the king, he confronted her with her confiscated throne and asked her whether she recognized it.

Had she not locked up her throne securely in the innermost secret part of her palace before leaving?

Seeing her Mighty Throne in Solomon's possession, the queen was convinced that he was a prophet and that she was no match for him – at least not militarily. The wise queen then gave a measured response: "[It is] as though it were the very one," adding, "We were given the knowledge beforehand and we had submitted" (Qur'an 27: 42). With the queen at the threshold of his palace and her throne in his possession, Solomon invites the Queen of Sheba to enter, but not before subjecting her to another test.

Rites of Passage

It is related that the devils and the *jinn* that God had assigned to serve at Solomon's court (Qur'an 34:12) feared that once he saw the beautiful Queen of Sheba he would instantly fall in love with her, that they would marry and have a son, and the *jinn* would never be freed of their bondage to Solomon and his progeny (Tha'labi 2002, 533). So, they tried to "incite him against" the queen by telling him that "there is something [wrong] with her intelligence and her feet are like the hooves of a mule[33] ... and she has hairy ankles, all because her mother was a jinn" (Tha'labi 2002, 534; Tabari 1991, 162).

Be that as it may, a highly curious Solomon set out to find out the truth of the queen's donkey-like hairy legs for himself. Mindful of the queen's approaching army, whose dust cloud had darkened the sky of his empire, Tha'labi tells us, Solomon ordered his devils and *jinn* to build "a palatial pavilion of glass, clear as water, and make water flow beneath it, and have fish in the water. Then he placed his throne above it, and sat upon it, and the birds, the jinn, and the human beings crowded around him" (2002, 534). With the stage impeccably set, Solomon invited the queen to enter his palace.

As the Queen of Sheba was about to cross the palace threshold, she perceived the entrance to the pavilion as "a spreading water" and so "uncover[ed] her legs" – lifting up her skirt – to enter, only to recognize

---

[33] In its Ethiopian version, it was not a mule but a goat, and all because the queen's mother had looked at that "handsome looking goat ... with greedy desire" (Koltuv 1993, 45). In its Senegalese version, it is a cows' hooves (Fallou Ngom, personal communication).

the "water" as slabs of smooth glass. Realizing the illusion, the queen said, "God, I have wronged myself [*zalamtu nafsi*] and surrender [*aslamtu*] with Solomon to God, the Lord of all Being" (Qur'an 27:44). Awakened to a new reality, the queen surrendered to God by accepting the new faith, and with that her story ends in the Qur'an. But not in the imagination of biographers and storytellers.

As the Queen of Sheba lifted up her skirt to cross the watery threshold, the story continues, Solomon stared at her bare legs.[34] After all, the purpose of that architectural marvel of the water palace was, from the medieval storytellers' point of view, to trick the Queen of Sheba into exposing her legs so that the king could see for himself whether she had donkey-like hairy legs! Lo and behold, the queen did not have the hooves of a mule, but her legs were ever so scruffy, with hair "twisted around" them. "Disgusted" by the sight, Solomon modestly averted his gaze (Tha'labi 2002, 535; Tabari 1991, 162). King Solomon asked his supernatural minions what might be the best way to remove the unsightly hair. He called on them, saying, "How ugly this is! What can remove it?" (Tabari 1991, 163). They suggested as mundane a solution as using a razor. But the king would not hear of it – castration anxiety? (Lassner 1993, 201; Hallpike 1969, 257). The king then turned to the *jinn*, but they feigned ignorance. At last Solomon sought help from his demons and devils, the *'afarit* – his ever-ready enablers. The demons finally found a solution, making a depilatory paste to remove the hair and leave the queen's skin smooth and silky (Tha'labi 2002, 536; Lassner 1993, 201).[35]

Muslim biographers have described the elaborate process of depilating the queen's hairy legs as a prelude to sexuality and cohabitation.[36] As a hairy queen, her gender is ambiguous. She is liminal in the sense that she is neither fully human nor fully *jinn*, neither truly feminine nor wholly masculine. She is an ambiguous creature with no recognizable place in the "natural" gender hierarchy of the patriarchal social order. Depilation aimed to "feminize" the queen by getting rid of her unsightly masculine leg hair, disabling her supernatural power (inherited from her *jinn*

---

[34] For a fourteenth-century image of Bilqis crossing the water, see https://commons.wikimedia.org/wiki/File:Balami_-_Tarikhnama_-_Bilqis_crosses_the_pool_covered_by_crystal_to_greet_Solomon.jpg.

[35] "Queen Hatshepsut of Egypt also used to have myrrh oil rubbed on her legs, and Queen Esther would have a six-month course of beauty treatment utilizing oil of myrrh" as part of her "preparation in the Persian King Ahasuerus' harem" (van Beek 1974: 45–46). My female students were delighted to learn that their concern with removing excess hair has such an illustrious history.

[36] On the association of sex and hair, see Bromberger (2007), Delaney (1994), Hallpike (1969), Leach (1958), and Haeri (1989, 222, fn. 23).

mother), and to "humanize" her by retrofitting her to the patriarchal gender hierarchy. The Queen of Sheba is silenced, her body is appropriated, and her throne is confiscated. She is no longer a sovereign queen, but a queen consort, a concubine – a *bilqis*; no longer a political agent but a subject.

With the queen's surrender to Solomon's faith, and her hairy legs depilated, did the king cease hostilities, marry her, and send her to his humungous harem? We read none of that in the Qur'an. God's concern is not with the queen's marital status. Nor does God arrange for the fabulous pair to get married and live happily ever after. Indeed, the queen's gender is immaterial to her leadership and governance. It is, rather, her faith that is at the center of the Quranic revelations. But in its medieval reconstructions, it is gender politics that takes the center stage. The struggle for war and peace and the recognition of the true faith was turned into the battle of the sexes, leading to the silencing of the queen and the objectification of her persona. Mystified by an inconclusive ending to the encounter between Solomon and the Queen of Sheba – be it romantic, legal, or both, in the Qur'an – storytellers and biographers have speculated at length as to what may have – could or should have – happened in the aftermath of this high-level gender encounter. Some have contended that Solomon did fall in love with Bilqis, married the queen, and gifted Ba'albak in greater Syria as her dowry (Mottahedeh 2013, 249). Subsequently, he established her as a ruler over her dominion and had the *jinn* build her three more palaces to expand her realm (Lassner 1993, 201). Others have maintained that Solomon married the Queen of Sheba, but sent her back to Yemen – where she continued to rule over her people – and visited her every few months (Lassner 1993, 62). The intermittent nature of his nuptial visitations has given some biographers the impression that Solomon might have taken the queen as his concubine, as her name Bilqis (from the Hebrew *pilegesh*, meaning "concubine," as noted above) may suggest. A different view holds that Solomon, still disgusted by – or fearful of – the sight of the queen's "masculine" hairy legs, had this "haughty" woman humbled by having her marry a man from among his companions, despite her objection to marrying when she already had dominion over her own people (Tha'labi 2002, 535–536; Tabari 1991, 164). Lassner muses that the queen's biggest disappointment must have been her ultimate rejection by Solomon: "This haughty woman who had never been touched by a 'blade' and trained great men as if they were wild stallions to be broken, will be rejected outright by the great stallion of them all" (1993, 85–86).

From then on, Tha'labi tells us, love and marriage were no longer possible between humans and the *jinn*, and humans could no longer see the *jinn*, though the *jinn* could see them (2002, 523). The renowned scholar of mystical Islam, Annemarie Schimmel, wonders why "love" is missing in this story, and why the meeting between the "miracle working Solomon" and the "Yemenite queen has not been transformed into a romantic epic as have so many other traditions in Persia. This Quranic story," she reflects, "would have been the fitting basis of a wonderful allegory about the spiritual power of the divinely inspired ruler and the love of the unbelieving woman who finds her way to the true faith through the guidance of his words" (1997, 59–60). But could love flourish in a relationship based on inequality, trickery, domination, and control?

Solomon and Sheba both show intense curiosity, and a desire to know the other. But the paths they take to unite with the other lead them to different results. Having heard of the wisdom and justice of the prophet-king Solomon, the queen embarks on a journey of discovery, hoping to unite "with one who has wisdom" through negotiating and building bridges, making peace, and possibly finding love. King Solomon too seeks unity with the other, but he does so through appropriation and coercion. In the Sufi literature one's soul is the abode of both 'aql (wisdom) and *nafs* (desire, the base instincts). Where 'aql is equated with masculinity, *nafs* is associated with the feminine and thus subordinate to 'aql, the male intellect and reason (Schimmel 2003, 70). The wise Queen of Sheba's leadership provides a counter-narrative to this dominant patriarchal discourse that is firmly enshrined in the thought structure of medieval sages and biographers. Love of her people motivates the queen to act rationally, wisely, and prudently, as a good leader should.

Whether he treated the Queen of Sheba as a concubine or a wife, King Solomon did not usher her into his own giant harem, and Muslim and Jewish biographers have written copiously about this. Or, might it have been that the queen did not wish to part company with her people, marry Solomon, and join his multiracial, multifaith harem? Biographers have paid little or no attention to the queen's wishes and agency. It is not her brilliant diplomacy and successful peace-making initiatives to avert a certain war that is utmost in the minds of patriarchal exegetes, but rather the control of this "haughty" – read autonomous – woman's body, and restriction of her mobility and sexuality through marriage. The water rite of passage is not seen as a transition to a new vision of reality – a new faith – but as the ruse of a lustful king who tricks the queen into lifting up her skirt so that he can see her blemished hairy legs.

Did the queen return to Yemen, having averted war and saved her paradisaical oasis? Would her people hail her as their savior once again, and receive her as their undisputed leader? Would they follow their queen and convert to the new faith? Would God lavish even more favors on her now that she was a believer? We do not know the answer to these questions, but ignorance has not prevented many storytellers and chroniclers over the centuries and across many cultural traditions from portraying politically active women as "Lilith," "haughty," "hairy legged," "wicked," "jinn," and "crooked" (President Donald Trump continues to refer to his defeated opponent as "crooked" Hillary). At best, such women are humbled through marriage. At the center of the social drama of the king and queen's encounter, as reconstructed by medieval biographers, lies the sexual politics of domination and submission, mediated through the authoritarian – lustful? – gaze and facilitated by removing problematic hair (i.e. a sign of ambiguous gender). Having submitted under Solomon's threat, the queen's high-level encounter with him ended in an uneasy truce that left the status of the queen and the nature of her relationship to the king unknowable, and thus subject to patriarchal wishful thinking and fanciful interpretations.

In historicizing the Queen of Sheba, she is systematically stripped of her individuality, autonomy, and authority; she is transformed into an imaginary consort of the king – but with some qualifications and ambivalence. While the patriarchal imagination celebrates the queen's political defeat and sexual submission, it is woefully deficient in judging her spiritual awakening or her independent acceptance of "the true faith (Islam)" (Wadud 1999: 40–42; see also Booth 2015, 140–141).

The Qur'an and the Hadith: Women, Authority, Sovereignty

In the preceding pages I have given my interpretation of the Quranic story of the Queen of Sheba interwoven with multiple – and often colorful – reconstructions by medieval Muslim exegetes and biographers. As a divinely chosen sovereign, the Queen of Sheba was the temporal and spiritual leader of her people. She commanded authority and respect among her advisers and military leaders, who were willing to go to war for her. Although alarmed, the Queen of Sheba was not cowed by the threat of war, but nor was she willing to drag her people into a destructive conflict. In taking this stand, she can be viewed as the quintessential model of a caring and wise leader. Indeed, she was mindful that "Kings, when they enter a city, disorder it and make the mighty ones of its inhabitants abased" (Qur'an 27:34). The queen pursued peace with the king, who was a much stronger adversary. She thus saved the lives of her people and prevented the destruction of her paradisaical community. As she was "historicized" in the patriarchal imagination of medieval biographers and exegetes, however, she was demonized as half-*jinn*, her sovereignty was delegitimized, her authority was usurped, and her autonomy was brought under the control of a husband.

In the Quranic revelations, neither is she the daughter of a *jinn* princess – and hence, not an imposter or a usurper ruler – nor is her sovereignty rejected by the rank and file. Besides, God gave the sun-worshiping queen a Mighty Throne that so powerfully confounded medieval Muslim sensibilities. The biographers conveniently overlooked the fact that the Qur'an draws parallels between the queen's Mighty Throne and God's Celestial Throne, identifying them in both instances as *'arsh-i 'azim*. As God the "All-merciful sits upon the Throne, and His Throne embraces the heavens and the earth," in the mystic philosopher Ibn 'Arabi's contemplation, he has "mercy upon all things (Chittick 1995)"[37] Graced with the "divine love," Ibn 'Arabi stated, the Queen of Sheba exhibited her love and compassion for her followers; negotiated peace and saved her people from certain destruction. But the sages' patriarchal predispositions precluded them from appreciating the queen's sagacious agency – be it in the political or the spiritual domain.

In the storytellers' interpretations, the story ends with King Solomon confiscating the Queen of Sheba's Mighty Throne, sending her back to Yemen with a new husband, and installing the queen's husband as the new ruler and king of Yemen. Solomon then appoints a *jinn* to serve her husband and to keep a watchful eye on the Queen of Sheba (Tha'labi 2002, 536). Clearly, the new king of Yemen, the queen's husband, needed supernatural help – as did King Solomon himself – to conduct affairs of state and to keep the queen away from the public and from politics, all but forgetting that – or maybe because – the queen's mother was a powerful princess *jinn*. Even if we were to grant the medieval biographers' wish to banish the Queen of Sheba to the private domain, deny her power in the public domain, and keep her under the watchful eye of her husband – and the *jinn*? – the queen would not disappear, nor her power instantly evaporate. Even pushed behind the walls of her palace and forced into silence, the Queen of Sheba refused to be forgotten and stayed alive in popular oral culture, reemerging as Sayyida Hurra Queen Arwa, better known as "the little queen of Sheba" in eleventh-century Yemen (Chapter 3) and as Razia Sultan, also known as Bilqis-i Jihan, "Queen of the World," in thirteenth-century India (Chapter 4).

---

[37] See also Elias (2014).

At the center of the Quranic story is a drama of faith and paganism, a story in which neither the queen's autonomy nor her authority is at issue. But in its medieval reconstructions and interpretations, the central issue of faith becomes secondary to political rivalry and the need for patriarchal conquest and domination. The encounter between the king and queen is interpreted as a drama of sexual politics, of domination and submission, of a zero-sum leadership competition. While the queen's political authority threatened the king, her hairy legs (implying masculine authority) disgusted him, and her supernatural power (her presumed maternal *jinn* ancestry) frightened him even more. He had to get rid of them all: the queen had to be dethroned, her sovereignty usurped, and her authority transferred to a husband of sorts – patriarchal domination consolidated.

Although by the Middle Ages the story of the Queen of Sheba had been incorporated into a rigid patriarchal sensibility and biases, and theoretically women were banished from the public domain, throughout Islamic history, many women wielded power behind the throne and several others have actually come to power and ruled as sultans, queens, prime ministers, and presidents, as I will discuss in the following chapters. The question is when and how the alleged Prophetic hadith "Never will succeed such a nation as makes a woman their ruler" emerged, and for whom and under what circumstances it was invoked. How did this hadith become so prominent that in 1988 it formed the basis for a legal suit brought against Benazir Bhutto, the democratically elected Prime Minister of Pakistan; and in 1999 derailed the presidency of Megawati Sukarnoputri of Indonesia? How to explain the difference between these two supreme sources of authority, the Quranic revelations regarding the sovereignty of the Queen of Sheba and the alleged Prophetic hadith warning against women's political leadership? I suggest we journey back in historical time to explore the sociopolitical dynamics of the rapidly growing Muslim community and revisit the role Aisha, Mother of the Faithful and beloved wife of Prophet Muhammad, played as a military leader in the battle of succession, popularly known as the Battle of the Camel.

'A'isha Bint Abu Bakr: Battle of the Camel, Battle for Succession

لَنْ يُفْلِحَ قَوْمٌ وَلَّوْا أَمْرَهُمُ امْرَأَةً.

Never will succeed such a nation as makes a woman their ruler.[1]

Prophet Muhammad

On December 656 'A'isha, the beloved wife of Prophet Muhammad and Mother of the Faithful (Qur'an 33:53), made an alliance with two cousins and companions of the Prophet to lead a fateful war against 'Ali, the Commander of the Faithful and the Prophet's paternal cousin. The plan was to unseat Caliph 'Ali in favor of one of her two allies. 'A'isha and the opposition lost the battle for succession, which has come to be known as the Battle of the Camel. In the aftermath of the battle, a Basran notable, Abu Bakra (d. 672), alleged that he had heard of the following Prophetic hadith: "Never will succeed such a nation as makes a woman their ruler." He claimed that when Muhammad heard of the ruling Persian queen (r. 631–632), he predicted doom and ruin were a woman to lead a nation. By displacing 'A'isha's defeat onto the Persian queen, Abu Bakra sought to delegitimize 'A'isha's military and political leadership. It was not until the twentieth century, however, that this hadith was thrust into global consciousness, with the election of Benazir Bhutto as the prime minister of Pakistan. A leading religious organization, Jama'at Islami (JI), filed a case in Lahore High Court in 1988, arguing that Bhutto's gender disqualified her from leading a Muslim state. The High Court dismissed the JI's case, but challenges to female political authority and leadership have persisted, and not just in Pakistan.

Before discussing 'A'isha's leading role in the Battle of the Camel, I introduce the Persian queen, Purandokht, whose sovereignty and leadership is historically intertwined with that of 'A'isha's involvement in the battle of succession – hence the hadith cited above. As Muslims, we hear much about the queen through repeated reference to this hadith but know little about her accomplishments and legacy.

Who was Queen Purandokht of Persia and how did she become the subject of an alleged Prophetic hadith?

---

[1] https://sunnah.com/bukhari/92. Variations on this hadith are reported that moderate Bukhari's version, the hadith beginning with *la* ("no, not") instead of *lan* ("never").

51

Purandokht: Queen of Persia

Before Purandokht (Boran in Arabic) had the chance to wear the crown, her brother Shiruyeh Qubad/Kawad – also her husband, according to some sources[2] – usurped the throne by orchestrating his father's murder,[3] the last of powerful – and legendary – Sasanid emperor Khosrow Parviz[4] (r. 591–628). Like father, like son: Khosrow Parviz had a hand in his own father's murder, though the real perpetrators were evidently his two maternal uncles, members of the powerful rival Parthian dynasty (Pourshariati 2008, 132). They had the emperor blinded and then murdered.[5] Shiruyeh Qubad, too, had all his brothers and half-brothers – all seventeen of them, whom he feared might have a legitimate claim to the crown – "exterminated" (Ghirshman 1954, 308). Shiruyeh Qubad's reign did not last long, however. Six or seven months into his rule, he met his demise, in 628, through either plague or poison (Pourshariati 2008, 178, fn. 967). With no viable male heir left standing, the two daughters of Khosrow Parviz, Azarmidokht and Purandokht, were the only ones "from the origin of gods" who had a legitimate claim to the crown (Daryaee 1999, 77; see also Emrani 2009, 7), but the powerful families of the elite were divided as to which daughter to support. Azarmidokht (r. 631), described as "a clever and very attractive woman" in many Islamic sources, was first to succeed to the throne. When her own general proposed marriage to her, Queen Azarmidokht had him murdered because she did not dare to refuse his proposal. The general's son in turn avenged his father by murdering the ruling queen (Gignoux 1987; Pourshariati 2008, 209–210). It was then that Purandokht became the queen of the Persian Empire.[6] Neither queen faced any overt religious opposition due to her gender. Their

---

[2] Marriage between royal siblings seems to have been the tradition among the pre-Islamic ruling dynasties in Iran (Tabari 1999, 404, fn. 996; Daryaee 1999, 77; Chaumont 1989).

[3] Shiruyeh Qubad is known for his cruelty and is condemned in Persian literature and history, not only for conniving to kill his father but also for coveting his father's wife, the legendary Queen Shirin. The poet Ferdowsi (d. 1020) writes that "This criminal," in Shirin's words, "whom the turning heavens mock, killed his own father for the sake of a crown and throne" (Davis 2004, Vol. 3, 488). Shirin preferred to commit suicide over the grave of her royal husband rather than submit to his son's indecent demand.

[4] The story of his love affair with Queen Shirin is immortalized by two of Iran's literary giants, Ferdowsi and Nizami (d. 1209). Khosrow's name is also spelled Chosero and Xusro, and Kasra/Kisra in Arabic.

[5] Patricide was at times matched by filicide. Fearing a serious challenge to his throne from his son, Emperor Hormozd IV at one point contemplated murdering his son Khosrow Parviz (Pourshariati 2008, 132).

[6] There seems to be a gap of at least two years in leadership between Shiruyeh's death in 628 and Azarmidokht's ascension to the throne. For such discrepancies, and a description of the sequence of the reigns of these two queens and a possible brief overlap, see Pourshariati (2008, 203–208).

sacral dynastic ties trumped any possible religious (Zoroastrian) objections, influential though the religious elites were (Emrani 2009, 4–5).

Once in power, Queen Purandokht, whose reign coincided with the last two years of the Prophet Muhammad's life, tried to clean up the political and social chaos created by her male predecessors. She told her people, "I will pursue righteousness and ordain justice" (Tabari 1999, 404). She "spread justice," brought stability to the empire, signed a peace treaty with Byzantium, treated her people with fairness and justice, revitalized the infrastructure, reduced the burden of taxes, and minted coins (Tabari 1999, 404; Daryaee 1999, 77). Noldeke makes astonishing claims about the queen's sense of social justice: she "wrote open letters" to her subjects, telling them "how she wished to do well by them" (in Rose 1999, 44). During her short reign (631–632),[7] an "amazing" number of coins were minted in her name, depicting her as the only Sasanid woman wearing the crown (Emrani 2009, 7), some of which shed light on her regency: the legend on one coin indicates that the queen "originated" from the gods and was the restorer of the Sasanids' rule (Daryaee 1999, 81; Pourshariati 2008, 217).[8]

Two of the most remarkable feats the queen was able to accomplish were the unification of the factional Iranian army and the successful mediation between the feuding Iranian aristocratic dynasties. Thus, it was under her royal watch that the united Iranian army scored its only victory against the invading Arab army; a victory that has come to be known as the Battle of the Bridge (Pourshariati 2008, 214–218; Saunders 1978, 50).[9] All the evidence indicates that the queen's agenda was to restore the monarchy and the empire, which had declined because of the murderous competition between the male contenders to the throne of Sasan, dynastic factionalism amongst the nobility, and the considerable influence of the Zoroastrian clergy (Hodgson 1977, 203). Faced with many disaffected contenders to the throne, the queen was unable to achieve all that she had set out to do. Nonetheless, she managed to bring about a semblance of calm and peace for her people.

Purandokht was strangled by one of the ambitious leaders of her own army. Factional rivalries and regicides, consequently, left the Persian

---

[7] The exact date of her reign is disputed, varying from 629–630 to 631–632 (Pourshariati 2008; Chaumont 1989).

[8] Emrani notes that neither Tabari nor Hamzah al-Isfahani (tenth century) or Sebeos (seventh century) made any negative comment regarding the queen's gender in their records; an exception is Tha'alibi (tenth–eleventh century), who invoked the aforementioned Prophetic hadith (2009, 8).

[9] Saunders (1978) and Morony (1986), however, place the date of Iranian victory two years after Puran's death, in 634. For explanations of the inconsistencies with dating in various sources, see Pourshariati (2008, 207–208).

throne of Sasan with fewer and fewer viable options. Strong winds of war were blowing from the Arab lands, and the internecine conflict with Byzantium had shaken the very foundations of the empire. At the queen's murder the empire descended into chaos, leading to the eventual disintegration and fall of the Sasanian Empire, and the Arab conquest in 651 (Daryaee 1999; Ghirshman 1954; Pourshariati 2008; Shahbazi 1990; Zarrinkoob 1957).

Contesting Succession, Arab-Style

Queen Purandokht ascended the throne as the result of murderous male rivalries over the crown of Sasan and crises of transition of power that left the empire bereft of a viable and worthy male heir. The rivalries, regicide, and communal tensions over the succession after the death of the Prophet of Islam were no less intense in the community of his companions. Political contentions and competition over succession began among the Prophet's companions immediately after his death – particularly since the Prophet left no explicit instructions for a successor, the Shi'ites claim at Ghadir Khumm notwithstanding.[10] 'A'isha, the indomitable wife of the Prophet, played a crucial role not only in the lives of the first two caliphs, but also contributed "to the destabilization of the third, 'Uthman" (Mernissi 1991, 5; see also Tabari 1997; Abbott 1942). By the time 'Ali b. Abi Talib (r. 656–661), paternal cousin and son-in-law of the Prophet, succeeded to the caliphate as the fourth caliph of the expanding Muslim community, a pattern of regicide had taken hold. Two of 'Ali's predecessors, caliphs 'Umar b. Khattab (r. 634–644)[11] and 'Uthman b. Affan (r. 644–656),[12] had been assassinated and the nascent community of believers was going through great turmoil, dissent, and division. Many of the Prophet's companions were his cousins – close or distant – hailing from various clans of the larger Qureish tribe, some of whom desired leadership and coveted succession to the caliphate after Muhammad's death (Tabari 1990; Abbott 1942; Hinds 1972; Madelung 2014). In the meantime, the Arabs had expanded their conquest and reached deep into

---

[10] According to Shi'ites, "on returning from the last pilgrimage to Mecca on the way to Medina at a site called Ghadir Khumm the Prophet chose 'Ali, his paternal cousin, as his successor before the vast crowd that was accompanying him" (Tabataba'i 1977, 68, fn. 6).

[11] A member of the larger Qureish tribe, the Caliph 'Umar was a close companion of the Prophet and his father-in-law. His daughter Hafza was married to the Prophet Muhammad.

[12] 'Uthman was a second cousin of the Prophet Muhammad and married to two of the Prophet's daughters, one after the death of the other, in accordance with Islamic law, which prohibits simultaneous marriage to two sisters.

Iran on its eastern frontier and into Syria and North Africa to the west. With the new wealth and riches confiscated from the conquered lands, the tribal Arab Muslim community became embroiled in clashes over economic control and political loyalty, escalating racial tensions and ethnic rivalries.

As the favored wife of the Prophet Muhammad and daughter of the first caliph, designated "Mother of the Faithful" in the Qur'an (33:6), 'A'isha had unparalleled social and political capital. Her special relationship with the Prophet, the controversy over her slander (the affair of the necklace, described later), her involvement in the Battle of the Camel, and contribution to hadith literature and the production of religious knowledge have been the subject of copious historical records and biographies – medieval and modern, ideological and revisionist, positive and negative, factual and fictional. One would be hard pressed to add much to this enormous recorded legacy of 'A'isha – easily the most written-about Muslim woman. Fourteen centuries later, her hold over the collective Muslim imagination remains strong, particularly in the area of religious authority, due to her contribution to our knowledge of aspects of the early Muslim community, specifically of the Prophet's personal life through her transmission of hadith. While her religious authority is acknowledged almost universally, her political agency and authority are the subject of much hand-wringing and conflicting commentaries, invariably leading to the invocation of the above-mentioned Prophetic hadith. Likewise, more is written on the story of her slander and vindication through divine revelations (Qur'an 24:11) than on her involvement in the Battle of the Camel.[13] Religious scholars uphold the example of her political activism as a warning against women's political agency. Biographical traditions equivocate on acknowledging her political authority and the extent of her culpability and accountability in the first Muslim civil war (*fitna*). Medieval Sunni and Shi'ite exegetes have historically adopted different and often conflicting perspectives on 'A'isha's life, legend, and legacy. They have particularly diverged on attributing blame and responsibility to 'A'isha for her involvement in the Battle of the Camel, with the Shi'ites, unlike the Sunnis, holding her fully responsible for initiating hostilities against 'Ali. In the course of history, however, Sunnis and Shi'ites have converged in their opposition to women's political activism, authority, and leadership, this though seems to be more pronounced among the former. As the histories of the life and legacies of Prophet Muhammad

---

[13] For a discussion of the slander, see Spellberg (1994, 66–100). While most of my Muslim students vaguely knew of the slander story, none had heard of the Battle of the Camel or 'A'isha's involvement in it.

and his wives were collected from oral sources, written and recorded by men more than a century and a half after the Prophet's death, it would be naïve to expect an "accurate" description of the events and an objective assessment of ʿAʾisha's role in the first Muslim civil war.

In the process of assembling the enormous recorded legacy of ʿAʾisha, much has been revisited and reconstructed continuously (by Muslims and non-Muslims) at various historical junctures, each time adding another layer of interpretation, fact, or fantasy, depending on the ideological, political, and sociocultural sensibilities of the writer and *his* time. I say "his" advisedly, for until well into the twentieth century, Muslim history was written primarily *by* men and *for* men. With the exception of a few members of the elite class, women were not educated, and their contributions were either minimized or omitted altogether. What follows is my reading of ʿAʾisha's military and political leadership in the Battle of the Camel and her determination to influence the succession following the Prophet Muhammad's death. As a popular and charismatic woman, ʿAʾisha capitalized on her honorific – almost sacral – Quranic designation of "Mother of the Faithful" to motivate her "sons" to join her in the battle to unseat a reigning caliph. ʿAʾisha's leadership in this dramatic communal conflict and her subsequent defeat constitute the most controversial and consequential aspects of her legacy, one that is traditionally held up as an argument against women's public presence and political leadership. Revisiting her determination to deploy her political capital to influence the succession to the caliphate, I highlight her charismatic leadership, her religious and political convictions, and her popular appeal. In the course of retelling the story of ʿAʾisha's involvement in the politics of succession, I discuss, via renowned tenth-century historian-biographer Muhammad Jarir al-Tabari (d. 923), the role that people – i.e. ʿAʾisha's soldier-sons – played in supporting or rejecting her as their leader.[14] I have also closely consulted the highly informative books by Nabia Abbott (1942) and Denise Spellberg (1994).

In Chapter 1 I discussed the Quranic story of the Queen of Sheba and argued that it was not her sovereignty as a woman that was at the center of the revelations, but her faith. In this chapter I contextualize the afore-mentioned hadith opposing women's political leadership. How are we to interpret the differences in these two sources of authority regarding women and political agency in Islam – one supporting, and the other opposing? ʿAʾisha's political authority and military involvement in the

---

[14] For a discussion of the significance of Tabari's historiography see Tayob, who argues that Tabari balanced his reporting based on three different sources: those of the apologists, more politically oriented non-apologists, and hadith reports (1999, 206–207).

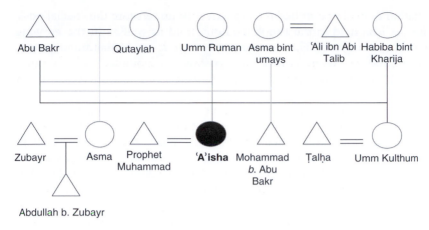

Figure 2.1 'A'isha Bint Abu Bakr's Genealogy

Battle of the Camel is the linchpin between revelation and tradition, as I discuss in the following pages.

Situating 'A'isha: Daughter, Wife, "Mother"

Born in Mecca circa 614 CE to Abu Bakr and Umm Ruman, 'A'isha – whose name befittingly means "life," "alive" (Figure 2.1) – was distinguished not only by her genealogical pedigree and marriage to the Prophet Muhammad, but also by the force of her personality and intelligence, as well as the nature of her relationship with the Prophet.[15] 'A'isha was married to the Prophet Muhammad at a young age,[16] and reportedly her charming personality soon established her as his favorite wife, captivating Muhammad's heart for the rest of his life.[17] 'A'isha was unique among the Prophet's wives; she was not only the sole virgin – a fact that has been given great historical weight – but also exerted significant political influence, particularly after the death of the Prophet. For her charismatic allure and beauty, the Prophet nicknamed her al-Humayra, "the little rosy one," and among her other epithets was *habibat habib Allāh*, "the beloved of the beloved of God" (Afsaruddin 2011). Such privileges –

[15] 'A'isha was not the only woman who enjoyed special relations with the Prophet. His first wife, Khadija, and her daughter Fatima also maintained an exalted place in the Prophet's heart, household, and beyond among Muslims of all branches of Islam.

[16] For discussions regarding 'A'isha's age at the time of her marriage to the Prophet Muhammad, see Kecia Ali (2014, chapter 5).

[17] For a description of 'A'isha's "special place" beside the Prophet and in his household, see Ibn Sa'd in Spellberg (1994, 29–31) and Stowasser (1994).

whether factual or ascribed retrospectively – underscore the special position 'A'isha held in the Prophet's household as well as in the growing
Muslim community. Having intimate knowledge of Muhammad's ways,
words, and character, 'A'isha was not slow "to capitalize on her reputation as Muhammad's favorite wife" (Abbott 1942, 97). Included in her
exceptional privileges in the Prophet's household were, according to the
later commentators: the fact that the Prophet received revelations in her
presence, died in her arms, and was buried in her chamber (Abbott 1942,
100; Afsaruddin 2011; Spellberg 1994).[18] When the Prophet of Islam
died in 632, 'A'isha was about eighteen years old. Privileged as the
Mother of the Faithful/Believers in the Qur'an, like Muhammad's other
widows, 'A'isha was nevertheless barred from remarriage (Qur'an
33:53).[19] Childless and widowed at an early age, and until her death in
678, she invested her enormous talent in the political, religious, and social
affairs of the rapidly expanding Muslim community, but not before leading a divisive and bloody civil war against the reigning caliph, 'Ali. The
"import of Aisha's life as an active force in the first Muslim community"
would, however, as Spellberg observes "be rendered entirely by men in
a social milieu vastly different from their subject's original Arabian setting" (1994, 11).

'A'isha's kinship affiliations within and across tribes and her marriage
to the Prophet Muhammad placed her at the center of the nascent
Muslim community, and endowed her with unrivaled social and political
capital. As a daughter, a wife, and a "Mother," she could not have been
better positioned, exercising power in the Prophet's household and commanding authority within the fast-growing community. Her status was
exalted and her influence, authority, and power far-reaching. Indeed,
'A'isha embodied the Foucauldian thesis that power is relational
(Foucault 1982; Newman 2004). Commentators invariably portrayed
'A'isha as intelligent, resolute, strong-willed, and vivacious. She was
clearly charismatic, easily capable of attracting large numbers of supporters, both male and female, including some of her own co-wives, who
were willing to follow her to war. Reading through the multiple and often
competing narratives of the tenth-century biographer-historian Tabari's
(1997) detailed report of the Battle of the Camel, one gets the clear
impression that 'A'isha had the courage of her convictions, and was
cognizant of the centrality of her role within the community. She

---

[18] She was held in such high esteem among the companions of the Prophet that the second
caliph, 'Umar, reportedly also asked to be buried in her chamber next to the Prophet and
Abu Bakr (Abbott 1942, 100).

[19] At his death the Prophet was survived by some nine wives, all of whom are distinguished
as Mothers of Believers.

commanded awe and respect; many were ready to die for her – or fight against her. She had little hesitation in speaking truth to power, as shown by her frequent testy exchanges with the Caliph 'Uthman and others: "And then Aisha spoke and she said plenty" (Abbott 1942, 110).[20]

In addition to having an extensive knowledge of the Quranic verses, 'A'isha possessed an admirable command of poetry, expertise that she utilized effectively to boost her soldiers'/sons' morale during the Battle of the Camel – as we shall see (Tabari 1997; Walker and Sells 1999, 58). Summing up the chroniclers' attempts to construct and reconstruct 'A'isha's legacy, Abbott writes:

Orthodox Islam conceded her first the honor of being superior in knowledge to any other Mother of the Believers and then to all of them collectively. Soon her great knowledge was reported to have exceeded that of all other women put together. Finally, she came to be considered among the wisest and most knowing of all people. (1942, 206)

Ultimately, what distinguishes 'A'isha as an extraordinary person – in all her complexity – is less her contribution to religious knowledge than her contested political authority, which she deployed during the Battle of the Camel. Her involvement in this battle has confronted religious and political elites with moral and legal dilemmas regarding representations of 'A'isha, and by extension any Muslim woman, as an autonomous political agent. 'A'isha's leadership of the dissenting faction and her active participation in the conflict over succession may not have seemed unusual in the sociopolitical dynamics at the time, but they had far-reaching implications for generations of Muslim women to come. Fourteen centuries later, a contemporary Egyptian historian warns that

The memory of Aisha should be pondered more than ever in our day. It never ceases saying [sic] to the Muslims: Look how this endeavor failed in the very heart of our Muslim history! We don't have to repeat it senselessly ... How can we do such a thing with the example of Aisha so fresh in our memory? (Sa'id al-Afghani, cited in Mernissi 1991, 7)

In the next few pages, I delve into Tabari's narratives of 'A'isha's role in the battle of succession, keeping in mind that his written record is based

---

[20] Apparently women of the Prophet's household had little or no hesitation speaking truth to power. Umm Salama, the aristocratic Meccan wife of the Prophet, questioned him for not including women in his divine message (Barlas 2006), and Fatima, the Prophet's beloved daughter, is reported to have pointedly contested Caliph Abu Bakr's decision to deprive her of her property inheritance, *fadak* (Gabbay 2014). 'A'isha is particularly known for her outspokenness and her "spirited rejoinders" to her parents and to Muhammad (Walker and Sells 1999, 77).

on multiple oral sources, remembered, reconstructed, and written from different and sometimes opposing perspectives.

'A'isha: Military Leader

In December 656, barely twenty-five years after the death of the Prophet of Islam, 'A'isha made a fateful political alliance with Talha b. 'Ubaydallāh[21] (597–656) and Zubayr b. Al-Awwam[22] (594–656), two companions and cousins of the Prophet Muhammad. The alliance was formed in fierce opposition to the fourth caliph and Commander of the Faithful, 'Ali b. Abi Talib (600–661), a paternal cousin of the Prophet and his son-in-law.

Even before 'Ali, however, the third caliph, 'Uthman, had been the subject of the trio's resentment. 'A'isha, Talha, and Zubayr were part of a vocal and growing opposition to Caliph 'Uthman and agitated against him (Hinds 1972, 464).[23] In the aftermath of the assassination of the second caliph, 'Umar (d. 644), the community of cousins, of which Muhammad had been a member, moved more aggressively to reassert its former tribal (i.e. Qureish) supremacy and regain its financial capital and social prestige (Hinds 1972). They opposed 'Uthman's policies, which aimed to centralize the growing Islamic territory and to maintain greater legal, political, and fiscal authority over the wartime spoils and their subsequent distribution (Tabari 1990, 242–243; Abbott 1942, 115; Afsaruddin 2011; Gleave 2008; Haider 2014; Hinds 1972; Madelung 2014; Saunders 1978, 78). What had particularly upset them, and others in the community, was 'Uthman's undisguised favoritism toward his own family and clan members, the Umayyads. They feared that the caliph was determined "to establish his caliphate on a dynastic basis" (Madelung 2014; Abou El Fadl 2001, 23; Hodgson 1977, 34–36; Saunders 1978).

---

[21] Talha was married to Umm Kulthum, a step-sister of 'A'isha (see Fig. 2.1). Reportedly, he "thought of marrying ['A'isha] after the Prophet's death, until the Quranic revelation of 33:53 made this impossible" (Stowasser 1994, 109). As a cousin of Caliph Abu Bakr and a close companion of the Prophet, Talha was dismayed when Abū Bakr appointed 'Umar as his successor: "He may well have harbored hopes of succeeding his cousin in the caliphate" (Madelung 2014; see also Abbott 1942, 102).

[22] Zubayr was also married to Asma, another step-sister of 'A'isha (see Fig. 2.1). 'A'isha adopted their son 'Abdallāh b. al-Zubayr. Zubayr also married Atikah, a widow of Caliph 'Umar's (Abbott 1942, 88). Zubayr's mother Safiyyah was a daughter of 'Abd al-Muttablib, the paternal grandfather of the Prophet and 'Ali (Tabari 1997, 126, fn. 827). He was also a serious contender for the caliphate (Madelung 2014).

[23] 'A'isha was not the only wife of the Prophet or the only Mother of the Believers to oppose Caliph 'Uthman. Umm Salama also shared the opposition's demand for the removal of 'Uthman (Abbott 1942, 107, 121), though she later opposed 'A'isha in the Battle of the Camel against Caliph 'Ali. For a detailed account of the opposition to Caliph 'Uthman and 'A'isha's role in it, see Tabari (1990) and Abbott (1942, 103–128).

One of 'A'isha's complaints – shared by some of her co-wives – was the reduction of the pension allotted to them by Caliph 'Umar (Abbott 1942, 95). Abbott further makes the point that one of the points of contention between 'A'isha and 'Uthman was the caliph's harsh treatment of people, who would then seek 'A'isha's mediation (1942, 111–112). Such incidents exemplify the public esteem for 'A'isha, the moral authority she commanded within the community, and her sociopolitical capital.

The Bedouin tribesmen also resented 'Uthman's attempt to enforce centralization and assert control over them "in the camp-cities of Kufa, Basra and Fustat," and the Medinans were concerned about "the rapacity of the Meccans" (Saunders 1978, 78). Finally, the opposition laid siege to the caliph's palace for several weeks. Talha "took possession of the treasury keys and maintained close contact with the besieging rebels" (Madelung, 2014).[24] As the opposition to 'Uthman grew, both Talha and Zubayr hoped, "with the backing of Aisha," to unseat the caliph and replace him (Abbott 1942, 118, 124). But sources also tell us that the opposition camp was divided from the beginning. The political rivalry between Talha and Zubayr was public knowledge. In a rare moment of unanimity among Sunni and Shi'ite commentators, a man involved is reported to have said: "If the victory had been ours we would have been caught up in civil war: Al-Zubayr wouldn't have let Talhah rule, nor would Talhah have let al-Zubayr" (Tabari 1997, 46–47). For his part, the eleventh-century Shi'ite scholar al-Mufid relates from 'Ali that each of the two men claimed the caliphate separately. Talha claimed it because he was a paternal cousin of 'A'isha and Zubayr did so because he was the son-in-law of her father, Abu Bakr. "By Allah, if they are victorious in what they want, then Zubayr will kill Talha or Talha will execute al-Zubayr, each in dispute over [the right] to the kingship" (al-Mufid in Spellberg 1994, 124).

As the "murderous" opposition to Caliph 'Uthman grew louder, however, 'A'isha became increasingly more ambivalent regarding her involvement (Abbott 1942, 123–125). Feeling uneasy about the siege of the caliph's residence, she decided to leave Medina for Mecca, despite the caliph's plea for her to stay.[25] Caliph 'Uthman was assassinated in the end, in 656, but much to the alliance's disappointment, neither Talha nor Zubayr was given the people's oath of loyalty – 'Ali was. With 'Uthman's murder, the community of Muslims was plunged into political and moral crisis. Under such chaotic circumstances, both Talha and Zubayr felt

---

[24] In keeping with tribal code of the blood feud, however, Talha and Zubayr sent their sons to stand guard at the gate of the caliph to ensure his physical safety (Abbott 1942, 126).

[25] The caliph sent an emissary to 'A'isha and implored her not to leave the city, knowing how influential she was with the opposition, but she refused (Mernissi 1991, 5; Abbott 1942, 123–124).

obliged to swear allegiance to ʿAli – but they recanted once they left Medina and became involved in agitation against ʿAli. Ultimately, the new caliph could hardly pacify the deeply polarized community of Muslims in the aftermath of the tumultuous murder of his immediate predecessor.

Failing to succeed ʿUthman to the caliphate, Ṭalḥa and Zubayr joined forces with ʿAʾisha again, turning their disappointment toward unseating ʿAli (Abbott 1942, 136; Tabari 1997, 43). Their battle cry now was that ʿAli was slow in avenging his predecessor's murder or, worse yet, had been complicit in it.[26] Hearing of ʿUthman's murder, ʿAʾisha rushed back to Medina, and on her way she heard of ʿAli's succession to the caliphate. Disappointed, she returned to Mecca and went straight to the mosque to address a gathering crowd:

People of Mecca, the mob of men from the garrison cities[27] and the watering places and the slaves of the people of Medina have conspired together … They spilled forbidden blood, they violated the sacred city, they appropriated sacred money, and they profaned the sacred month. By Allah! One of Uthman's fingers is better than a whole world of their type. (Tabari 1997, 38–39)

Framing her provocative rhetoric in terms of class and race, ʿAʾisha and the alliance referred to ʿAli's supporters as "The *riffraff* of provincials and *outsiders* from the tribe," and described Kufa as a "garrison town." When a skeptical citizen asked Zubayr why they should go to war against Caliph ʿAli, he reiterated, "The commander of the Faithful (Uthman) has been attacked and killed with neither blood revenge nor excuse … By the riffraff from the garrison towns and outsiders from the tribes assisted by Bedouin and slaves" (Tabari 1997, 55; parenthesis original). Ṭalḥa and Zubayr may have coveted the caliphate and so resented ʿAli even more than ʿUthman – time was running out for them.[28] But ʿAʾisha reportedly had an additional motivation. Once, during the Prophet's lifetime, ʿAʾisha was slandered and accused of adultery, following an incident that has come to be known as the affair of the necklace or the "story of the lie" (*ifk*). In a lull during the battle

---

[26] One of those involved in the political opposition and eventual death of Caliph ʿUthman was Muhammad b. Abi Bakr, a step-brother of ʿAʾisha whose widowed mother had married ʿAli (see Fig. 2.1). He was brought up by ʿAli, with whom he had strong bonds of affection and solidarity.

[27] Early on during the reign of the first two caliphs, the nomads had created problems of law and order. To prevent them from asserting their power against the state, they were recruited into the Islamic armies and were settled in "garrison towns away from the desert and the home territories of their tribes" (Donner 1981, 251 ff).

[28] Caliph ʿUthman was not unaware of the other companions' ambition for the caliphate. He knew that his long reign would reduce the chances of his rivals, as he indicated, "My life has been long to them and their hopes of governing have been deferred, and so they seek to hasten [God's] decree [by murdering me] (Tabari 1990, 242–243; brackets original). See also Jack Goody on the issue of longevity of a ruler and the impatience of successors, who may be motivated to commit regicide (1966, 9).

against the Banu Mustaliq tribe, 'A'isha left her palanquin in search of a missing necklace, only to return to find that the caravan had packed up and moved away. She was brought back to the campsite a day later by a young male companion of the Prophet. Thereafter, accusations of adultery against a wife of Muhammad spread like wildfire.[29] Insisting on her innocence, 'A'isha remained steadfast, even though she was initially not believed by many, including her own parents and her husband. With Muhammad's reputation at stake and his enemies clamoring against him, 'Ali advised the Prophet to divorce 'A'isha. Muhammad resisted the idea, and she was eventually vindicated through divine revelations (Qur'an 24:11–20). Although 'A'isha was only fourteen years old, she exhibited wisdom and understanding of Muhammad's precarious position in the community. She expressed gratitude to God and not to Muhammad, for if she were to do so, he would be left vulnerable to his enemies' accusation of receiving revelations on demand (Walker and Sells 1999).

Whether 'A'isha's objective was to retaliate against Caliph 'Ali for her earlier humiliation, to avenge the assassination of the third caliph, 'Uthman, or to unseat the fourth caliph in favor of her kinsmen she moved resolutely. From Mecca, 'A'isha sent letters to Arab-Muslim leaders and dispatched emissaries to various provinces to recruit soldiers and warriors to fight against 'Ali and his supporters.[30] She and her allies also had a "public crier" to inform the people of Mecca that the Mother of the Faithful was departing to avenge the blood of 'Uthman. Over a thousand soldiers are reported to have answered her call, enticed by the promise of receiving full funding, which included horses (Abbott 1942, 138). Calling it a "true campaign of information and persuasion," Mernissi writes that 'A'isha must have learned her "military tactic" by observing the Prophet Muhammad – a military leader par excellence (1991, 54). Whether 'A'isha was writing letters to notables inviting them to join her in the war against Caliph 'Ali or addressing the public in the mosque, she always referred to herself as "Mother" and to the people as her "sons," regardless of their social class.[31] Invariably, 'A'isha addressed her letters: "From

---

[29] For a thorough discussion of this incident, see Spellberg (1994); Walker and Sells (1999).

[30] Abbott makes the point that 'A'isha did not know how to write but learned to read the Qur'an, but she does not make it clear who then wrote these letters – if they were written at all – and what the source of her information is. Mernissi, however, specifies that 'A'isha sent the letters with messengers to all the notables of the city, explaining the reasons why she rebelled against 'Ali (1991, 54).

[31] I have not come across any situation in which 'A'isha would refer to her "daughters" in public or private gatherings. One wonders whether other women were in attendance at such meetings and the term "son" was used generically here to refer to people of both sexes. Schimmel notes that in the Quranic phrase "the believers are brothers" (Qur'an 49:10) sisters/women are included (1997, 45).

Aishah bint Abi Bakr, Mother of the Faithful, beloved of the Messenger of God, to her devoted son ... " (Tabari 1997, 79–80). In one such letter to a certain Zayd b. Suhan, she wrote, "When this letter of mine reaches you, come and assist us in this undertaking! If you don't, then at least make the people abandon Ali." Zayd b. Suhan (a Kufan opponent of the third caliph, 'Uthman), responded, "If you withdraw from this undertaking and return home, then I will be your devoted son. If you don't, I will be the first to break with you" (Tabari 1997, 79–80; Abbott 1942, 153). In calling herself "Mother" and framing her authority to command in kinship terms, 'A'isha communicated a double message to her followers, symbolically and literally: that as her sons they had an obligation to respect, obey, and defend their mother, and that as a mother she would nurture and protect her sons.

In the end, history has recorded that a wife of the Prophet Muhammad, Mother of the Faithful, and two close companions and cousins of Muhammad formed a formidable alliance to unseat 'Ali, the Commander of the Faithful, himself a companion, cousin, and son-in-law of the Prophet. The murderous rivalries, the feuds, the battle of succession, all happened within the family.

Reading through Tabari's gripping narratives of the unfolding – and contentious – sociopolitical drama in Mecca and Medina, one gets the distinct impression that 'A'isha was the indisputable leader of the alliance – later medieval equivocations notwithstanding. With all eyes on her, every strategic and crucial decision was either made by her or carefully run by her. When, for example, Talha and Zubayr, who had fled Medina subsequent to 'Ali's accession to join 'A'isha, reported to her the unfolding chaos in that city, 'A'isha advised them on how to approach the gathering storm, reciting the following verse:

> Were the leaders of my people in accord with me
> I would deliver them from the rope-halters and from ruin.
>
> (Tabari in Abbott [1942, 13])

In another instance, when on the road to the battlefield, disputes broke out among Talha, Zubayr, and Marwan (a cousin of 'Uthman) as to who should lead the prayer, it was 'A'isha who successfully mediated between them, ultimately deciding on her nephew, Zubayr's son (Tabari 1997, 46).

Meanwhile, in Basra, Medina, and Kufah, people began soul-searching, pondering whether to join 'Ali the Commander of the Faithful or 'A'isha the Mother of the Faithful, or remain neutral (Tabari 1997, 90). Many of the Prophet's companions and newly converted Muslims refused to join 'A'isha against the reigning caliph, but others who shared her objectives answered her call. That she was a woman seemed irrelevant to them, but not who she was. 'A'isha also asked her co-wives to accompany her in this battle (Abbott 1942, 138). Hafza, 'Umar's daughter and 'A'isha's sister/ co-wife, decided to join her, but was prevented from doing so by her brother, who reminded her of the Quranic command for the Prophet's wives to stay secluded (Abbott 1942, 138–143). Umm Salama, another widow of Muhammad and a devoted follower of 'Ali not only refused 'A'isha's invitation, but also pointedly and publicly rebuked her for her divisive political action (Spellberg 1994, 132).[32] The rest of 'A'isha's co-wives declined to join her once the designated battlefield was changed from Medina to Basra (in southern Iraq), and bid her a tearful goodbye. "There has never been a day more full of tears for or against Islam"; a day that has come to be known as "the Day of Weeping" (Tabari 1997, 41, 55). It was not unusual for women to participate in battles at the time, and so 'A'isha's adventure was considered neither out of the ordinary by 'A'isha herself nor odd by the rank and file – at least not to a good number of them.[33] The Prophet Muhammad himself was accustomed to taking a few of his wives to battle. He would often choose by "lot" which of his wives, usually two at a time, would accompany him (Stowasser 1994, 108). Biographer Ibn Sa'd (d. 845) reports that the Prophet said of Umm 'Umara Nusayba: "Whenever I looked to the right or left [in the battle field] I saw her fighting in front of me," showcasing his "delight" in her participation in the fighting (Mayer 2000, 140; Afsaruddin 2010b, 115). Women also participated in the Battle of Siffin (657), but as Maya Yazigi states, no mention of this is made in the first-century Islamic sources (2005, 438).

From Mecca, 'A'isha, Talha, and Zubayr decided to move to Basra rather than to commence the battle in Medina, as they had greater popular support in Basra. On their way, 'A'isha became transfixed upon hearing dogs barking in the distance. Was it an omen? Gripped by fear, she hesitated and refused to continue toward the battlefield. She recalled the Prophet's admonishment to his wives to beware of the barking dogs of al-Haw'ab and interpreted the barking as a warning for her to withdraw and return to Mecca (Spellberg 1994, 120–125). She was persuaded to reconsider by her nephew, Zubayr's son, and the army moved on (Tabari 1997, 140, 68; Abbott 1942, 144). Whether this incident actually happened as was reported or is a revisionist rewriting by the later biographers who pieced together 'A'isha's political legacy is not clear. Whatever the

---

[32] For spellbinding exchanges on the subject between the co-wives 'A'isha and Umm Salama, see Spellberg (1994, 132–134); Abbott (1942, 139–141).

[33] Nabia Abbott (1942, 20–21) gives several historical cases of pre-Islamic Arab queens and military leaders, including one of Queen Mawia, who upon the death of her husband, established herself among the Syrian Arabs and defeated the Roman Empire (373–380 CE). See also Southern (2008, 93–94).

case might be, this incident clearly formed a pivotal moment in the narrative of the Battle of the Camel regarding ʿAʾisha's role in this first Muslim civil war. Some have argued that the objective of this remembrance/reconstruction was twofold: to show the costly consequences for the Prophet's wife of disobeying his warning, and displacing blame onto ʿAʾisha's companions, who insisted on going ahead with the war (Spellberg 1994, 120–125).[34] The Shiʿites do not exonerate Ṭalḥa and Zubayr, but they also blame ʿAʾisha, as exemplified in the comment of the eleventh-century Shiʿite scholar, al-Mufid: "By Allah! I know that she is the one who rides the camel" (Spellberg 1994, 124). For Tabari, ʿAʾisha's moral ambivalence rehabilitates her on a personal level (Tayob 1999, 207). Others have interpreted ʿAʾisha's apparent reluctance to go through with the war as a part of her growing pessimism following the desertion of her soldiers and other prominent individuals, most notably that of her wavering brother-in-law, Zubayr (Abbott 1942, 142–143).

At the edge of the battlefield, the warring camps also hesitated and sought ways to negotiate peace. But their hard-won bargain was frustrated by rogue members of both camps, and so a bloody battle ensued in the nascent Muslim community. Thus began the first Muslim civil war.

An arrow – it is unclear whether it came from a friend or foe – killed Ṭalḥa early on.[35] A regretful Zubayr also had second thoughts regarding the entire political drama, and deserted the battlefield only to be followed by some disgruntled soldiers and killed (Tabari 1997, 158–159). In her red *howdah*, perched on her famous white camel Askar, ʿAʾisha was surrounded by opposition forces.[36] Her soldier-sons rallied around her camel, holding its reins and preventing anyone from getting too close. Watching the battle from her camel, ʿAʾisha called out to one Kaʿb[37] and ordered him to "Leave the camel," commanding him to "Go forward." Then "holding the Book of Almighty and Glorious Allah," she called them to advance (Tabari 1997, 131). Kaʿb was killed, and again ʿAʾisha in her *howdah* addressed her army: "My sons! [Remember] the recompense [of Allah]!" Like a general ordering his forces, ʿAʾisha

---

[34] In the later reconstructions of the Battle of the Camel, Ṭalḥa and Zubayr are held solely responsible for initiating the hostilities and for encouraging ʿAʾisha to go to war. A disaffected soldier rendered the highly charged event in a poem: "Her curtains have been ripped down by Ṭalḥa and al-Zubayr / No further tale needs to be told about them!" (Tabari 1997, 62).

[35] Madelung (2014), however, writes that ʿUthman's cousin Marwān "treacherously" killed Ṭalḥa, while fighting on the same side in the battle.

[36] For a sixteenth-century image of the battle, see: https://commons.wikimedia.org/wiki/File:Muhammad%27s_widow,_Aisha,_battling_the_fourth_caliph_Ali_in_the_Battle_of_the_Camel.jpg.

[37] Apparently he had personally led ʿAʾisha's camel to the war front, hoping to avert major clashes (Abbott 1942, 158).

raised her voice: "Allah! Allah! Remember Almighty and Glorious Allah and the reckoning" (Tabari 1997, 131–132, brackets original; Abbott 1942, 159).[38]

'A'isha was closely engaged the entire day of the battle, and switched between reciting the Qur'an and poetry to boost the morale of her soldier-sons and to encourage them to fight on. At one point in the thick of the battle, 'A'isha turned to her right and then to her left, asking her soldiers to identify themselves and tell her to which clan or tribe they belonged. Hearing their kinship, genealogy, and tribal affiliation, she would complement each soldier with appropriate words of praise and encouragement: "Tribesmen of Ghassan . . . we used to hear tell of your prowess with the sword! Keep it up today!", further elaborating her praise with the verses "The Ghassani protector fought with their swords, / as did Hinb and Aws and Shabib."[39] Turning to the soldiers on the other side, 'A'isha heaped praise on them: "They came at us with swords and armor as though they were / Judging from their impenetrable strength, Bakr b. Wa'il." She continued to inquire about the soldiers' lineages across the entire squadron, continuously cheering on the fighting of her "sons": "Bravo! Bravo! Abtahiyyah swords and Quraishe swords."

And on and on the fierce battle went.

Though brave men were holding the reins of the camel and defending "their Mother," a soldier from the opposite camp was finally able to hamstring her camel. The wounded animal fell and let out a "bellowing cry not heard before," and 'A'isha's *howdah* came crashing down to the ground. Her red carriage was so pierced by arrows that it resembled a "hedgehog," though she herself suffered only minor scratches (Tabari 1997, 140, 155; Abbott 1942, 162). The Commander of the Faithful then ordered Muhammad b. Abi Bakr,[40] a younger half-brother of 'A'isha and a staunch supporter of 'Ali, to watch over 'A'isha's safety and well-being – which he did to 'A'isha's delight (Tabari 1997, 156). And so, in December 656, the first Muslim civil war came to an end.

Honoring her as the Mother of the Faithful, 'Ali treated 'A'isha respectfully, and afterward selected "forty prominent Basran women" to accompany her back to Mecca (Tabari 1997, 170). Who were these women? Had they participated in the civil war? To which tribe, clan, or class did they belong? Tabari provides no details. Might one infer that

---

[38] Despite 'A'isha's small stature, Tabari tells us, she had a powerful and commanding voice (1997, 60; Abbott 1942, 146).

[39] This line and the next few citations of poetry are from Tabari (1997, 135–136).

[40] See fn. 26.

other women were actually present or involved in this political conflict? Possibly.[41] People came to see ʿAʾisha off as she said farewell to them:

My sons, some of us criticized others of us, saying they were slow or excessive. But don't let any of you hold it against any others over anything you might hear about this. By Allah! There was never anything in the past between me and Ali other than what usually happens between a woman and her male in-laws. (Tabari 1997, 170; see also Abbott 1942, 165)

Then ʿAli spoke: "By Allah, men! She has spoken the truth and nothing but the truth. That was all there was between us. She is the wife of your Prophet now and forever" (Tabari 1997, 170; Abbott 1942, 165).[42] With these words of regret and reconciliation, ʿAʾisha, Mother of the Faithful and beloved wife of the Prophet, was reintegrated into a chastened community. She lived to a ripe old age, and "continued to be widely revered by her contemporaries for her knowledge." She was "consulted by the senior Companions (akābir) for her detailed understanding of inheritance shares (farāʾid)" (Afsaruddin 2011). It is also important to note that ʿAli did not criticize ʿAʾisha's allies for "forming an alliance with a woman against him." But he did fault Ṭalḥa and Zubayr for reneging on their previous pledge of loyalty (bayʿa) to him, their leader and Commander of the Faithful (Fadel 2011, 34). It was their political disloyalty that led to disorder and chaos in the nascent community that ʿAli condemned. Nor did ʿAli take the opportunity to scold ʿAʾisha personally or belittle her for her political leadership as a woman in the battle for succession. For her part, ʿAʾisha took her defeat gracefully, yet her political and military legacy has continued to be a subject of contentious debate throughout the history of the development of Islam in the Muslim world, focusing squarely on her gender.

Sons, Soldiers, Supporters

Who were the young men, the "soldier-sons" who followed ʿAʾisha into the battlefield? Historical accounts of the first century of Islam – collected and recorded by men over a century and a half after the Prophet Muhammad's death – neglect to report on the political activities and involvement of ordinary people. Tabari, though focusing on the elite, provides a rich

---

[41] Commentators do not tell us whether women were also present at this gathering. Given that forty Basran women were to accompany ʿAʾisha, I would guess they may have been present then, which suggest some level of tolerance for women's political activism and public participation – at least of the elite women – at the time.

[42] ʿAli's defense of ʿAʾisha as Muhammad's wife "now and forever" reconfirmed her prestige within the community, and was followed by ʿAli's supporters who likewise defended her reputation (Spellberg 1994, 109).

drama of the battle of wills and wits, swords and spears between the supporters and soldiers of ‘A’isha and ‘Ali – whether historical fact or reconstructed narrative of a particular historical moment. Acting as a political leader, ‘A’isha reportedly reached out to the public either through writing letters and sending out messengers bearing letters to various notables in the expanding Muslim world or by speaking directly to the general public in the mosques. It is remarkable, at a time when women are not allowed to enter mosques in some contemporary Muslim countries, let alone speak publicly, that not only were they not barred from attending mosques at the dawn of Islam, but they participated actively in public events – ‘A’isha is but one example. For her part, she did not seem shy or hesitant about addressing the gathering crowds at the mosques or in other public arenas, and by all accounts she was an adept political orator and communicator. Neither the political elite nor the public at large was unanimous in its response to ‘A’isha’s call to arms against the reigning caliph, nor did either group support ‘Ali unanimously; some did, some did not, while others found ways to remain neutral or even left the city or went into hiding (Tabari 1997, 110–111). The point is that ‘A’isha’s voice was not stifled and she was not censored by either the political elite or the public, as evidenced by the fact that many willingly followed her to war. But her leadership did not go unchallenged either – leadership seldom goes uncontested. In public gatherings held in the mosque, ‘A’isha was sometimes challenged by those who questioned her political motivations, objectives, and sincerity – but not her place as a woman. In one instance, reported by Mernissi, she was confronted by an irate man in the mosque, who said:

[A]fter the death of the Prophet, you selected a man from among you without consulting us [the common people ...]. After his death, you got together and you named another [caliph], still without asking our advice ... You chose ‘Uthman, you swore your allegiance to him, still without consulting us. You became displeased with his behavior, and you decided to declare war without consulting us. You decided, still without consulting us, to select ‘Ali and swore allegiance to him. So, what are you blaming him for now? Why have you decided to fight him? (1991, 56)

Mernissi interprets such episodes as indicative of freedom of expression, a precedent set by the Prophet that reflects the tolerant and democratic nature of the early Islamic community (1991, 55). Tabari, on the other hand, does not take a political stand one way or another, and offers no interpretation of the unfolding events. He records multiple narratives, both contending and corroborative. Some stories give detailed descriptions of the battle scene, specific people, and community notables involved or kept away. Others highlight the fighting soldiers, those holding the camel's reins and their unwavering defense of 'A'isha as they fought on and often lost their heads, before another brave soldier-son took hold of the reins and continued fighting. Throughout, however, Tabari tells us, 'A'isha was present in the middle of the battlefield, shielded in her red *howdah* atop her white camel Askar, giving heart to her soldiers and supporters, her "sons."

In describing the drama of the battlefield, Tabari sets the stage for the expression of a whole range of rhetorical and oratorical poetry, recited by soldiers and supporters on either side. The poems range from praising or mocking 'A'isha or 'Ali to boasting of the bravery of the soldiers' devotion to their warring leaders, to ridicule, to insult, to exaggeration, to lamentation and regret.[43] Below, I include a sample that highlights the drama and dynamics of the Battle of the Camel, the Muslims' first battle for succession.

One supporter, expressing loyalty to 'A'isha and her camp, recited:[44]

> We, Banu Dabbah, are the allies of the camel;
>> We take the field against death whenever death dismounts.
> We lament the death of ibn Affan[45] with tips of spears
>> Death, we want it more than honey!

Another supporter of 'A'isha, who killed several notables from 'Ali's camp, boasted:

> I strike out at them but I do not see Abu Hasan.[46]
> This is the biggest grief that could be!

The theme was picked up by another valiant soldier:

> The sword healed us of Zayd and Hind
>> completely and the two eyes of Adi.
> We kept fighting them all day until nightfall
>> with sturdy spears and sharp swords.

A staunch supporter of 'A'isha, Ibn al-Samit, praised her soldiers:

> Go off Dabbah! For the land is wide
>> to your left. Death lurks in the valley
> A fighting force like the rays of the rising sun,
>> A force with a torrent that flows with force.
> So we will stand up to you in every battle,
>> holding Mashrafiyyah swords, striking and not weakening.

---

[43] Poetry was so much a part of the cultural repertoire of the public that in the Battle of Siffin women supporters of 'Ali recited poetry to express their feelings about and support for 'Ali (Yazigi 2005).
[44] The poems cited are taken from Tabari (1997, 138–145).   [45] I.e. 'Uthman.
[46] I.e. 'Ali.

As the tide of the war turned against 'A'isha's forces and some of her soldiers fled the battlefield, one soldier cried out:

> Mother of ours, 'Aysha! do not flee
>> All your sons are heroes brave.
> Mother of ours, wife of the prophet,
>> wife of the blessed and the guided!

Holding the reins of 'A'isha's camel, 'Amr b. al-Asharf struck with his sword anyone who came near him. But a soldier from 'Ali's camp came close and addressed 'A'isha:

> O Mother of ours! O best Mother we know!
>> Do you not see how many a brave is being wounded?
> His head and wrist made lonely?

Tabari tells us that both soldiers fought to the death, one defending 'A'isha, the other 'Ali (1997, 141–142, 145).

Regardless of their political allegiance, however, the soldiers invariably respectfully referred to 'A'isha as the Mother of the Faithful. In the aftermath of her defeat, however, when a certain Ammar, who was also tasked with protecting the Mother of the Faithful, "rebuked" her for "shedding the blood of her 'sons'," 'A'isha did not hesitate to "disown him as her 'son'" (Abbott 1942, 162). All throughout the battle, 'A'isha showed the courage of her convictions, the strength of her character, and the command she had over her followers. In defeat, too, she maintained her dignity by staying out of politics for the rest of her life.

Some Reflections

'A'isha's involvement in the conflicts over the succession to the caliphate highlights her charismatic personality and her determination to effect change within the political leadership of the burgeoning Muslim community. It is reported that she once challenged Caliph 'Uthman for his undue nepotism and confronted him before a crowd that had gathered in the mosque. The caliph finally lost his temper and chided the Mother of the Faithful: "What have you to do with this? You were ordered to stay at home" – a reference to the Quranic revelation (33:59) requiring the seclusion of the wives of the Prophet. The bystanders did not accept the caliph's scolding quietly; some sided with Caliph 'Uthman while others supported 'A'isha's right to speak out – who but a wife of the Prophet could speak truth to power? In the end, it was Caliph 'Uthman who gave in to public opinion (Abbott 1942, 111). Was the caliph's public castigation of 'A'isha because of her gender, or is the report a medieval rewrite of their testy encounter? Not clear. But even if the former, 'Uthman's gender-specific retort came as a last resort, after a protracted and contentious public dispute. The point is that 'A'isha's presence in the public domain, in the midst of the crowd and challenging the caliph, was not considered out of order. In fact, some expected it of her. Her leadership was not challenged on the basis of her gender – not unanimously. Rather, it was her political challenge to the reigning caliph that provoked his retort, though even then he eventually relented and made some concession to 'A'isha's right to speak and, by extension, to the public's objection to 'Uthman's nepotism.

Despite her popularity and charisma, 'A'isha lost the Battle of the Camel, but not because she was a woman or for want of support from the political elite and her soldier-sons. Had she won the battle, the narrative of opposition to women's political leadership and military expeditions would have taken a different trajectory in Muslim societies – alas, history is written by the victors. The fact is that she lost, and with that the political legacy of her military misadventure and audacious political adventure against the reigning caliph, as argued by Spellberg, was ultimately "transformed into a convenient component of the medieval construct which defined all women as threats to the maintenance of Islamic political order" (1994, 109). Her political legacy poses a threat that has become all too real since the advent of the twentieth century and the political awakening of women across the Muslim world. Mobilizing their resources, women – and some of their male supporters and reformists – demand legal equality and political representation. Collectively, they challenge the lopsided gender hierarchy and the monopoly of male privilege and domination of the political and spiritual domains. While a growing number of Muslim women scholars (primarily outside of their own countries, for fear of persecution) have brilliantly reinterpreted the Qur'an and rendered novel interpretations of the revelations,[47] women's collective demand for political restructuring and gender justice in many Muslim societies poses an even greater threat to their conservative patriarchal political systems. Little wonder then women's agitations for political representation have provoked backlash from the "fundamentalist" and "Islamist" camps, even in some officially "secular" Muslim societies. As modernity globally resulted in women's awareness of the injustice of their historic inequality, it also led to religious revivalism in much of the modern world – contrary to popular expectations. In the Muslim world, religion is thus deployed as a political weapon to enforce a medieval patriarchal gender hierarchy to safeguard and maintain male

---

[47] See the Preface fn. 3.

privileges and political domination. Consequently, the purported Prophetic hadith cited earlier in this chapter has gained greater popularity among the religious and political elite in Muslim societies. As we will learn in Chapters 5 and 6, this hadith was invoked in attempts to prevent Benazir Bhutto and Megawati Sukarnoputri from standing for election and assuming state power.

Hadith Remembered

Caught between the threats of an imminent civil war waged by a wife of the Prophet of Islam against the reigning caliph and a cousin of the Prophet, one man made an assertion that has reverberated since. This man was Abu Bakra (or Bakara, d. 672), a freed slave and a late convert to Islam who became a companion of the Prophet Muhammad and eventually a Basran notable (Mernissi 1991, 49–57). Fearing the consequences of civil war and a battle for succession, he decided against joining either faction. Kaukab Siddique argues, however, that Abu Bakra was actually fighting in 'A'isha's camp and continued to support her until the very end (1986, 57). In any case, it was not until *after* the war's end and 'A'isha's defeat that Abu Bakra voiced the alleged hadith, "Never will succeed such a nation as makes a woman their ruler," attributing it to the Prophet Muhammad upon becoming aware of a ruling queen in Iran. Finding his exit strategy, Abu Bakra justified his political decision on the basis of 'A'isha's gender and legitimated his refusal to take part in the first Muslim civil war by invoking the Prophet Muhammad. Whether Abu Bakra refrained from getting involved in the raging civil war or regretted his participation afterward, he seized the moment to represent the first Muslim civil war in terms of gender politics and to displace the blame onto Queen Purandokht of Persia – a woman leader of a country recently conquered. It was, after all, only a few years since the defeat of Iranians by the Arabs and the fall of the Sasanid Empire in Iran. Further, whether Abu Bakra knew of this prophetic hadith first-hand or it was reconstructed by medieval hadith narrators many decades later, remains unclear. In either case, the articulation of a Prophetic hadith at the moment that the sociopolitical situation demanded, highlights a situation of tradition-making, aptly characterized by Stowasser as "sunna-in-the-making" (1994, 115). Remarkably, the famed historian Tabari makes no mention of Abu Bakra or of this hadith in his detailed descriptions of the unfolding hostilities during and after the Battle of the Camel (1997). Similarly, Nabia Abbott makes but one fleeting reference to Abu Bakra and his recollection of this hadith before dismissing it as a "singleton" (i.e. a hadith reported from a single source – and thus unreliable) (1942, 175–176). Citing Ibn Hanbal (d. 855), Abbott then goes on to say that "Mohammed, who took the advice of his wives Khadijah and Umm Salamah and who referred in the Qur'an to the good government of the Queen of Sheba, was not likely to utter such sentiment" (1942, 176). Muslim exegetes, however, have by and large endorsed Abu Bakra's assertion, based on the authority of the ninth-century hadith collector Bukhari, and have historically attempted to exclude women from political office and leadership – but not universally and not always successfully, as we will discuss shortly. Nonetheless, in time the hadith opposing women's political authority gained political capital and currency to mask the authority of the Quranic revelations regarding the Queen of Sheba and her sovereignty. It has continued to be the major religious justification for excluding women from politics and the public domain in contemporary Muslim societies.

Some scholars have debated the credibility of Abu Bakra, and rejected the authenticity of this hadith.[48] I further suggest three interpretations, the first of which overlaps with that of Fadel (2011). First, it is possible that the Prophet of Islam, finding Purandokht's sovereignty extraordinary, commented negatively on her reign, particularly since her father, Khosrow Parviz, had rejected the Prophet's call to submit to Islam (Morony 2012). Muhammad might have found the moment opportune to humiliate a formidable adversary by connecting its impending misfortune with the gender of its leader. The Prophet's saying was thus intended for that particular case only and was not meant as a general rule (see Ibrahim 2016). Second, I argue that the assumption of the universality of the prohibition of this hadith is problematic. The Prophet of Islam received divine revelations regarding the sovereignty of the Queen of Sheba (Qur'an 27). Attributing the aforementioned oppositional hadith to him is thus highly irregular. In a similar situation, when faced with the Sunni claim that temporary marriage (*mut'a*) is prohibited (*naskh*) in the Qur'an, the Shi'ite *ulama'* countered that if *mut'a* had been cancelled in the Qur'an, Muhammad would have known it and banned it (Haeri 1989, 62). Last, and more important, is 'A'isha's silence on the veracity of this hadith. Never slow to speak truth to power, 'A'isha is conspicuously silent on this matter that has directly involved her reputation. She chastised Abu Hurareh for attributing

---

[48] For example, see Fatima Mernissi (1991), Abou El Fadl (2001), Mohammad Fadel (2011), and Kaukab Siddique (1986).

a misogynist hadith to the Prophet (Mernissi 1991; Brown 2018, 73). Why would she remain quiet and not make any comment one way or another now that her own legacy was at stake?

Moreover, as one of the major contributors of hadith, particularly those having to do with Muhammad's private life (Schimmel 1997, 10; Abou El Fadl 2001), 'A'isha consistently applied the principle of checking the hadith against the Qur'an (Nadvi 2013, 240). This principle was later "formulated and agreed upon by all jurists and traditionists," meaning that "if a hadith is contradicted by a Quranic verse, and there is no way of reconciling them, then the hadith will be 'left'" (Nadvi 2013, 240). Why then was the hadith "Never will succeed such a nation as makes a woman their ruler" not "left" by eminent medieval authorities, the exegetes, the jurists, and the religious scholars – those who have knowledge of the Book? Surely they were/are not unaware of the unquestioned authority of the Qur'an and the hierarchy of the sources of authority in the Islamic tradition. In her critique of medieval Muslim exegeses of the Quranic story of creation, the Pakistani scholar Riffat Hassan (1985) likewise highlights Muslim scholars' misrepresentation of the evenhanded Quranic story of Adam and Eve while relating its patriarchal Biblical reconstruction in which Eve (not named in the Qur'an) is solely held responsible for deceiving Adam, and seducing him to disobey God by eating the forbidden fruit. Clearly Muslim exegetes found it expedient to abide by Abu Bakra's exclusionary rule, which appealed to their patriarchal sensibilities. By projecting the prediction of doom to the Prophet Muhammad, Abu Bakra – or later commentators – made it possible for these eminent scholars to ignore the dubious origins of this hadith.

Unlike Purandokht, 'A'isha was not a ruling queen, yet their political legacies are intertwined through the aforementioned alleged Prophetic hadith. 'A'isha was a political and military leader who wielded enormous authority in both domestic and public domains. Her story is included in this book on Muslim women rulers because of her active involvement to influence the course of succession in the Islamic world, and because the legacy of her political agency is frequently invoked to justify ideological and religious opposition to Muslim women's political authority and leadership. 'A'isha was admired by many in her society during her lifetime and throughout history – notwithstanding some Shi'ite opposition.

Reminiscent of the esteem the Queen of Sheba commanded as a sovereign, 'A'isha's gender did not make her actions seem odd to her supporters or deter them from following her to the battlefield. Nor was her actual presence on the battlefield leading the army a cause of dissent or anxiety among her generals or the rank and file. This is not to say that her military leadership was not contested. Civil war is always contested; some support it, some don't, and some want no part of it. 'A'isha's gender was initially immaterial as the competition over succession to the caliphate was gathering force. Ṭalḥa and Zubayr both capitalized on their kinship ties to 'A'isha and on her political authority to help them clinch the caliphate. Her gender became the most objectionable issue retroactively, however, in the revisionist medieval rewrites of the eighth and ninth centuries – given her spectacular loss in the battle for succession.

In the face of such an apparently impeccable discourse of opposition, what other sources of authority did actually enable Muslim women to come to power and wear the crown, as it were? Did women rulers contravene public morality and socio-religious norms? What sociopolitical structures and cultural mechanisms enabled them to ascend the throne in medieval Yemen and India, or in modern Pakistan and Indonesia? I suggest we look into the dynastic power and the dynamics of the father-daughter relationship, and it is to this themes that I turn in the next four chapters.

Part II

Medieval Queens: Dynasty and Descent

3   Sayyida Hurra Queen Arwa of Yemen: "The Little Queen of Sheba"

> By Allah! O fair of face, thou shalt sweep away the dynasty of the Sulaihids and thou shalt rule over their kingdom.
>
> Hamdani (1931, 509)

On October 1130 the tenth Isma'ili Fatimid imam-caliph,[1] al-Amir bi-Ahkam Allah,[2] was assassinated in Cairo by a Nizari, a member of a rival Isma'ili faction, in the belief that the latter's legitimate right to the succession had been usurped some thirty-five years earlier. Just a few months prior to his assassination, al-Amir had sent an official letter (*sijill*) to the Sayyida Hurra ("the Independent Noble Lady") Queen Arwa of Yemen, announcing the birth of his son and legal heir, Abu'l Qasim al-Tayyib, to much local rejoicing. Pledging allegiance to the infant heir, the queen ordered the letter read in the public square and had the news of al-Tayyib's designation as the legitimate heir to the Fatimid caliphate spread far and wide. But in the aftermath of the leadership chaos that followed the assassination of the imam-caliph in Cairo, the child "disappeared," never to be seen again.[3] Faced with the crisis of succession, Queen Arwa moved quickly and decisively to proclaim the missing infant al-Tayyib as the rightful heir of the assassinated imam-caliph al-Amir. Laying thus the foundations of Tayyibi Isma'ilism, she strengthened it by creating the new post of "supreme missionary" (*da'i mutlaq*), in order to safeguard the newly formed Tayyibi Isma'ili mission. She could do so because of her own supreme position as *hujja*,[4] spiritual leader – the second highest-ranking position in the Isma'ili religious hierarchy, after the imam. The

---

[1] Regarding who can or cannot be called imam-caliph, see Lawrence (2006, 78).

[2] Al-Amir was the "last in line of direct father-to-son successors to the caliphate, a fact so rare in Islamic history," writes Walker, "that later mediaeval authors insisted on noting it" (2016).

[3] For the controversy surrounding the existence and disappearance of al-Tayyib, see Hamdani (1931); Hamdani (1974); Stern (1951); Walker (1995). Following al-Amir's assassination and the subsequent disappearance of al-Tayyib, the question of who should be addressed as *imam* (i.e. a direct descendant of Ali, the first Shi'ite imam) in the fractured Isma'ili leadership was contested.

[4] For a description of *hujja* and its role and function within the Fatimid Isma'ili religious hierarchy, see Hamdani (1974, 276); Calderini (1993); Walker (1993).

queen's timely intervention in the ongoing Fatimid battle of succession changed the course of the history of the Isma'ili community by achieving two objectives simultaneously: it distanced the Sulayhid dynasty of Yemen from the weakening Fatimid dynasty in Egypt and disentangled the newly formed Tayyibi Isma'ili *da'wa* (religious mission) from the political authority of both Fatimid and Sulayhid dynasties, effectively separating the state from the "church" (Hamdani 1931, 515).

Who was Sayyida Hurra Queen Arwa of Yemen and how did she come to be known as the "Great Queen of Arabia"[5] and the "Little Queen of Sheba"?[6]

Situating Sayyida Hurra Queen Arwa

Sayyida Hurra Queen Arwa of the Isma'ili Sulayhid dynasty in Yemen is one of the most impressive and politically astute Muslim women rulers. Her sovereignty is unique in that she held both political and spiritual authority simultaneously. The historiography of the Queen of Yemen and the key role played by her in the succession, preservation, and continuation of the Tayyibi Isma'ili community would not have come to light had it not been for the felicitous unearthing of some Tayyibi Isma'ili sources that had been kept secret for centuries by the scholarly elites primarily for fear of persecution. The Isma'ili elite in Yemen concealed "its literature and doctrine from the outer world" by forming a "secret organization" (Hamdani 1931, 506). Hamdani attributes the secrecy and the preservation of these sources partly to Queen Arwa's foresight, while Delia Cortese attributes the secrecy primarily to the *da'i mutlaq*, whose authority rested on his being the exclusive keeper of Isma'ili esoteric knowledge on behalf of the "disappeared" imam (Daftary 1999, 128; de Blois 1983). Whatever the origins of the secrecy, two of the primary sources that have come to light and form the foundation for subsequent works on the Sulayhid dynasty in Yemen are *Tarikh al-Yaman* (*The History of Yemen*) by the historian Umara al-Yamani[7] (d. 1174), translated

---

[5] Hamdani (1931, 505).

[6] "Bilqis al-Sughra" (Bilqis the Younger) is how Queen Arwa is popularly known in present-day Yemen. A visiting Yemeni scholar at Boston University once told me, "We usually associate [Arwa] with the Queen of Sheba and refer to her as the little Bilqis" (i.e. Queen of Sheba). She then went on to tell me, "By the way, my sister's name is Bilqis. Usually when a family has a daughter called Bilqis, her younger sister would be named Arwa" (personal communication with Arwa Eshaq, visiting scholar, Dept. of Anthropology, Boston University, May 22, 2013). Still standing in present-day Yemen are a mosque in San'a known as Jami' Arwa, and a major highway in Aden named Tariq al-Malika Arwa (Hamdani 1974, 259–260).

[7] Husain Hamdani finds the work of Umara (also Omurah) to be "the most detailed and authentic version" of all the scattered references to the Sulayhids in various Arabic works (1931, 506).

into English by Henry Cassels Kay (1892); and '*Uyun al-akhbar* (*Eyewitness Reports/Accounts*) by Idris Imad al-Din b. al-Hassan (d. 1468), which is primarily based on Umara's account (Sayyid 2002, 16).[8]

Biographers and historians are unanimous in their praise of Queen Arwa's intelligence, political shrewdness, and personal charisma. In one instance, for example, she is described as "a woman of great piety, integrity, and excellence, perfect intelligence and erudition, surpassing men even and how much more [than] women with no thought beyond the four walls of their chambers" (Idris in Hamdani 1931, 510). In another, the queen is said to have been "well-read and, in addition to the gift of writing, [she] possessed a retentive memory stored with the chronology of past time. Nothing could surpass the interlinear glosses, upon both verbal construction and interpretation, inserted in her own handwriting in the pages of books that she had read. Our Queen was decidedly a woman of high literary caliber" (Umara, 39 in Kay 1892; Hamdani 1931, 509). The sources did not miss an opportunity to comment on her physical characteristics, though I wonder how many people might have actually seen the queen in person. One writes: "Saiyida was of fair complexion tinged with red; tall, well-proportioned, but inclined to stoutness, perfect in beauty of features, with a clear-sounding voice" (Umara, 39 in Kay 1892; Hamdani 1931, 509). Another says: "Sayyida was not only endowed with striking beauty, but was also noted for her courage, integrity, piety and independent character as well as intelligence. In addition, she was a woman of "high literary expertise" (Daftary 2006, 93). These accolades notwithstanding, we also need to remember that the existing biographies, the earliest of which is that of the twelfth-century Umara, were written a few decades after her death, with much based on oral culture and history.

---

[8] The seventh volume of Idris' book, *The Fatimids and Their Successors in Yaman*, is translated by Ayman Fu'ad Sayyid (2002). As a Tayyibi *da'i mutlaq*, what gives Idris' records particular historical value – notwithstanding the ideological slant of his historiography – is his collection of official missives and letters, known as *Sijillat al-Mustansiriyya*, of imam-caliph al-Mustansir (Sayyid 2002, 21; Hamdani 1933). Unless otherwise stated, all references to Umara al-Yamani are from Kay's translations, and those of Idris Imad al-Din from Sayyid's translation. The contemporary scholars who have examined these sources extensively and written about the Sulayhid dynasty in Yemen, the Tayyibi *da'wa*, and the Fatimid imamate in Egypt, and whose work I have incorporated into this chapter, include Husain Hamdani (1931, 1933); S. M. Stern (1951); Abbas Hamdani (1974, 1950); I. K. Poonawala (1977); Farhad Daftary (1993, 1998, 2006); Paul Walker's many publications; Samer Traboulsi (2003); G. R. Smith (2012); and Delia Cortese and Simonetta Calderini's (2007) comprehensive book on the Fatimid women. Almost all these sources cover some of the same ground, though focusing on different personalities, events, and historical controversies. As it would be tedious to cite all or even most of them here, I cite one or two in order to minimize repetition, though credit is due to all of them.

Sayyida Hurra Queen Arwa effectively governed Yemen for fifty-four years, though she had de facto political authority for seventy-one years: first as a queen consort in collaboration with her husband al-Mukarram bi Allah (1067–1084), then as the queen regent of her son (1084–1094), and finally as the queen – a sovereign in her own right until her death in 1138. Her sovereignty in Yemen was closely intertwined with three successive Fatimid imam-caliphs in Cairo, starting with al-Mustansir Billah (1029–1094). What distinguishes her as a seasoned politician is her balancing act of paying allegiance to the Fatimid imam-caliphs in Cairo while maintaining a degree of administrative independence and autonomy in Yemen. In this she might have been helped by the physical distance between Cairo and Yemen. The growing political, economic, and spiritual clout of the Sulayhid Queen Arwa coincided with the battle of succession, the weakening, and decline of the Fatimid dynasty in Egypt. Ultimately, however, her death effectively ended the Sulayhid dynasty.

Situating Arwa: Family Background

Arwa was born circa 1047 (or 1048) to Ahmad b. Ja'far b. Musa al-Sulayhi and al-Radah bint al-Fari b. Musa (Umara, 38 in Kay 1892). Upon her husband's death (no date is given), Radah married Amir b. Sulayiman al-Zawahi, the son of a former *da'i* (Isma'ili missionary) and member of an allied tribe who subsequently became a political rival of his step-daughter, Queen Arwa (Hamdani 1931, 509). With the death of her father, the young Arwa[9] joined the household of her paternal uncle, 'Ali b. Muhammad al-Sulayhi. As a member of one of the largest and most powerful Sulayhid tribes (Figure 3.1), 'Ali b. Muhammad managed to consolidate his power around 1063 by bringing all of Yemen under his own control, and thus under that of the imam-caliph al-Mustansir in Cairo,[10] who in turn appointed him the *da'i* of the Yemen (Hamdani 1931, 506). As an ardent supporter of the Fatimids in Egypt, 'Ali b. Muhammad al-Sulayhi subsequently strengthened the *da'wa* in Yemen, which became one of the most

---

[9] There is some controversy as to whether Arwa was her given name or that of her daughter (Stern 1951, 197, fn. 5). Umara refers to her as Sayyida, or al-Malika (Queen) Sayyida. Abbas Hamdani argues that she was known as Sayyida al-Hurra with Arwa as her given name (1974, 259–260). Arwa is a Quranic girl's name, meaning "gracefulness and beauty," "softness," and "liveliness," among other things (http://quranicnames.com/ar waa/).

[10] Shi'ites distinguish between caliphate – actual political leadership – and imamate, the theoretical right to leadership, based on blood kinship (Mottahedeh 1980, 14). Stern stresses the immense importance of the imam for Isma'ilis, who stands at the very center of the religious system. On the imamate depends "the continuity of institutional religion as well as the personal salvation of the believer" (Stern 1951, 194).

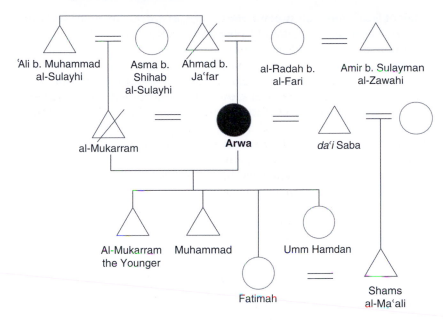

Figure 3.1 Queen Arwa's Genealogy

important geopolitical and trading outposts of the Fatimid dynasty on the shores of the Indian Ocean (Halm 2014; Cortese and Calderini 2007, 128). ʿAli b. Muhammad al-Sulayhi managed to keep Yemen firmly in the imam-caliph's service in Cairo, ensuring that Egypt would also become dependent on Yemen. In return, the Fatimids threw their full support behind the Sulayhid government and the *daʿwa* in Yemen (Traboulsi 2003, 98).

Arwa was brought up under the supervision of her paternal uncle's wife, Asma bint Shihab – another intellectually and politically formidable Ismaʿili woman. Beloved of her husband, Asma was his close companion and cousin, and collaborated with him in the management and governance of the state.[11] Early on, the royal couple recognized young Arwa's aptitude and intelligence and set out to provide her with the best education and training.[12] It is reported that one day Arwa told her aunt Asma of a dream she had in which she "swept the king's palace." Upon hearing this, Asma exclaimed, "It is as though I had shared my vision . . . By Allah!

---

[11] For the fairy-tale story of their love and marriage, see Umara, 21–22 in Kay (1892); Hamdani (1931, 507).

[12] The Fatimids had generally a positive attitude toward educating women, and provided sessions at the al-Azhar mosque for ordinary women and at special halls in the Fatimid palace for elite women (Daftary 1999, 118).

O fair of face, thou shalt sweep away the dynasty of the Sulaihids and thou shalt rule over their kingdom" (Umara, 39 in Kay 1892). Arwa married her paternal cousin al-Mukarram b. ʿAli in 1066. The new bride was so esteemed by her uncle/father-in-law that he gifted her the annual revenue of the port city of Aden as her bride price (Cortese and Calderini 2007, 129–130). Al-Mukarram was unexpectedly thrust into the political limelight, however, following the untimely death of his elder brother, the heir apparent.

As fate would have it, in an expedition in 1067 against the Najahids of Zabid, the Sulayhids' perennial enemy, ʿAli was defeated and decapitated, and his wife Asma and other women accompanying him were taken captive. The women were held in a fortress where the severed heads of ʿAli b. Muhammad and his brother were placed in their full view (Idris, 58 in Hamdani 1931; Umara, 31 in Kay 1892). Reportedly, the ever-resourceful Asma managed to smuggle the message of her whereabouts in a loaf of bread that she passed to a beggar through her barred window, thus informing her son of her captivity. Al-Mukarram promptly attacked the fortress, freeing his mother and her companions, and ordered the severed heads of his father and uncle to be taken down (Idris, 60 in Hamdani 1931). "At the moment" of freeing his mother, writes Umara, al-Mukarram "was struck by the wind, a shudder passed over him, and his face was contracted by a spasm. He lived many years thereafter, but was continually subject to involuntary movements of the head and spasms in his face," which prevented him from active political and public involvement (35 in Kay 1892; Hamdani 1931, 510).[13]

Al-Mukarram succeeded his father in both of his capacities, as king and daʿi of the Ismaʿili Sulayhids.[14] His high position brought his wife Arwa into closer proximity with the affairs of the state. The queen mother Asma, however, continued to be in charge of political affairs and governance, controlling sensitive strategic information and managing all state and financial matters (Cortese and Calderini 2007, 129). Asma did not observe veiling, which, according to Umara was a "sign of her exalted rank over the men from whom other women are secluded" (35 in Kay 1892). She was a patron of art and architecture, and one court poet wrote that:

> She hath impressed upon beneficence the stamp of generosity.
> Of meanness she allows no trace to appear.

---

[13] Cortese and Calderini, however, place the time of al-Mukarram's facial paralysis several years later, shortly after his mother's death in 1074 (2007, 130).

[14] For an informative discussion of the role and function of Ismaʿili daʿis, see Cortese and Calderini (2007, 14–27).

I say, when people magnified the throne of Bilqis[15]
"Asma" hath obscured the name of the loftiest among the stars.[16]

Until her death in 1074–1075 the queen mother Asma continued to be the de facto power in the state's affairs. Husain Hamdani finds the Sulayhids "singularly fortunate in having had two distinguished women who exercised great influence not only on the careers of their husbands, but in public affairs and the administration of the country" (1931, 507).

Queen Consort: Power "Behind" the Throne

Until the queen mother's death, her niece/daughter-in-law Arwa is not reported to have had many public roles or to have performed any official functions. But one could well imagine how she might have learned from Asma simply by observing her or assisting her in various official duties, given the close relationship between the two women and the ease with which Arwa replaced her mother-in-law after her death. With her mother-in-law's death and her husband's paralysis, Arwa was propelled into the political limelight and there began the life of Yemen's Great Queen, the Sayyida Hurra, "The noble lady who is free and independent" (Mernissi 1994, 115). Reportedly, it was al-Mukarram himself who asked her to take charge of the state because he "honored the counsel of his wife and had great faith in her shrewdness and intelligence" (Hamdani 1931, 509). But the historian Umara attributes different motivations to al-Mukarram's wish to switch roles with his wife. He had, in fact, given "himself up to the pleasures of music and wine,"[17] leaving the queen "alone in charge of the affairs of the kingdom" (40, in Kay 1892). Umara seems uneasy about this gender role reversal, not so much because he doubts Arwa's political talent, but because he is not sure how to rationalize it culturally. Arwa was young and beautiful. Accordingly, Umara has Arwa begging her husband to spare her the trappings of power and let her have her "personal freedom," because "a woman, who was desired for the marriage-bed, could not be fit for the business of the state" (Umara, 40, in Kay 1892). Whether the Sayyida Hurra was genuinely reluctant to accept the challenge of political power or would express her presumed unwillingness to govern in such culturally imprudent terms is open to debate. In practice, she proved to have few, if any, qualms about her gender or the extent of her political authority. Cortese and Calderini find Umara's

---

[15] The majesty of the "Throne of Bilqis" is a popular expression among Arabs. See Chapter 1.
[16] Umara, 22 in Kay (1892); Hamdani (1931, 508); Cortese and Calderini (2007, 129).
[17] See Sayyid for a different characterization of al-Mukarram's intentions (2002, 19–20).

prudish rationalization to be a projection of male anxieties about potential dishonor and "sexual subjugation" (2007, 130) – in case she were taken captive in one of the many tribal conflicts, and sexually molested.[18]

Arwa lost no time in firmly establishing her authority.[19] With the reversal of their roles, says Husain Hamdani, the queen "assigned to her husband his domestic role, while she energetically took up the responsibilities of running the state in the troubled times that synchronized with her rulership" (1931, 511). The young queen sent a *sijill* to the Fatimid imam-caliph al-Mustansir in Egypt, requesting his decision for a replacement for a *da'i* in India. Responding positively to her request in 1075, Imam al-Mustansir gave the queen control over the *da'wa* in India, stressing that she should look after the affairs of India and Oman (Idris, 69–70 in Hamdani 1931).

One of Arwa's prudent political decisions early on was to move her capital from San'a to Dhu Jibla in central Yemen.[20] Ostensibly, the move was justified on the basis of al-Mukarram's health, but it was also because San'a was becoming a hotbed of rebellion – resistant to the Sulayhids' dominance and a threat to her leadership. In a show of force, the astute queen rode at the head of a large army to Dhu Jibla to inspect the site of her new residence. There the "people ... gathered together around Sayiddah's stirrup, acknowledging her authority" (Umara, 40 in Kay 1892). To convince her reluctant husband to make the big move, she set him a test. She asked him to look out of the palace window in San'a and in Dhu Jibla and report on what he saw people carrying in these two cities. In San'a, he saw people carrying weapons and drawn swords; in Dhu Jibla, he saw them carrying "vessels filled with ghee or with honey." Life among these industrious people, the queen told her husband, was much preferable. And so in 1074 they transferred the seat of power from San'a to Dhu Jibla[21] (Umara, 40–41 in Kay 1892; Idris, 68 in Hamdani 1931; Hamdani 1974, 263). While officially her husband was the king and Queen Arwa the power behind his throne, in reality she was very much the bona fide power and ran the state. In keeping with tradition, however, the queen had *khutba*s recited in

---

[18] In a concession to tradition, Mernissi writes that Queen Arwa, aware of her own youth and desirability, veiled while conducting state business (1994, 147), but she does not provide any sources for this assertion. I have not seen references to the queen's veiling in other primary sources cited in his chapter.

[19] Almost at the same time, Zainab al-Nafzawiyya, a Berber queen, was also sharing power with her husband in Morocco (Mernissi 1994, 205, fn. 4).

[20] Jiblah was the name of a Jewish potter and the palace was built where he used to make his pottery. The city was founded in 1065 and named after him (Umara, 40 in Kay 1892).

[21] They built a second palace further up the mountain and converted the first one into a "cathedral mosque," containing the tomb of the queen (Umara, 41 in Kay 1892), where people still visit her shrine to pay their respects.

the name of her husband, the nominal head of the state. Mersnissi, though, notes that the queen was also mentioned in the *khutbas*: "May Allah prolong the days of al-Hurra the perfect, the sovereign who carefully manages the affairs of the faithful"[22] (1994, 115–16). More importantly, Daftary notes that the queen's name was "mentioned in the *khutba* after that of the Fatimid caliph-imam al-Mustansir" (1999, 121), which reveals the respect and authority the Sayyida Hurra commanded. Twenty years after al-Mukarram's death, coins were still minted in his name "as if frozen in time," and even in Umara's time (the late twelfth century) (37 in Kay 1892; Cortese and Calderini 2007, 134).

With her royal husband retreating further into the recesses of the palace, Arwa's role in state affairs became more prominent. Her gender and visibility fueled the revival of age-old conflicts and intensified tribal rivalries, animosities, and competition for geopolitical domination. Surrounding herself with a few loyal supporters and advisors, Queen Arwa set out to subdue various rebellions. She was particularly bent on avenging her uncle/father-in-law's gruesome beheading, and for that she planned a shrewd trap. Capitalizing on the local perceptions of traditional gender roles, the queen instructed one of her allies to convey to Sa'id al-Ahwal (Sa'id the Squint-Eyed), the leader of the Najahid tribe, that because her husband was stricken with paralysis, she was in charge of the government, which meant that now Sa'id was "the most powerful king in Yemen" (Umara, 41 in Kay 1892). She further coached her ally to propose to al-Ahwal a joint attack on her state from two fronts for a quick victory. Her enemy "fell into the trap," and the queen's army "fell upon him and crushed his forces" (Hamdani 1931, 511). For good measure, she then had Sa'id beheaded and "hung below the window of the palace" in full view of his womenfolk. Thus avenged, the queen reportedly said: "O that thou hadst eyes, Lady Asma, wherewith to see the head of the squint-eyed slave below the window of" his wife[23] (Umara, 42 in Kay 1892; Hamdani 1931, 511; Cortese and Calderini 2007, 133).

Back in Cairo, the imam-caliph al-Mustansir, a grand-nephew of the high-spirited and formidable princess Sitt al-Mulk (discussed in the Introduction), was caught up in the ethnic rivalries between his mother and her African collaborators/slaves and the Turkish mercenaries in charge of the army. Imam al-Mustansir was the son of al-Zahir, the seventh Fatimid imam-caliph,[24] and his slave/concubine Rasad, who

---

[22] Reciting the *khutba* and minting coins were the two main criteria for sovereignty in medieval Muslim societies (Mernissi 1994, 73).

[23] Mohammed Shakir disputes the veracity of these events (1999, 53 ff).

[24] He owed his throne to Princess Sitt al-Mulk, his paternal aunt, who played a crucial role in ensuring his ascension to the Fatimid throne. See the Introduction, p.15-16.

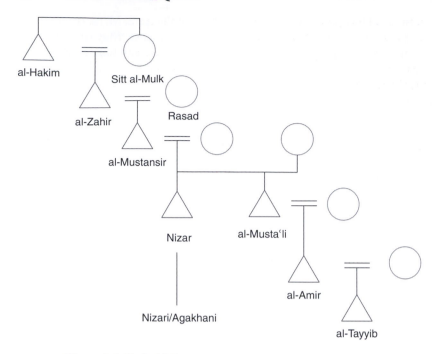

Figure 3.2 Fatimid Dynasty

was Nubian or Sudanese – some say Ethiopian (Figure 3.2). Many of the Fatimid caliphs did not marry, but had numerous slaves/concubines of all racial, ethnic, and religious backgrounds (Cortese and Calderini 2007, 110). While such racial diversity and ethnic plurality within the polygynous royal palaces allowed for a degree of tolerance toward minorities, more frequently it led to fierce and deadly competition among the concubines, who would jockey for positions of power and favor. Al-Mustansir was only six or seven years old when his father died in 1036, catapulting him to a position of political and religious authority as the eighth Fatimid imam-caliph. His mother Rasad became particularly prominent after the death of the young imam's powerful *wazir* in 1044–1045. She seized control immediately and retained all political power, effectively remaining the queen regent for "a long period of time" (Daftary 1999, 118; Cortese and Calderini 2007, 110). Rasad was one of the most powerful and formidable concubines/mothers/regents during the long reign of her son. The ethnic animosity between the Turks, Arabs, and Africans, reportedly stirred up by Rasad – the so called "evil genius of al-Mustanṣir's reign" (Gibb and Kraus 2015) – provoked murderous battles between 1064 and 1071, leaving the state's treasury empty and the soldiers exhausted. With the eventual victory of the Turks over the black slaves, Rasad fled to Baghdad with her daughters in 1069, though this account is disputed. In any case, her power and influence within the royal court was much reduced (Cortese and Calderini 2007, 113).

Queen Regent: Political *and* Spiritual Authority

After a long illness, al-Mukarram died (1084), but the astute Queen Arwa kept her husband's death secret for almost a year. Such concealment, says Jack Goody, was not unusual: whenever succession was to occur immediately after the death of a ruler, the changeover tended to create a period of crisis (1966, 10). The queen rightly perceived that her society could be torn apart, as it had been in the aftermath of her father-in-law's murder, and that certain ambitious local leaders might try to dislodge her.[25] She thus bided her time until she received the official letter, the *sijill*, from imam-caliph al-Mustansir.

Upon hearing of al-Mukarram's death, al-Mustansir sent a *sijill* to Queen Arwa, dated 1085, expressing his condolences and promptly appointed her son, al-Mukarram al-Asghar ("the Younger") as the successor and heir to the Yemeni *daʿwa* and the queen as his regent (Traboulsi 2003, 93; Hamdani 1931, 511; Idris, 70 in Hamdani 1931).[26] The imam-caliph instructed the queen "to act in her son's interest and to assist him in gaining the loyalty of the members of the *daʿwa* in Yaman" (Idris, 70 in Hamdani 1931). Aware of the young king's age and anxious of the chaos that might lie ahead, imam-caliph al-Mustansir found it necessary to reinforce the queen's hold on power with the following command to the Yemenites: obey the queen or face "rejection as infidels, with the anger of God, the Prophet and the imams falling upon them" (Traboulsi 2003, 99, 101). The imam-caliph then went on to take an action that remains unparalleled in history: he appointed the queen *hujja* of Yemen and India – as noted above, the highest rank after the imam in the Ismaʿili religious hierarchy. As a *hujja* and representative of the imam-caliph, "Arwa became the religious figure whose example was to be followed by the community of believers. She

---

[25] For the chaos and the raging internal wars that arose in the aftermath of ʿAli b. Muhammad's death, see Idris (58–67 in Hamdani 1931).

[26] As the majority of the Fatimid imam-caliphs were young children when they ascended to the throne, traditionally their mothers would act as regent and some became quite powerful. Al-Mustansir's mother Rasad, as mentioned, was one of the most powerful queen mothers, though because of her intense meddling in the internal affairs of the Fatimid court, mothers' regency became increasingly restricted (Cortese and Calderini 2007, 114). See Walthal (2008) for similar cases in Japan and China.

also became the ultimate authority for all the *da'i*s of her *gazira* [sector]"
(Traboulsi 2003, 99, bracket mine; Daftary 1999, 122). Queen Arwa's
simultaneous leadership of the state and the religious establishment is
unique in the Muslim world, and has never been held by another woman.

Religion, Gender, and Spiritual Authority

How to explain the appointment of a woman into this highly patriarchal
sacred order? Did Arwa have the requisite knowledge and the experience
for such an exalted position? What stance, if any, did the religious establishment take? To begin with, the imam-caliphs were considered the
highest religious authority, and "God's sole, infallible representatives"
(Walker 1995, 240). Imam-caliph al-Mustansir himself realized that his
elevation of Queen Arwa was extraordinary and unprecedented, but he
had been convinced by the elite of the *da'wa* that the queen, "the Lady,
the Righteous, the Faithful, the Powerful, the Preserver of Religion . . . the
Supporter of the believers, the Cave of the followers . . . the Supporter of
the Commander of the Faithful and the Protector of the Blessed
Followers" had received the "wisdom and science of the imam"
(Traboulsi 2003, 101). Further, not only did the religious elite not object
to the queen's elevation, they found ways of justifying it. Al-Sultan al-
Khattab (or al-Hattab, d. 1138), a high-ranking *da'i*, scholar, and court
poet who held the queen in high esteem,[27] advanced an intriguing argument in favor of her appointment as *hujja* (Traboulsi 2003, 104–105;
Daftary 1999, 122). Al-Khattab supported his opinion with an idea that
has long resonated among the Sufis and within mystical circles, though
Traboulsi interprets that as a "theological escape." Al-Khattab contended that the human body is merely an "envelope" (*qumus*) and has
"no real importance and does not indicate a person's sex" (Traboulsi
2003, 105). Rather, it is a person's knowledge – primarily religious and
esoteric – that determines one's sex. Presumably, only a male can attain
perfection in religious knowledge (i.e. knowledge is power is male).[28] The

---

[27] In one of his poems in praise of Queen Arwa, al-Khattab writes: "She was the Banu
Sulayhi's pearl / who brought light to a place of darkness" (Cortese and Calderini 2007,
133–134). His "loyalty to Sayyida Hurra and his military services to the Ismaili cause
contributed significantly to the success of the early Tayyibi *da'wa* in difficult times." He
was killed in 1138, a year after the queen passed away (Daftary 1999, 127). For detail on
al-Khattab's background, see Hamdani (1974, 267); Poonawala (1977).

[28] In a variation on the theme, in the Greek and Roman traditions, it was the "voice" that
was quintessentially male. A Roman woman "whose natural condition did not manage to
keep her silent in the [Roman] Forum" and was able to defend herself in the court
"really had a man's nature behind the appearance of a woman . . . a woman speaking in
public was . . . by definition not a woman" (Beard 2017, 11, 17). Such was the obsession

female, perceived to be of lesser intelligence, was believed to be inherently incapable of such perfection (Traboulsi 2003, 105). "Tradition never tires of reminding us," reiterates Schimmel, that "when a woman walks in the way of God, she cannot be called a 'woman'" (1997, 19); she is a man.[29] Occasionally, however, a few women – e.g. Khadija, Fatima, and Sayyida Hurra – might reach such a level of perfection of esoteric religious knowledge that they are no longer female, even if their "body envelope" is that of a woman.[30]

The twelfth-century historian Umara vacillates between views regarding the institutional authority of the imam-caliph's decree and the extent of Queen Arwa's spiritual authority (Cortese and Calderini 2007, 137). But the fifteenth-century Idris, himself a Tayyibi da'i mutlaq, has no misgivings about viewing the imam's decision as comprehensive and the queen's spiritual authority as valid (70–71 in Hamdani 1931). Some modern scholars equivocate, however. Traboulsi, for example, finds Idris's certainty far from reassuring because the imam's decree "survives only in quotations in" Idris's own 'Uyun al-akhbar (2003, 99, fn. 10). Traboulsi does not dispute the granting of spiritual authority to Queen Arwa, but interprets the imam-caliph's action as political rather than religious because of the types of activities that were assigned to her (2003, 99). Likewise, Daftary accepts that the imam granted the status of hujja to Queen Arwa, but he comments that in her case, "the term hujja was also used in a more limited sense" (1999, 122). For Abbas Hamdani, her institutional authority was also more concentrated on "the temporal side" (1950, 157). Husain Hamdani, on the other hand, believes that al-Mustansir "gave both functions, temporal and spiritual, into the charge of the Queen," and that he also "entrusted the [da'wa] mission of India and Sind to her care and leadership" (1931, 514). Cortese and Calderini (2007, 136) position the imam-caliph's action on a solid religious foundation, arguing that the imam-caliph, as a Fatimid Isma'ili Shi'ite, must have had in mind the incomparable models of the women of the Prophet's household, such as Khadija and Fatima.

with the sex of leaders that the coins commemorating the Sasanid Queen Azarmidokht (c. 631–632) depicted her with beard (Emrani 2009, 9).

[29] Political authority and sovereignty are perceived to be a challenge not just for Muslim queens. Commenting on the European queens, William Monter writes, "King may have no female form, but political power has no sex." He continues: "As Simone de Beauvoir once noted, Europe's most successful women rulers 'were neither male nor female – they were sovereigns'" (2012, 41).

[30] For further discussion and other examples see Traboulsi (2003, 105–106).

With her newly expanded spiritual authority, Queen Arwa continued to manage the affairs of the state in her dual capacity. Officially, however, her son al-Mukarram al-Asghar was in charge of the state, and the *da'i* Lamak b. Malik was in charge of the *da'wa* administration (Idris, 70–71 in Hamdani 1931; Hamdani 1974, 271). The queen appointed her cousin, *da'i* Saba b. Ahmad al-Sulayhi, to head state security. She also gave him an important position within the *da'wa*, and charged him with her sons' education (Idris, 71 in Hamdani 1931). As she was a relatively young widow with small children, some tribal leaders, including some of her own allies, assumed she would be unable to hold onto her demanding administrative position. A few considered this moment of transition an opportune time to challenge the queen's authority, seeking to overthrow her and take control of the Sulayhid state. Her step-father Amir b. Sulayman al-Zawahi for one found fault with *da'i* Saba's decisive defeat by one of the state's old enemies in 1086, and staged a rebellion against Saba and the queen (Idris, 72 in Hamdani 1931; Traboulsi 2003, 100). While the two leaders were fighting it out, the queen sent a missive to the imam-caliph in Cairo, seeking his support (Idris, 72 in Hamdani 1931). Fearing that the collapse of the Sulayhid state would be catastrophic for the well-being of the Fatimid Empire, al-Mustansir responded promptly (Traboulsi 2003, 100). Not only did the imam-caliph write a *sijill* in support of the queen, sent to both *da'i* Saba and *da'i* Amir, he also wrote to the tribal leaders asking them all to cease the infighting. Astonishingly, they did (Idris, 73 in Hamdani 1931; Hamdani 1934, 315, 319). Nonetheless, biographers have marked the conflict between these two leaders – and former allies and advisors to the queen – as a major catalyst in the weakening of the Sulayhid dynasty and the beginning of its decline (Hamdani 1974, 265). In a few years, however, both of the queen's potential rivals were dead: *da'i* Saba al-Sulayhi died in 1097–1098 and Amir b. Sulayman the following year. The queen outlived both of them and from then on was free of major political rivalries from within her tribe (Traboulsi 2003, 103; Idris, 78 in Hamdani 1931) – but not before another close encounter with her cousin *da'i* Saba.

Marriage, Autonomy, Authority

The infighting and challenges to the queen's political authority were not the only arenas in which the queen had to fend off male relatives, competitors, and tribal rivals. Marriage and sexuality were other domains in which the queen was potentially vulnerable and had to fiercely protect her honor and autonomy. Three incidents tested both her resolve to remain independent and her ability to face the ongoing personal and political challenges to her authority in the years following her husband's death.

As a young widow, Queen Arwa was perhaps the most sought-after woman of her time. With little or no stigma attached to widowhood, women, particularly among the elite, were often sought after and remarried not long after a husband's death. The social standing of widows in the early days of Islam was quite unlike the cultural perception of the inauspicious widowhood in many modern Muslim societies.[31] Most of the Prophet Muhammad's wives were either widowed or divorced. Caliph ʿAli b. Abu Talib married a widow of the first caliph, Abu Bakr, and al-Zubayr, another cousin/companion of the Prophet, married Atiqa, a widow of the third caliph, ʿUmar b. al-Khattab. Not surprisingly, perhaps, da ʿi Saba – Queen Arwa's commander-in-chief, her cousin, and her sons' tutor – desired to marry her. Umara describes da ʿi Saba as "Ill-favored [and short in stature]," a man who appeared "disadvantaged" in the saddle. But Umara adds that he was of a "benevolent and of generous disposition" and "an accomplished poet" (43 in Kay 1892). Not surprisingly, too, the queen refused his proposal. She was, after all, Sayyida Hurra, the Free and Noble Lady. Refusing to take no for an answer and offended by her rejection, Saba decided to win her over by force – a tribal custom? – and took his army to Dhu Jibla to compel her to accept his demand (Umara 45–46 in Kay 1892). The queen "was not the type of woman to submit to intimidation," however, and immediately mobilized her own forces to counter her chief of security. The two armies fought for several days without a decisive victory for either side (Hamdani 1931, 512; Umara, 46 in Kay 1892). Given the prolonged stalemate, one of the queen's step-brothers advised her suitor to take his case to the imam-caliph in Cairo and seek his mediation. Happy to have heard a reasonable solution, da ʿi Saba ceased hostilities, withdrew his forces, and dispatched two messengers to al-Mustansir, imploring the imam-caliph to intercede with the Sayyida Hurra. The imam-caliph welcomed the idea (Umara, 46 in Kay 1892; Idris, 73 in Hamdani 1931, 512).

Did the imam-caliph wish to temper his earlier dramatic decision to elevate the queen as *hujja*? Did he think the Sayyida Hurra needed a measure of male control or that as a da ʿi and a Sulayhid male, Saba would be a better guardian of the Fatimids' political and economic interests in Yemen? Whatever his motivations, al-Mustansir decided to act on da ʿi Saba's request.

The imam-caliph dispatched a missive and a special envoy to Yemen. Being an eunuch, the envoy was allowed to "enter into the presence of the queen" and to deliver the message to her personally (Umara, 46 in Kay

---

[31] For an example from Pakistan, see the chapter "The Crime of Being a Widow" in Haeri (2002).

1892). The stage was impeccably set. Inside the queen's palace, she was surrounded by her standing ministers, secretaries, and the official of the Fatimid state. Once in the queen's presence, al-Mustansir's eunuch read out the imam's letter:

The Prince of the Faithful returneth salutations of peace unto the Honorable Lady, the Queen Sayyidah, the Favored, the Pure, the Unparagoned of her time, Sovereign Lady of the Kings of Yaman, the Pillar of Islam, the Treasure of the Faith ... Our lord, the Prince of the Faithful, gives thee in marriage to the Daʿy, the Unparagoned, the Victorious ... (Umara, 46–47 in Kay 1892)

The imam's envoy further informed the queen that *daʿi* Saba had arranged a "dowry of hundred thousand dinārs in money, and the equivalent of fifty thousand dinārs in the articles of a rarity and values, in perfumes and in robes" (Umara, 47 in Kay 1892; Idris, 73 in Hamdani 1931). With all eyes on her, the queen received the imam's support for Saba's proposal graciously. Offering neither a yea nor a nay, the "Little Queen of Sheba" channeled her grand ancestor's reply to Solomon upon receiving his threatening letter to submit (Qurʾan 27:32). Turning to her advisors, she asked for their counsel (Umara, 47 in Kay 1892). After much discussion and cajoling, she finally gave her nominal consent – for disobeying the imam was sacrilegious.[32] Saba was overjoyed. He rushed to Dhu Jibla, arriving at her palace gate with his army in tow. He set up camp there, hosting "profuse feasting" and spending money on "his soldiery, a sum equal to the dowry he paid to the princess." He remained there for months but, alas, did not receive permission to enter the palace; the queen kept him waiting at the gate (Umara, 48 in Kay 1892). Heartbroken and humiliated, he finally sent a secret message to the queen, begging her to allow him to save face by receiving him in her palace, "that it might be believed by people that the marriage was consummated." The queen accepted his plea, and Saba was able to enter. He did not, however, have the good fortune to spend time with her, and their marriage was never consummated. Queen Arwa sent to him one of her female slaves who bore a striking resemblance to her. Suspecting the ruse, Saba never looked at her, and upon his departure the next morning, he told the slave girl: "Tell our lady that she is a precious pearl, to be worn only by whoever is worthy of her" (Umara, 48 in Kay 1892). Having lost face and humbled, Saba realized his own folly, acknowledging that "no person could be fitly compared to her, she whose people called her their Mistress." He then departed, and they did not meet again (Hamdani 1931, 512; Umara, 48 in Kay 1892). Abbas Hamdani, however, credits

---

[32] On the significance of obedience in Ismaʿilism, see Calderini (1993).

Saba with "gallantly" withdrawing his offer of marriage upon noticing Arwa's reluctance (1974, 266). Traboulsi sees the queen's "disobedience," discreet though it was, as the beginning of the Fatimids' change of attitude toward her, for they were "no longer willing to support her after the death of her sons" (2003, 102). But he is unclear what kind of support the Fatimids actually denied her. Practically speaking, the imam-caliphs in Cairo did not seem to have been in a position to discipline the queen. She was already declared a *hujja*, to whom obedience was due; she was "immensely popular" and strongly supported by her people. In fact, the regime in Egypt had come to depend on her economically, politically, and religiously. The Sayyida Hurra retained her throne for another forty-four years, outliving three successive Fatimid imam-caliphs, as I shall discuss shortly.

Another family drama involves the queen's daughter, Fatima, and her son-in-law, Shams al-Maʿali. As a member of the larger Sulayhid tribe, Queen Arwa and her family were involved in several marriage alliances. The queen herself had once been married to her cousin al-Mukarram, and her daughter Fatima and the queen's younger sister were both married to two sons of *daʿi* Saba – the same man who had sought to marry Arwa. As the story goes, Sayyida Hurra received a letter from Fatima informing her of her husband's second marriage.[33] Furious, the queen promptly moved to punish her wayward son-in-law by bringing the force of her army upon him. The army smuggled out Fatima, who was disguised as a man, and reunited her with her mother. Meanwhile, her soldiers kept Shams al-Maʿali under siege "until he was expelled from his domains" (Cortese and Calderini 2007, 133; Umara, 49 in Kay 1892). Shams al-Maʿali sought help from his father's former allies in Cairo, but to no avail – none apparently wished to offend the queen. Later Shams al-Maʿali returned to Yemen to claim his father's fortress, but he was poisoned and died in 1101, a fate reportedly arranged by a close ally of the queen (Umara, 49 in Kay 1892). Fatima died two years after her mother, in 1140. No other details are provided about her life after escaping her husband's fortress. While Husain Hamdani finds the queen a judicious "administrator," on occasion and of necessity, he opines that she had "to display qualities that betokened inflexibility of purpose, hardness of heart and severity" (1931, 516).

The last incident also involves matters of the heart and honor. It illustrates yet again the queen's ability to face challenges to her sovereignty. It is the story of al-Mufaddal, a loyal servant of the queen whose leadership qualities had early on gained her confidence (Hamdani 1931,

---

[33] This incident seems to have occurred after *daʿi* Saba's death.

512). Following the death of her husband, al-Mukarram, Arwa assigned Mufaddal to the fortress of al-Takar – where she spent her summer months – and put him in charge of a war against a few rebellious tribes (Idris, 78 in Hamdani 1931). Idris tells us that in Ramadan of 1111 and during al-Mufaddal's absence, a group of Shafiʿi jurists rebelled against the queen and took hold of the fortress. Al-Mufaddal then rushed to al-Takar and immediately laid siege to it. In response, the rebel jurist leader exacted an unusual revenge: he ordered all of al-Mufaddal's concubines to put on their finest clothes, go onto the roof of the fortress, and play their tambourines (Idris, 80 in Hamdani 1931). In horror, al-Mufaddal watched the women of his harem dancing in full view of the public. Dishonored, a disheartened al-Mufaddal committed suicide in a jealous rage (Idris, 80 in Hamdani 1931, 512–13). At the death of al-Mufaddal, the queen took her army to a place near the fortress of Dhu Jibla while simultaneously suing for diplomacy. She was "very scrupulous in the observance of treaty obligations," and offered a settlement to the jurists. They submitted to the queen's authority and returned control of the fortress to her, upon which the queen honored her promise to guarantee their safety and property (Hamdani 1931, 513).

These three incidents – and likely others for which we have no written record – illustrate the Sayyida Hurra Queen Arwa's skill at preserving her rule as well as her ability to discipline her subjects and to negotiate challenges to her political authority.

The Great Queen of Arabia: Mistress of Her Own People

Al-Mukarram al-Asghar's life was short; he died in 1094 soon after his younger brother passed away. After the death of her two sons, Arwa was no longer queen consort or queen regent. She was now the Great Queen of Arabia: the political head of the Sulayhid dynasty and spiritual leader, *hujja*, of the Ismaʿili *daʿwa* in Yemen and India. Traboulsi characterizes the period after the death of the queen's sons as "one of the survival of the fittest" (2003, 102), but her dexterity in facing challenges to her regime enabled her to stay in power for another four decades.

Back in Cairo, in the meantime, imam-caliph al-Mustansir lay on his death bed as his long life neared its end. He had lived to an old age; his fifty-eight years on the throne (1036–1094) made him the longest reigning Fatimid caliphs in Egypt. The reigns of al-Mustansir and Queen Arwa overlapped for almost twenty-seven years, spanning crucial moments in the survival of the imam-caliph in Egypt and the growing power and clout of the queen in Yemen. Al-Mustansir's death in 1094 ushered in the Fatimid's first major bloody battle over succession and the subsequent

regicides that weakened the foundations of the Fatimid political establishment. As primogeniture was not necessarily an Isma'ili rule of succession,
al-Mustansir's powerful and manipulative *wazir*, al-Afdal b. Badr al-
Jamali,[34] bypassed the imam's first son, Nizar, and declared the imam's
youngest son as the new caliph and leader of the Isma'ili Fatimids with the
royal name of al-Musta'li (Walker 1995, 262). But as the power struggle
over the succession raged, the necessity to prove the heir's legitimacy
became urgent. Until then, succession for the Isma'ilis meant "the divine
right personified in the legitimate heir" (Stern 1951, 194), and for ten
generations the succession had passed on smoothly from father to son.
But as the crisis of succession intensified, the Fatimid royal women who
had vested interests in the outcome of this political drama became actively
involved (Cortese and Calderini 2007, 38). Nizar's full sister is reported
to have testified against her brother and supported al-Musta'li, possibly
under threat by the wily *wazir* (Walker 1995, 256–257; Cortese and
Calderini 2007, 38–39). Meanwhile, the young al-Musta'li's mother
dispatched a letter to Queen Arwa in 1096, reiterating her son's legitimate
right to the Fatimid throne and seeking her support. Detailing the
expanding hostilities between the two brothers,[35] the queen mother
ended her letter by restating the indispensable position the Sulayhid
queen had always held for the Isma'ili *da'wa* in Cairo (Idris, 77 in
Hamdani 1931; Cortese and Calderini 2007, 38). The new imam-
caliph himself quickly followed suit, and personally wrote to the queen,
also in 1096, expecting support (Hamdani 1934, 320). The queen swiftly
acknowledged al-Musta'li's legitimacy and threw her support behind him
(Daftary 1999).

Having the (mis)fortune of being born into a polygynous royal harem,
al-Mustansir's first-born son Nizar had had to face competition not only
from his half-brothers but also from two willful *wazir*s, who had monopolized power and wealth in his father's court. A year later, Idris reports,
Nizar was captured, imprisoned, and eventually killed (77 in Hamdani
1931). And with that, the Isma'ilis split forever into the Nizari and
Musta'li factions, with further divisions yet to come. The queen remained
close to al-Musta'li and his successor al-Amir, both of whom bestowed
several more honorific titles on her (Daftary, 1999). At this point, Queen
Arwa was in her late forties, and she had overcome many political uphea-
vals and challenges to her position as both temporal and spiritual leader.
By all measures she was an experienced and seasoned politician. As she

---

[34] Afdal was a son of Badr al-Jamali, al-Mustansir's powerful *wazir* (d. 1094), who replaced
his father just before imam al-Mustansir's death in the same year (Walker 2017).
[35] There were actually several brothers, of whom at least three laid claim to the Fatimid
throne (Walker 1995, 262).

became more secure in her position and enjoyed popular support in Yemen, the Fatimid factionalism and turmoil in Egypt grew deeper. It motivated the queen to keep her distance and act more independently, and in that the physical distance between Egypt and Yemen worked to her advantage. The most consequential battle over the succession that directly involved the queen was yet to come – some thirty-five years later in October 1130. It was ignited by the assassination of al-Musta'li's son and successor, the imam-caliph al-Amir in Cairo.

Al-Musta'li – Tayyibi Isma'ilis

Al-Musta'li's reign was short. In less than six years he was dead, in 1101. During his rule, he recognized Queen Arwa and her chief *qadi* (judge), Yahya b. Lamak,[36] as leaders of the Yemeni *da'i* (Idris, 78 in Hamdani 1931) – once more reinforcing the queen's political and religious authority, and underscoring Yemen's geopolitical importance for the Fatimid regime in Egypt. When al-Musta'li's son al-Amir bi-Ahkam Allah was declared imam-caliph and assumed the mantel of the Musta'li faction of Isma'ilism, the queen promptly pledged her allegiance. Born in 1096, al-Amir was barely five years old and, like many of his predecessors, he fell under the domination of his shrewd and powerful *wazir* al-Afdal b. Badr al-Jamali, whom he had also inherited from his father. For the first two decades of his reign, al-Afdal "excluded him almost entirely from the government" (Walker 2016). The imam-caliph would not be able to rid himself of his meddlesome *wazir* until 1121. Rumors claimed that it was the frustrated imam-caliph himself who had al-Afdal vanquished, despite his elaborate show of mourning at his death (Walker 2016). With the Fatimids' dynastic discord simmering and political dissatisfaction ongoing, Queen Arwa had already distanced her administration discreetly from Cairo while at the same time maintaining official relations with the imam-caliph. She felt increasingly dissatisfied with the regime in Cairo, though she continued to pay tribute to the imam and occasionally received gifts from him (Daftary 1999, 124).

In 1119, after a period of almost twenty years, imam-caliph al-Amir appointed *da'i* Najib al-Dawla as his representative in Yemen, ostensibly to defend and keep the peace there. Sources are divided regarding the objectives of Najib's mission to Yemen, however. Traboulsi argues that Najib was chosen by the powerful *wazir* al-Afdal in order to bring the state of Queen Arwa under strict administrative control of the Fatimid court

---

[36] Yahya b. Malik was the son of the queen's former chief *qadi* and *da'i*, who had served in her court until his death in 1098. Yahya in turn served the queen until his death in 1126.

(2003, 103; Hamdani 1974, 267). But Husain Hamdani finds that Najib's mission was to serve Arwa, to "render assistance to the Queen in any manner" she desired (1931, 513). As before, the queen obeyed the young imam's order and installed Najib as her commander-in-chief. Apparently Najib's initial victories over the Sulayhids' perennial tribal enemies inflated his ego and encouraged him to entertain removing the queen from power and replacing her. In his eyes, Sayyida Hurra was old and feeble-minded and needed to step down, and so he rebelled against her. But the astute queen was well experienced in thwarting male competitors. She swiftly staged a counter-attack, laying a vigorous siege against al-Najib's troops, and in time taught him a lesson in humility. The queen based her brilliant military strategy on "fake news!" She ordered large sums of Egyptian money to be distributed among al-Najib's rival tribal leaders, while spreading rumors among his soldiers of his largess toward the enemy's mercenaries. Angered by their leader's inexplicable charity toward the enemy, al-Najib's mercenary soldiers abandoned him. Deserted, defeated, and humiliated Najib returned to the queen, apologized, and submitted to her authority. The shrewd queen told him: "Perceivest thou, the artifice accomplished by her of whom thou hast said that her mind is weakened?" (Hamdani 1931, 513). Having managed to make himself and his army "odious" in Yemen, in 1129 imam-caliph al-Amir finally recalled Najib al-Dawla to Egypt. But he never arrived. On his way to Cairo, Najib was "accidentally" drowned by his enemies, who "spread the news that he was carrying a mission on behalf of the Nizar" (Hamdani 1931, 513). While the queen rejected the allegation of treason leveled against Najib, she successfully concealed her own alleged responsibility for the drowning of the caliph's envoy. She nevertheless continued to obey the commands of the young Fatimid caliph in Egypt (Idris, 83 in Hamdani 1931).

Back in Egypt, happy times seemed to have returned to Cairo. In March 1130 it was announced that a son named Abu'l-Qasim al-Tayyib had been born to imam-caliph al-Amir. But the historicity of al-Tayyib's birth has been doubted and debated. Stern refutes the doubters (1951, 197), writing that the news of al-Tayyib's birth was received with many public festivities and ceremonies: "Misr (i.e. Fustat) and Cairo were decorated, music was played in the streets and at the gates of the palaces. New suits of clothes were issued to the troops and the palaces were decorated ... This continued for a fortnight ... Then the child was brought in ... Pieces of gold dinars were strewn over the head of the people" (Stern 1951, 196–97; Walker 2016, Idris, 85 in Hamdani 1931). Daftary likewise cites al-Khattab's eyewitness account of the celebrations surrounding the child's birth (1999, 126). More historically significant,

however, is the *sijill* that al-Amir sent to Queen Arwa in Yemen, announcing the birth of al-Tayyib and confirming his designation as heir. Upon
receiving the letter, the Sayyida Hurra informed all the *da'is* and the
public, and promptly and publicly pledged her allegiance to the infant
future imam. Once again, the caliph's official missive highlights the significance of Queen Arwa's strategic position for the Fatimid Isma'ilis. In
this connection, Idris tells an anecdote that underscores the imam-
caliph's and the queen's esoteric knowledge – hence their close cooperation and her qualification as a *hujja*. Al-Amir had reportedly given
a certain *sharif* "letters and a tattered garment" to be delivered to the
queen in Yemen. Upon receiving them, she wept at the sight of the
tattered garment. She understood the message of death and demise that
imam-caliph al-Amir was communicating to her (84 in Hamdani 1931).
Not long after al-Amir's premonition came true. He was stabbed to death
by a devotee of Nizar as he made "his way through the streets in a large
procession", leaving the fate of the infant heir hanging in the balance
(Idris, 85 in Hamdani 1931; Stern 1951, 198). What became of the child,
al-Tayyib, is anyone's guess. According to some accounts, al-Amir's
cousin, who was charged with al-Tayyib's guardianship, had the child
taken away from the palace, never to be seen again (Stern 1951, 198).
Some think he was killed, others believe that he went into concealment
(*sitr*) and remains hidden from view to this day. Only those closest to him
knew of his whereabouts (Idris, 86 in Hamdani 1931).

Frustrated with the evolving – and intensifying – regicidal political
crises of succession in Cairo, Queen Arwa finally severed her administrative ties with the Fatimids and turned her attention to laying the
foundations of the Tayyibi Isma'ili sect in Yemen and beyond (Daftary
1999). As a *hujja* with religious authority, the queen moved swiftly to
establish the new rank of *da'i mutlaq* (supreme missionary with absolute
authority) in the Isma'ili religious hierarchy.[37] She appointed the first *da'i
mutlaq* of the Tayyibi *da'wa*, and charged him with leading the "*da'wa* on
behalf of the hidden Imam [al-Tayyib] and to assume custody of the
literature of the (earlier) Fatimid Ismaili *da'wa*" (Sayyid 2002, 2). This
was politically a bold and strategic action that challenged assertions that
the queen's spiritual authority as *hujja* was "primarily honorific and not
executive" (Hamdani 1974, 273). Theoretically, one may grant the
queen's marginality as a *hujja* vis-à-vis her gender. No other Muslim
woman had been named *hujja* before, or has been since, in the Isma'ili
religion. But what she did as a *hujja* at that critical moment in history
renders moot the theoretical presupposition of her marginality. While her

---

[37] See Hamdani (1974, 272, fn. 1) on the ranks of the Isma'ili *da'wa* hierarchy.

title may have been initially conceived as ceremonial, when the opportunity presented itself, she did not hesitate to intervene authoritatively in the Fatimid conflicts of succession. Her historic achievement was to establish the Tayyibi *da'wa* and to separate it from the political structures of both the Fatimids in Egypt and the Sulayhids in Yemen (Hamdani 1974, 272; Daftary 1999, 126). The queen clearly demonstrated that she intended to use her authority both politically and religiously. Neither the *da'i*s in Yemen at the time nor the newly appointed *da'i mutlaq* objected to the queen's extraordinary action. In fact, under the Sayyida Hurra's supreme guidance and patronage this branch of Isma'ilism consolidated its power in Yemen (Daftary 1999, 127); her gender was irrelevant to her decision, and the religious elite clearly recognized that. In the end, the queen's "greatest achievement" was her "establishment of the Isma'ili Taiyibi Mission" in Yemen and Gujarat, India, where they are known as Bohras (Hamdani 1931, 515; Daftary 1999, 126). Creating the office of *da'i mutlaq*, the queen set the Tayyibi *da'wa* on a course that has continued to the present day.[38] Meanwhile, al-Amir's death and the violent struggle over the succession in Egypt sealed the Isma'ili schism between the Nizaris and the Tayyibis, hastening the rapid decline and demise of the once-powerful Fatimid dynasty in Egypt, which came to an end in 1171.[39]

The Great Queen of Yemen, the Little Queen of Sheba: Some Reflections

[R]eal histories, as both durations and events, are shaped by practices within and against existing "structures."

Ortner (2006, 9)

The Sayyida Hurra Queen Arwa emerged from within a particular patriarchal dynasty at a specific historical juncture in the Yemeni culture of the eleventh and twelfth centuries. She was an elite member of the Sulayhid tribe, trained and supported by the lineage's patriarch and *da'i*, 'Ali b. Muhammad. She married the heir to the throne, also a *da'i*, whose infirmity and early death facilitated her ascent to the highest political office. The Sulayhid dynasty of Yemen was a satellite ally of the Fatimid Isma'ilis in Egypt, supporting and supported by the latter – the fates of the two states were intimately interconnected. Queen Arwa came to power through an accident of history, but she made history in taking on the helm

---

[38] By the sixteenth century, however, the Tayyib *da'wa* further split into Da'udis and Sulaymanis (de Blois 1983, 3; Sayyid 2002, 3).

[39] For a history of schism among the Isma'ilis, see Daftary (1993).

of the state and becoming a powerful local sovereign with long-term global consequences.[40] She was an exception to the rule not only in being the first Isma'ili woman sovereign, but also in simultaneously holding the highest religious authority, as *hujja* – a privilege enjoyed by no other Muslim woman ruler before or since. Ceremonial though her title of *hujja* might have been from the view of the male political elite, the queen had no doubt about her own legitimacy and little hesitancy to use her authority as political situations demanded. She did so in the aftermath of imam-caliph al-Amir's assassination in Egypt and moved promptly to structure and transform the Tayyibi Isma'ili religious hierarchy.

The Sayyida Hurra was an admirably fast learner in the games of realpolitik. Educated and trained early on under the supervision of her remarkable mother-in-law, Queen Arwa manifested intellectual discernment, political acumen, and personal charisma. Throughout her unusually long reign she demonstrated self-confidence and acted decisively to preserve her throne, whether against her state's enemies or insubordinate family members. She did not hesitate to use her political authority to influence social change in the composition of her political/religious administration, nor did she dither in taking independent action to alter the rigidly structured Isma'ili clerical hierarchy. Sometimes she used her gender as "capital" to mislead her adversaries; other times she displayed vindictiveness and inflexibility. Faced with the momentous prospect of a contested succession after the murder of the Fatimid imam-caliph al-Amir, she acted independently in establishing and appointing the new religious role of *da'i mutlaq*. In so doing, the queen distanced the Tayyibi religious authority, not only from the ongoing Fatimid politics of succession, but also from the Sulayhid state in Yemen. She thus put the Tayyibi Isma'ili branch on a solid and independent foundation, disentangling it from the whims of temporal authority, and enabling it to survive autonomously. Had the queen not had political authority and had she not firmly established her political domination in Yemen, she would not have been able to influence the course of events, religious and political, so decisively.

The Sayyida Hurra ruled effectively for seventy-one years, and as she gained more experience as sovereign, she was able to wield greater political leverage in her relationship with the increasingly younger and

---

[40] In a conversation I had with Dr. Farhad Daftary, director of the Ismaili Institute in London, he contended that had it not been for Queen Arwa in Yemen and Hassan Sabbah (leader of the Nizari branch) in Iran, Isma'ilism would not have survived. After breaking away from the Fatimids in Egypt, Daftary said, both Sabbah and Arwa were able to operate autonomously and founded these two independent branches of Isma'ilism. Both moved from within the tradition and followed similar paths; Sabbah was a *da'i*, and the queen was a *hujja* – higher in status (London, February 4, 2016). See also Daftary 1999, 124, 127).

inexperienced Fatimid caliphs in Egypt. Unfazed by the social, political, and military roller-coaster in Egypt, and tribal infighting in Yemen, she performed a delicate balancing act of diplomatic deference and obedience to the Fatimid imams in Cairo while exercising authority and autonomy in Yemen. She managed to keep the powerful and competing Yemenite tribal leaders in check, while delivering justice and ensuring the welfare of her people, who called her their "Mistress." The queen was highly respected, and not just by her own people. Even when the *da'wa* split again after Caliph al-Amir's death and the leading *qadi* in Egypt took a hostile stance toward the queen and her *da'wa*, he could "never come out openly against her and showed her due deference because of her high reputation and popularity in all Yaman" (Hamdani 1974, 265).

Traboulsi argues that the "Fatimids exhausted every possible political and religious means to cover the queen's deficiency" (2003, 107), presumably meaning her gender. But exactly what they did, he does not specify. Probably the three Fatimid caliphs whose reigns coincided with that of the queen – and many more members of the political elite – were mystified by the queen's gender, political acumen, and longevity. Nonetheless, they all made sure to keep her happy. All three caliphs, al-Mustansir, al-Musta'li, and al-Amir, responded promptly and positively to her requests, given the extent of their dependence on her government for political, economic, and religious support. Holding the queen in "special regard" (Idris, 70 in Hamdani 1931), al-Mustansir appointed her *hujja*, al-Musta'li sought her political support, and al-Amir trusted her with the fate of his son's succession. In all these cases, it was political pragmatics on the ground that guided their actions, though couched in religious ideology and doctrinal principles. As a ruling queen with political authority, she was in a position to demand reciprocity in political transactions with the three Fatimid imam-caliphs in Cairo. Acknowledging al-Mustansir's pragmatism in appointing the queen a *hujja*, Traboulsi concludes, "The reign of the Sulayhid queen is a paradigmatic historical case of the inseparability of religion and state" (2003, 107). Theoretically he is correct, for after all it was imam-caliph al-Mustansir who appointed the queen as both temporal and spiritual leader of Yemen. But in fact the queen effectively separated religion from politics, thereby ensuring Tayyibi Isma'ilism's survival, unaffected by the fall of both the Fatimid in Egypt and the Sulayhids in Yemen.

Little Queen of Sheba and the Prophetic Hadith

We might pause here and ask whether the alleged Prophetic hadith, "Never will succeed such a nation as makes a woman their ruler," played any role in imam-caliph al-Mustansir's decision to appoint the queen as a religious leader, a *hujja*. For one thing, this hadith does not resonate as strongly among the Shi'ites,[41] and still less among a dynasty that claimed descent from the Prophet's daughter Fatima and took her name. Did Yemen suffer under her sovereignty? Evidently not! She was "immensely popular" and people called her "their Mistress" (Hamdani 1931, 512). Sources underline the way Queen Arwa maneuvered to position her regime in Yemen as indispensable to the Fatimid imam-caliphs in Egypt: "At that time," writes Sayyid, "Yaman was the only region that was considered safe due to the political power held by the Sulayhids, who ruled there on behalf of the Fatimids" (2002, 2). And so to raise her rank to that of *hujja* with the ultimate religious authority over the Sulayhid domains, was perhaps "The best, or possibly the only step to be taken for the time being" (Traboulsi 2003, 99). Arwa's gender was perceived as of little or no consequence – if not actually an asset.

At several junctures when her authority was threatened, Queen Arwa showed resolve and charisma by planning highly intelligent political and military stratagems. She had the murderer of her father-in-law and the Sulayhids' perennial enemy, Sa'id "the Squint-Eyed," misled, trapped, captured, and destroyed. She taught a humiliating lesson to the haughty Najib al-Dawla – her Fatimid-appointed Egyptian commander-in-chief, who assumed she was old and feeble-minded – before having him "accidently" drowned on his way back to Cairo. The Sayyida Hurra did not tolerate disloyalty from close members of her family either. She punished her unfaithful son-in-law, who had dared to take a second wife and had him banished from his palace. But she played a delicate diplomatic balancing act when the imam-caliph al-Mustansir ordered her to marry her cousin and commander-in-chief, *da'i* Saba. As a loyal follower of the imam-caliph she did not wish to disobey him openly – disobedience was, after all, an impious act – yet she had no intention of becoming a co-wife to Saba's multiple wives. Taking her cue from none other than the Queen of Sheba, Sayyida Hurra consulted with her advisors publicly, but refused discreetly to consummate the marriage.

When she was asked to step into her royal husband's shoes to govern, tribal leaders did not think she had what it took to be a political leader; that the challenge of authority would be too much for a woman, let alone a young one; that she could be maneuvered out of power quickly. She proved them wrong, and her long rule testifies to her political acumen and charisma. At every turn of events, it seems, she simply thwarted men in authority, but sought the collaboration and advice of a few good men to

---

[41] Abdul Karim Soroush, personal communication, Boston 2015. See also Rafiq Zakaria (1989, 13, 15).

continue with the functioning of her government.[42] She would not have been able to do so had she not been highly intelligent, and had she not had the strong support of the political and religious elites, and of her people, behind her.

In the meantime, while the male elite was trying to justify Arwa's position as both a queen *and* a *hujja*, as a sovereign *and* a religious leader, she continued to govern and her people continued to live their lives contently under her leadership – life went on as the political and religious elites argued among themselves. As for the people of Yemen, the gender of their leader was irrelevant. If anything, Arwa's womanhood was, for all practical purposes, for the better, as they lived in peace for as long as she was their sovereign. The queen cleverly and competently controlled her domain, ruled her people with justice, created networks of economic transactions across the Indian Ocean, and was not anxious about her own sex (i.e. whether she was "in reality a male" in a female "body envelope") or her gender performance. Nor did she doubt her own legitimacy, intelligence, or competence to govern her people; her popularity underlined her legitimacy. The queen was a highly effective political leader and a true believer.

The Sayyida Hurra Queen Arwa died at the ripe old age of ninety in 1137–1138 and was buried in the cathedral mosque in Dhu Jibla that she had built. Her grave has become a pilgrimage destination for "Muslims of diverse communities," though they "are not always aware of her Ismaili Shi'i connection" (Daftary 1999, 128). There was no person of significance of the Sulayhid dynasty to succeed her. She bequeathed all her wealth, jewelry, gold, and other valuables to the cause of the Tayyibi *da'wa* (Idris, 90 in Hamdani 1931; Hamdani 1931, 516). The Sayyida Hurra Queen Arwa is still remembered fondly in Yemen, where she is affectionately referred to as the "Little Queen of Sheba," and her shrine is visited by locals and foreigners. She remains the Great Queen of Yemen.[43]

---

[42] No references, however, are made to her having any wise female advisers – not even her daughters – nor of her mentoring other women for leadership, as her mother-in-law had done for her.

[43] For a few decades after the queen's death, however, some members of the Sulayhid dynasty held on to "some scattered fortresses in Yemen," but to no avail (Daftary 1999, 127).

4   Razia Sultan of India: "Queen of the World Bilqis-i Jihan"

> The gentle breeze cleaned the surface of the earth of worries and the aggrieved bird sang a song of joy. A new order was set up in the world and the remains of the old regime disappeared. Philosophers said to one another, "It is Venus who is going to rule." The world from end to end became like the exalted paradise when the insignia of prosperity manifested itself ... The principal officers of the old regime arranged a beautiful durbar in which the army chiefs placed a golden throne. They made the daughter of the Solomon of India occupy it according to the advice of the grandees of the State. Before her stood the harem like servants attending on kings – inside the seraglio all the women and outside it, the lion-conquering men. The chiefs bent their heads toward her, fully resolved to carry out her order.[1]   Husain (1938, 253)

On April 3 of the year 1240 Amir Ikhtiyar al-Din Altunia, a onetime ally turned adversary of Razia Sultan, the fifth sovereign of the Delhi Sultanate, tricked her out of the royal court and the capital city, Delhi, the center of her popular support and power base. The sultan was defeated, arrested, and imprisoned in a fortress, kept under the watchful eye of none other than Amir Altunia himself. Whether it was "the artful queen" who then tempted the rebellious Amir, or a regretful but ambitious Altunia, in a surprise move captor and captive decided to marry.[2] The two joined forces and in October of the same year moved to regain Razia's throne. In her absence, however, some of the same formidable Shamsi *amir*s,[3] the military elite who had facilitated Razia's ascent to the throne of Delhi in 1236, removed her from power and crowned her younger half-brother. The newly married couple had little chance of victory, as their mostly mercenary soldiers defected to the imperial army. They were defeated, taken captive, and on October 13 of the same year "attained martyrdom at the hands of Hindus" (Juzjani 1963, 462).

---

[1] This passage is from *Futuh al-Salatin*, also known as the *Shah Nameh* of India by the fourteenth-century poet Isami, which has been edited by A. S. Usha (1948). I cite both Husain and Usha.

[2] Ishwari Prasad (1931, 84).

[3] The ethnically Turkic military-political elite and former slaves (*ghulam*) of Razia's father, Sultan Shams ud-Din Iltutmish - hence, Shamsi (described later).

Who was Razia Sultan?[4] How did she come to ascend the throne of the Delhi Sultanate, and how did the political tide turn against her?[5]

Situating Razia: Daughter of the Solomon of India

Razia was born in Delhi to Turkan Khatun and Shams ud-Din Iltutmish around 1205 (Figure 4.1). Her mother was a daughter of Qutb al-Din Aybek, who had laid the foundations of the Mamluk/slave dynasty of the Delhi Sultanate.[6] "Though ugly in external appearance" (Ishwari Prasad 1931, 74), Aybek started life as a "high-spirited and open handed" loyal slave of Muiz al-Din Muhammad Sultan Ghuri and rose rapidly in the ranks to be appointed to the prestigious position of "Lord of the Stables" (*amir-i akhur*) of the sultan[7] (Brijbhushan 1990, 4–5; Ayalon 2012).

Manumitted before the death of his benefactor, Qutb al-Din claimed independence upon his master's death and established himself as Sultan of Delhi in 1206. Little is known about his daughter, Turkan Khatun, whom he arranged to be married to his favorite slave, Shams ud-Din Iltutmish, who succeeded his master upon the latter's death (Juzjani 1963, 440–452).[8] Juzjani, a contemporary of Sultan Iltutmish and the court chronicler, describes the sultan as "endowed with excellent disposition and comeliness," and the fourteenth-century poet Abdul Malik Isami

---

[4] Various spellings of her name include Razia, Raziya, Raziah, Raziyyat, Radiyya, and Ridiya. I have adopted Razia, the most common.

[5] The primary sources on Razia Sultan's life and leadership are fairly restricted (Jackson 1999, 182–183). The only eyewitness account is that of her contemporary biographer-chronicler Minhaj al-Din Siraj Juzjani (d. 1266), author of the *Tabaqat-i Nasiri*. A judge, an imam, and a public orator (*khatib*), Juzjani was from a family of distinguished scholars and clerics of Turkic ethnicity. I have used his book extensively in this chapter. His manuscript is translated from Persian with extensive commentaries and footnotes by Major H. G. Raverty, which I have also consulted for this chapter. Raverty gives a biographical sketch of Juzjani, and of the extant copies of the manuscripts that he consulted to prepare his translation. All references to Juzjani and Raverty are from Volume 1 of their respective works, unless otherwise specified. All translations from Juzjani's *Tabakat/Tabaqat-i Nasiri* are my own unless otherwise stated. Another fourteenth-century biographer is Abdul Malik Isami, whose book of poems the *Futuh al-Salatin* (completed in 1350) I have also used. Lastly, there is the account of the famed Arab traveler, Ibn Battuta (d. 1369), translated by H. A. R. Gibb (1971). All references to Ibn Battuta are taken from Gibb.

[6] For a thorough discussion of the Delhi Sultanate, see Sunil Kumar (2010); Ishwari Prasad (1931).

[7] For a discussion of the specificities of slave (*ghulam*) ownership in medieval Muslim states, the nature of slaves' loyalty to their master, and the "enduring ties of affection" between slave and master, see Mottahedeh (1980). Many of these slaves were trained to become military leaders.

[8] Variations of Iltutmish's name include: I-Yal-Tamish (Raverty, 1970), Talmish (Ibn Battuta), Altamsh, and Altamish. See Gibb (1971, 629, fn. 47) and Brijbhushan (1990, 6) for a brief discussion of the different spellings.

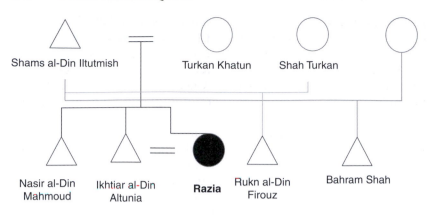

Figure 4.1 Razia Sultan's Genealogy

praises him as the "Solomon of India." Originally from the Qara Khitai of Olberlie (Ilbari) tribe in Central Asia – known for its greater tolerance of women's autonomy and individuality[9] – Shams ud-Din was reportedly lured away from home at a young age in a manner reminiscent of the Quranic story of Josef (Qur'an 12). He was sold to a merchant from Bukhara by his envious brothers, or cousins (Juzjani 1963, 441). He was treated well, trained, educated, and resold several times before eventually being purchased by Qutb al-Din Aybek. Shams ud-Din so impressed his master with his charisma, personality, and achievements that Qtub al-Din manumitted him and arranged for his daughter Turkan Khatun to marry him. She was her husband's senior wife in the sultan's harem and lived in "purdah" in the "Turquoise Palace," leading a pious life (Juzjani 1963, 457; Raverty 1970, 638). Upon Qutb al-Din's death in 1210, Iltutmish claimed the throne, defeating his other rivals, including a son of his benefactor who, after a brief reign of one year, proved incompetent (Ishwari Prasad 1931, 76). High-ranking slaves could apparently marry their master's daughter, but needed to be free men to ascend the throne. Iltutmish was thus paid a visit by a delegate of jurists, headed by Delhi's Grand *Qadi*. Realizing their intention, the astute sultan raised "a corner of the carpet upon which he was sitting produced for them a deed formally attesting to his enfranchisement." Afterward, the religious delegation "unanimously" sworn allegiance to Iltutmish (Ibn Battuta in Gibb 1971, 630; Mernissi 1994). A brave warrior and a just statesman, Iltutmish was also intensely religious (Brijbhushan 1990, 11;

---

[9] At least two princesses ruled the Qara-Khitan Empire in Turkestan in the middle decades of the twelfth century (Jackson 1999, 189).

Ishwari Prasad 1931, 81). He endowed the construction of mosques, patronized the *ulama*, and "projected Delhi as the 'Sanctuary of Islam' in a world facing the Mongol holocaust" (Kumar 2010, 239; Auer 2009, 7). Once in power, however, Razia exhibited a more pragmatic approach to religion than her father, which might have motivated some heterodox Muslim minorities to rebel early in her reign, as I discuss below.

A fast-growing urban center and a cosmopolitan city, Delhi had gained such great prominence by Juzjani's time that it was simply referred to by the honorific *hazrat* (majesty).[10] A century later, Ibn Battuta describes Delhi as "a vast and magnificent city, uniting beauty with strength. It is surrounded by a wall whose equal is not known in any country in the world, and is the largest city in India, nay rather the largest of all the cities of Islam in the East" (in Gibb 1971, 618). The heart of the city and the hub of all political activities, administrative planning, and harem intrigues, however, was the royal court.[11] With the Mongol hordes on its threshold, this grand city provided a safe haven from death and destruction.[12] Poets and painters, writers and scholars, artists and craftsmen fled to Delhi not only to survive the Mongol invasion, but also to benefit from the patronage of the royal court. The move toward art and education that had started prior to the Shamsi dynasty was accelerated by Razia's father, Sultan Iltutmish, who established several colleges and *madrasa*s throughout northern India, including the magnificent and renowned Nasiriya College, named after the Sultan's first-born son and heir-designate (Mobasher 2013, 110). These educational centers were richly endowed and attracted a number of eminent professors from all over India (Brijbhushan 1990, 65). Later, in the second year of her reign, Razia Sultan appointed Juzjani – the court historian – as the director of Nasiriya College in Delhi, which in Kumar's view far superseded in significance the positions of "qazi, *imam*, and *khatib* of Gwalior" that Sultan Iltutmish had already given him (2010, 224–225).

Razia had benefited from her father's educational policies and artistic patronage; she was well-educated and could "read the Quran with correct pronunciation" (Mobasher 2013, 111). Juzjani is silent on how the life of this young woman might have been lived in her father's royal court.

[10] For a description of Delhi's grandeur and its material resources, see Juzjani, 440–444; Ibn Battuta in Gibb (1971, 618); Kumar (2010, 124); Brijbhushan (1990, 56–74). The Qutub Minar monument in Delhi is but one example of a memorial to Iltutmish's greatness and to Delhi's grandeur (Ishwari Prasad 1931, 81).
[11] See Ibn Battuta for description of the Mamluk royal courts (Gibb 1971, 657–709; Brijbhushan 1990, 25–26).
[12] Ishwari Prasad (1931, 79) believes that what saved India from Mongol invasion was its intolerably hot weather.

However, he does underline the close relationship between father and daughter, and the sultan's "firm belief in the wisdom of his daughter," and admiration of her political talent and aptitudes (1963, 458; Mobasher 2013, 111). Brijbhushan faults Juzjani, however, for not enlivening his narrative on Razia's reign with anecdotes, as he had done so for the other rulers – all men – who preceded or succeeded her to the throne of the Delhi Sultanate.[13] Nor did Juzjani comment on her appearance, as he has done for other leaders; for example, Qutb al-Din Aybek possessed "no outward comeliness"; Iltutmish was endowed with "comeliness, intelligence and goodness of disposition"; and Rukn ud-Din was "of handsome exterior" (Raverty 1970, 630). What about Razia? asks Brijbhushan. "Was she tall or short? Was she Amazonian in proportion or slightly built? Did she have any physical defects? Was she autocratic and domineering or soft spoken and of pleasant disposition?" (1990, 118) Silence! On the other hand, Juzjani was highly complementary of Razia's half-brother and the last of the Shamsi sultans, Nasir al-Din Mahmoud Shah (1246–1266), under whose patronage he completed the *Tabaqat-i Nasiri*. Medieval biographers and chroniclers, according to Richard Bulliet (2003), were generally reluctant to write about women, particularly women not related to them through kinship or marriage. Gavin Hambly, on the other hand, observes that medieval chroniclers had few qualms about recording women's biographies (1999, 4). Juzjani seems to fall in the former category. However, we do not know whether local gender norms inhibited him from writing in greater detail about Razia, or whether his bare-bones description of her reign reflected the fact that his own benefactors were Razia's half-brother and successor Nasir al-Din Mahmoud and his *wazir*, the wily Turkic Shamsi Amir Ghiyas al-Din Balban, who had opposed Razia's ascension to power. It could also be that Juzjani's own Turkish ethnicity, as well as his position as a judge and a prayer leader in a local mosque, played a role in his restrained account of Razia's reign.

With so little historical information on Razia Sultan, it may come as a surprise to learn that she is today a folk hero in India and a widely admired queen,[14] and that the story of her rise and fall is a subject of ongoing cultural fascination. Reminiscent of the story of the legendary

---

[13] Even though Juzjani describes her successor, her brother Bahram Shah, as "blood thirsty [*khunriz*]," he composes panegyrics in his name, signing off with a customary reference to himself in the last line: "As with Minhaj Siraj, people pray you stay on your throne forever" (463). Some references use his first name, Minhaj, while others use his last name, Juzjani. I have adopted the latter.

[14] Razia is part of a proud line of women rulers and political leaders in India, be they Hindu, Muslim, or Christian. Some better-known ones are Begum Samru (c. 1753–1836), a Muslim convert to Christianity; the Begums of Bhopal, four successive generations

Queen of Sheba, the bare outline of Razia Sultan's sovereignty – particularly the unresolved intrigue of an alleged "romance" with her loyal Ethiopian slave/adviser – has tantalized scholarly and popular imagination, leading to the production of numerous documentaries,[15] romanticized blockbuster movies,[16] and long-running television melodramas.[17] Books on Razia Sultan also exist in several categories, ranging from adult literature[18] to children's books to comic strips.[19] These works creatively imagine, improvise, and reconstruct what it might have been like to be a young, politically active princess growing up in the Delhi royal court and become a charismatic sovereign queen of medieval India, when political competition for the crown was murderous and loyalty to the sovereign was at a premium, and when a close-knit Muslim minority of primarily Turkic ethnicity ruled over the majority Hindus and a smattering of Muslims. Creative representations of Razia's life revolve more often than not around her presumed interracial forbidden love affair with her father's loyal slave and her last-minute – and rather pathetic – marriage of convenience to her reported childhood friend and longtime ally, *Amir Altunia* – another slave-*amir* in her father's court. What the multiple narratives of the rise and fall of this formidable young queen all agree on is her charismatic personality, her sense of justice and equity, and her sensitivity to the lives of the masses – both Hindus and Muslims – who supported her and stood by her throughout her reign. For Raverty, however, only Juzjani's eyewitness account has the "authority" to comment on personalities and events of the period. He writes that "all other works since written, merely copy from him and add their own fertile imaginations" (1970, 638). Raverty is correct in asserting the primacy of Juzjani's written account, but his quick dismissal of the power of oral culture is unwarranted. The story of a female sultan in thirteenth-century India and the extraordinary circumstances of her life and leadership in the magnificent Delhi court cannot – and should not – be limited to those few

---

who ruled Bhopal, mother to daughter (1819–1926); and Indira Gandhi (1917–1984), to name a few.

[15] "History of India – Delhi Sultans and Their Historical Importance," www.youtube.com /watch?v=EpvZ5ag9WXw; "Once Upon a Sultan," www.youtube.com/watch? v=PpcW1KIpYjo.

[16] *Razia Sultan*, written and directed by Kamal Amrohi (1983), www.youtube.com/watch? v=mUxvmOOrtHc; *Razia Sultan*, written by K. P. Kathak and directed by Devendra Goel (1961), www.imdb.com/title/tt0381528/.

[17] *Razia Sultan*, www.youtube.com/watch?v=Khr8CUJt3sM. As of October 2015, 170 episodes had been made.

[18] *Razia: Queen of India*, by Rafiq Zakaria, and *Sultan Razia, Her Life and Times: A Reappraisal*, by Jameela Brijbuhshan (1990), to name a few.

[19] *Razia and the Pesky Presents* by Natasha Sharma (n.d.). "It's nice to get presents but not if they are challenging your right to rule as a woman."

written pages. The people of Delhi were not unaware of the uniqueness of this royal princess; they loved her, supported her, and helped propel her to the throne of Delhi when she needed them. The people seem to have spun a more nuanced – if also more fanciful – narrative of who Razia Sultan was. The story of her life and legacy and her path to power has become the stuff of legend in India, wrapped in many layers of fact, fiction, and fantasy.

Drama of Succession: Contesting the Crown

Sultan Iltutmish died on April 4, 1236, and with that the rivalry over the Shamsi crown reached a crescendo. This "Solomon of India," like his namesake and many other kings, sultans, *amir*s, and other men of power, had multiple wives and possibly many more concubines and slave girls – even he may not have known how many! Juzjani and Raverty identify some ten to twelve of his offspring, all of whom, with the exception of Razia, are male (Juzjani 1963, 451; Raverty 1970, 625). Razia was Iltutmish's eldest and perhaps only daughter.[20] The head of the sultan's harem, Shah Turkan (or Terken), was a Turkish slave/concubine/wife of Iltutmish. She patronized "the ulema, Sayyids, priests and recluses" (Raverty 1970, 631), which set in place powerful networks of loyal supporters within the royal court. Initially, the sultan named his first-born son, Nasir al-Din Mahmoud – also the name of his youngest son and the last sultan of the Shamsi dynasty – as his successor (Juzjani 1963, 454). As fate would have it, however, the son predeceased his father by a few years (d. 1229), and from then on the issue of which of the children from his multiple wives and concubines the sultan had actually designated as his successor was hotly contested.

Court chronicler Juzjani repeatedly underlines the close and affection-ate bond between Sultan Iltutmish and his daughter. He notes the sultan's acknowledgment of his daughter's political talent and his appreciation of her aptitude for leadership. But did the sultan actually designate his daughter as his heir? Which of his two eldest children had the sultan specifically named as his successor – his daughter Razia from his senior wife, Turkan Khatun, or his second oldest son Rukn ud-Din Firuz from his favorite wife, Shah Turkan? Juzjani gives two accounts. In one, he underscores Razia's fitness for leadership, noting that she was particularly tested when the sultan charged Razia with overseeing state

---

[20] Raverty, however, writes that Razia was probably not Iltutmish's only daughter, but he does not provide any evidence (1970, 635, fn. 1). In the melodramatic reconstruction of Razia's rise to power for the contemporary Indian television series, she is portrayed as the spirited younger sister of Shazia.

affairs while he was away on a military expedition to Gwalior in 1231. She fulfilled her duties so skillfully during her father's absence, and the sultan was so impressed by his daughter's signs of "sovereignty and high spirit," that even though "she was a girl and sheltered [*mastureh*]"[21] he ordered his secretary to draw up a decree and named his daughter as his heir-apparent (Raverty 1970, 638; Juzjani 1963, 458; Brijbhushan 1990, 12; Habibullah 1976, 97). To highlight the sultan's bold and contentious step, Juzjani relates that several of the *amir*s and ministers of Iltutmish's inner-circle went to see him and asked:

Why would the Sultan nominate a daughter as "king of Islam" when he has several sons? "Tell us the wisdom [*hikmat*] of your action," they implored the king, "for we do not understand it."

"My sons," responded the Sultan, "are given over to the follies of youth: none of them is fit to be king and rule this country, and you will find there is no one better able to do so than my daughter ... It will become clear to you after my death." (Juzjani 1963, 458; see also Lane-Poole, 1903, 74)

The leaders remained unconvinced. But "it came to pass as that wise King had predicted" (Juzjani 1963, 458).

Peter Jackson doubts the attribution of this passage to Juzjani. He argues that at the time of this episode Juzjani was still in Gwalior and not in Delhi, and so could not have personally observed the writing of the decree (1999, 183). Rather than challenging the veracity of Juzjani's observation, Kumar cites another passage in which Juzjani refers to the return of the royal father and son to Delhi, where "the people had their eyes" upon the son, Rukn al-Din (2010, 455). Raverty, however, dismisses all the skeptics and contends, "The people may have had their eyes upon him, but I-yal-timish had already named his talented daughter, Raziyyat Khatun, as his successor" (1970, 631, fn. 9). Habibullah agrees: her nomination was given wider publicity because her name was included "in a new series of the silver *tankah*" coins (1976, 97).

In the end, Shah Turkan, the sultan's favorite slave/concubine/wife plotted with his Turkish military slaves/*amir*s to give the "green Canopy of the State" to her son Rukn al-Din and declare him king (Brijbhushan 1990, 14–15; Lane-Poole 1903, 74). Razia acquiesced, much to the chagrin of her devoted slaves/supporters, but she remained watchful. No sooner were the coronation ceremonies over than "Rukn al-Din opened the treasury, and indulged in seeking pleasure [*Ishrat*] and ... because of his indulgence in

---

[21] Raverty and others have translated *mastureh* as "veiled." This translation is slightly off. Although one meaning of the multivalent *mastureh* is "covered" or "veiled," a more contextually relevant meaning here would be "chaste" more generically, "sheltered," but not necessarily a veiled woman (http://dictionary.abadis.ir/?LnType=dehkhoda,fato fa,moeen,amid&Word=%D9%85%D8%B3%D8%AA%D9%88%D8%B1%D9%87.

debauchery [*lahv va la'b*], the affairs of the state remained neglected"
(Juzjani 1963, 455). As the saying goes, "a brilliant ruler's son is apt to be
a failure." Rukn al-Din fully realized his father's prediction. The young king
was "a handsome, generous, soft-hearted, convivial, young fool, who spent
his money upon singers and buffoons and worse, and swaying drunk upon
his elephant through the bazaars [he] showered red gold upon the admiring
crowd"[22] (Lane-Poole 1903, 73; Juzjani 1963, 457). The young sultan's
mother, Shah Turkan, effectively assumed control of the palace and "seized
the opportunity to pay off old scores in the *harem*" (Jackson 1999, 184).
Raverty finds the queen mother a cunning and vengeful woman; Firishta
characterizes her as "a monster of cruelty"; Ishwari Prasad thinks she "had
an inordinate love of power" (1931, 82); and Rafiq Zakaria's historical novel
presents her as a woman who would put "Lady Macbeth to shame" (1966,
148). Juzjani rationalizes Shah Turkan's cruelty and vengefulness as
a reaction to the "envy and jealousy" the queen consort must have experienced in the harem. He suggests that in retribution she "brought misfortune
upon" her co-wives once in power, and in her tyranny and cruelty, she
destroyed some of them (1963, 455). Raverty finds Juzjani's characterization of the queen mother too charitable and writes that, on the contrary,
Shah Turkan "envied and was jealous of the others through their having
taken her place. No sooner did she obtain an opportunity than she had the
noble women – free-born women – who had been married to the late Sultan,
put to death with much degradation" (1970, 632, fn. 5). Ultimately, Rukn al
-Din Firuz Shah proved utterly incapable of running the affairs of state, and
left the governing to his mother, "till her savage cruelty caused a general
revolt" (Lane-Poole 1903, 73; Jackson 1999, 184).

Barely six months into his reign, the treasury was dwindling rapidly,
political chaos mounting, and popular dissatisfaction with the sultan's
moral corruption growing. Fearing imminent personal danger from her
vengeful stepmother, Razia made her intentions public. On a November day
in 1236, aiming judiciously for maximum publicity, she addressed a huge
crowd at "the mosque for Friday prayers"[23] (Brijbhushan 1990, 14;
Mernissi 1994, 95). Clad in a red dress, customarily worn by people with
grievances, and in the name of her father, Razia addressed the restive
crowd.[24] She appealed to the public for protection against her ruthless

---

[22] While not disputing Rukn al-Din's zeal for pleasure, Kumar (2010, 256–260) considers
the sultan's patronage of the elephant keepers not foolish but a strategic move to create
a power base independent from that of his father's formidable Shamsi slave-*amir*s, which
nonetheless provoked their resentment and opposition to the young sultan.

[23] Ibn Battuta describes it as "the terrace of the old castle adjoining the great mosque"
(Gibb 1971, 631). Juzjani makes no reference to this episode.

[24] According to Ibn Battuta, those seeking justice wore a red "dyed garment [*kaghzi
pirhan*]" so that they would be easily identified and their grievance redressed (Gibb

stepmother, who was bent on eliminating any and all actual or potential threats to her reigning son, and to herself. The queen mother, Razia told the crowd, had already had one of her younger brothers – a "youth of great worth and promise" – blinded and then put to death, and was now scheming to destroy her (Juzjani 1963, 455; Raverty 1970, 633). Isami reports in verse that she pledged to the people that she would prove herself to be better than any man, and vowed that if she was unable to deliver on her promises the people had the right to "take my crown away" :

ز مردان اگر بهتر آیم مرا / بدارید برجائی فرمانروا
وگر خود دگرگونه بینید کار / برید از سرم افسر شهریار.   (Usha 1948, 132)[25]

Moved by her plea, the discontented people of Delhi "attacked the royal palace and seized Shah Turkan" (Brijbhushan 1990, 13; Ibn Battuta, 631). Faced with the havoc wreaked by Rukn al-Din and his mother, the Turkish Shamsi *amir*s reconsidered their earlier opposition to Razia's enthronement, deposed her brother, crowned Razia Queen of India, and pledged allegiance to her (Juzjani 1963, 456). Learning of the developing crisis, Rukn al-Din rushed back to Delhi, where he was promptly arrested and jailed. There, mother and son met their death.

The contestation of the succession and transition of power was rapid, relentless, and ruthless. It was all over in less than a year, following Sultan Iltutmish's death on April 4, 1236. His son Rukn al-Din wore the crown for only six months and twenty-eight days before being defeated and dethroned by his sister Razia, who was promptly crowned on November 19, 1236 and assumed power as Razia Sultan Queen of India.

At the age of thirty-one and unmarried, Razia became the first and the only female ruler of the Delhi Sultanate. She had realized her father's dream that she would be a successor worthy of wearing the crown as Sultan of India.

Uneasy Lies the Head that Wears the Crown

Razia had, for the moment, won the crown. But the battle of succession was far from over – they seldom are. She was now faced with the more intricate task of balancing power and keeping in check the ambitions of the Turkish Shamsi *amir*s, the military-political elite who had helped

---

1971, 630; Mernissi 1994, 95; Athar Ali 2012). Traditionally, Persian kings would allocate a safe space in the royal court (*shadgan*) for people to voice their grievances without fear of retribution (Davis 2004, Vol. 3, 485).

[25] Transliteration of Isami's text: "ze mardan agar behtar ayam mara / dedarid bar ja'i farmanrava / va gar khod degarguneh binid kar / barid az saram afsar-i shahriyar."

bring her to power. Unlike her brother Rukn al-Din, Razia owed her crown not just to the loyalty of her father's devoted military, the Shamsi *amir*s, the provincial governors and *iqta '*-holders,[26] but also to the citizens of Delhi, who brought down Shah Turkan (Jackson 1999, 184–185). Indeed Brijbhushan (1990, 15) credits the public for turning the tide in Razia's favor and, unlike Jackson, thinks that she had no reason to feel beholden to the political-military elite. Calkins concurs. In his view, the basis of Razia's authority and legitimacy rested on her popularity among the people of Delhi and the political support she received from them (1968, 907). In time, however, her popularity among the people – Hindus and Muslims – provoked the ire of the Shamsi *amir*s, who disdained the people because of their different races and ethnicities. The elite had almost formed themselves into a "caste" system with a sensibility one might refer to as "castizisation" of Muslim consciousness (Brijbhushan 1990, 77; Lane-Poole 1903, 62).

But who were these Shamsi *amir*s who formed the military and political elite? Juzjani describes them as "*turkan-i hadrat*," the Turks of the court or the capital, who were the special slaves (*ghulam*s) of Iltutmish (Jackson 1999, 185). They were primarily of Turkic ethnicity, and were alternately called Shamsi after Iltutmish's first name, or *Chihilgani*, "the Forty slaves," presumably because there were forty of them.[27] They had a strong sense of loyalty to their master and formed a formidable power group (Jackson 1999, 185; Hambly 1972).[28] The Shamsi throne was thus "a purely Turkish throne supported by Turkish nobles" (Brijbhushan 1990, 12). They acted as the power brokers in the politics of the sultanate, though, as Kumar argues, they were far from forming a "monolithic bloc," or creating a close-knit hierarchy of power and privilege (Singh 2010). By and large, after Iltutmish's death, they remained in the service of the sultan's successors and supported them as long as the sultans did not threaten their privileges and position. The strong emotional bond of

---

[26] *Iqta '* generally means "the assignment of lands for a fixed value." This practice was introduced in medieval India by the "Turkish conquerors." Accordingly, Sultan Iltutmish had over two thousand *muqti*s, holders of *iqta '*, who were assigned the revenue of a village in return for military service. The *muqti*'s tenure was not permanent but depended on the sultan's whim (Khan 1983, 5; Katuzian 2013)

[27] Kumar explains that the number forty should not be taken literally but symbolically, for at the time the number forty was synonymous with "many" (2010, 158). He has categorized all twenty-five Shamsi *ghulam*s identified by Juzjani (Vol. 2, chapter 22, 3–89) and systematically classified them in a useful chart according to their seniority, rank, and positions in the court of Iltutmish, and later in courts of his five children who succeeded him to the throne (Kumar 2010, 242–253).

[28] For further definition of the Shamsi *ghulam*s, or forty slaves and competing theories regarding their identity, formation, and function, see Hambly (1972).

loyalty that had tied the Shamsi slaves to Iltutmish, however, was for the most part lacking in their relations with his children (Kumar 2010, 254).

For the purpose of this chapter, we need to know the names of a few of the Shamsi *amir*s who played crucial roles – real or imagined – in helping Razia to gain power and then, later, in instigating her downfall. Chief among them was Ikhtiyar al-Din Altunia[29] (Altunapa in Jackson's account), who held the position of chief Canopy-Bearer – a mid-level position in the administrative hierarchy of the Iltutmish court. He was promoted to governorship of Baran in Razia's court (Jackson 1999, 185). While Juzjani mentions Altunia's name in relation to his uprising against Razia and his hasty marriage to her, others, particularly contemporary popular sources, have reportedly depicted him as a childhood friend of Razia, madly in love with her and wishing to marry her.[30] Another mid-level *amir* was Malik Ikhtiyar al-Din Aitegin,[31] who was given the *iqta'* of Nandana and was raised to the pivotal rank of *amir-hajib* (military chamberlain) in Razia's court (Jackson 1999, 186).

The third and most important character was Jamal al-Din Yaqut, Iltutmish's devoted Ethiopian slave, and not one of the Turkish Shamsis. Yaqut, like the other Shamsi *ghulam*s, was inherited by Razia, but unlike many of the politically ambitious and opportunist slave-*amir*s, he remained unwavering in his devotion to her. He stayed by her side, kept her counsel, and eventually became one of the highest-ranking individuals in Razia's court. Being black, an outsider, and of a different ethnicity, Yaqut had little social standing among the political elite, the Forty *amir*s, and his elevation by Razia Sultan provoked intense racial hatred and resentment among the former. Their friendship eventually proved destructive to Razia's sovereignty and lethal to Yaqut. Rafiq Zakaria in his historical novel conceptualizes a triangle of love-hate relationships among Raiza, Yaqut, and Altunia – a theme that is also highlighted in popular movies and television melodrama. Zakaria finds it probable that Razia loved both men at the same time, though the intensity of her feelings for them may have been expressed differently. In Zakaria's recreation, Yaqut and Altunia are initially tolerant of each other and solidly behind their sovereign. But Altunia's intense jealousy, racism, and personal ambition eventually overwhelm both his tolerance of Yaqut and his loyalty to his sovereign. In his blockbuster popular

---

[29] Number 11 in Juzjani (1963, 20–22), and in Kumar's chart (2010, 245).

[30] Raverty, Kumar, Jackson, and Brijbhushan make no mention of the prior friendship between Razia and Altunia, only the position he held in her father's court and later on in her court. Perhaps the fact that Razia eventually married him has given rise to the popular belief that the two – or at least Altunia – may have entertained romantic feelings.

[31] Number 12 in Juzjani (1963, 22–23) and in Kumar's chart (2010, 246).

melodrama, *Razia Sultan* (1961), Devendra Goel depicts a love triangle, dramatizing Altunia's love for Razia and his consuming jealousy of Yaqut. In the 1983 movie production by Kamal Amrohi, however, Altunia's treachery is highlighted while Yaqut is portrayed as Razia's beloved, with whom she finally elopes. We may never know how melodramatic these relationships were in real life. But they were significant in the rise and fall of Razia Sultan, Queen of India.

Challenging the Sultan's Authority: Siege of Delhi

> The [lioness] showed so much force
>   that brave men bent low before her.[32]

With Razia's coronation, "all things returned to their usual rules and customs," though, as often happens in moments of political transition, rebellions erupted in various corners of the kingdom (Raverty 1970, 639; Juzjani 1963, 458). One of Razia's half-brothers, Ghiyas al-Din Muhammad, who had earlier rebelled against Rukn al-Din Firuz Shah, continued with his insurgency in Awadh (Juzjani 1963, 455), possibly egged on by some of the Shamsi *amir*s, including Balban the Lesser.[33] But it remains unclear whether there was any systematic coordination among the opposition (Kumar 2010, 254). Ghiyas al-Din died unexpectedly and suddenly, removing one potentially serious rival to the young sultan's throne[34] (Jackson 1999, 185). A more serious threat, simultaneously, came from some of the disgruntled Shamsi *amir*s and devotees of Razia's father.[35] Ignoring their master's wishes, they challenged Razia's authority and laid siege to Delhi (Brijbhushan 1990, 18; Jackson 1999, 184; Kumar 2007, 586). "Even when Shah Terken was overthrown in Delhi by yet another faction," writes Jackson, "and Firuz Shah himself was arrested and put to death . . . the insurgent amirs refused to recognize Radiyya, who had been enthroned in his place, and besieged her in the capital" (1999, 184). Accordingly, some had felt passed over for rewards and promotion during Firuz Shah's brief reign, and felt further threatened by Razia's ascension to the throne.

---

[32] A verse in a poem praising Razia by the famed Amir Khusraw Dehlavi (d. 1325).

[33] As a low-ranking "page" in Iltutmish's court, slaves such as 'Izz al-Din Balban had weak ties to their master and still weaker to his successor; they had no hesitation in breaking away from Delhi and seeking their fortunes elsewhere (Kumar 2010, 254).

[34] Raverty thinks that "He was probably put to death," but by whom? Was it instigated by Razia Sultan? Raverty does not make this clear (1970, 633).

[35] At the time of assuming power, Sultan Iltutmish found himself in a similar situation. Some Turkish slaves of Qutb al-Din Aybek, his predecessor and father-in-law, opposed him and left Delhi to join forces against the new sultan (Juzjani 1963, 444).

With the siege of Delhi lasting for some time, Razia took on the challenge. Riding her elephant and leading her army, she "came out of her city and pitched camp on the banks of Jamuna where several pitched battles took place between those loyal to the sovereign and to her enemies" (Brijbhushan 1990, 18; Juzjani, 458; Raverty 1970, 640). Was Razia in *purdah*, veiled, as she led her army onto the battlefield atop her elephant? Was she appropriately dressed for combat? Juzjani makes no comment one way or another.

Witnessing Razia's determination and her army's strength, the rebellious Shamsi leaders had second thoughts and scattered. Certain of harsh punishment for their disloyalty, two of the seven high-ranking rebellious *amir*s switched sides, expressed contrition, and pledged allegiance to the sultan. These repentant *amir*s then joined the sultan's army and vowed to defeat the remaining renegades. A plan was hatched to summon the rebellious *amir*s to a secret conclave with the intention to capture, imprison, or eliminate them. Hearing rumors of this plot, the insurgent *amir*s fled, with Razia's army hot in pursuit. They were captured and "eliminated either in the battle or by strangulation in prison" (Brijbhushan 1990, 18). The insurgency collapsed, the siege of Delhi was lifted, and the last of the rebel leaders fled to the foothills of the Himalayas, where he died in isolation and of natural causes (Jackson 1999, 184; Raverty 1970, 640; Juzjani, 458–459). With Razia's successful breaking of the siege of Delhi, "the Kingdom was pacified, and the power of the state was widely extended," writes Juzjani. "From the territory of Lakhnawati [Western Bengal] to Diwal and Damrilah [lower Sind], all the Maliks and amirs manifested their obedience and submission" to Razia Sultan (Raverty 1970, 641; Juzjani, 459). Law and order was at last restored.

Confident of her popular support, in a politically calculated and religiously judicious move, Razia Sultan reached back in history to conjure up further legitimacy. Invoking the Queen of Sheba, her legendary predecessor, Razia had coins minted in her own name. One legend read "Bilqis-i Jihan," Queen of the World,[36] and another indicating her royal designation, *al-Sultan al-'Azam Jalalat al-Dunya wa al-Din Raziyah*, meaning broadly "the glory of the earthly world and of the faith" (Mernissi 1994, 89; Saleh 2004, 85). The commemoration in the coinage of Razia Sultan also attested to her independence, and the public's esteem. Whereas early on her father's name was included on the coins, by 1237–1238 she felt secure enough to have coins minted with her name

---

[36] Bilqis being the popular name for the Queen of Sheba (Badriye Ucok Un cited by Mernissi 1994, 89).

alone (Jackson 1999, 187). Displaying remarkable political acumen, Razia Sultan was determined not to rely solely on her father's soldier-slaves. If some Shamsi *amirs* and political elite assumed that the reign of a young female ruler signaled a turning point in their fortunes, they had miscalculated. Much to the surprise of the senior *amirs*, Razia did not stay in the shadows as these political courtiers and military leaders had expected. The sultan demonstrated striking political initiatives, which greatly disappointed many of her military advisers and leaders (Jackson 1999, 186; Kumar 2007, 586). The bonds of loyalty and emotional relationships that had sustained a mutual devotion between her father and his soldier-slaves had already been weakened, if not totally broken, by the time Razia ascended the throne (Kumar 2010, 254).

Razia Sultan was apparently not unaware of the Shamsi *amirs'* ambition and their reach for power, and she did not wish to be in their grip. She acted self-confidently, had a good sense of her own authority and independence, and felt secure in her relation with the public from which she drew affirmation and support. She tried hard to strike a balance of power and privilege among her father's Turkish slave-*amirs* who formed the political elite while pursuing her own agenda of making a difference in the lives of the masses who had supported her bid for power. However, her trust in the extent of her army's loyalty proved to be misplaced, and her belief in her own ability to keep them under control a miscalculation. As Mottahedeh put it, "A [wo]man who did not give sustained patronage had less chance of ending [her] career of governmental service alive" (1980, 91).

Protecting the Faith: Upholding the Status Quo

Political rivalries and contestation of her sovereign authority were not the only arenas that prompted Razia to strategize wisely and act decisively. Religious life was another domain that tested her tolerance of diversity. Muslim conquerors and invaders who came to India lost no time in proselytizing and propagating their religion, which for the most part was that of Sunni Islam, the established state religion. India's polytheistic civilization and tolerant attitude toward other religions offered fertile ground for all branches of Islam to establish roots, become integrated, and flourish. These included Shi'ism and Isma'ilism and their various divisions and subdivisions – not to mention several prominent Sufi orders. In Chapter 3 I discussed the policies and politics of the eleventh/twelfth-century Yemenite Queen Arwa, who with unparalleled political acumen and spiritual authority ensured the survival of the Tayyebi Isma'ili in Yemen, and facilitated the sect's spread further east by dispatching missionaries and traders to India. By the thirteenth century, Isma'ilis had firmly established themselves in Delhi, attracting new converts and expanding their power base (Bazmee Ansari 2012).

Finding the moment opportune, by 1237 a large number of religious minorities defied the center and the sultan, who as the head of the state also represented the state religion – if only nominally. Gathering under the umbrella of a certain "Nur Turk,"[37] whom Juzjani defines as "quasi-learned [*danishmand-guneh*]" followers of "*qaramateh* and *mulahideh*" – perceived as heretical by the majority of the Sunni ruling elite[38] – came together from all over India, including Gujarat, Sind, and the periphery of Delhi, to congregate in Delhi (Raverty 1970, 646; Juzjani, 461). Having been long oppressed by orthodoxy, they expressed their grievances by publicly denouncing the Sunni *ulama'* as reactionaries and "whipped up the populace into a frenzy of rage against the ecclesiastical establishment" (Brijbhushan 1990, 17; Mernissi 1994, 94). After heavy fighting in and around the mosque and the bazaar, "worshippers who had fled to the roof tops joined in the fray" threw "bricks and stones on the heads of the rebels" (Juzjani, 461; Brijbhushan 1990, 18). Faced with such a public spectacle, Razia Sultan acted swiftly and decisively. The uprising and the revolt were effectively defeated and the opposition suppressed. Ironically, it was the female sovereign, the victorious Razia Sultan, who successfully defended religion and guaranteed the supremacy of the state religion and the continuity of the privileges of the clergy who had raised no objections to her sovereignty (discussed later). She lived up to her royal designation as the glory/protector of the world and religion, *Jalalat al-Dunya wa al-Din*.

Calm before the Storm

چو از عهد رضیه بر آمد سه سال

دگر سکه زد عالم بد سگال.

When three years of her reign had rolled by,
the malicious world struck a different coin.

(Isami, 133; Husain 1938, 253)

With the religious rebellions and political revolts subdued, a sense of normalcy and calm returned to Delhi, and Razia turned to the serious task of supervising, governing, and disciplining. Momentarily secure in her royal court, she granted various positions to a number of junior court

---

[37] For a discussion of Nur Turk and his uprising, see Kumar (2010, 204–207).

[38] Qaramateh split from Isma'ilism in the ninth century (Daftary 1993, 123; Poonawala 1977, 5–6). See Kumar (2010, 202 ff) for a fuller discussion of the "*qaramateh* and *mulahideh*" and the diversity of religious practices in early thirteenth-century India.

pages and mid-level slaves of her father, including granting the *iqta‘* of Baran to Altunia. She promoted a few to the senior ranks and reshuffled others from one position to another. She "neutralized" rebel leaders and forced some "powerful administrators" into retirement (Kumar 2007, 586). Razia elevated Ikhtiyar al-Din Aitegin to the very important and highly sensitive position of *amir hajib* in her court and appointed Jamal al-Din Yaqut Lord of the Stable (*amir-i akhur*), another highly coveted position. Once Razia Sultan started exercising her authority, making her own decisions, and forging new alliances, the entrenched political-military elite began to agitate against her. Hoping to "rule from the shadows," her father's military and political supporters, the Shamsi *amir*s, who had helped her ascend the throne became resentful at having been outmaneuvered and managed by a young woman. Adding insult to injury, two years into the sultan's reign, the two major cities of Ranthambor and Gwalior, which represented major victories for her father, were lost to Hindus. This territorial loss deepened the Shamsi *amir*s' dissatisfaction with Razia Sultan. What particularly annoyed the political elite was her charitable attitude toward the natives and her fairness toward non-Turkic individuals, among whom she gave titles and distributed *iqta‘* governorships (Jackson 1999, 187–188). She initiated reforms in her government, reduced or removed taxes, and included some Hindus in her court (Zakaria 1966, 124–125). Isami highlights her popularity with the public in the following line:

همه شهر و بوم است هوا خواه من
که بودم نکوخواه هر مرد و زن.

Everywhere people are my supporters
because their welfare is my concern.   (Isami, 138)

The straw that broke the proverbial camel's back was the sultan's elevation of her Ethiopian *amir*/slave Yaqut in her court, and her increasing reliance on him in the face of numerous crises and rebellions. That finally ignited the anger of the Shamsi *amir*s against their sovereign and unleashed their military might against the young sultan.

The final curtain in the Razia Sultan's reign was drawn on April 1240, when she had just returned to Delhi from a battle in which she defeated the insurgency of the *muqti* of Lahore. No sooner had she settled back in the court than *Amir* Altunia – her former advisor and supposed childhood friend and "suitor" – staged an insurgency in Tabarhindh. Unbeknownst to Razia, her trusted chief Chamberlain Aitegin had entered into a treacherous secret deal with Altunia of Baran, plotting to dethrone her. Their three-pronged strategy was to strike before Razia and her army had the chance to unwind, to isolate her from her devoted advisor Yaqut, and to cut her off from the people who formed her power base in Delhi (Juzjani, 460). Razia Sultan and her army quickly regrouped and left Delhi in order to put down Altunia's rebellion, leaving the treacherous Aitegin in charge of the court. With the queen out of the royal court and away from Delhi, her Ethiopian adviser Yaqut was immediately seized and unceremoniously murdered. En route to the battlefield, some of the Shamsi *amir*s and mercenaries deserted Razia Sultan and joined the opposition's camp. Razia Sultan's army was defeated and she was arrested, "fetters set on her legs." She was sent to none other than Altunia's fortress in Tabarhindh (Isami, 136; Husain 1938, 255, fn. 1). Back in Delhi, the Shamsi *amir*s wasted no time in crowning Razia's younger half-brother Bahram Shah.

Eager to wear the crown, the young Bahram Shah had to face the ignominy of having the treacherous Aitegin impose himself as his regent. Aitegin also married the young sultan's widowed (or divorced) uterine sister, thus becoming Bahram's brother-in-law as well (Kumar 2010, 261). But in less than two months Bahram Shah had grown so offended by his regent's reach for power and appropriation of the sultan's prerogatives that he had Aitegin stabbed to death in full view of all in the royal palace. He then abolished the office of regent altogether (Juzjani, 463–464). Bahram Shah's two years of power "were spent in plots and counterplots, treacherous executions, and cruel murders, and he was killed after a siege of Delhi by the exacerbated army" (Lane-Poole 1903, 76).

With Aitegin's death and the abolishment of the regency, Altunia's hopes of reaping greater rewards and gaining a firmer foothold within the new sultan's palace crumbled. In the meantime, Razia was imprisoned in his fortress and kept under his watchful eye. Zakaria imagines that the two met frequently and presumably their former sentiments were rekindled between them. And so they had a change of heart, and tied the knot: Altunia no longer wished to be her jail keeper, and Razia no longer resisted marriage. But why now, and why in captivity, did Razia Sultan accept Altunia's marriage proposal? Hadn't he betrayed her? While her true motivation may remain a mystery, she seems to have killed two birds with one stone: she saved her honor and proved the baselessness of the malicious accusations of her illicit relationship with Yaqut. Zakaria reckons that Altunia would never have married her had the accusations been true (1966, 139). Moreover, she motivated Altunia, one of the Shamsi *amir*s, to champion her cause and help her regain her throne. In revenge and regret their interests merged: she would regain her crown and Altunia – with Yaqut out of the picture – would be her husband and closest companion and adviser. They mobilized their armies and set out toward Delhi, but before they reached the blessed city and joined forces with her devoted supporters, they were confronted by the imperial army of Razia's brother. With little in the way of scruples, some of the Turkish *amir*s and mercenaries broke rank once again, deserting their commanders and joining Bahram Shah's camp. The couple's army was routed, and Altunia and Razia were both captured and killed on October 13 in the year 1240, barely six months after the siblings had rekindled their battle of succession yet again.

In death, as in life, multiple narratives describe the circumstances under which Razia met her demise. Rafiq Zakaria objects to Juzjani holding "Hindus" responsible for Razia's death. He finds this prejudicial toward Hindus and ignominious for Razia. He prefers a nobler ending for this extraordinary Queen of the World, *Bilqis-i Jihan*. He finds an arrow piercing her heart more befitting of her departure of this world (1966, 126). Athar Ali holds her brother Bahram Shah responsible for her death, for he coveted her throne and did not hesitate to destroy her. Lane-Poole (1903, 76) has Razia and Altunia fleeing "into jungles," where they were killed – how and by whom is not clear. Ibn Battuta, ever-curious "ethnographer" that he was, makes the following observations. When Razia's troops suffered a defeat, she fled:

Overpowered by hunger and strained by fatigue, she repaired to a peasant whom she found tilling the soil. She asked him for something to eat. He gave her a piece of bread which she ate and fell sleep; and she was dressed like a man. But, while she was asleep, the peasant's eyes fell upon a gown (*gaba*) studded with jewels which she was wearing under her clothes. He realized that she was a woman. So he killed her, plundered her and drove away her horse, and then buried her in his field. Then he went to the market to dispose of one of her garments. But the people of the market became suspicious of him and took him to the *shihna* (police magistrate) ... There he was beaten into confessing his murder and pointed out where he had buried her. Her body was then disinterred, washed, shrouded, and buried there. (Ibn Battuta in Gibb 1971, 632; see also Mernissi 1994, 97)

Mourning her loss, the local people – her faithful supporters – made Razia a saint, building a dome over her grave, which is still visited by "pilgrims" who seek "blessings from it" (Mernissi 1994, 97; Ibn Battuta in Gibb 1971, 632). By the time I visited Razia Sultan's grave in March 2016, it was but a very small and humble – though serene – courtyard, dwarfed and encroached upon from all sides by haphazard and unattractive multistory urban constructions (Figure 4.2). It is located at the dead end of long, narrow, and winding alleyways in Bulbuli Khana, near the Turkman Gate in old Delhi.[39] To the

---

[39] There are at least two other locations said to be Razia's grave. See: www.youtube.com /watch?v=MMVjRiaLSmg; www.youtube.com/watch?v=treik17-gaU.

Figure 4.2 Razia Sultan's Tomb in Old Delhi

left of the two slightly elevated stone graves were stretched rows of reed prayer mats, facing the *qibla*, where the local shopkeepers would go to perform their daily prayers. No one was there when I entered the little graveyard-shrine, and no one knows exactly whether this is, in fact, the actual resting place of the most celebrated queen of India. If it is, to whom does the other grave belong – to Altunia her husband? Or Shazia her sister? Regardless, a plaque at the gate

Figure 4.3 Government Plaque Identifying Razia Sultan's Tomb

of the enclosure officially identifies the site as the burial place of Razia Sultan, Queen of India (Figure 4.3).[40]

Razia Sultan ruled for three years, six months, and six days, during which time she was able to expand the state's territory, bring a level of

[40] based on archeological findings, however, Brijbhushan believes that the graves belong to neither Razia nor her husband or sister, but to two Sufi saints (1990, 21).

peace and prosperity to her people, patronize the arts, and support educational institutions (Mobasher 2013). Had it not been for the greed of mercenary political elites and their growing racial hatred, ethnic rivalries, and unproven allegations of sexual impropriety, she would most likely have ruled for much longer[41] – she possessed the necessary political wherewithal and enjoyed popular support. She was "The People's Queen" (C.Lal 2018). In the end she lost her crown and her head not just because she was a woman ruler, but because of the fickle and disloyal military elite whose economic interests and political power she challenged, the treachery of those who should have remained close allies, and the murder of her devoted supporter Yaqut. Nonetheless, given the explosive dynamics of the intersectionality of gender, race, caste/class, and ethnicity, as well as the challenges of patriarchal power and authority, the fact that she lasted as long as she did is significant and a tribute to her political charisma and acumen. She proved her father right.

Shame of the Sultan, Honor of the State

عنان تافت دولت ز پیرا منش
چو گردی سیه دید بر دامنش.

Good fortune turned its back on her
When it saw black dust on her skirt.[42]   Juzjani (1963, 23)

Did Razia have an improper relationship with Yaqut, her Ethiopian slave-adviser? No one really knows. In the end, the scarcity of the facts has not stopped anyone from guessing, rumor-mongering, and making claims. The harm had been done, and the perception of it was there, as poignantly expressed in the poem cited above. The rumor of the female sultan's moral lapse and her presumed illicit relationship with her African slave gradually became the defining narrative of her sovereign life. By the time Ibn Battuta visited India a century later, it was taken as historical fact that the virgin Queen of India had sexual relations with her black slave-advisor, and that the proof of it was her "unveiling." Ibn Battuta wrote that she had "relations with a slave of hers, one Abyssinian" and that she "used to ride abroad just like the men, carrying bow and quiver and without veiling her face." After that "the people agreed to depose her

---

[41] That her brother Nasir al-Din, "the weak and puppet sultan" (Raverty 1970, xxviii), stayed in power for almost twenty years was primarily because he effectively left the state's affairs in the charge of the shrewd Shamsi *ghulam* and his father-in-law, Ghiyas al-Din Balban Ulugh Khan, who not surprisingly crowned himself sultan after Nasir al-Din's death.

[42] Zakaria disputes the attribution of this poem to Juzjani (1966, 137).

and marry her to a husband" (in Gibb 1971, 631). In Ibn Battuta's view, she had transgressed political, racial, sexual, and gender boundaries, offenses for which she was punished, put in her place and obliged to marry.

But where did this rumor come from? And what does Juzjani, the court chronicler who was in the position to give an eyewitness account, have to say on this matter? When recounting the first three years of Razia Sultan's reign, Juzjani makes no comment regarding the nature of Razia's relationship with Yaqut, nor to her physical appearance or her attire while leading her army in and out of Delhi on military expeditions. Then, following his description of the royal redistribution of positions, power, and privileges, he pontificates on her Ethiopian slave Yaqut, writing that he found "favor [*qurbati*] with the Sultan," which "provoked the jealousy [*ghairat*] of the Turkish Maliks and amirs" (Juzjani, 460). As if that insidious insinuation was not enough, Juzjani immediately adds that "Sultan Razia set aside women's clothing and came out of veiling, purdah. She wore a robe [*qaba*] and put on a hat [*kulah*] and appeared among the people [*khalq*]." He ends his provocative account by noting that Razia Sultan "sat on an elephant, and allowed herself to be seen by all" while leading a military expedition into Gwalior (Juzjani, 460; Raverty 1970, 642, fn. 3). In barely three sentences, Juzjani condemns the sultan, supplying her opponents with the rallying cry they were looking for. *Ghairat* is a highly charged, complex, and primordial concept with multiple connotations and overlapping meanings. The emotional force that moves *ghairat* is honor, and honor is male-centered and acted out in public (Frank 1994; Haeri 1995). Inaction is not an option; it is dishonor. Here Juzjani implies that the Turkish Shamsi *amir*s and the political elite had no choice but to act to remove the source of dishonor and restore their honor (i.e. the honor of their master and, by extension, the honor of the state). Juzjani first puts the blame on Yaqut, who acted improperly by getting too close to the sultan (i.e. while helping her mount her horse). Then he provides incontrovertible "proof" of Razia Sultan's lapse of judgment (i.e. appearing unveiled in public and adopting male attire), which leads his readers to conclude that the female sultan had acted improperly and immorally. Isami, the fourteenth-century poet, takes up the cue and embellishes the narrative:

I am told that a slave of Ethiopian race used to stand by her side when she mounted her horse. With one hand he used to hold her arm and help her to mount her horse firmly ... When the grandees of the State noticed liberties he took openly, they felt scandalized and said to one another privately: "from the way this demon has made himself more powerful in the State than other servants, it would be no wonder if he found his way to seize the 'royal seal.'" (Isami, 134; Husain 1938, 253–254)

But how would Yaqut seize the "royal seal," and in whose possession was the precious item? With "royal seal," Isami conveys a double meaning: he refers to the actual royal seal and metaphorically to the young female sultan's virginity – the precious "capital" of the state and the sovereign. It is shameful enough to lose one's virginity, but it is particularly dishonorable to lose the "royal seal" to an Ethiopian man – that would be unbearable to the ethnically conscious Turkic political-military elite. How could they tolerate a mixed-race progeny as part of the Shamsi dynasty? Isami becomes graphic:

All women are in the snare of the devil; in privacy, all of them do Satan's work. Confidence should not be placed in women; devils should not be relied upon. At no time can faithfulness be expected of women ... When the passions of a pious woman are inflamed, she concedes to an intimacy even with a dog. (Isami, 134; Husain 1938, 254)

Was all this hue and cry a power grab and male conspiracy against the female sultan? Possibly. To begin with, as Raverty points out, Razia Sultan did not ride horses but elephants (1970, 643, fn. 3). But one could imagine that she may have ridden both, depending on the occasion, in which case Yaqut might have helped her mount. After all, Yaqut was the Lord of the Stable! It was his job to provide appropriate mounts for the queen! Finally, we should clarify the overused category of "people." It was not "the people" who deposed Sultan Razia, but a treacherous and resentful "suitor" and a onetime ally, and the racially motivated Turkish political elite whose power base she had threatened.

Marriage, Concubinage, and Challenges of Authority

We may pause here and ask why was Razia not married by the time she took the helm of the state? She was crowned at the age of thirty-one, well past the normative marriage age for both Muslims and Hindus.[43] One could well imagine that as the sultan's daughter, she would not have been lacking in serious suitors. Juzjani is silent on what may or may not have been the circumstances surrounding her marriageability, or what may have inhibited her – or men around her – from entering into matrimonial relations. Why did her father Sultan Iltutmish not arrange for her to marry one of his own loyal slave-*amir*s, as his own father-in-law had done for him? Did Razia express reservations about marriage? Or was it that the

---

[43] See also Brijbhushan (1990, 118).

sultan himself did not find any of his devoted *amir*s worthy of his daughter? Juzjani gives no clue, and we may never know the answers to these questions. But they remain, and motivate us to imagine a few scenarios for the celibacy that lasted well into the last few months of Razia's life.

To begin with, it may be that by her time the Hindu custom of dowry[44] and marriage hypergamy (women marrying into higher social status within a particular caste) had found a foothold among Indian Muslims.[45] If so, father and daughter would have found it unpalatable to follow the tradition as it would put them in a symbolically inferior and awkward situation.[46] On the other hand, her reluctance – if that were the case – may have had something to do with the contractual form of Islamic marriage.[47] As a married woman, Razia would have been at risk of losing her autonomy and independence – if not necessarily her crown – given the ensuing unequal rights of spouses that legally oblige a wife to obey her husband. Legally, he could have prevented her from holding a public post and restricted her mobility. Would Altunia, for example, have stayed on the sidelines and allowed his wife to run the state? Did he ultimately marry her in hopes of sharing power, or displacing her once they regained her throne?

A more vexing possibility is the legality of polygyny and slave ownership in Muslim societies. Potentially – and often actually – polygyny poses a threat to women's marital security, not to mention happiness. But it could be particularly challenging for a female sovereign. Muslim men are legally permitted to marry up to four wives simultaneously, and to maintain as many slaves/concubines as they wish or their harems can contain. A married Razia Sultan could have found herself in a highly undesirable – and administratively untenable – situation were her husband to take a second wife and extend his harem by multiple concubines. How would a female sultan deal with her co-wives – permanent, temporary, and concubine – each of whom would be vying to secure her own position by getting the patriarch's attention, if not actually working to replace the queen. On the other hand, she could have had her serious rivals eliminated – as her stepmother Shah Turkan had – and formed alliances with

---

[44] Dowry payments involve transfer of money, goods, and gifts from the bride's family to the groom and his family. See Goody and Tambiah (1973). By the fourteenth century the custom was so well-entrenched that Firoz Shah Tughlak (r. 1351–1388) adopted the Hindu customs of dowry and provided dowry for orphaned Muslim girls (Brijbhushan 1990, 119).

[45] Kumar, however, argues that although the "structures of symmetry" were the matrimonial norm in thirteenth-century South Asia, they were frequently violated by Iltutmish's slaves. The hasty marriage of Altunia and Razia is one example (2007, 586).

[46] On hypergamy, Tambiah writes, "The wife-givers are persistent gift givers and lavish hosts while they are at the same time excluded from intimate social contact with the receivers as this would smack of equality" (1973, 97).

[47] See Haeri (1989), chapters 1–3.

a few more compliant co-wives. In either case, she would have had to divert her attention from affairs of state to the intrigues and intense politicking within the harem.

Faced with such a possibility, what options would or could a female ruler have in medieval India or Egypt? Could a reigning queen prevent a Muslim male warrior leader from owning slaves and having sexual relations with his concubines in a culture where slave girls were highly prized, and often gifted to a sultan or men of power? Would she – or her father – be farsighted enough to include a conditional clause in her marriage contract, a prenuptial agreement of sorts, to restrict her potential consort's right to subsequent marriages? That they could do according to the tenets of Islamic law, but they could not forbid him from remarriage altogether.

The jilted queen could arrange for the elimination of a competitor or her husband or both, either through poisoning or assassination.[48] The spirited Mamluk Queen of Egypt, Shajarat al-Durr, did precisely that. Beautiful, educated, and highly intelligent, Shajara "is one of the best known sultanas" and is "never ignored by historians" (Mernissi 1994, 202, fn. 7). Similar to Razia, Shajara was of Turkish ethnicity; unlike Razia, she entered the palace of the king not as a princess but as a slave. Shajara became the favorite slave/concubine/wife of the last Ayyubid Sultan, Malik al-Salih, and ushered in the Mamluk dynasty of Egypt. She reached the zenith of authority when she was crowned the Queen of Egypt by the Mamluks following her husband's death in 1250. She kept his death secret from the caliph in Baghdad for some time until plans could be set in place for her own eventual enthronement. Coins were minted in her name and *khutba*s recited on Fridays. She defeated Louis IX of France, "preserved the lives of French prisoners . . . and ransomed the French king for 1,000,000 bezants and liquidated the Crusaders' holdings in Egypt" (Duncan 2000, 51–53). But before the year was out, the short-sighted Abbasid patriarch in Baghdad terminated her authority. The caliph belittled the Mamluks for allowing a woman to ruler over them, and insulted their honor by threatening to send a man to rule Egypt if one could not be found among them (Duncan 2000, 53). Thus challenged, the Mamluks obliged, and the queen obeyed. She agreed to marry and relinquish the leadership to a man.[49] She was not about to marry any man, however. She maneuvered to marry the same man the caliph had tasked to lead Egypt (Mernissi 1994, 92). Shajara abdicated in favor of her new husband, Aybek, whom she forced to divorce his wife

---

[48] See the Introduction, p.14.

[49] Compare Shajara's "pathetic" obedience, in Mernissi's words (1994, 90), with that of Queen Arwa's diplomatic resistance to the Fatimid imam-caliph a century earlier. See also Chapter 3.

before marrying her. Thus ended the brief period in which she reigned supreme in her own name. Over the next seven years, however, she was effectively ruling Egypt and maintaining peace and stability in the country.[50] Things fell apart, however, when she learned of her husband's marriage to the daughter of the lord of Mosul. Finding herself an unwilling co-wife, and fearing the imminent possibility of losing her power, Queen Shajarat al-Durr was outraged. She lured Aybek to her bath – yes, another *hammam* – and had soap rubbed in his eyes before her eunuchs murdered him (Duncan 2000, 53, 57). Alas, her crime was soon discovered and that spelled the end of her reign. The disgraced queen was brought into the presence of the murdered king's first wife and "the latter's slaves beat Shajara to death" – some say with their wooden clogs – before "tossing her corpse over the wall of the Citadel. Her remains were collected in a basket after three days and interred in her mausoleum" (Duncan 2000, 53). Whether this account of the queen's fall from power is true or is embellished, her tomb in Cairo is still visited by pilgrims (Mernissi 1994, 98).

Not all sovereign queens would take such extreme and vengeful actions, of course. They could divorce their husbands. Islamic law does allow for the dissolution of marriage, assuming that the husband agrees to it. But breaking up a royal marriage would be highly undesirable and politically costly. Divorce (*talaq*) is legally the unilateral right of the husband, though the Prophet of Islam frequently said "of all things permissible, divorce is the most blameworthy." Faced with a husband's reluctance to divorce, a queen could invoke the divorce of the *khul'* kind which, unlike *talaq*, is a bilateral and contractual form of separation. But in that case not only must she forgo her enormous bride price, she would also have to satisfy her husband's monetary demands for separation. Further, a royal divorce would stigmatize the queen and cost her social capital and popular support. Some seven hundred years later, the sentiment hasn't changed much in South Asia. In the words of a prominent Pakistani woman, "In our society marriage may be purgatory, but divorce is hell" (cited in Allen 2016, 88).

On the other hand, as much as a queen's spinsterhood could help her maintain her royal authority, it would threaten the dynastic line – unless, of course, she had younger brothers, half-brothers, or nephews who had survived successional fratricide.

---

[50] For the diversity of the interpretations of the life and legacy of Shajara, see Duncan (2000).

All things considered, therefore, from Razia Sultan's point of view the least problematic option was to remain single.[51] Whatever the hypothetical or actual reasons may have been, Razia remained single, maintaining her autonomy and independence.[52] In that she seems to have had her father's support. Whether her hasty marriage to Altunia was one of convenience or the result of a rekindled childhood love or other reasons, it seems to have weakened Razia's position and may have hastened her demise. Their alliance gave the imperial army and the Turkish *amir*s greater incentives to confront the duo forcefully and violently.

As a female sovereign, Razia's personal life fascinated the multitudes – then and now. It has inspired numerous individuals to conjure up scenarios as to what might have – should have – been the life trajectory of the young female sultan in the royal court. The most colorful reconstruction of palace life and courtly intrigues is the long-running Indian TV melodrama, *Razia Sultan*, on her rise to sovereign power. How might she have maintained her royal authority while keeping her Turkish military elite's ambitions in check? How might she have tried to maintain an administrative balance in her multiracial, multiethnic court while maintaining her connection to the people at the bottom of the sociopolitical hierarchy? Was there a triangle of love, hate, and jealousy between Altunia and Yaqut, one of the same race and ethnicity as the sultan and the other an Abyssinian outsider? Did she keep an eye on the ambitious and cunning *amir*s, with their sense of caste and racial superiority? How did she relate to the people, her power base, who were apparently nonentities as far as the Turkish military-political elite were concerned? With so many questions and so few historical facts, popular speculations, rumors, and folk narratives abound, as I have tried to highlight in the preceding pages. Given the extraordinary circumstances surrounding her rule, the ongoing rebellions and disturbances on the outskirts of Delhi, and the growing disillusionment of the military-political elite trying to maneuver the female sultan, it would not be surprising if Razia Sultan found the company and counsel of Yaqut reassuring. He was a safe haven in that boiling political cauldron of scheming half-brothers vying for her throne,

---

[51] Whether by choice or force of circumstances – i.e. no suitable match – some Fatimid princesses, including Sitt al-Mulk (see Introduction), remained unmarried. Maria Szuppa writes of several Safavid royal women who remained unmarried while being active in politics (2003, 144). This was also true of some Mughal princesses. Benazir Bhutto writes of women of her paternal lineage who remained unmarried because of a lack of a suitable match – often among their own clan of cousins (1988, 29, 31).

[52] Queen Elizabeth I of England (sixteenth century), Queen Christina of Sweden (seventeenth century), and Queen Elizabeth of Russia (eighteenth century) all remained unmarried - the latter by force of circumstances - despite palace pressure on them to do so, if only to continue the dynastic line.

disgruntled racist Turkish *amirs*, and rebellious local leaders–and who knows what intrigues were going on inside her father's – and her brother's – harem? It is precisely at the moment when the sultan is beleaguered on several fronts and weakened politically that the court biographer Juzjani comments on her social lapse and sexual "transgressions," asserting that Razia Sultan cross-dressed and appeared unveiled in public, that her "unveiling" – presumably a symbolic gesture of revealing the self – provided "proof" of her "immoral" relationship with her black slave.

Cross-Dressing: the Sin of Visibility

Exactly when did Razia Sultan, the commander-in-chief and military warrior (*lashkar kish*), adopt male attire and appear "unveiled" in public, allowing herself to be seen? She had been on military expeditions throughout her reign, as recorded by Juzjani, leading her army in and out of Delhi while perched on her elephant. No mention is made of her attire or her veil – off or on. Nothing is said by Juzjani until well into the third year of her reign, when political conflicts were mounting. One could reasonably assume that Razia Sultan was acting and dressing appropriately for her role as a ruler, projecting authority while leading her army. Raverty is right that the word "sultan" comes from the root word *sulta*, which signifies to have or possess power, to rule (i.e. be a sovereign). It is therefore equally applicable to both a female and a male ruler, and does not have anything to do with "affectation of the superior sex," or with "her assumption, subsequently, of male attire when she rode forth" (1970, 637, fn. 8).

Further, how different were male and female attire for the ruling elite in thirteenth-century India? We may not know the fine details of gender-specific Indian clothing at that time, but as Raverty notes, there wasn't really that much difference between clothing for men and women. Other than "the tunic and the head-dress," the other items of clothing were identical,[53] and that is the costume Razia seems to have adopted (1970, 638, fn. 1). Mernissi interprets Razia Sultan's "cross-dressing" as intended to facilitate her leading of military expeditions, and to enable her to "walk among people, to keep in touch with her power base and listen to their complaints" (1994, 96). Alyssa Gabbay notes that imperial women living in cultures influenced by Persian and Turko-Mongol traditions "could have worn tunics and other male attire without causing an

---

[53] The present-day Pakistani and Punjabi two-piece *shalwar* and tunic is stylistically the same for both men and women, though women drape a long rectangular scarf, known as a *dupatta*, over their shoulders and choose more colorful fabrics.

uproar" (2011, 56). Writing about medieval Egyptian clothing, Leila Ahmed similarly observes that "Outer garments, such as cloaks, could be worn interchangeably by either sex" (1992, 118). The European traveler Francesco Romano wrote of sixteenth-century Safavid women that "All Persian women – and particularly in Tauris – are wanton, and wear men's robes, and put them over their heads, covering them altogether" (Szuppe 2003, 143). Ultimately, it was not so much Razia's crossdressing or "unveiling" that provoked the Turkish amirs to remove her from the throne, but the threat – perceived or actual – to their authority, power, and privileges. For as Jackson notes, however scandalous her unveiling "might have been to the Tajik ulama of Delhi, it would surely have had less impact on the Turkish military" (1999, 189).

While the extent and form of Razia's cross-dressing may be debated, the real cross-dresser may have been her royal brother Rukn al-Din Firuz! In the 1961 film version of *Razia Sultan*, he is depicted wearing women's clothing while dancing coquettishly with a see-through black veil – and he does so during the call to prayer! The film's director may have gotten his inspiration from a statement by Juzjani. While praising Rukn al-Din for his generosity, Juzjani faults him for wasting his time in the company of "dancers, impersonators, effeminate men and eunuchs [*mukhannisan*]" (457). Raverty translated *mukhannisan* as Ganymede, the beautiful youth carried off to Olympus by Zeus to be the cupbearer of the gods. I would guess that Juzjani was referring to the *hijras*, the well-known Indian "third gender," also known as "neither men nor women," who were traditionally professional male cross-dressers and dancers (Nanda 1998).[54]

Hadith Remembered

Let us pause finally and ask what role, if any, the religious establishment played in the war of succession between the two siblings contending for the dynastic throne? Apparently, it took another three hundred years, muses Kumar, before a sixteenth-century jurist and scholar of hadith "asked the awkward question: how was it that the '*ulamā*' of the age accepted a woman as a ruler?" (2010, 287). While we may never know whether individual jurists and scholars of Islam contemplated the same awkward question at the time, we do know that there was no institutional opposition to Razia's leadership. It "would take a great deal of ingenious interpretation," observes Habibullah astutely, for *shari'a* "to countenance the idea, but Iltutmish could perhaps count on his docile ecclesiastics to

---

[54] For a comprehensive discussion of various early hadiths on *mukhannathan* from Mecca and Medina, see Rowson (1991).

overlook this departure from a law that was, in any case, continually being reinterpreted all these centuries" (1976, 96). It was, after all, Razia's father who patronized the *ulama'* and under whose watch Delhi became a "sanctuary of Islam." A strong authoritarian caliph or sultan trumps the "church," even as the former pays lip service to – and is legitimated by – the latter. At least it did in medieval Muslim India. And Razia successfully subdued the rebellious religious minorities and restored clerical dominance. Besides, dismayed by her royal brother's excesses and debaucheries, and fearing chaos and crisis of governance, the *ulama'* may have found Razia the only legitimate and suitable successor to Iltutmish: she had acted wisely and proven her political talent, and her other half-brothers were all too young.

Most conspicuous, however, is the silence of the court scholar and chronicler Juzjani who, as a prayer leader and a judge, was well familiar with *shari'a*. He recorded no objection to Razia's ascension to the throne. She raised Juzjani's status considerably by appointing him to the directorship of the prestigious Nasiriya College, founded by her father. Not only did he not express any overt objections to Razia's political leadership, he even praised her as "just" (*'adil*), "guardian of her people" (*ra'iyat parvar*), and the only successor to Iltutmish worthy of being called a "military leader" (*lashkar kish*). Juzjani's pragmatism is not lost on Kumar either. He was "trapped by the conditions of his services and his conscience," since it was Razia who elevated his position (2010, 289). Juzjani thus could not "condemn Raziyya outright for immodesty, nor could he criticize the Shamsi slaves for raising a woman to the throne" (Kumar 2010, 289). One could, however, interpret Juzjani's accepting – or not overtly oppositional – attitude regarding Razia's leadership not just as calculating and pragmatic, but also a sign of genuine belief in the dynastic legitimacy of her rule. Moreover, as a man of faith he must have been well familiar with the Quranic revelations regarding the Queen of Sheba and her sovereignty, and so may have found Razia's sovereignty not out of bounds. Be that as it may, ultimately the opposition to Razia's authority came not from the religious establishment or an appeal to the alleged Prophetic hadith, but from the senior political-military elite: the loyal Shamsi slaves of her father's whose fear of losing their own power and privilege increased as their hopes of manipulating the young queen diminished. And thus they moved to remove her from the throne.[55]

[55] It is an historical irony that upon ascending the throne some twenty-five years after Razia's tragic death, Ghiyas al-Din Balban, a Shamsi *ghulam*, effectively curtailed his colleagues' privileges once and for all, making Razia's reign appear as their golden age in retrospect (Jackson 1999, 191; Lane-Poole 1903, 82).

Years later, in stark contrast to her brothers' reigns, Razia Sultan, the only Shamsi leader distinguished as a *lashkar kish* by Juzjani, was memorialized as "a great monarch: wise, just, generous, a benefactor to her realm, a dispenser of equity, the protector of her people, and leader of her armies" (Lane-Poole 1903, 74). Juzjani ends the exaltation of her leadership qualities with the following lamentation: "she had all kingly qualities except her sex, and this exception made all her virtues of no effect in the eyes of men. May God have mercy upon her" (Lane-Poole 1903, 74; Juzjani, 457). God did. Men did not.

Part III

Contemporary Queens: Institutionalization of Succession

5 Benazir Bhutto: A Queen "Without Parallel"

Such were the paths that Sassi pursued
paths that would have cost heroes their lives!
The towering mountains are as flat as the steppes
to the mind and eye of love.

Shah Abdul Latif in Schimmel (1997, 148)

On December 27, 2007, Benazir Bhutto, the twice democratically elected Prime Minister of Pakistan, was gunned down at a huge political rally at Liaqat Bagh in Rawalpindi. She had returned to Pakistan to yet another enthusiastic public welcome after eight long years of self-imposed exile, in order to stand for election to a third term. Some twenty years earlier, she had scored a spectacular electoral victory to become the first woman prime minister of a Muslim-majority society. The response had been euphoric. Her election electrified Pakistanis, millions of Muslims, and the wider world. Following the mysterious midair explosion of the plane carrying General Zia ul-Haq – the military strongman who had ousted her father in a military coup and executed him in 1979 – her electoral victory was more than a dynastic and personal triumph. It also heralded a new era, more tolerant and equitable, and a more democratic leadership in Pakistan.

Who was Benazir Bhutto, and why was she assassinated?

Situating Benazir: The Bhutto Dynasty

The history of the feudal family into which Benazir was born is a long and illustrious one.[1] Their landholding in Sindh was so vast that it reportedly

---

[1] If the primary sources on medieval queens and sultans are rather limited, the number of books and articles written about Benazir Bhutto, films and documentary made about her life, interviews, and the media exposure she has had is staggering. This chapter is based on extensive interviews I conducted with close family members, friends, and associates of Benazir Bhutto in Cambridge, Massachusetts, London, and Lahore in February and March of 2016. These include Ambassador Peter Galbraith; Sanam Bhutto (Benazir's sister); Ambassador Wajid Shamsul Hassan; historian and journalist Victoria Schofield; Senator Aitzaz Ahsan; the prominent human rights lawyer Asma Jahangir, who sadly passed away in February 2018; Professor of Psychology Durre Sameen Ahmed; Naheed Khan (Benazir's personal friend and assistant) and her husband, Senator Safdar Abbasi.

prompted Richard Napier, the British conqueror of Sindh, to tell his driver to wake him up when they were out of the Bhutto land (Bhutto 1989, 29)! To prevent partitioning of the land and keep it within the family, marriages were routinely arranged within the family, and cousin marriage dominated. No Bhutto child, male or female, married outside of the extended Bhutto family, and the parental rights and obligations to arrange their children's marriage were sacrosanct. Benazir's paternal grandfather, Sir Shah Nawaz Khan, was the first to break this pattern of clan endogamy, but only after he had first married his cousin and sired a couple of children. He later fell in love with a Hindu woman who converted to Islam to marry him; and from this union was born Zulfikar Ali Bhutto in 1928, Benazir's father.[2] When he was twelve, it was arranged for Zulfikar to marry his cousin Shirin Amir Begum, who was eight years his senior. He agreed to the marriage only after he was bribed with a "cricket set from England," after which, he returned to his school and she to her own family, reportedly never to spend intimate time together (Bhutto 1989, 31). Benazir's mother, Nusrat, was born in Iran in 1929 to Shi'i parents of Kurdish ethnicity. She came from an urban cosmopolitan merchant family in which women did not observe veiling and drove their own cars. Zulfikar and Nusrat married in 1951,[3] and the fact that one was a Sunni and the other a Shi'i was irrelevant to them and their children later on.[4] It was during the summer solstice, June 21, 1953, that Benazir – literally meaning "without parallel" or "one of a kind" – was born into this multiethnic, multi-faith, cosmopolitan, and feudal dynasty (Figure 5.1). She was the first of four siblings. From early childhood, Benazir and her brothers and sister were indoctrinated into the "ancestral moral code" of loyalty, patronage, and principle that formed their sensibility and guided

---

They experienced the elation of her election; shared her frustrations at being unable to get her projects implemented; suffered the heartaches of her being twice dismissed, slighted by her former friends in the UK and USA, and the fall out with her mother and brother; and felt the foreboding excitement of her return to Pakistan to run for a third term as prime minister. They also carry the sorrows of the tragedy of her untimely death with them at all times. They all became visibly sad and pensive as they recounted various events and stories of her life to me.

[2] Zulfikar means "sword" in Arabic. The sword reportedly belonged to Prophet Muhammad, who gave it to Ali, his cousin and son-in-law – hence Zulfikar Ali. See www .vajehyab.com/?q=%D8%B0%D9%88%D8%A7%D9%84%D9%81%D9%82%D8% A7%D8%B1).

[3] Zulfikar Ali Bhutto secretly married for a third time to Husna Sheikh in December of 1971, and had a daughter, Shameem (Lone 2016).

[4] Such cross-faith marriages are not unusual in Pakistan – or in other Muslim-majority countries – at least they were not until recently, specifically until 9/11 and the US invasions of Afghanistan and Iraq. The family with whom I lived when I first went to Pakistan in 1987 was religiously mixed: he was a Shi'i and she was a Sunni. See also Benazir Bhutto on this issue. (2008, 55–56).

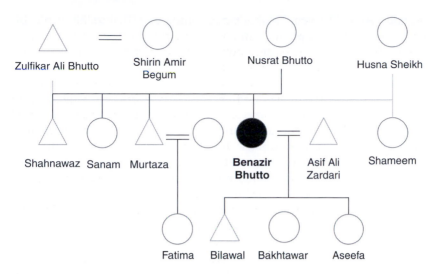

Figure 5.1 Benazir Bhutto's Genealogy

their public comportment (Bhutto 1989, 31). She was called Pinkie, apparently due to the color of her rosy cheeks. Years later, she would occasionally tell people "it was because of her leftist politics".[5]

Present-day Pakistan, partitioned from India in 1947, is composed of four major provinces: Sindh, Punjab, Baluchistan, and the North West Frontier (renamed Khyber Pakhtunkhwa in 2010).[6] Culturally diverse and ancient, each province carries a distinct ethnic and linguistic legacy, forming together a multicultural, multiethnic, and multilingual nation-state. Although based on a constitutional and representational polity, the Pakistani state has remained weak, the political elite struggling to build or to fortify its democratic institutions. By and large, the politics of person-alities, patronage, and loyalty form the foundation of the state. Presently, at the very core of the political system lies a major divide between a deeply rooted aristocratic feudalism and corporate business, with a military/ *mulla* alliance either supporting or challenging the civilian government as the political situation demands. As one of the most popular feudal dynasties from Sindh, the Bhuttos hold a particular mystique for a vast majority of people, and as one Pakistani said to the prize-winning

[5] Peter Galbraith, personal interview, December 2, 2015, Cambridge, Massachusetts. All quotations of Galbraith are from this interview.
[6] See Aitzaz Ahsan on Indus culture (Muslim/Pakistani) as separate and distinct from Indian and Hindu culture (2013).

journalist Anatol Lieven, "Nobody can compare to [Benazir Bhutto]. All other leaders are pygmies by comparison" (2011, 242).

Benazir and her siblings grew up in a world of privilege, power, and prestige. In her autobiography, she describes a happy and carefree childhood and young adulthood for herself and her siblings. Sanam, Benazir's younger sister, whom I met and interviewed in London, stressed that the siblings had "some hierarchy" tied to age from "elder to younger," but not to gender.[7] "You see, in Sindh somehow the fathers are a little shy of their eldest son, they are a little formal." But with the girls, their relationship is "very loving." With her parents often away on governmental assignments and state visits, the young Benazir was provided with the best private education, first at a boarding school in northern Pakistan, where for the first time she learned to make her own bed, polish her shoes, and "carry water for bathing and tooth-brushing back and forth from the water taps in the corridors" (Bhutto 1989, 38). Her father was particular about his children's education and adamant that they learn about the society in which they lived. He intended to make them understand that they were part of the larger world – particularly that of Pakistan and its geopolitical position in relation to the superpowers (Bhutto 1989, 37). His words of wisdom, political instructions, and philosophical advice to her are interspersed throughout her autobiography.

The intellectually formative years for Benazir began with her attendance at Radcliffe College in 1969. While taking courses in government at Harvard University, she began to appreciate the differences between democracy and dictatorship, rule of law, and arbitrariness. She became keenly sensitized to issues of authority and representation, that where authority is wanton and not supported institutionally, people have no reason to obey it. She developed a sense of what bonds leaders and followers and took that lesson to heart (Bhutto 1989, 51). Years later, by the time she had started campaigning for the office of prime minister, the people had become the source of her political strength and inspiration. She felt more comfortable with ordinary people than with those of her own feudal class; she trusted them, said Asma Jahangir who knew Benazir from childhood.[8]

After thirteen years of military dictatorship, in 1970 General Yahya Khan (r. 1969–1971) finally agreed to allow a general election. But Benazir's hopes for the restoration of a democratic civilian government

---

[7] Interview, London, February 2, 2016. All quotations of Sanam Bhutto are from my two interviews with her.

[8] I interviewed Asma Jahangir in Lahore, February 2016. Halfway through our conversation, we were joined by Asma's journalist daughter, Munizae Jahangir. Quotations of Asma and Munizae are taken from this interview.

in Pakistan turned into a nightmare as a brutal civil war soon broke out between East and West Pakistan. With India intervening on behalf of East Pakistan, the latter finally broke away from the union and declared independence. Benazir was in her second year at Harvard University when her father summoned her to join him in New York. He was representing Pakistan at the United Nation's Security Council regarding the ongoing conflict between India and West Pakistan. Sitting behind her father, the eighteen-year-old Benazir observed first-hand the "behind the scenes" political intrigues and public performance of international actors and their diplomatic negotiations. Feeling politically cornered, her father broke up the meeting, tore up the resolution, and walked out – and with that Bangladesh became a new nation-state on the world map.

Back at Harvard, Benazir was no longer known as Pinkie from Pakistan, but Pinkie Bhutto, the daughter of the President of Pakistan (Bhutto 1989, 59). She was in her third year at Harvard University when on June 28, 1972, she was once again summoned by her father to accompany him to Simla, India, for bilateral peace talks. Zulfikar Ali Bhutto was to meet with Prime Minister Indira Gandhi to negotiate the terms of disengagement between India and Pakistan. On their way, the father gave his daughter a lesson in diplomatic conduct: "You must not smile and give the impression you are enjoying yourself while our soldiers are still in Indian prisoner-of-war camps. You must not look grim, either, which people can interpret as a sign of pessimism" (Bhutto 1989, 60). On her father's side, ironically, it was the young Benazir who became the center of the media attention:

people lined the streets to stare at me. Cheering crowds began to follow me everywhere: past the old cottages and country gardens planted by nostalgic British inhabitants years before; on my arranged visits to a doll museum, a handicraft center, tinned fruit factories, and a dance program at a convent where I ran into several of my older teachers from the convent in Murree. When I walked down the Mall ... the crowds grew so huge that the traffic had to be stopped ... Letters and telegrams piled up welcoming me to India. One even suggested that my father appoint me Ambassador to India! (Bhutto 1989, 61)

How to explain this phenomenon? Benazir herself provided an answer – one that she tried to realize years later when she was first elected prime minister. The reason for the "overwhelming" public and popular attention she received in India, Benazir's autobiography explains, was not a "diversion" to the drag out political negotiations, as her father had said, nor was she an object of fascination due to a dynastic parallelism that people saw with her counterpart, Indira Gandhi. It was because she "symboliz[ed] a new generation"; she was not born in the undivided

India, but in the newly established state of Pakistan. She was a Pakistani proper, different and yet very familiar:

I was free of the complexes and prejudices which had torn Indian and Pakistanis apart in the bloody trauma of partition. Perhaps the people were hoping that a new generation could avoid the hostility that had now led to three wars, burying the bitter past of our parents and grandparents to live together as friends. And I certainly felt it was possible as I walked the warm and welcoming streets of Simla. (Bhutto 1989, 62)

Benazir truly cared about peace with India, her friend Victoria Schofield stressed to me in interview. She cared about Kashmir and was hoping to reach out and remove the burden of mutual animosity.[9] One of the first diplomatic moves she made as Prime Minister of Pakistan was to extend an invitation to the then Indian Prime Minister, Rajiv Gandhi, and his wife.[10] But if Benazir's idea was to bring down the tension with India, argues Ayesha Siddiqa, a military specialist, her action tended to sideline the military.[11] Siddiqa's observation underscores diplomat Peter Galbraith's assertion that the military viewed Benazir's interest in India as a "security risk," which in turn led to a degree of insecurity in her relations with the Pakistani Army. Compensating for that, Benazir would at times ratchet up the anti-Indian rhetoric, particularly in her second term as prime minister.

It was also at Harvard and later at the University of Oxford that Benazir formed some of her most influential and enduring friendships, most notably with Peter Galbraith and Victoria Schofield, with both of whom I conducted extensive interviews in Cambridge, Massachusetts and London. "The extraordinary thing about her," said Schofield, "was the ripple effect with various people who meant a lot to her. She was the central figure [in their lives] and she is gone now. But all the others are still holding hands in different manners and ways." Throughout her college years, her father was intimately involved in Benazir's progress, kept a watchful eye on her educational activities, and often wrote her long letters. He was cultivating a deeper relationship with his daughter while also meticulously imparting to her his political insights regarding government, state, and society. By the time Benazir had finished her degree at Radcliffe, the father-daughter relationship had strengthened both emotionally and intellectually. "My father adored her," said Sanam Bhutto.

---

[9] I interviewed Victoria Schofield in London, February 2016. All quotations of Schofield are from this interview.

[10] Rajiv's visit to Pakistan was part of the summit of the South Asian Association for Regional Cooperation (SAARC), held December 29–31, 1989.

[11] Personal communication, April 24, 2018, Boston.

Benazir's charismatic personality manifested early and blossomed at Oxford. Educated and sophisticated, Benazir returned to Pakistan triumphantly in 1977, having completed her studies at Harvard and Oxford. She was now poised to embark on diplomatic missions as her father's representative. But it was not to be.

Benazir had just celebrated her twenty-fourth birthday when on July 5 her father's handpicked chief of the army, General Zia ul-Haq staged a military coup against him.[12] Despite national and international pleas to free Mr. Bhutto, General Zia remained steadfast in his decision to execute Mr. Bhutto, and he did so on April 4, 1979. Having unconstitutionally overthrown a democratically elected government, General Zia embarked on a multipronged strategy to solidify his position. Domestically, he legitimated his military takeover by embarking upon a massive Islamization program. He brutally stifled the opposition and enacted the Hudood Ordinance, which was primarily aimed at restricting Pakistani women's mobility and activities – personal, legal, and political:

> Within a few years of Zia's rise to the top slot, he got so used to the propagation of his sham Islamization that he started to give the impression of a man with a mission, with faint outlines of an aura of a Messiah already dimly visible. A man who loves power, is already riding a tiger, and bears the conviction that Allah wants him to stay there can become a very ruthless man [*sic*]. (Abbas 2005, 108)

Internationally, it was the height of the Cold War. With the Soviet Union poised on the threshold of Afghanistan, General Zia was actively wooed by the USA to bring Pakistan solidly into the Western camp. The United States generously rewarded General Zia with sophisticated weapons and foreign aid, much to the detriment of the Pakistanis.[13] Although the Pakistanis might have initially benefited from the injection of US money into their economy, they eventually inherited a divided, polarized, weaponized, and ideologically oppressive country. "The US," said Sanam,

---

[12] Was it Henry Kissinger's warning to Mr. Bhutto that had come true? In her autobiography, Benazir writes, "I didn't want to believe the United States was actively destabilizing the democratically elected government of Pakistan. But I kept coming back to a remark Henry Kissinger had made to my father during a visit to Pakistan in the summer of 1976." Unable to persuade Mr. Bhutto to abandon the "Reprocessing Plant Agreement" with France, Mr. Kissinger finally warned Bhutto to "Reconsider the agreement with France or risk being made into 'a horrible example'" (Bhutto 1989, 86–87). See also Brooke Allen on the role of the USA and the CIA in overthrowing Mr. Bhutto and ushering General Zia into power (2016, 57–58).

[13] The USA collaborated with Saudi Arabia to send financial and military aid to Pakistan, which strengthened not only the Pakistani intelligence services and military, but also radical Islam, Wahhabism, and Talibanism (Bennett 2010, 67).

"gave the dictator billions of dollars, but only a few millions of aid to Benazir. What message of democracy are you sending?"

As General Zia went on a campaign to stifle dissent and silence the Bhutto family and its supporters, the still imprisoned Mr. Bhutto ordered his young sons Mir Murtaza (b. 1954) and Shahnawaz (b. 1958) to leave the country. Benazir and her mother, Begum Nusrat Bhutto, stayed behind to look after the affairs of their jailed father and husband, only to become the subject of Zia's unrelenting harassment. Mr. Bhutto's brutal treatment and ultimate execution affected his children differently. Forced into exile, his young sons were deprived of seeing their father and of the opportunity to grieve properly when he was hanged. The injustices of Zia's betrayal turned these young men into avenging angels. The chance to stand by her father, on the other hand, to provide him emotional solace and closely witness his stoicism in the face of death, strengthened Benazir's determination and engendered a different sensibility in her, one that might have deeply influenced her own resolve to return to Pakistan in 2007. Her experiences, painful though they were, motivated her to follow a diplomatic path while keeping her father's legacy alive. Turning grief into political awareness and activism, Benazir wrote:

Now, in the nightmare that had engulfed Pakistan, his cause had become my own. I had felt it as I stood by my father's grave. At that moment I pledged to myself that I would not rest until democracy returned to Pakistan. I promised that the light of hope that he had kindled would be kept alive. He had been the first leader of Pakistan to speak for all of the people, not just for the military and the elite. It was up to us to continue. (Bhutto 1989, 18)

Under the leadership of Begum Bhutto and Benazir, the Pakistani opposition was finally able to coalesce in early 1981 and form the Movement for the Restoration of Democracy. The movement would have been much more effective had it not been sidelined by the hijacking of a Pakistani airplane, allegedly orchestrated by Murtaza Bhutto in the same year (Anwar 1997, 95–111).[14] General Zia thereafter increased pressure on the Bhutto women, subjecting Benazir particularly to harsh treatment in her confinement. Sanam recalls receiving a torn piece of cardboard on which Benazir had hastily jotted down the news of her impending transfer to an unknown location (Figure 5.2).[15]

---

[14] Fatima Bhutto, Murtaza's daughter, downplays the effect of the hijacking on the Movement and accuses her aunt of having "hijacked the movement as a personal vehicle for her political ambition" (2010, 239).

[15] I am grateful to Sanam Bhutto for allowing me to take this photograph.

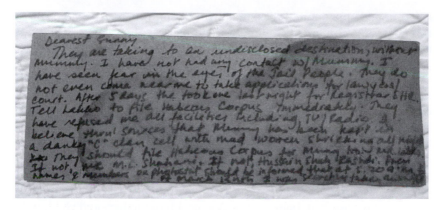

Figure 5.2 Benazir Bhutto's Hurried Note to Her Sister Sanam from Her Jail

Between 1977 and 1984, Benazir spent more than five and a half years either in prison or under house arrest. The US administration under President Ronald Reagan banned any high-level contact with the Bhuttos and conveniently overlooked Zia's atrocious human rights violations. That was of the "greatest help to Zia," recalled Ambassador Galbraith. Thanks to Peter Galbraith's political lobbying, particularly when it became clear that holding her in such inhumane conditions would affect US foreign aid to Pakistan, Zia finally released Benazir from jail and allowed her to leave the country. In 1984 she left for London, where she assumed the leadership of the Pakistan People's Party (PPP) and set out to revive her father's legacy and to direct the party from exile.

By 1986 Zia felt secure enough in his position to ease off the repression, and announced a no-party election. Benazir Bhutto returned to Pakistan in the same year, intending to participate in the electoral process and seek the office of the prime minister. She was well aware of her society's cultural traditions and religious conservatism, and so carefully navigated the invisible yet sacred boundaries of the state, society, and religion. Mindful that her youth and gender would put her at a disadvantage in this feudal society, she agreed to an "arranged" marriage with Asif Ali Zardari, covered her hair elegantly with a white *dupatta*,[16] and avoided shaking hands with male dignitaries. The intellectual incompatibility between Benazir and Zardari stunned some of her friends and relatives, and her head covering displeased many more middle-class and educated Pakistani women. When I brought up such objections to Asma Jahangir,

---

[16] The *dupatta* is a long scarf and an essential part of Pakistani women's three-piece suits.

she sounded impatient. "I disagreed with her putting on a *dupatta*. It was not necessary. But anyway, she did it and felt secure doing it. It did not mean that she became compliant and conservative – not at all."

Reflecting on Benazir Bhutto's legacy, in the following pages, I discuss the dynamics of power politics in Pakistan that held her in its vortex. Evaluating her policies, whether effective or not, is not a major consideration in this chapter. Much has already been written on that subject, and is easily available, though it must be said that Benazir was unconstitutionally dismissed from office twice and before her governments had a chance to realize her objectives. I will mention a few that specifically affected Pakistani women, however, which include the first women's bank, a women's police corps, and the Lady Health Workers, a "gender targeted program" that hires women to go to remote villages to help improve the health of mothers and children.[17] What interests me is the trajectory of Benazir's involvement in the dynastic power struggle and the deadly competition over electoral politics in Pakistan. In her first term she was up against the entrenched male political elite and army generals, the "deep state" or the "establishment," as it is known in Pakistan – and her gender and youth only added to the misogyny and resentment showered upon her by the representatives of the traditional establishment. Her second term was marked by dynastic competition and the battle of succession between sister and brother – Benazir and Murtaza – that ultimately undid both her relationship with her brother and her administration. Seeking a third term, an older and more experienced Benazir returned home to her "beloved Pakistan" from exile, determined to bring the country "back to democracy," and to act as a "catalyst for change" (Bhutto 2008, 1–2). It was not to be. She was assassinated.

Benazir's eternal resting place in Larkana, similar to that of the Yemenite Queen Arwa, has become a pilgrimage center for many Pakistanis – and her cult is steadily growing, stories of her miracles are spreading fast. The poetics and politics of Benazir's life and legacy, much like those of the mystical figures of legend Sassi and Sohni, will continue to be told and retold for years to come – sympathetically or otherwise. But ultimately, as divined by the thirteenth-century Persian mystic philosopher, Maulana Jalal al-Din Rumi:

هرکسی از ظن خود شد یار من / وز درون من نجست اسرار من

For what they think they hear me say, they love me
None gaze in me my secrets to discern. (trans. Franklin Lewis (2007, 362))

---

[17] I thank Raza Rumi for bringing the Lady Health Workers to my attention. Presently, this program covers millions of women, helping them with immunization, maternal care and planning, and child nutrition. See www.who.int/workforcealliance/knowledge/resources/casestudy_pakistan/en/.

First-Term Prime Minister: "In Government, but Not in Power"

In the terrible tumult of the tide
the mighty crocodiles,
powerful alligators gathered beyond number
in the stream ...

Shah Abdul Latif in Schimmel (1997, 158)

On an anxious day in April of 1986 Benazir Bhutto returned to Pakistan after two years of exile in Europe. She was determined to carry on her beloved father's legacy. As her plane circled the skies over Karachi airport, Benazir was not sure what to expect – neither from a terrorized and brutalized public nor from the general who had executed her father in 1979 and made himself president. What she saw on the ground, however, took her breath away. She was "shocked at the huge crowd awaiting her," observes Libby Hughes, and "When her feet finally touched the land of her birth, she knew she was where she belonged" (2000, 60, 95). The PPP had expected a few hundred thousand supporters to turn out for Benazir. Well over two million had gathered at Iqbal Park, where she was to address the crowd (Bhatia 2008, 20–21). "Her arrival in Lahore," writes the late Pakistani scholar Eqbal Ahmad, "was an event without parallel in the sub-continent's history. Gandhi, Nehru, Jinnah: no one ever had a public reception like hers" (1998). The goddess had returned.

But why was Benazir so popular? What did she represent to the public in this conservative and patriarchal society that the military and the male political elite did not? In the cultural context of South Asia, says Durre Ahmed, a professor of psychology, Benazir represented the "Goddess," the "Grand Mother," or "Bari Ammi Jan" (beloved mother), as she put it humorously.[18] In the sociohistorical consciousness of South Asians, Ahmed asserts, it is the goddess/mother who symbolizes authority and has the power of life and death; she is worshiped and loved, and in turn protects her children – or punishes them:

Look at posters of Goddess/Bari Ammi Jan! You can draw parallels between these images and the resonance of that with Benazir. The Great Mother/Goddess rules over life, death and rebirth. There you have the colors of the PPP flag [red, black and green]. And of course the biggest shrine to Bari Ammi Jan, one of the key places, is Rajasthan, and Benazir Bhutto is from Sindh.[19]

---

[18] Personal interview, Lahore, February 2016.
[19] Rajasthan in India and Sindh in Pakistan share borders as well as culture, language, and traditions.

Energized by the outpouring of love she received from her fellow Pakistanis, Benazir began campaigning for election with renewed energy and enthusiasm. If people subconsciously perceived her as the Ammi Jan, Benazir knowingly situated herself as part of the larger Pakistani family, as their "sister." As she campaigned from province to province and from town to town, she would tell her audiences, "People say I am a young girl, all alone without the protection of father or brother. But aren't you my brothers? Won't you protect me?" People would respond with "greater frenzy, 'yes, yes, yes'" (Zakaria 1989, 7). Wherever she went, Benazir was welcomed by ever more enthusiastic crowds, women included. It was not just that she was her father's daughter; she represented the face of a new, a different, a charismatic leader. She had that "magnetic quality that is charisma," in Charles Lindholm's words (1990, 7). Emerging from the trauma of witnessing her father dragged through the political mud and subjected to a military execution, and abused under a harsh and punishing military dictatorship, millions of Pakistanis felt relieved and comforted by this fresh face of authority, and by her youth and gender. She was a breath of fresh air – indeed, an unparalleled leader.

As fate would have it, General Zia vanished in a mysterious plane explosion in the skies over Islamabad – divine justice? – having decided to finally hold a national election in 1988.[20] This decision did not mean that the general had finally seen the light and decided to allow a democratic transition of power. Rather, it was another attempt to out-maneuver Benazir, who had married a year earlier and was expecting her first child. Zia's calculation was that she could not withstand the rigors of campaigning and that the public would shy away from supporting a pregnant woman (Bhatia 2008, 22; Hughes 2000, 105–106). Benazir saw through the ruse, recalled Pakistani journalist Marvi Sirmed, and in response attended "political rallies with her intravenous drip in her hands."[21] Much to the humiliation of the acting president, Gholam Ishaq Khan – who had been a close ally of the late General Zia and was one of the country's top-ranking military generals – Benazir Bhutto's party, the PPP, won ninety-two seats. The spy master Hamid Gul, head of the notorious Inter-Service Intelligence (ISI) – a military institution known for its manipulation of politics – was convinced that unless there

---

[20] *The New York Times* considered the KGB to be the culprit in Zia's death. See Kaplan (1989). His death, similar to Benazir's, has remained a mystery.

[21] "Being a woman never hindered her," writes Marvi Sirmed (2011): "I cannot forget her coming to the political rallies with her intravenous drip in her hands ... When she was expecting Bakhtawar during her premiership, the crisis was once again carefully chosen to coincide with the dates of her delivery. She did not make herself absent from her office for more than 48 hours."

was a credible political alliance to oppose the PPP, "the latter would run away with the election by a landslide." He cobbled together the Islamic Democratic Alliance (Islami Jumhuri Itihad, IJI), bringing together the Muslim League,[22] Jamaat-e-Islami (JI), and a host of other right-wing religious parties. "This was the first time the army supported and used religious parties in electoral politics" (Abbas 2005, 134; Lieven 2011, 211). Nawaz Sharif, a protégé of General Zia, ran on the IJI ticket and won fifty-four seats. In the end, Benazir's party fell short of winning the majority outright.[23]

The United States had sent a delegation, including Peter Galbraith, to observe the election. Galbraith accompanied Benazir Bhutto to Larkana, her ancestral village, and together they watched the election returns. Benazir won the election, despite the rigging that in some precincts denied her an outright majority. Galbraith advised her to ignore the cheating, though he had no doubt that rigging had occurred. He told her to instead highlight the monumental event that had just happened: a young, modern, educated Muslim woman had won the national election in Pakistan! "She really had good judgment," said Galbraith. He remembers the scene on their way to catch a flight back to Karachi:

> People were lining up ten feet deep to cheer her. It was such a moment! In the plane, the pilot handed her three roses, and we flew to Karachi. There were half a million people there. Then the press conference, and the first question she gets: "Aren't you too young for this position?!" She said, "Well, it is not the age, but the mandate!"

President Ishaq Khan, however, was relentless in his opposition to Benazir and the PPP, and tried everything possible to deprive Benazir of her victory. He even tried to persuade her mother to form the government, said Galbraith. It was not until two weeks later that a reluctant Mr. Khan succumbed to pressure from Benazir's national and international supporters – including a phone call from President Reagan[24] – and called on her to form her cabinet. The military unenthusiastically pledged allegiance.[25]

---

[22] The main party associated with Pakistan's founder, Mohammad Ali Jinnah (d. 1948), which has since splintered.

[23] Perhaps this should not come as a surprise to anyone, writes Lieven. Because of Pakistan's plurality of smaller parties and deep ethnic division, no party ever wins an absolute majority (2011, 206).

[24] "Ishaq Khan's inability to resist this [American] demand only showed the truth in the old Pakistani saying that the most important person in the country is not the head of the state, or even the army chief, but the American Ambassador – known to cynical Islamabad insiders as 'the Viceroy'" (Allen 2016, 98).

[25] Articles 90–100 of the 1973 Constitution describe the appointment of a newly elected government in Pakistani. The president calls on the members of the assembly who have

And so, on December 4, 1988, a young and democratically elected Muslim woman was sworn into the exalted office of the Prime Minster of Pakistan. At thirty-five years of age, she was the first Muslim woman prime minister charged with the leadership of a modern Muslim society. The majority of Pakistanis were ecstatic, and the feeling of euphoria and the anticipation of a new beginning were palpable. I was in Pakistan just before the election and witnessed the public's adoration of Benazir Bhutto during her political campaign. The slow-moving cavalcade, the exuberant dancing men – and some women – in front of her motorcade, and the sheer number of red rose petals strewn on her path would be the envy of any politician. As the country celebrated, however, Chief of the Army Staff Mirza Aslam Beg,[26] President Ghulam Ishaq Khan, and head of the ISI Hamid Gul,[27] the so-called Troika, sulked.[28] "The hostility that Benazir aroused among many of the generals who ran the Pakistan army also extended to key officers in charge of the military intelligence agency, MI (military intelligence) and ISI" (Bhatia 2008, 81). They had done their best to vanquish Benazir's father and to banish her. Now they had to stand behind her at attention, watch her take the oath to the highest political office, and pledge allegiance to her. Pakistani poet Habib Jalib (d. 1993) describe the situation succinctly:

> The ones with guns are scared of an unarmed girl
> Light of courage is shining, spreading because of an unarmed girl
> They are scared, trembling and dying
> The Mullas, tradesmen, generals and braves alike, of an unarmed girl
> Do not talk about freedom, they say, do not meet the people,
> Say the insensitive, oppressors with black hearts, to the unarmed girl.

Benazir Bhutto's political leadership of a conservative and ethnically and linguistically divided society heightened existing tensions within and

---

demonstrated a majority able to form a government. The prime minister must then face a vote of confidence within ninety days of their appointment, and the military pledges allegiance to the new government. I am grateful to Ayesha Siddiqa for providing me with these details. For the text of the articles, see www.pakistani.org/pakistan/constitution/part3.ch3.html.

[26] Mirza Aslam Beg was the only member of General Zia's entourage who did not accompany him on the plane that fateful day when it exploded in midair, killing all aboard, including the American Ambassador Arnold L. Raphel.

[27] Following General Zia's death, Hamid Gul took up the anti-PPP mantle, encouraged by his army chief, Mirza Aslam Beg (Nasir 2015).

[28] In October of 2012, Pakistan's "Supreme Court ordered the government to begin criminal proceedings against former army and spy chiefs in an election-rigging case that dated to the 1990s. During the hearings, Gen. Aslam Beg, a former army chief, and Lt. Gen. Asad Durrani, a former chief of the powerful ISI Directorate, were accused of distributing money to an alliance of right-wing political parties that opposed Benazir Bhutto's Pakistan Peoples' Party" (Masood 2012).

among the religious and political domains. The JI and a few other religious leaders, having gained greater visibility and voice under General Zia's unabashed Islamization policies, found the moment opportune to challenge her leadership. The JI filed a case against her in the high court, based on the Prophetic hadith: "Never will succeed such a nation as makes a woman their ruler."[29] The irony of it was the blatant hypocrisy of the political elite. They "resorted to Muslim tradition only after their failure in the election" (Mernissi 1994, 1). "Confronted" by their duplicity, said Asma Jahangir, the JI had to back away: they had supported Fatima Jinnah for president against Ayub Khan in 1964.[30] Their case against Benazir was promptly thrown out of court. "They tried, but the people were with her." Benazir reached out, however, and ultimately was able to achieve political alliances with some religious parties, including with the Jamiat Ulema-e-Islam (JUI), during her time as prime minister. "She knew how to manipulate them," journalist Munizae Jahangir told me in Lahore, "and basically fed Maulana Fazlur Rahman [leader of the JUI] whenever she needed him."

One of the first democratic decisions Benazir and her cabinet took, according to Senator Aitzaz Ahsan, was to announce the release of all prisoners sentenced by the court martial tribunals under Zia:[31]

We believed they were political prisoners and the first effective announcement ought to be the release of those prisoners. These added up to something like 10,000 prisoners. We were, I must admit, a little raw and were not informed of bureaucratic processes.

Not surprisingly, continues Senator Ahsan, the announcement faced stiff opposition from President Ishaq Khan, who was the "kingpin of our military regime and had been finance minister of General Zia. He obliged us to look at each case individually, which would have taken a long time," and would have "deprived Benazir's government of its dramatic effect and luster." This was a period, recalls Ahsan, in which President Ishaq Khan opposed anything Benazir wanted to do. He would "hold the rule book in front of her, and the bureaucracy was loyal to President Ishaq." Those in the army leadership resented her because they thought she had been imposed upon them by international pressure in the aftermath of

[29] See Charles Amjad Ali (1989, 125–126) for a discussion of the religious opposition to Benazir Bhutto.

[30] For an imaginary "trial of Benazir," and the JI's objections to her political leadership, see Zakaria (1989).

[31] This section is based on my interview with Senator Aitzaz Ahsan in Lahore, February 2016. He was the interior minister in Benazir Bhutto's first cabinet. Zia's regime had rounded up and detained PPP members "in the tens of thousands" and incarcerated them in inhumane conditions (Allen 2016, 53).

Zia's sudden death. They pointedly ignored the will of the Pakistani people who had democratically elected Benazir.

Benazir's young government was particularly "put through the wringer" in relation to Afghanistan and the decisions she was forced to make. The beginning of her first term, said Ahsan, coincided with the approaching deadline set by the Geneva Accord. Under the terms of this agreement, the Soviet Union was to leave Afghanistan and withdraw all its forces by February 10, 1989. Pakistan was a signatory to this agreement. But by the time Benazir's government took the helm, the Pakistani military had already hatched a plan to "fill the vacuum after the Soviet withdrawal." Ahsan paused: "Look! We need to make an important distinction here: we were in government but not in power." The main advocates of this policy were President Ishaq Khan, himself a Pathan and an old-school hardliner on Afghan policy, the army chief Mirza Aslam Beg, the ISI chief General Hamid Gul, and a few other senior members of the foreign office and the defense establishment. Their assumption was that the Soviet withdrawal would create a political vacuum, which would then present a golden opportunity for Pakistan to "literally occupy Afghanistan," and that "Pakistani army and military troops would be received with garlands and welcoming cheers from the crowd"[32] (Ahsan). The army's strategy was to first take over Jalalabad, the town closest to Pakistan, and so the plan came to be known as the Jalalabad Operation.[33] Benazir Bhutto's government was kept in the dark, but when she became aware of the plan, she opposed it. She insisted that the parliament and the National Assembly be informed of the decision, because "we thought if we were to be a party to such a major decision, the parliament would hold us accountable one day." Bhutto and her government challenged the "vacuum" theory; they believed that what the Soviets would leave behind was "fortresses" in every big town and that there would be no possibility of overrunning these fortresses (Ahsan).

On January 28, 1989, the National Assembly met and, according to Senator Ahsan, presented and debated the views of the three factions: the civilian government opposing the plan; Hamid Gul and the ISI advocating it; and the National security adviser listening in:

Hamid Gul's message was that we take Jalalabad in a month, Kabul in the next three months, and by God's grace we would be on the banks of the Oxus within

---

[32] General Zia had reportedly long dreamed of evicting the Soviets and establishing Afghanistan as a satellite state (Kaplan 1989), and so this planning could have been a push to realize his dream posthumously.

[33] An impatient Gul wanted to establish a government of the so-called *mujahedeen* on Afghan soil, with Jalalabad as the seat of the new administration (Nasir 2015).

a year! At that point the opposition – and we had a large opposition – started shouting Allah-u Akbar – yes, it is true! And the PM and I knew that we had lost the argument; that we would not be able to stand in the way of the Jalalabad Operation. But we had put down our dissent in black and white and had discussed our reservations elaborately, explicitly, and unambiguously – they are still on the record.

The Jalalabad Operation began in mid-March, less than a month after the Soviet withdrawal on February 10, 1989. By April it became clear that the operation was a failure. Too many dead bodies were being brought back, and by the end of May there was a clear realization – and, finally, an acknowledgment – of defeat. How did Hamid Gul justify his military operation? He didn't, Ahsan told me: he felt he owed no explanation to the public. He was committed to the cause of Islam! Hamid Gul passionately believed in "Afghan *jihad*" and tried to have a direct say in Afghan policy beyond his ISI years (Nasir 2015).

A furious prime minister decided to sack Hamid Gul as the head of ISI, for his disrespect for the civilian government. Did she have the constitutional right to get rid of him? Ahsan asked rhetorically. The embattled prime minister was mindful that her action might create crises leading to her removal. Consequently, "we arranged for her to leave for Turkey and to be out of harm's way in case of such eventuality." Ahsan continued:

Having consulted the appropriate agencies and institutions, it became clear that the PM had the constitutional right to get rid of her trouble-making spy master. So, Nasirullah Baber, retired major general and special assistant to the PM, immediately ordered all doors to be locked, took the two secretaries with him to his office, and recommended the transfer of Hamid Gul back to the army. He took the files to the tarmac for signature by the PM, who was about to board a flight to Turkey. She signed the dismissal of ISI Hamid Gul and flew off to Turkey, whereupon General Babar announced the decision. This all goes to show how embattled she was in her first term – there were so many events!

"Hamid Gul *was* the ISI," said Ayesha Siddiqa to me.[34] Benazir "thought that she could control the military by appointing her own man" as the head of ISI, but the military wanted the head of the ISI under *its* own control – hence the tension between the army and Benazir. Nonetheless, Ahsan stressed, the entire establishment was working "against us, but we survived a vote of no confidence in 1989," though the state "used all its coercive machinery against us." But this was not the only vote of no-confidence that Benazir's administration survived. In their antipathy toward Benazir, the chief of the army Mirza Aslam Beg and President Ishaq Khan hatched a blatant plan to topple Benazir's government and to bring Nawaz Sharif, a handpicked protégé of

---

[34] Personal communication, Boston, April 24, 2018.

General Zia, to power. Revelations emerged in 2009 from a former ISI officer, who confessed his organization's plan to bring down the PPP government of Benazir Bhutto in 1990. It was a covert plan, code named "Operation Midnight Jackal." They adopted a two-pronged strategy: to bribe PPP deputies to defect from the party and to deceive them with the "fake news" of her impending dismissal by the president for corruption. Their message was clear: "her MPs and ministers would be better off switching sides in order to keep their positions" (Lieven 2011, 211).

Benazir's election and the working of her government were marred by incessant plots by various political and military operatives who worked to entrap, topple, and remove her. Although the entire establishment was working against her, she made a comeback at every turn and enjoyed popular support:

Chastened by the no-confidence motion, we spent some time reflecting on it. It could have succeeded. On my suggestion we took a retreat for three days away from Islamabad, and went back to the drawing board. We improved our governance, and it was at that time that Ishaq Khan and the army chief and the military bureaucracy became convinced that she could not be removed, that she would have an effective government and probably would win the next election, too. That is when they began to seriously turn. They feared, however, that if the democratic government was to be removed, there might be a reaction from the West and the US. So when on the first of August 1990, Saddam Hussein invaded Kuwait, on the sixth of August Benazir Bhutto and our government was removed by a presidential decree and sanctioned by the full backing of the army. (Ahsan)

Peter Galbraith also became pensive when recalling the United States' preoccupation with the invasion of Kuwait and Saddam Hussein, which led to taking its eyes off the unfolding political events in Pakistan. Certainly the military wanted Benazir out, and President Ishaq Khan definitely did not like her. He was in his seventies, and he had to put up with this charming Western-educated woman in her thirties, with her husband, a baby, and Western friends, to boot. It was just too much for this elderly Pathan patriarch.

Ishaq Khan brought seven charges of corruption against Benazir, for which a special court was created. But she was acquitted of all seven charges, with Aitzaz Ahsan acting as her legal counsel. "She was dismissed precisely because there was no valid ground for dismissing her government," said Ahsan. In fact, she was "consolidating her grip over the politics of Pakistan, which later became evident because she won the election for the second time. She started and ended with a hostile president and a hostile army chief," summarized Aitzaz Ahsan (who was not included in Benazir's second government).

Benazir stayed in Pakistan and became an effective member of the opposition to the government of Nawaz Sharif, and in 1993 she won a second term.

Second-Term Prime Minister: Family Feud and Battle for Dynastic Succession

The sun is sinking behind the trees
while the rising mist of dusk turned red.
Oh, Mother! I have been killed
in the darkness.

Shah Abdul Latif in Schimmel (1997, 144)

Back in 1993, Ishaq Khan was still president. He subjected Prime Minister Nawaz Sharif to the same fate as Benazir, and unceremoniously dismissed him based on similar charges of corruption – apparently the standard means to dismiss a civilian government. Nawaz Sharif, in turn, successfully challenged the president in the Supreme Court. But the constitutional crisis that was created by the president's arbitrary dismissal of elected prime ministers was eventually resolved by General Abdul Waheed Kakar, the chief of the army who pressured both men to step down. It was then that a general election was held, and on October 20, 1993, Benazir Bhutto was sworn in as the Prime Minister of Pakistan for the second time. More politically experienced in her second term, Benazir was now also more personally beleaguered. She had a better awareness of the dangerous political landscape in Pakistan and in the region, and was determined to forge a closer relationship with the army. But she now had to grapple with another "Troika," of the three men closest to her personally and politically. Two were her husband Asif Ali Zardari and brother Mir Murtaza, who detested each other, and the third was Farooq Leghari, a member of an aristocratic feudal family from Baluchistan. He was Benazir's long-time friend, and handpicked for president. Eventually, all three men contributed to her downfall in October 1996. None of the three, however, had her charisma and intellectual depth, as her friend Victoria Schofield told me in London;

She didn't have many intellectual equals. Her husband wasn't intellectually her equal. She couldn't sit and discuss lofty issues of governance at that time with him – given her own education and the position she held. She was a force of nature; heads would proverbially turn. But when you look at individuals like that, it is a lonely position without someone to mentor them.

Hemmed in by the military and the opposition, this time around Benazir leaned more heavily on her husband to counterbalance the scheming male political elite. Sanam believes that it was the press that isolated her sister and pushed her to rely more on her husband. Asif did not disappoint her; he stood by her and bore his long-term imprisonment for charges of "corruption" with forbearance, never betraying his wife. He wept openly when he recalled the moment of his wife's assassination and death in a video documentary made by Duane Baughman (2010).[35] During her second term as prime minister, Benazir expanded the scope of her husband's power and influence, giving him the portfolio of the federal investment minister and appointing him chairperson of the Pakistan Environmental Protection Council. As Zardari became more involved in her administration, he came to be known as "Mr. Ten Percent," for his alleged take from the national and international financial deals and treaties made in the country. Senator Aitzaz Ahsan believes that this is where things went wrong.

Even more pressing politically and challenging personally was Benazir's brother, Murtaza. He was agitating to return to Pakistan and demanded to take the leadership of the PPP. "In those days," writes Raja Anwar, Murtaza "considered himself the one and only political heir of Zulfikar Ali Bhutto and the undisputed leader of his party" (1997, 194). Their mother, Begum Nusrat Bhutto, supported his demand to return to Pakistan, while his prime minister sister asked him to wait. Murtaza had charges of air piracy pending against him, and as a prime minister, Benazir was bound by law to hold off granting him permission to return to Pakistan. Having languished in Zia's jail off and on for several years, Benazir had distanced herself from Murtaza and denounced Al-Zulfikar Organization (AZO), her brother's revolutionary movement, and its violent tactics (Paracha 2010).[36] Time and again and in different interviews Benazir stressed the differences in their political strategies, reminding all that she and her brother had chosen different political movements to lead.[37] But

---

[35] Many Pakistanis did not – and do not – believe his sincerity. I arrived in London a day or so after Benazir's assassination. The first thing my driver, who happened to be Pakistani, said was that Zardari had his wife killed because he wanted to replace her. That he became president in the aftermath of her death seems to lend credence to such conspiratorial beliefs.

[36] A "socialist guerrilla outfit," the AZO had the objective of avenging Bhutto's death. Almost all of its members "belonged to the lower-middle-class and working-class strata of society and had faced stiff jail sentences, torture, and lashes of Zia's Islamist tyranny" (Paracha 2010). Many of them also lost their lives in the cause of the AZO. See also Anwar (1997, Appendix V, 220).

[37] "She had better judgment," Peter Galbraith told me, choosing a diplomatic path. Faced with their father's impending execution, she reached out to Victoria Schofield to write up the account of her father's trial, and contacted all those intellectuals she had come to

Murtaza was ambitious and restless and took the risk of returning to Pakistan – the law seems to matter little to male feudal lords.[38]

Murtaza was a handsome, brash young man with a "dashing domineering personality – like his father," Ambassador Shamsul Hassan said to me in London.[39] As a feudal man born to riches, he had a sense of entitlement to the leadership of his father's party. Murtaza and his younger brother, Shahnawaz, had left Pakistan right after their father's arrest. The latter had feared that as the young men of the Bhutto family, they would not be safe in Pakistan. Unable to prevent their father's execution, Murtaza turned to armed struggle, and Shahnawaz followed his lead. "They acted angrily – understandably. They allowed themselves to be defined as terrorists, particularly after the hijacking [of a Pakistani airplane]. After that the boys couldn't be a credible opposition. Murtaza potentially could have been" (Galbraith). Youthful and hot-blooded, he wanted to incite revolution against General Zia and his military dictatorship in Pakistan.[40] After Bhutto's hanging, writes Anwar, "a Murtaza seething with rage and determined at all costs to avenge his father's death arrived in Kabul in 1979 with a promise of PLO [Palestine Liberation Organization] arms and no programme beyond causing harm to the rulers of Pakistan and any of their servants and associates" (1997, 87). He took up residence in the pro-Soviet Afghanistan, where he had clout and was given protection by Dr. Mohammad Najibullah, head of the Afghan security unit known as KHAD.[41] There he founded an armed movement, Al-Zulfikar Organization – adopting his father's name, Zulfikar, meaning the "sword" (i.e. of justice). While in Afghanistan, Murtaza and Shahnawaz married two Afghan sisters, though by the mid-1980s, both marriages had become marred

know while at Harvard and Oxford – e.g. Noam Chomsky. "Of course we all got engaged trying to save her father."

[38] Two books are of particular importance in this section. One is by Murtaza's daughter, Fatima Bhutto (2010), and the other by a PPP devotee of Murtaz, Raja Anwar (1997), who accompanied him in Afghanistan. He lost Murtaza's trust, and was subsequently jailed in Afghanistan for two and half years. Both books are very valuable in providing firsthand information about Murtaza and his political activities, but give diametrically different pictures of the man, his life, and his legacy.

[39] I interviewed Ambassador Wajid Shamul Hassan, a longtime friend of the Bhutto family, in London on February 8, 2016. He also keeps an active weblog on Pakistan and related issues (www.news18.com/blogs/author/wajid-shamsul-hasan-12638.html).

[40] "My father knew my brothers," said Sanam to me in London. "Their hands were aristocratic hands. They had never done a day's work in their lives! And my father said: 'You can't fight the American army, the Pakistan army, the ISI.' I think they just got isolated."

[41] "It is an irony of history that in 1976, Zulfikar Ali Bhutto had the Supreme Court of Pakistan declare the National Awami Party (NAP) a pack of traitors because of its links with Kabul. Yet here, three years later, was his son seeking Afghan assistance to set up a guerrilla base to operate against Pakistan" (Anwar 1997, 228–229, fn. 4).

by bitter tension and conflict. Following a happy night of family reunion in 1985 – the last time the family was ever together – Shahnawaz was found dead in his hotel room. Speculations about the cause of his death range from a serious quarrel with his wife to suicide, to poisoning by the ISI. Benazir held the ISI responsible for his death.[42]

Fatima Bhutto, Murtaza's daughter and a potential dynastic contender, dismisses such speculations and holds her aunt Benazir Bhutto accountable in her younger brother's death. She reached this conclusion after tracking down Jacques Verges, "the controversial French lawyer" and the "family's advocate" at the time of his death in 1985. Reflecting on Shahnawaz's death some thirty years later, Jacques Verges seemed to have the answer Fatima Bhutto was looking for. He told her that the reason for Benazir's reluctance to accept the CIA's offer to investigate Shahnawaz's death was "because she worked with them." But what would Benazir gain by not pursuing Shahnawaz's death? Fatima asks perceptively. Verges reasons that Benazir viewed her brothers as political rivals and so moved to eliminate her dynastic competitors. Clarifying further, he continues, "I am not surprised that it would benefit her for one brother to be disposed of before the other . . . Imagine to be killed by your own sister." Fatima is puzzled: "But why Shah[nawaz] first? He wasn't in charge, my father was." Verges concludes, "Among the two brothers, the strongest was Mir [Murtaza]. Perhaps it was necessary to get Shah out of the way because he was the weaker one" (2010, 258–260). Fratricide is of course the thread that runs through the history of dynasties. But in 1985 General Zia was alive and well and Benazir was nowhere remotely close to clinching dynastic power in Pakistan.

Nevertheless, Murtaza bided his time, determined to sabotage the regime of General Zia while traveling between Kabul, Damascus, and Delhi, making high-level contacts and establishing networks of support. Murtaza's most notorious political involvement came in early 1981: with the cooperation of three devoted members of AZO, he successfully orchestrated the hijacking of a Pakistan International Airlines plane en route from Karachi to Peshawar. The hijackers forced the plane to land at Kabul airport, where Murtaza opened up negotiations with General Zia, who reluctantly agreed to release a few PPP political prisoners – but not before the hijackers had killed an innocent man and thrown his

---

[42] Zia's regime attributed Shahnawaz's death to alcohol and drug abuse (Paracha 2017), whereas the Pakistan Ambassador to France at the time, Jamsheed Marker, posited a fight between the two brothers. In an interview in 2010, he disclosed that Shahnawaz and Murtaza had an "ugly" fight that night regarding the division of millions of dollars given them by Libya's Muammar Gaddafi. Tired of AZO, and against Murtaza's wishes, Shahnawaz wanted to branch out and spend the money on tourism (Niaz 2018).

body out onto the tarmac.[43] Murtaza was now considered an outlaw and barred from returning to Pakistan; he was sought for crimes of air piracy.[44]

With General Zia dead and Benazir in power, Murtaza finally returned to Pakistan against his sister's wishes. Upon arriving at Karachi airport in 1993 he was promptly arrested and taken to Landhi jail, where he was kept for eight months.

But how was it possible for Murtaza to return to Pakistan to begin with, given that he had charges of sedition and air piracy pending against him? For that we need to look into the intricacies of the labyrinthine political feudalism in Pakistan, where personal and political relationships continue to crisscross and alliances shift unscrupulously. Murtaza intensely disliked his brother-in-law, Asif Zardari.[45] He was convinced that his sister's "negative attitude" toward him was all Zardari's doing. Zardari was also intensely disliked by Jam Sadiq Ali, a "former PPP big wig . . . chucked out by Benazir from the party" and Chief Minister of Sindh and a member of a feudal ruling dynasty that dated back to the eighteenth century.[46] The enemy of his enemy became his enabler. Murtaza sought Jam Sadiq Ali's mediation to facilitate his return to Pakistan, and the latter contacted Nawaz Sharif, who had succeeded Benazir as prime minister in 1990. Sharif, Benazir's long-time political rival, in turn sought the intervention of some members of the ISI, who were "licking" their "lips in anticipation" of luring Murtaza back to Pakistan (Sethi 1993).[47] Clearly, they expected that Murtaza, heir to the family's dynastic leadership, would wrestle the PPP chairmanship from Benazir, weaken her and the party in the process, and by default strengthen Nawaz Sharif and his party. Sharif would then be rid of them both, and Jam Sadiq would have avenged his honor. Little did Sharif know that he would soon be dismissed on the same charges as Benazir had, and Jam Sadiq died in 1992 before he could actually see the result of his divide-and-rule political intrigues. Murtaza, however, did not disappoint them:

[43] See Raja Anwar's detailed account of Murtaza's al-Zulfikar and its operation, including some details of this hijacking (1997, 95–111). See also Bashir (2014).

[44] Murtaza's daughter, Fatima Bhutto, however, believes that her father rejected his followers' plan for hijacking "in no uncertain terms" and that once the deed had taken place, he pleaded with the hijackers to release the prisoners (2010, 220–221).

[45] Murtaza is reported to have had Zardari's photograph hung in the visitor's bathroom at the Bhutto residence (Anwar 1997, 203).

[46] Benazir had apparently offended Jam Sadiq Ali by appointing him to a minor position in her first government because she did not want to offend her new feudal in-laws. Insulted, Jam Sadiq Ali sought help from his longtime friend, President Ishaq Khan, who was eager "to teach Benazir a lesson," and appointed him "Chief Minister of Sindh" (Anwar 1997, 200).

[47] Paracha (2010) believes that the plan was actually hatched by Jam Sadiq Ali and "some ISI sleuths" who brought Nawaz Sharif on board.

Till the day he was tragically killed, Murtaza spent all his efforts trying to undermine Benazir's second government, but the truth was, his short stint as the agency's trump card came to an end as soon as it was realized that the majority of the PPP voters had rejected his claim of being the party's "true heir." (Paracha 2010)

As for the ISI, Ambassador Shamsul Hassan told me, "They hated Murtaza and the Bhuttos. They wanted Murtaza to come back, only to keep him as a thorn in his sister's side." While visiting Murtaza in jail, Shamsul Hassan told him point-blank: "Look, the ISI brought you here to kill you." But Murtaza accused him of being a sycophant and "Benazir's *chamcha* [henchman], just trying to please her." No sooner had he been released from jail in May of 1994 – thanks partly to his prime minister sister (Sethi 1993) – than Murtaza demanded the mantle of his father's party leadership and claimed that it was rightfully his. In that he had the backing of his mother, who as the co-chair of the PPP, seemed to have assumed – indeed, expected – the natural devolution of the dynastic leadership to her son. Begum Bhutto campaigned for Murtaza during the 1993 election and accordingly went door-to-door to solicit votes for him, when he was still in jail (Shamsul Hassan). Not only did Benazir not accede to his – and her mother's – demands, she had her mother removed as the co-chair of the party, much to the latter's anger. After all, Benazir was also a feudal lord. This not only widened the rift between the siblings, more significantly, it alienated mother from daughter. Faced with opposition from Benazir and the party, Murtaza, like many other disgruntled members of the political elite, started his own breakaway faction of the PPP in 1995, calling it Shaheed Bhutto.[48] However, like many other such splinter parties, "While the new grouping managed to create some sort of a skeleton presence in Sind, it failed to generate excitement in other provinces of the country" (Anwar 1997, 202). Sanam Bhutto commented that "You see, usually in our part of the world when one person is successful, the whole family backs them; stands behind them. Behind the scene you can beat each other, pull each other's hair out. But in the public domain, in front of people, you unite. My brother didn't do that."

Primordial Conflicts: Family Feud

Mother-Daughter Relationship

The family feud escalated as Begum Nusrat Bhutto invested her political capital and maternal love in the cause of her son. It turned deadly quickly. Why would she, a woman of elegance and courage, twice elected to the

---

[48] *Shaheed* means "martyr."

National Assembly and co-chair of the PPP, openly and actively support her son against her daughter – a sitting prime minister? Begum Bhutto had previously stood by her daughter and shown grace and resolve in the face of Zia's extreme cruelty. Why would she now turn against her daughter? Let us entertain three possibilities. First, the cultural context of patriarchal feudalism in which she lived. In that context, sons are preferred and the norm is for them to follow their father into positions of power and privilege; they "assume de facto power even before they earn it."[49] Benazir herself provides a clue:

> I remember [my mother] said how her own family longed for a son. When a son was born, they would cuddle him, spoil him. Now I remember that she always said how disappointed everybody else was when I was born; how she wanted a son to give her security. And now I wonder whether everybody else was disappointed, or was she perhaps disappointed? Perhaps in her own culture, a son was more important than a daughter.[50]

On the other hand, far from being disappointed, Mr. Bhutto had maintained a close relationship with his daughter throughout the highs and the lows of his life, and had taken her along on various diplomatic missions.

Second, it could be that the circumstances surrounding Mr. Bhutto's incarceration and execution had prevented him from cultivating a closer and warmer relationship with his sons. For that matter, Begum Bhutto was keenly aware of and sensitive to Murtaza's forced absence from Pakistan, which prevented him from "rightfully" assuming the leadership of the party. Begum Bhutto may have thought that it was time for Murtaza to enjoy equal opportunity to carry the mantle of leadership. Sanam Bhutto was sympathetic to her brother, but noted that his anti-state actions disqualified him for statesmanship. Najam Sethi, the editor-in-chief of the *Friday Times* weekly, sums up the family dynamics: "Benazir Bhutto is the undisputed leader of the Peoples Party ... Murtaza Bhutto doesn't stand a snowball's chance in hell of capturing his father's party" (1993).

Lastly, it could have been the result of wounded pride and an old grudge that Begum Bhutto nursed against her daughter which was exacerbated by Benazir's unwillingness to share power. Begum Nusrat Bhutto, writes Brooke Allen, was "a powerful woman in her own right and accustomed to her share of political clout," and "might have been chafing under Benazir's imperiousness for years" (2016, 119). According to Allen, days before being executed, Zulfikar Bhutto entrusted the leadership of the party to his wife – Benazir was too young then (2016, 48). Either by choice or by

---

[49] Interview with Adil Najam, October 24, 2014.
[50] Benazir Bhutto in an interview with Michael Noll in his documentary, *Benazir Bhutto: Duel In Pakistan* (2010, 46:1–24).

force of circumstances, Begum Bhutto shared the chairmanship of the party with her daughter. But by the time Benazir left Pakistan in 1984 and settled in London, she was the public face of the party. She called the shots and was considered the leader of the PPP. So long as Murtaza was out of the country, the mother would throw her support behind either her son or her daughter as the situation demanded. But the residual resentment seemed to bubble to the surface once Murtaza returned to Pakistan and tipped the balance of maternal love toward him.[51]

Whatever the reasons, the family tension came to a head when brother and sister made separate plans to commemorate their father's birthday on January 5, 1994, at the site of his grave at their ancestral home, Larkana. Murtaza was still in jail, but representing him was his mother, who was to lead a few of Murtaza's loyal "emotionally charged young men" to place a wreath at Mr. Bhutto's grave (Anwar 1997, 202). Benazir pleaded with her mother: "Mummy, why create this incident in Baba's grave. Don't do that; it is a sacred place. Why don't I go in the morning and you go in the evening . . . everybody gets to pray separately. That way there would be no incident."[52] Begum Bhutto rejected her daughter's request and in the company of her son's followers, went ahead with their plan. Not surprisingly a brawl broke out, with the police moving in to disperse Murtaza's followers. It was then that Begum Bhutto publicly denounced her daughter – "I had no idea I had nourished a viper in my breast, " (Burns 2007) – and accused Benazir of mistreating the opposition, of talking about democracy but acting like a dictator, even "worse than Zia!"

Death of a Brother

Once darkness descends and overcomes you,
you'll lose sight of his tracks again.

Shah Abdul Latif in Schimmel (1997, 147)

Murtaza was relentless in his challenges to his sister's administration.[53] He accused Benazir and her husband of embezzlement, calling Asif Zardari a thief (*chor*) and referred to her government, in which Zardari served, as "Asif Baba and the forty thieves" (Bhutto 2010, 360).[54]

---

[51] Fatima Bhutto also argues that her aunt usurped both her mother's and her brother's leadership privileges. "But as soon as Mir came back . . . Benazir ousted her mother from her honorary party post. She was terrified that her mother might try to overturn her decisions and welcome Mir into the Party" (2010, 361).

[52] Interview with Michael Noll, *Benazir Bhutto: Duel In Pakistan* (37:41–56).

[53] For a discussion on the Bhutto sibling relationship see Anna Suvorova (2015, 217–249).

[54] Fatima Bhutto notes that her father's substituting "Asif" for "Ali" – hence "Asif Baba and the forty thieves" – became "an instant hit . . . I am proud to note" (2010, 360).

Tensions were building between Zardari and Murtaza, and Begum Bhutto's belated mediation between her children in early 1996 came to naught – rumors of a near-reconciliation notwithstanding. Not long after, the family tragedy reached the point of no return: Murtaza was gunned down in front of his home just as he celebrated his forty-second birthday. What exactly happened is anybody's guess. Asif Zardari and Benazir Bhutto instantly became the prime suspects. But by all accounts Benazir was genuinely heartbroken and wept when she heard of her brother's assassination. Indeed, without exception, I was told of her grief by everyone I interviewed. Benazir blamed the ISI and its endless hatred of the Bhuttos. Fatima Bhutto and Murtaza's supporters accused Zardari of orchestrating the murder, and Fatima holds her aunt accountable for her father's death in her memoir (2010, 259–260). Raja Anwar puts the blame squarely on Murtaza himself for his arrogant behavior and for throwing his weight around with the police.[55] Anwar links the incident specifically to a confrontation between Murtaza and the police just four days before the shootout. Ambassador Shamsul Hassan recalls the tragedy:

Benazir arrived the very same night and went to the hospital. Murtaza's body had been flown to Larkana. The next day was the burial, and tempers were running high. Murtaza was surrounded by his people and they would not see Zardari. We talked to Murtaza's people. They said, Benazir could come, but Asif could not. Murtaza was hated by them [the ISI] and they thought that if they could not do anything to Benazir they must do something to Murtaza. And they knew attention would be focused on Benazir and Zardari. I had this strong suspicion that there are some elements that did not want Benazir to continue [i.e. to complete her second term]. Prime Minister Bhutto accused the ISI of having a hand in this matter, and I could see that she was right. The ISI must have collaborated with the CIA.

The objective was not to kill Murtaza, believed Shamsul Hassan, but to injure him and teach him a lesson:

Dead or injured, Murtaza would be a heavy weight on Benazir. The ISI saw Murtaza as a successor to Benazir because, if for whatever reasons Benazir was gone, he would win the election hands down against anybody. But he would be a rebellious political leader – a nuisance to the army. If he lived, he would be the worst possible enemy to Benazir Bhutto. Dead or alive they used Murtaza against Benazir.

---

[55] This was not the first time Murtaza had had "run-ins" with the Karachi police. After a few incidents in the early 1970s, his father quickly dispatched him to Harvard University in 1973 (Paracha 2017).

Prime Minister Bhutto hired "five senior Scotland Yard detectives" to go to Pakistan and investigate the murder (Shamsul Hassan).[56] Heartbroken and politically beleaguered, Benazir was vulnerable. Her mother was slowly slipping into Alzheimer's, and her husband was accused of corruption and abuse of power. It was then that Benazir's long-time friend and her own handpicked man for president, Farooq Leghari, found the moment opportune to dismiss her government, and did so in October of 1996, on charges of corruption. Leghari "fell into the hands of the establishment, and backstabbed her," Asma Jahangir said to me in Lahore:

> Let us give Leghari the benefit of the doubt and assume that he dismissed her because of some corruption. But Leghari was no less corrupt. So, corruption cannot be the cause for a person who himself indulges in corruption. He probably felt that he was an alternative leader. The establishment builds you up … What is happening in Pakistan today [2016] is a rerun of the same thing. Leghari was a feudal lord, and opposed land reform. He was able to get a judgment from the court [in his favor], saying that land reform was illegal, because his own land was reformed – and he got his land back; this is how heartless he was. Pakistan is so corrupt!

Senator Safdar Abbasi likewise told me that Leghari "wanted to be in charge and play around with the next prime minister."[57] He was not so much against Benazir because of her gender, interjected Senator Abbasi's wife Naheed Khan, but because "his ambitions prevailed. He couldn't resist wishing himself in a more powerful position." Abbasi and Khan furthermore told me of the sad irony that Benazir's chief of the army, Jahangir Karamat, had warned her about Laghari. Aitzaz Ahsan, however, believes that the main reason for Benazir's dismissal was the undue influence of her husband.

So, what became of Farooq Leghari? "He was a nobody," said Asma Jahangir. He started his own party, but "people in our country are very savvy – very savvy. All the breakaway parties – what is happening to them? Have they survived? No!" Leghari died from a longstanding heart ailment in 2010, but not before clashing with Nawaz Sharif and being forced to retire in 1997. Soon after dismissing Benazir's government, Leghari had Zardari arrested and put in jail – where he was kept for the next eight years, without charges being brought against him.

Faced with the sole responsibility of taking care of her three young children and her increasingly frail mother, Benazir relocated her family to Dubai in 1998.

---

[56] See also Heraldo Munoz for further detail (2014, 65–69).
[57] Senator Safdar Abbasi and Naheed Khan are a political couple who worked very closely with Benazir Bhutto, both when she was in and out of power. I interviewed them together in Lahore, February 2016.

Would-Be-Third-Time Prime Minister:
"Chronicle of a Death Foretold"

She who yearns for Sahar
does not look for ferry or boat.
To him who thirsts after love,
the rivers are but steps to climb.

Shah Abdul Latif in Schimmel (1997, 160)

In October 2007 Benazir Bhutto returned to Sindh, her homeland in
Pakistan, to contest the premiership for a third time. She had lived in
self-exile in Dubai for the previous eight years. As she descended the
steps of her chartered plane, she paused, looked up to the sky, breathed
the air of her home country, and raised her hands to pray – tears running
down her cheeks. She stood "on the soil of Pakistan in awe ... I was
home at long last. I knew why. I knew what I had to do" (Bhutto
2008, 1). She had finally returned, her father's words perhaps ringing
in her ear: "Remember, whatever happens to you, you will ultimately
return here. Your place is here. Your roots are here. The dust and mud
and heat of Larkana are in your bones. And it is here that you will be
buried."[58] Dressed in the green of Islam and Pakistan's flag, Benazir had
worn an armband with Ali's name inscribed on it; Ali is the Muslims'
fourth caliph and the Shi'ites' first imam –incidentally, it is also the
middle name of both her father and husband. As her motorcade moved
slowly – very slowly – toward the tomb of Pakistan's founder,
Muhammad Ali Jinnah (d. 1948), to pay her respects to the father of
the nation, a huge bomb struck Benazir's convoy, killing nearly two
hundred people, but sparing her – for the moment. She was not fazed.
After a whole night talking to her lawyers and others, early the next
morning she called on Naheed Khan to accompany her to several
hospitals to call on the injured. "That was amazing! Nothing stopped
her from reaching out to the people. People were her strength," said
Naheed. She held a press conference, journalist Munizae Jahangir told
me in Lahore, in which she said, "this was not the job of any political
party," and so "she was not going to blame the Taliban but the hand
beneath the seven veils." Years earlier, during her second term in office,
she had told Michael Noll, "I don't think any true Muslim would make
an attack on me" (2010, 49:00).

Benazir flew back to Dubai to see her children in what turned out to be
their last reunion. In the meantime, the top PPP leaders had contacted
Baitullah Mehsud, a well-known Pakistani Taliban militant, to sound his

---

[58] Zulfikar Ali Bhutto to Benazir in 1969 on the occasion of her departing for Harvard
University (Bhutto 1989, 17).

position on Benazir. "Identify your enemy," he told them pointedly. "I am not your enemy. I have nothing to do with you or against you or with the assassination attempt on you on October 18."[59] In the aftermath of her assassination, when all eyes were on Baitullah Mehsud again, he would say, "the people who killed her father and brothers are the same people who also killed her" (Asma Jahangir).

Local and international requests for greater protection for Benazir Bhutto went nowhere. As in her first return home from exile, Pakistan had once again suffered a military takeover in 1999, this time by General Pervez Musharraf. The difference between the two military dictators, as articulated by Peter Galbraith, was:

Musharraf was not a sadistic murderer; that was Zia. Zia was really a sadist and a murderer. Musharraf put on the air of an old school scotch-drinking British-Pakistani military officer, not a man who would personally dirty his hands. But I think he absolutely saw the opportunity to get rid of Benazir and took advantage of it.

But why would Benazir Bhutto return to Pakistan, knowing of the dangers awaiting her?

It was six years after 9/11 and the US "war on terror" against al-Qaeda and the Taliban had dragged on. The US invasions of Afghanistan and Iraq had left the region in tatters, and Pakistan, with her large numbers of Taliban and their sympathizers, was in a particular quandary. General Musharraf, who had ousted Nawaz Sharif,[60] the democratically elected prime minister, in a military coup in 1999, was confronted with a stark choice: either stand by the USA in its "war against terror" or continue supporting the Taliban. He chose the former, which gladdened the hearts of the American government. The general was then showered with billions of US dollars in military and economic assistance. But by 2006 Musharraf's half-hearted policies regarding the Taliban had made it evident that the Bush administration's partnership with Pakistan had paid little in the way of dividends:[61]

2007 was perhaps the worst year in Pakistan's legal and political history as the president misused his powers through a series of unlawful acts: on 9 March 2007

---

[59] Baitullah Mehsud to Senator Saleh Shah, "[S]ome enemy of Benazir was deliberately attempting to spread misinformation that he [Mehsud] wanted to kill her" (Noorani 2005). I am grateful to Munizae Jahangir for providing me with this information.

[60] The arc of history caught up with Nawaz Sharif once again: he was dismissed for alleged "corruption" form the post of prime minister for the third time in 2017.

[61] The distrust and duplicity were mutual, as Pakistan and the USA pursued their own national interests: Pakistan's intelligence agencies pragmatically preserved ties with Islamist extremists, "just as once the United States found it expedient to ally with people like bin Laden and other Jihadists against the Soviet Union" (Munoz 2014, 220).

Musharraf dismissed the chief justice of Pakistan and on 9 November 2007, he issued a decree firing over sixty judges of the superior judiciary. Musharraf then managed to get re-elected as both the chief of the army and a serving general. Lawyer protests were ruthlessly suppressed, violating the 1973 constitution. (Shafqat 2009, 93)

Musharraf was beginning to lose his allure for the West, as General Zia had done before him. Having put all its eggs in Musharraf's basket, the USA began to have second thoughts. Sadly, history sometimes does repeat itself. It was then that Benazir became once again politically visible to the West (Schofield). She had been shunned since her second ousting in 1996, and because of the pending allegations of corruption against both Benazir and her husband, she had become toxic for the governing elite in the USA and the UK. The same people who had befriended her while she was in power now actively avoided her. "They were so discourteous," recalls Shamsul Hassan. Schofield concurs:

Given all that is going on with Da'esh [ISIS], people are now thinking how extraordinary that this woman was in that society! We are now waking up to the Islamic – well, I don't like to use that word – but you know, the extremist characteristics. You know, we should have understood, how extraordinary it was that this woman is there; how good for women it is that she is there. But what did we do in the West, in the media? We started worrying about allegations of corruption! And we pulled her down, because we felt she'd become corrupt. We didn't look at what corruption means, how corruption manifests itself throughout that society, etc., etc. She had to be preserved at all costs ...

Knowing Benazir's political appeal and charisma, and feeling threatened by her politically, Musharraf had also warned American and European government officials against meeting with her. In the meantime, like Zia before him, Musharraf enhanced his power and position through consti-tutional amendments[62] – e.g. banning any two-term prime minister from running for a third term – a proposal specifically aimed at disqualifying Benazir Bhutto, but applied to Nawaz Sharif also.

In the meantime, recognizing the historical significance of the moment, and in anticipation of the upcoming election in late 2007, Benazir Bhutto and Nawaz Sharif met in London in May of 2006 and signed the "Charter for Democracy."[63] The former political rivals promised to join forces to strengthen democratic institutions and vowed to return to Pakistan – one

---

[62] Musharraf enacted the Seventeenth Amendment of the Pakistan Constitution (2003). Article 63(1)(d) allowed the president to hold on to the office of chief of army staff (https://en .wikipedia.org/wiki/Seventeenth_Amendment_to_the_Constitution_of_Pakistan).

[63] https://web.archive.org/web/20090519022229/http://www.ppp.org.pk/elections/cod .html

from Dubai and the other from Saudi Arabia[64] – to contest the election. But exactly when that would be neither leader specified. Both of them faced several court cases, and unless they could find a way to get them dismissed, they would face jail upon arrival in Pakistan.

Now there was a change of attitude in the UK. The foreign secretary Jack Straw decided to pay a visit to Benazir. Mr. Straw stressed that the UK and the USA wanted Pakistan to have a stable democracy and wished to see a more inclusive and pluralistic government, according to Shamsul Hassan. The Americans did not necessarily wish to replace Musharraf – they had invested heavily in him – but only to encourage a military-civilian power-sharing arrangement, and for that they wished to have Bhutto and her party actively involved. Strangely, however, they did not want her to return to Pakistan. They knew of her strong popular support; that if she were to return to Pakistan it would upset the general's hold on power – and the American's vested interest. "The British and the Americans love the army.[65] They trust the army. Especially the British," said Sanam:

My sister would go from pillar to post to get things done. They'd say she is mad; the army pushed her. They played a double game with her. American foreign policy is about them, not about others – from Vietnam till now, from the Korean War till now. When do they care for others? It is so hurtful – so hurtful!

Negotiations started in earnest and became particularly intense between the US Secretary of State Condoleezza Rice, Benazir Bhutto, and General Musharraf. With American support, the deal would allow Benazir to return and run for a third term and General Musharraf would remain president for another term (Bowley and Masood 2007). A meeting was arranged between Musharraf and Benazir Bhutto for July 26, 2006 while they were both in New York City – "but the negotiations didn't get anywhere" (Shamsul Hassan). Benazir then suggested a one-on-one meeting with Musharraf. A date was set for January 24, 2007, though where the two should meet became an issue. Musharraf wanted to see Benazir at the Pakistani Embassy in Abu Dhabi but she suggested her home. Finally, they met at the palace of the Amir of Abu Dhabi. Their talk lasted three hours, and later Benazir told Ambassador Shamsul Hassan that the first thing Musharraf said to her was how unpopular she was; that she had impoverished Pakistan:

She said that she got annoyed with him, but remembered that her American friends had told her not to break up the talks. She told Musharraf they should

---

[64] Nawaz Sharif was exiled to Saudi Arabia in the aftermath of Musharraf's military coup of 1999.

[65] Haqqani (2005, 311–312), likewise, faults US support for the Pakistani military because it made it difficult for a weak secular government to move away from the rhetoric of Islamist ideology.

leave it to the people to elect whom they want, and whoever gets elected the other should quit. But Musharraf said no, it is not legally possible, etc. Finally, he said, "I won't allow you to come back. I won't allow you to become prime minister for the third time." Benazir said, "My people have waited for me for a long time. Irrespective, I am coming back. And I am going to campaign for my party and we are going to contest the election." She also told him he should give up his uniform if he wanted to remain president.

The US-brokered Musharraf-Bhutto power-sharing deal had reached an impasse.[66] By September of 2007 she was refusing to meet Musharraf again – there was no point. But there was a lot of hype in Pakistan about her impending return. On October 3 she held a crucial party meeting in London to announce both the date of her return to Pakistan, and the en masse resignation of members of her party from the parliament. The night before her departure from London on October 3, Benazir's friend Lady Olga Mitland, a former Tory MP, hosted a farewell dinner party for her at the Royal Air Force Club that was attended by over 150 "leading lights," Ambassador Shamsul Hassan recalled:

I was sitting next to Benazir; my cell was switched off while the dinner was on. Usually she would receive calls from Richard Boucher and the State Department on my mobile phone. Dinner ended around 22:30 pm and we returned to the hotel where she and Asif Ali Zardari were staying. The person involved with the negotiation with Musharraf, Rahman Malik, came running to tell me, "They are trying to contact you. Condoleezza Rice wants to talk to Benazir." First we thought it was a prank call and did not get it. Three times the call came in, and finally I got it. It was the US State Department. I said, "Is this the Secretary of the State?" "Yes," she said, and then I gave Benazir the phone. They talked for about one and half hours.

One of the reasons for Condoleezza Rice's phone call was that Musharraf had become desperate when he learned of her party members' planned collective resignation. It would leave him short of the electoral college votes he needed to be re-elected as president. At the same time, Shamsul Hassan said, Benazir told Secretary Rice that she did not trust Musharraf, and that they did not agree on anything. But Rice reassured Benazir that everything would go as planned, that Musharraf would have to keep his word. Still doubtful of Musharraf's sincerity, Benazir told her, "You know, he is never going to keep his word." Condoleezza Rice said that the American Ambassador to Pakistan, Ann Paterson, was her personal friend and that Benazir should stay in touch with her, that any time she had a problem, to just let her know. Musharraf subsequently sent Benazir

[66] Benazir's attempt to reach a power-sharing deal with Musharraf upset Nawaz Sharif, who found her duplicitous in her negotiations with him. But she made amends later (interview with Asma Jahangir, Lahore, February 2016).

and her party a draft of the National Reconciliation Ordinance – which granted general amnesty to politicians to return to Pakistan, that the election would be held in 2007 or 2008, and that the two-term limit would be lifted[67] – that came to be known as the Musharraf-Bhutto power-sharing deal, brokered by the USA. As for Benazir's security, Condoleezza Rice again tried to persuade her not to go back, but witnessing Benazir's determination, she said that security would be provided.[68] On October 4, 2007, Benazir publicly announced October 18 as the date of her return to Pakistan. Her enthusiastic "supporters threw flower petals and lit firecrackers, chanting: 'Long Live Benazir! Prime Minister Benazir!'" (Bowley and Masood 2007).

On the ground, events were moving fast and neither Benazir nor Musharraf truly kept their word – nor were the Americans truly honest brokers. Musharraf was not eager to have Benazir back in Pakistan, knowing of the enthusiasm she would generate and the near certainty of her electoral victory. Benazir was well aware of her position and told an interviewer, "Musharraf is scared of me because I symbolize democracy; and he is scared of the people of Pakistan." The general "was even vaguely threatening" her about what might happen to her if she were to return to Pakistan ahead of schedule. "Your security," he warned her ominously, "is based on the state of *our* relationship" (Munoz in Allen 2016, 139); he would "protect" her, said a former Pakistan ambassador to the US, only if she were "nice" to him (cited in Munoz 2014, 184). According to Peter Galbraith, Musharraf "had given pretty explicit threats: 'if you return you'll be killed, unless you honor this deal that allows me to stay the president.'" Allen chides the US government for being "penny-wise, pound foolish," and not protecting the security of its "investment." Instead, it recommended Blackwater to take over her security (2016, 139). But Benazir refused the appointment.[69] Sanam was angry:

You send her to pave the way for your benefit, and this is how you treat her? A friend of ours went to the American embassy, saying "Protect her, protect her." But Musharraf said, "No, she doesn't have the status; she doesn't have this, she doesn't have that." Shocking, no? But you know, once it is over, it is over. Once you are dead, you are dead!

Shamsul Hassan, at the same time, marveled at how stoic Benazir was, and how she was able to read his mood; he was peeved at not being asked

---

[67] This ban was legally removed in 2010 under the Eighteenth Amendment of the Constitution.

[68] According to Munoz, "Benazir's security was a sort of addendum to the larger agreement that was never negotiated" (2014, 184).

[69] Fatima Bhutto claims that it was Benazir who tried to hire Blackwater for her security but that they declined (2010, 258).

to accompany her on her chartered flight to Pakistan. The reason, Benazir told him, was because "something horrible" was going to happen to her. Why then risk it and go, asked Shamsul Hassan. "Tell me," said Benazir rather philosophically. "Which death is better: death for a cause or under a bus?"

She had chosen the style of her own death; her death was foretold.

Benazir Bhutto was returning home, and nothing could stop her; she had already embarked on her journey home to her beloved Pakistan. She was willing to risk death for unification with her people. Every bit a Sindhi heroine, like her legendary folk sisters Sassi and Sohni, Benazir was willing to brave the hardship of hot deserts, the towering mountains, and the rushing waters of the rivers to reach home. She knew of the dangers that lay ahead. In a sense, she "had died before she died," as a Sufi motto would have it.[70] Both Asma Jahangir and Durre Ahmed told me of the foreboding feelings they had when they heard of Benazir's plan to return to Pakistan.

Back in Pakistan, Benazir campaigned enthusiastically in all four provinces. She galvanized PPP supporters and followers, and in speech after speech she demonstrated her courage. She launched "a frontal attack on religious extremists and terrorists. She emerged as the only Pakistani leader willing to take on the terrorists, and she forcefully argued that democracy was the only alternative to an authoritarian military dictatorship. At the time of her death, she was the most popular, credible and legitimate political leader in recent history" (Shafqat 2009, 94; Bhutto 2008; personal interview with Rumi 2018). "Listen to her speeches given during that time," said Victoria Schofield:

They all rested with the individual; the idea that you could make a difference, that there should be a national reconciliation, and a genuine determination to fight extremism. It goes back to Thomas Carlyle and his idea of history and a few good men.[71] These ideas mirrored in a way the conversations she had with her father in jail. All these years later, very few people in that period had her charisma. People were looking to her as the leader. What she got from attending the National Prayer Breakfast[72] was regaining her sense of self-worth, which had been taken away from her, particularly after the death of her brother. They gave her the strength to

---

[70] "[T]hey who die before they die do not die when they die." Schimmel (1997, 152).

[71] In his famous essays *On Heroes, Hero-Worship, and The Heroic in History*, Carlyle (d. 1881) explains that "the key role in history lies in the actions of the 'Great Man', claiming that 'History is nothing but the biography of the Great Man'" (https://en.wikipedia.org/wiki/Thomas_Carlyle; also http://history.furman.edu/benson/fywbio/carlyle_great_man.html). If only he had known about Benazir Bhutto and other "Great Women" of history, whose biographies are gendering history.

[72] A yearly event held in Washington, DC, on the first Thursday of February; Benazir Bhutto attended several.

believe that "I can go back and I can make a difference." This was the philosophy she had in her head when she went back to Pakistan in 2007. In some of my last conversations with her, when she talked about going back, it was that she wanted to leave a legacy. The fifty-four-year-old woman was totally different from the thirty-five-year-old woman.

Benazir's enthusiasm to be with the people and her rousing speeches were reaching a crescendo. She was tireless in reaching out to, and spending time among, the masses. In her white *dupatta* and green *kurta*, she could be symbolizing Fatima, Zainab, or Aisha – quintessential Muslim women leaders. But she also resembled millions of ordinary Pakistani women; she was one of them, and they saw themselves in her. "People felt secure with her," said Asma Jahangir. "They identified with her. She awakened them. She came to symbolize the have-nots and the oppressed." She was a role model *par excellence*: "Even the color of women's dresses changed when she came to power; their veils became brighter! She signified freedom," and hope.

On her white land cruiser, waving at the enthusiastic crowd and her jubilant supporters, Benazir basked in the euphoria of the reunion.[73] She was home at last, among her adoring supporters. Then a shot rang out. She slumped and fell down – never to rise again. She was gone. Pakistan cried:

There was not a single dry eye that day; from the richest to the poorest in a country of 130 million – well, maybe with the exception of a very few. The whole country was shut down. There was a realization that we did not do her justice – the way they [the army] humiliated her, the way she was badgered, the way corruption was made a symbol of her life values – all were wrong. This country is very corrupt.[74]

It was an even bigger tragedy, according to Schofield, "Because she was poised with that strength [of leadership]. Her stature, her composure, and the way she bore herself." She was "a seasoned politician in her fifties, and that was taken away. Not that anybody who took her away recognized that."

Why was Benazir Bhutto murdered? Who would have benefited from her demise?

The high expectations raised by the American-brokered power-sharing deal was doomed from the beginning. Benazir's alliance with Nawaz Sharif, also an old nemesis of Musharraf, threatened the general even

---

[73] Disbelieving Benazir's sincerity, Allen describes the "dangling Koran overhead," and Wilkinson writes sarcastically of the "Third coming of Pakistan's empress . . . on a truck bedecked like a large howdah on a medieval elephant of war" (Allen 2016, 141, fn. 8).

[74] Interview, Asma Jahangir in Lahore, February 2016.

more. Did the general-president wish loudly that someone "would get him rid of this troublesome woman?" Did the Taliban have a hand in her assassination? (Bennett Jones 2017). Asma Jahangir and her daughter Munizae – and many others – hold the state and General Musharraf squarely responsible for Benazir's assassination – he had a lot more to gain by her death. Asma did not discount the idea that the purported Taliban leaders, such as Baitullah Mehsud, may have also wished for her demise.[75] But she was convinced of the state's role in her murder. We may never know who assassinated Benazir Bhutto. But why she was killed is ultimately as important as who killed her. It is no mystery why General Musharraf wanted her dead and why he failed to provide adequate security for her. Pushing for a UN investigation committee, Galbraith believed that Musharraf felt that "Benazir had dissed him," dishonored him. "He wanted Benazir dead, but I don't believe he plotted her murder. I believe Musharraf and the ISI knew that there would be an assassination attempt and allowed it to happen." Akbar Ahmad, too, believes that "Musharraf may have wanted it, but lower ranking military officials had greater sympathy with the Taliban" (2008, 4–5). By eliminating Benazir Bhutto, one of the most popular leaders Pakistan had seen in its short but troubled history, the establishment effectively killed two birds with one stone: the general got rid of his most troublesome rival and the democratic alliance between Benazir and Sharif – which could have had the potential to pull Pakistani society out of her perennial political turmoil – another serious threat to the general(s), was effectively demolished. Heraldo Munoz, the UN Commissioner appointed to investigate Benazir Bhutto's murder, stressed that

Musharraf certainly bears political and moral responsibility in the assassination, as he did not provide the security that Benazir had so urgently requested and was entitled to receive as a former prime minister, especially considering that she had been the target of a failed assassination attempt in Karachi on the eve of her homecoming on October 18. (2014, 182)

As a matter of fact, Munoz states that just four days after the October 18 bomb blast, an Interior Ministry letter had instructed "all provincial governments to provide stringent VVIP-level security" for former prime ministers but pointedly did not include Benazir Bhutto's name. Munoz finds this "discriminatory and inexcusable" (2014, 183). Asma Jahangir believes that the "Establishment, the deep state and whomever the deep state controlled wanted her dead. They had infiltrated her party; even

---

[75] The Chief of Army Staff, General Ashfaq Parvez Kayani, however, doubted that the Taliban killed Benazir (Dawn 2013). On the other hand, he did not rule out the ISI – or some rogue members of the agency.

now her party is infiltrated." Marvi Sirmed agrees: "All through her life she struggled against the hegemony of the oppressive deep state that used every jape that they could, and against right-wing rhetoric that was nauseatingly misogynist and anti-people" (2011). But who are the "Establishment" and the "deep state?" This is the mystery that finally led Heraldo Munoz to fall back on fiction, the Spanish play *Fuente Ovejuna*, to provide potential clues to the reasons for Benazir's tragic murder. He concluded his investigative reports by stating that the whole "village" might be complicit in her murder:

Al-Qaida gave the order, the Pakistani Taliban executed the attack, possibly backed or at least encouraged by elements of the Establishment; the Musharraf government facilitated the crime by not providing her with adequate security; local senior policemen attempted a cover-up; Benazir's lead security team failed to properly safeguard her; and most Pakistani political actors would rather turn the page than continue investigating who was behind her assassination.[76] (2014, 185)

But finding the "village" as a whole responsible for Benazir's murder does injustice to the people – millions of "villagers" loved her and deeply mourned her violent end, then and today. They had no reason to want her dead. Did the top echelons of the "village," her political opponents, want her dead? We may never know for sure, but clearly many benefited from her demise.

Some Reflections: "Seeking the Beloved"

Love is a fire set by God. (a Sufi saying)

The daughter of a powerful feudal dynasty from Sindh, Benazir Bhutto was thrust onto the Pakistan's political landscape by the draw of destiny; she became a force of nature and has left an indelible mark on Pakistani political culture and structure. She succeeded her slain father to the high office of Prime Minister of Pakistan and set out to revive his legacy and to establish one of her own. Neither father nor daughter is politically blameless, and both provoke intense and conflicting reactions from the public. Many Pakistanis, particularly educated men – and some women – are quick to point out that she got where she did because she was her father's daughter. As with other women rulers, Benazir's persona and her position are primarily evaluated through a gendered lens; her failings are attributed to her gender – "she couldn't even get the Hudood ordinance thrown

---

[76] See Munoz's reflections on the conflicting reactions to his report by the male political elite and the military in Pakistan (2014, 187–203). It reads like theater of the absurd.

out" – and her achievements to her dynastic ties. Although her pedigree helped, Benazir Bhutto contested the elections in a highly patriarchal and conservative society and won twice, despite the powerful military/*mulla* alliance against her. And while she paid tribute to the legacy of her father, Benazir Bhutto shifted his policies and rhetoric in quiet but important ways. Indeed, she reshaped them, says journalist Raza Rumi.[77] Where the father was a bully and a tyrant – notwithstanding his populist discourse – the daughter managed to change the political worldview of her party. Where Mr. Bhutto was a hyper-nationalist, a hypermasculine revolutionary, Benazir feminized domestic and foreign policy. She shifted the national narrative from socialist rhetoric to democratic discourse – peace with India and broader trade relations (Galbraith; Rumi). She was adamant in her efforts to institutionalize democratic changes in Pakistan and paid with her life.

A daughter of Sindh, Benazir Bhutto finds her spiritual parallels in her legendary sister-seekers Sassi, "who died on the path," and Sohni, "who died by drowning" (Schimmel 1997, 140); all three anticipated their own demise and found their union in death. She knew she was going to die, according to her sister Sanam. "She said goodbye to everybody – heart-breaking!" After eight years of living in exile, Benazir's first and last wish was to return home to her beloved Pakistan, and to unite with her people, her source of power and support. She knew of the dangers that lay ahead, of "the beasts" that would face this "unarmed girl," to paraphrase Pakistani poet Habib Jalib, quoted above. And yet she proceeded. Her fearlessness and determination to return to Pakistan and stand for election were not born purely of political ambition, though some may argue just that. Her cause was also, I believe, imbued with a sense of destiny and steeped in South Asian mysticism. Her prayer of gratitude as she descended the steps of her plane to set foot on the soil of her homeland in October 2007 was not merely a seasoned politician performing for the crowd, as Allen and Wilkinson would have it. It was, I believe, an expression of her genuine trust in God (*tavakkul*) and of thanksgiving for finally arriving home. Her long self-imposed exile helped cleanse her soul and gave her time and space to contemplate, to gain insight and wisdom. With her husband in jail, her mother slipping deeper and deeper into memory loss, and her children needing her care, she had time to reflect on her "self" and to re-evaluate her personal and political priorities. The last trial was to return home, to her "beloved," and leave her faith in God's hands. In Maulana Rumi's mystical language, she was no longer an inexperienced, "raw" (*kham*) leader but one transformed into one with

---

[77] Personal communication, Boston, February 4, 2018.

experience, "cooked." The famed eighteenth-century Sindhi mystic poet, Shah Abdul Latif (d. 1752), echoes Rumi, "The fire called 'separation' cooks the raw one / and frees him from all hypocrisy" (in Schimmel 1997, 150). Politically, Benazir had become a far more formidable adversary, and that's what threatened General Musharraf and her political opponents most seriously.

The political atmosphere in Pakistan continues to be precarious, and so to render any definite view on Benazir's political legacy would be unwise. However, ten years after her assassination, her lifelong mission to foster democracy in Pakistan has nearly become ingrained in the fabric of Pakistani political structure, despite the powerful counter-currents of religious extremism and military interference. As the first woman prime minister of a Muslim-majority country, Benazir Bhutto put Pakistan on the map, allowing the land and its people to be seen in a more positive light. The issue of female leadership, however, is not unusual in Pakistan; it is paradoxical. Fatima Jinnah, sister of Pakistan's founder Mohammad Ali Jinnah, ran for president against the military dictatorship of Ayub Khan (1958–1969) and she had the full backing of the JI, Pakistan's largest and most powerful religious party. But Fatima Jinnah lost. As history is written by the [male] victors, not much is said about her; she did not have the stature of Aisha, the beloved of Muhammad, to galvanize opposition to – or support for – women and political leadership. Benazir Bhutto, on the other hand, won her election – and not just once, but twice; and she was poised to win the election for a third time. She had created huge excitement as well as deep anxieties with the promise of her return. Less than three months after Benazir's assassination, Fahmida Mirza was elected the first woman speaker of Pakistan's National Assembly (2008–2013) – almost at the same time Nancy Pelosi became Speaker of the House of the Congress of the United States of America. Nawaz Sharif's daughter, Maryam, is widely expected to follow in her father's footsteps, and the media never fail to draw a parallelism between them and Benazir and her father.[78] The general consensus in Pakistan presently converges on the legitimacy and objectives of democracy, the political system Benazir Bhutto had hoped to cultivate in her country – no matter how far off its realization on the ground may be.

Young, beautiful, and charismatic, Benazir ignited a political romance with millions of people from all strata of her society, but particularly with women, the dispossessed, and the have-nots. She celebrated her marriage among the poor in Lyari, an impoverished neighborhood of Karachi, and

---

[78] Although charges of corruption and possible jail sentences are hanging over Nawaz Sharif's head, no one can be sure how the fate of father and daughter may evolve.

gave birth to her son, Bilawal, in a hospital in the same neighborhood. She was their goddess, their Bari Ammi Jan, sister, and "lover," all folded together and then some. She shares the distinction of being the head of a Muslim nation not only with several other contemporary women rulers from South Asia – including Indira Gandhi of India, Khalida Zia and Sheikh Hasina of Bangladesh, Bandaranaike (mother and daughter) of Sri Lanka – but she also shares the spotlight with the likes of Razia Sultan from thirteenth-century India (see Chapter 4) and the Begums of Bhopal, the four generations who ruled Bhopal from 1819 to 1926, mother to daughter (Khan 2000). Benazir's popularity and the ease with which she connected with people, as well as the public's unabashed adulation wherever she went, were unparalleled in her society – and remain so. It provoked the resentment of the powerful, the male elite, the Establishment. The USA's and the UK's half-hearted support of Benazir during her third run for the premiership and their push for a power-sharing government added to this anger. Musharraf did not mince his words, or hide his envy: "It appears in the West that if a person speaks good English, it is very good. A person who doesn't know good English is quite unpopular in the West. And if he or she happens to be good-looking, then it's better" (quoted in Munoz 2014, 182).

That Benazir was a woman and beautiful added to her charismatic authority and further intensified male political rivalries. She had become a popular icon and inordinately influential with the public. As she herself said, "I am a threat to dictatorship. I am a threat to the extremists." From the moment she was first elected to the highest office in Pakistan, the Establishment found it challenging to take orders from a civilian government, much less from a young woman. Her election upended Pakistani patriarchal power and privilege, age and gender hierarchies. The only way to stop her, it seemed to her political rivals, was to disable her physically – to eliminate her, not through the ballot box and fair competition but through intimidation and violence. It had become increasingly clear to the political elite that if elections were held fairly and freely, Benazir Bhutto would likely win.[79] While male political leaders saw her as a formidable female competitor, the people saw her as a charismatic leader with "specific gifts of the body and spirit," in a Weberian sense – her gender intensifying their sense of attachment and surrender. She was also – and continues to be – an inspirational role model for millions of Pakistani women. Benazir Bhutto was murdered not so much because she

---

[79] On the backroom dealings and money spent to defeat Benazir Bhutto time and again, see Nasir (2015).

was a woman politician; there are in fact quite a few of them in Pakistan. Nor because the JI brought a suit against her based on the Prophetic hadith that allegedly warns against women's political leadership. The suit was thrown out by the Lahore High Court for what it was: a politically motivated attack with little support from the public or grounding in religion and piety. Who killed Benazir Bhutto is still a mystery, but by all indications she was assassinated because she had become a *powerful woman*, a formidable and popular political leader without parallel. It was this serious challenge to the "establishment," the male elite, and its traditional monopoly of power and privilege that had to be met at all costs; even at the cost of annihilating her. Religion was used to give a thin veneer of justification. As she crossed the dangerously rapid waters of politics in Pakistan, Benazir Bhutto knowingly risked her life to unite with the people. But her legend lives on in the cultural memory of Pakistan – and not just politically.

> In Sohni's experience
> black is the night and unbaked the jug,
> and no raft made of goatskin;
> and all for the sake of her Beloved
> no leisure and no rest.
> To Love the river seemed
> a dry and level road.   Shah Abdul Latif in Schimmel (1997, 165)

6 Megawati Sukarnoputri: "Limbuk Becomes Queen"

> Limbuk, as a representative of the younger generation, is now appearing outside the bounds of the palace and has a new freedom. This is perhaps in keeping with the age of *reformasi*, as many societal values are under review.
>
> Pausacker (2002, 293)

On Monday July 23, 2001, Megawati Sukarnoputri was sworn in as the fifth president of Indonesia, following the impeachment and removal of President Abdurrahman Wahid. She was elected president by the People's Consultative Assembly (MPR), the highest state institution that until 2004 would elect the president and vice president of Indonesia.[1] Less than two years earlier, the same statewide organization had rejected Megawati's bid for president in favor of Mr. Wahid even though her party, the Indonesian Democratic Party of Struggle (PDI-P), had won the highest percentage of votes and garnered the largest number of seats in the parliament, while that of Abdurrahman Wahid had won barely a third as many and was lagging behind Golkar, the former president Suharto's party of the New Order.[2] At the time, Megawati was rejected for the office of president primarily because she was a woman. At issue was consideration of the application of the purported Prophetic hadith, "Never will succeed such a nation as makes a woman their ruler." That Megawati was a woman about to clinch the presidency of the largest Muslim country had discombobulated not just some religious party leaders, who hastily invoked the hadith, but also threatened the prerogatives of the male political elite, men such as Amien Rais[3] and

---

[1] In 2004, president and vice president were elected directly for the first time on the basis of one person, one vote, and limited to two consecutive five-year terms. The law obliged presidential and vice presidential candidates to be elected as a pair (Dagg 2007, 51).

[2] The origin of the New Order is traced to the power struggle between President Sukarno and General Suharto. In March 11, 1966, a politically weakened Sukarno was pressured to transfer power to General Suharto, who a year later ousted Sukarno and was declared the new president (McIntyre 2005, 93).

[3] Amien Rais is a Ph.D. scholar, a political leader of the Democratic Mandate Party (PAN), and head of Muhammadiyah, one of the largest modernist and reformist religious organizations in Indonesia. He became one of Megawati's main opponents. See Dennett (2010, 185); Hefner (2000).

Abdulrahman Wahid,[4] who until then were known for their balanced views on gender equality and commitment to democratic reform. Finding the moment opportune, the reformist male political elite hastily joined forces and threw their support behind Mr. Wahid, who emerged as the MPR's compromised candidate. Faced with widespread protests and the threat of rioting by Megawati's disappointed supporters, Megawati was voted in as Mr. Wahid's vice president.

Who is Megawati Sukarnoputri and how did she become president of Indonesia in the face of opposition from a spectrum of religious and political elite figures who had rejected her for the same position first time around?

I started this book by juxtaposing revelation and tradition as reflected in the Quranic story of the Queen of Sheba's sovereignty and the alleged Prophetic hadith against women's political authority, following ʿAʾisha's leadership in the Battle of the Camel. My discussion of the ongoing battles for succession and the challenges of women's authority and sovereignty is brought full circle with the fierce political opposition to Megawati's candidacy for president. Interestingly, however, the whole contentious debate fizzled out when Megawati actually became president two years later. What happened? In this chapter I discuss the intense political rivalry over the presidency following Suharto's fall, and the appeal to the Prophetic hadith to disqualify Megawati for president. Ultimately, it becomes clear that it was not so much genuine religious conviction that sought to block women's political advancement, but the intense anxiety of the male elite who realized their political dominance was in serious jeopardy.

Situating Megawati Sukarnoputri: Family Background

A child of postcolonial Indonesia, Megawati was born on January 23, 1947. She was the eldest daughter of Sukarno (also spelled "Soekarno," 1901–1970), Indonesia's national hero and first president, and Fatmawati (1923–1980) his third wife (or second, according to McIntyre, 2005). The name Megawati is derived from the Sanskrit *meghavatī*, meaning "she who has a cloud," as in a rain cloud. She was

---

[4] Abdurrahman Wahid was the grandson of the founder of Nahdlatul Ulama (NU), one of the largest Islamic organizations in Indonesia, and served as its national chair for almost fifteen years. As a scholar, teacher, and enlightened politician, Wahid is seen as a saint (*wali*) by millions of Indonesians, and was popularly known as Gus Dur (Bennett 2010, 184). Wahid was the chairman of the National Awakening Party (PKB). See Fic (2003); Hefner (2000, 167–169); McIntyre (2005, 157).

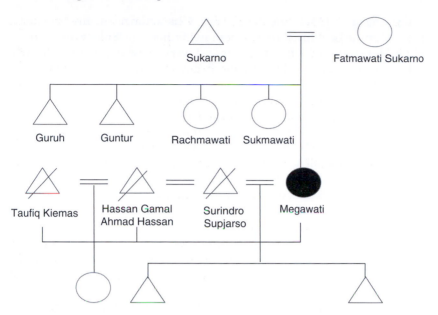

Figure 6.1 Megawati Sukarnoputri's Genealogy

so named because it was raining when she was born (Figure 6.1).[5] Both of her parents claimed a distinguished and aristocratic heritage; her father was the son of a Javanese patrician father and a Balinese Brahman mother, and her mother, Fatmawati, was a descendent of the Sultanate of Inderapura.[6] As the leader of the anti-colonial and nationalist movement, Sukarno led the resistance against the Dutch, for which he was detained and jailed. Sukarno was a charismatic politician and a prolific polygamist – he married nine wives officially. Fatmawati married him in 1943, and with him she had five children. Offended by Sukarno's zest for multiple marriages, she refused to be a senior co-wife to Sukarno's fourth wife, Hartini, and left the palace in 1954, shortly after the birth of their last child Guruh. Fatmawati died of a heart attack in 1980 in Malaysia. Their eldest son, Guntur (b. 1945), whose name means "thunder," was unhappy about his father's remarriage and left his palace with his mother. The other children continued to live with their father. As the eldest daughter, Megawati seems to have developed the "motherly qualities" that she is known to have exhibited

---

[5] www.newworldencyclopedia.org/p/index.php?title=Megawati_Sukarnoputri&oldid=999830.
[6] https://wikivividly.com/wiki/Fatmawati#cite_ref-4.

as a young child (McIntyre 2005, 143). Characterized as his "mother's son," Guntur kept his distance from his father – to Sukarno's regret – while Megawati had a much closer and warmer relationship with their father (Bennet 2010, 180; McIntyre 2005). Sukarno reportedly discussed more serious matters with Megawati and Guntur, as "he thought they were old enough to understand." Like Zulfikar Ali Bhutto of Pakistan, Sukarno brought his daughter along on overseas trips, including one to "the Nonaligned Movement in Belgrade" (McCarthy 1999). Later in her life, when in 1967 the little-known general Suharto (also spelled "Soeharto") removed her father from power and placed him under house arrest, Megawati left college to stay by her father's side until his death in 1970. Sukarno was not given a proper state funeral and his will was ignored by Suharto, who had installed himself as president. He was buried in Blitar, next to his mother's grave (Ariyanto 2015). The emotional suffering of the last three years of Sukarno's life and that of his children are vividly described by Megawati's younger sister, Rachmawati, in her memoir (McIntyre 2005).

Megawati married three times, first to Lieutenant Surindo Supjarso in 1968. Their marriage ended in tragedy when the lieutenant died in a plane crash in 1970; his body was never found. Megawati was pregnant with their second son at the time of her husband's death. In 1972, she became infatuated with Hassan Gamal Ahmad Hassan, an Egyptian diplomat, and eloped with him, much to her family's chagrin. The marriage, however, did not last long. Megawati was obliged by her family to dissolve her marriage two weeks later at the Islamic Court of Jakarta. The annulment relied on her family's reasoning that the death of Megawati's first husband was not yet determined, even though more than a year had passed since his disappearance. Despite the tragedy of her first marriage and the trauma of the second, McIntyre notes, Megawati remained characteristically stoic and betrayed no emotions (2005, 147–148; see also Bennet 2010, 181). Silence in the face of personal distress and political crisis became her trademark. She married Taufiq Kiemas, her third husband, in 1973, with whom she has a daughter. Taufiq died in 2013.

Megawati was born in Yogyakarta in postcolonial Indonesia and grew up in the religiously syncretic island of Java. Her personality and sensibilities were by and large formed within her father's polygynous palace, and her worldview was influenced by Indonesia's precarious political structure and its religiously diverse and mythologically rich cultural environment. Megawati and her siblings lived "dangerously" through the period in which their father was removed from power and they were unceremoniously forced to leave the president's palace in 1967. She witnessed her once-charismatic and articulate father rapidly declining, sinking into silence, and ultimately disappearing into the eternal stillness of death. As Megawati left the domestic domain in the mid-1980s and shed her stereotyped image of "housewife" to become an active political member of her father's party, her aloofness in public became a topic of baffled fascination, mainly for the male political elite and media pundits. Was her much-noted "silence" a legacy of the memory of her father's suffering and his ultimate silence in death that was indelibly etched in her mind? Or was it an effective political stratagem to stay safe while conveying a deafening protest in the face of Suharto's stifling policies? Was it calculated and strategic, or was it rooted in the Javanese syncretic *abangan* and mystical traditions?[7] Whatever it was, her quiet leadership resonated loudly with the public. They appreciated her carefully choreographed politicking and saw her suffering and her family's forced political isolation as reflective of "their own long isolation" (Hefner 2000, 175). She was, after all, Sukarno's daughter and a legitimate defender of his legacy and charisma. True to a Weberian model of charismatic authority, Megawati emerged as a leader at a time when Indonesian society was in the grip of both social and political crises. As the daughter of a former savior and charismatic leader of Indonesia, Megawati was "perceived to have a direct connection with supernatural or sacred power." She seemed to possess the ability to articulate "a new vision" for a new movement (Weber in Keyes 2002, 248–249).

Megawati entered politics at a pivotal moment in Indonesian history. It coincided with the last decade of Suharto's increasingly oppressive regime and his desperate attempt to hang onto presidential power by all means necessary. Fearing a rapid loss of his popularity, Suharto made political alliances with some hardline Islamist parties to further fortify his power base – similar to actions taken by General Zia-ul-Haq in Pakistan in the aftermath of his military coup against President Bhutto, Benazir Bhutto's father (see Chapter 5). The enthusiasm generated by Megawati's appearance on the political scene in Indonesia almost coincided with that of the political rise and fall of Benazir Bhutto in Pakistan. Megawati's quick rise to power inspired new productions of shadow plays with plot lines that improvised on the mythical character of Limbuk (discussed below), reflecting the changing role and status of Megawati and, by extension, that of Indonesian women.

---

[7] The term *abangan*, meaning a nominal or syncretic Javanese Muslim, was introduced to scholarship by Clifford Geertz in his influential book, *The Religion of Java* (1964). For a critique of Geertz's use of *abangan*, see Ricklefs (2006).

Indonesia is one of the most intriguing, complicated, and complex societies, where different religions, cultures, ethnicities, languages, beliefs, and practices have historically converged. Consisting of several thousand islands, Indonesia is a crossroads of indigenous animism, Hinduism, Buddhism, Christianity, and Islam, enmeshed with some modern philosophies and political ideologies. Indonesia also lies at the juncture of many cultures' trading relationships, material exchanges, cultural dialogues, and aesthetic expressions. It was within this culturally syncretic and religiously pluralistic society – particularly that of the dominant culture of Java – that the artistic tradition of shadow play, *wayang*, found its distinct characteristics (Anderson 2009; Pausaker 2004).[8] The *dalang*s, the puppeteers/storytellers, have historically shown sensitivity to sociocultural change and political transformations. The significance of *wayang*s as venues for social and political communications and education are brought out by Haryoguritno (2002). Describing the evolution of *wayang*s from pre-Hindu to the Hindu, to Majapahit Empire, and lastly to Islam in Indonesia, he writes, "Islam used *wayang* as a means of proselytizing, and *wayang* acquired new spiritual values and culture from Islam" (2002, 363). Under Sukarno and Suharto, *wayang* evolved further to reflect the changing sociopolitical dynamics of the time. Haryoguritno stresses, "If we consider that wayang ... is the result of a type of concoction that consists of ingredients, including animism, mythology, legends, history, imagination, aspiration, impression, and cultural expression, it is unlikely that wayang will gradually disappear" (2002, 363). Shadow plays have, for example, creatively reflected the rise and fall of Suharto's authoritarian regime and his attempt to forge an ever-closer alliance with certain Islamist parties toward the end of his regime. The "production of meaning in wayang," writes Weintraub, "through language, discourse, and music – is intersected by social struggle over power and authority" (2004, 233). Reflecting the ongoing power plays, Weintraub further notes, *wayang*s "force us to reconcile the seemingly contradictory themes and tensions ... of popular entertainment (often understood as the 'only' escape and hence not to be taken seriously) and state politics (often understood as a privileged form of power and hence to be taken very seriously)" (2004, 233). There are different genres in *wayang*, but the strict gender hierarchy once present in almost all of them is now changing. One of the minor characters in the universe of *wayang* mythology is Limbuk.

---

[8] *Wayang*s were often performed at private parties or in public on various governmental occasions (Pausacker 2004).

Limbuk was a palace servant who traditionally lived in the innermost section of the court (*kadhatona*) where women lived in the royal palace. Traditionally, Limbuk was a minor presence and did not speak much, given her lowly status. Nor did she have a significant role to play in the male-dominated *wayang*s (Pausacker 2002, 268); she was just there; cloistered, voiceless, and invisible. Not surprisingly, female mythical characters such as Limbuk were less prominent in the many variations of the myths that were written or performed, nor were they creatively appropriated to critically represent political elites – whether negatively, positively, or ambivalently – as agents of social change. As Megawati gained greater political visibility, Limbuk began to move out of the inner recesses of the royal court to play bigger, more vocal, and less frivolous roles.[9] Limbuk represents the voice and visibility, recognition and acknowledgment of women's changing status in the Indonesian political landscape. Limbuk's symbolic change of status represents for Indonesians a glimpse of their own long-suppressed citizenship and political agency; the clown-servant becomes queen – in control and in charge of her own political destiny. With the rise of Megawati to the vice presidency and eventually to the presidency, a few *dalang*s seized the moment to retrieve Limbuk to give voice to aspects of Megawati's character, personality, and political activities. Pausacker (2004, 231–232) makes a brief reference to one Hersri Setiawan,[10] who, upon the elevation of Megawati to the presidency, wrote the play *Limbuk Becomes Queen*.[11] Not having been able to get hold of this *wayang*, hard as I tried, I wonder whether Hersri Setiawan intended it to be a positive social commentary, or sarcastic, ironic, or humorous – or all of the above – regarding Megawati's rapid rise to presidency. Regardless of his intention, I find Pausacker's reference to Limbuk's "breaking out" and the parallelism between the mythical and historical women reflective of social and political changes in gender politics in Indonesia.

Megawati and Limbuk as women could no longer be ignored either in the political life of Indonesia or in the much-loved and frequently performed shadow plays. I see Limbuk's crossing of the threshold of the restrictive palace and into the limelight of the palace courtyard as a rite of passage, symbolic of the changing women's roles and gender politics in

---

[9] My discussion of the mythical character of Limbuk is informed by Pausacker (2002, 2004) and Anderson (2009).

[10] Hersri Setiawan is a writer and former political prisoner who was sent into exile on Buru Island, Maluku, in the late 1960s. See Krismantari (2016).

[11] Other *dalang*s also produced *wayang*s depicting Abdulrahman Wahid's political decline and Megawati's rise. One was produced right after Wahid's impeachment, called *Arimbi Becomes Queen*, in which the links between *wayang* characters and political figures, says Weintraub, were hard to miss (2004, 219).

Indonesia. The transition also represents more than a symbolic performance of Megawati's political action (i.e. transitioning from being a "housewife" to becoming a President of Indonesia – one of the most visible positions in society). It also represents the active and impressive role that Indonesian women – and ordinary people – have played in supporting Megawati and thus making this transition possible. In that, the leader and her followers have helped move their society from an autocratic system, a one-person show, to a more open and democratic one. Limbuk is no longer a voiceless character whose occasional presence in public would be considered out of place and farcical, scorned and ridiculed, as it once was. I am told that some Indonesians use the clown-servant Limbuk as a way to insult or make fun of the first lady of Indonesia, a "housewife" becoming a "queen."[12] Obviously, that is not my intention here. On the contrary, it is to reappropriate a neglected feminine symbol and give it a new interpretation. It is in the lasting power of the *wayang*, this tradition-steeped institution, to be creatively mined in very many variations and from multiple perspectives (Pausacker 2004).

My objective here is to look at Megawati's presidency through the prism of the *wayang*, as a cultural phenomenon and not just a political one. I do not intend to draw a one-to-one correspondence between the realities of a fierce power struggle in the rapidly changing Indonesian political landscape and the imaginative representation of mythological stories and characters. But I found this popular means of raising public awareness regarding sociopolitical changes in Indonesia, with its possibilities of supporting or satirizing duplicitous and hypocritical politicians, an effective vehicle for producing politically informed local knowledge that is educational as well as entertaining.[13] In other words, I found the *wayang* "good to think with."

Reclaiming a Dynastic Legacy: Into the Rapid Waters of Indonesian Politics

> She was a housewife. He was a dictator. Yet Megawati Sukarnoputri was the one person in Indonesia Suharto feared.   McCarthy (1999)

After a relatively long period of political inactivity and with her children grown, in 1987 Megawati was ready to test the political waters and run for a seat in the Indonesian parliament. What had long dissuaded her and her siblings from trying their hand at politics was Suharto's authoritarian

[12] Siti Nurjanah, personal communication, Boston, April 2018.
[13] On initiatives of the New Order government to include education about birth control, family planning, and child-rearing in the 1970s through *wayang* performances, see Pausacker (2002, 287). See also Haryogurinto (2002, 362–365).

policies and the punishing political system he had engineered in
Indonesia. But what personal and sociopolitical factors precipitated
Megawati's change of heart and her willingness to brave the rapid waters
of Indonesian politics, particularly in the heyday of Suharto's authoritarian New Order? Surprisingly, it was initially Suharto himself, who provided the impetus for Megawati to run for political office.

Whether it was political expediency to highlight his "democratic"
credentials or a genuine change of heart, in the 1980s Suharto seems to
have felt strong enough to soften his stance on his predecessor and
decided to rehabilitate the image of Sukarno. Recognizing Sukarno as
a national hero, Suharto held a public ceremony in 1986, which Megawati
attended. For the first time since he had installed himself as president of
Indonesia in 1967, he saw the possibility of allowing Sukarno's children to
participate in the election (Bennett 2010, 181):

> Which particular member of the Soekarno family was not as important as the
> opportunity to employ the family name and everything it represented, as a means
> of garnering badly-needed popular support for the party during a period when the
> Partai Persatuan Pembangunan (PPP, or United Development Party), the sole
> representative of Islamic groups in the New Order electoral system, had emerged
> as the only serious challenger to Golkar. (Ziv 2001, 77)

After two decades of Suharto's oppressive regime, many Indonesians
yearned for a democratic society, free from the tight grips of the Suharto
family's "mafia" network, which controlled much of the country's financial
and political resources.[14] Evidently, in Suharto's political calculation, getting
members of Sukarno's family involved in the Indonesian Democratic Party
(PDI) and allowing the party to display Sukarno's posters and symbolism
would do much to revitalize the moribund party politics. The PDI was
regarded as the party of the proletariat, and the prevailing sentiment was
that "there was nostalgia for a figure like Soekarno" (Wibisono 2009, 84). It
was also the product of a forced merger in 1973 of Sukarno's PNI
(Indonesian National Party) and Christian parties.[15] Moreover, it was one
of only three political parties allowed to function alongside Suharto's own
dominant New Order party, Golkar. Behind this political maneuvering lay
his attempt to achieve at least two objectives: one, to dress up his authoritarian image by touting "democratic" credentials, thus continuing to silence his
unhappy citizens; and, two, to counterbalance the growing popularity of the
United Development Party (PPP), the third party permitted to operate, by
encouraging the visibility of the more pliant Islamists in Indonesia: "The

[14] For an exposé of Suharto and his children's wealth, see Colmey and Liebhold (1999). See
also Berger (2008).
[15] For a discussion of party restructuring by Suharto, see Hefner (2000, 99–101).

divide-and-conquer strategy, long central to Soeharto's rule, had taken an ominous turn indeed" (Hefner 2000, 167).

Initially none of Sukarno's children accepted the "invitation." But by 1987, at her husband's encouragement, Megawati stood for election as one of the "opposition" candidates, and both husband and wife easily won their seats. Sukarno's children did not all respond the same way to Suharto's apparent change of heart. Of Megawati's two younger sisters, the ever-contrarian sister Rachmawati[16] was uncompromising regarding her father's legacy and did not want to give Suharto the satisfaction of thinking he had co-opted her father's children (McIntyre 2005, 231; Lanti 2002, 115), and Sukmawati refused to run for election because she found the PDI "insufficiently radical" and "too unwilling to challenge the government" (Bennett 2010, 181; Eklof 1999, 39).[17] On the other hand, Megawati took a more pragmatic approach to family loyalty and was therefore able to gain greater political grounding (McIntyre 2005, 153). Her joining the PDI was welcomed enthusiastically by her father's followers, millions of young people who looked back admiringly to their national hero, and the pro-democracy reformers who were poised to exploit all the Sukarno symbols they could. To them Megawati represented an "authentic" leader of the opposition to the Suharto regime (Ziv 2001, 76), even if Suharto initially had something to do with her running.

What Suharto and his supporters, including his own daughter, Siti Hardiyanti Rukmana (popularly known as Mbak Tutut),[18] had not anticipated, however, was the speed with which Megawati was able to capture the public's imagination and become a popular icon of the opposition. Suharto and company soon came to regret their strategy to empower the PDI. They huddled around the political drawing board to map out Megawati's defeat through expulsion from her party and the political domain. They became particularly frantic in 1993, when, despite their best efforts the PDI overwhelmingly elected her as its leader, a position she still holds as I write (2018).

Chairwoman of the Indonesian Democratic Party

> The fundamental assumption of practice theory is that culture ... constructs people as particular kinds of social actors, but social actors, through their living on the ground, variable practices, reproduce or transform ... the culture that made them.   Ortner (2006, 129)

---

[16] See *The Jakarta Post* for some charges brought against her in 2016–2017.
[17] Megawati's two younger sisters were "angry" at Guntur for not "scolding" Megawati for entering politics (Siti Nurjanah, personal communication, Boston, MA, May 27, 2018).
[18] *Mbak* is a respectful term meaning something close to "miss," or "sister."

Megawati had rapidly scaled the political hierarchy and by 1993 was cata-
pulted to political prominence. Her agreement to run for the chairmanship of
the PDI was courageous and inspiring not only for party members but also for
many of her supporters (McIntyre 2005, 156). Suddenly, Megawati was at
the center of an "hysterical campaign" during which "Hundreds of supporters lined streets outside, praying and fasting for her success, even sleeping
there" (Bennett 2010, 182). Despite the best efforts of Suharto and his
supporter to sabotage Megawati's party leadership, she was finally ratified
as the chairperson of the PDI in 1994, becoming the first woman party leader
in the history of Indonesia (Yulianti-Farid 2015, 10). But Suharto could not
live with that reality and witness the rising power of Sukarno's popular
daughter. The irony is that Suharto's daughter, Mbak Tutut, almost the
same age as Megawati, was also involved in national politics, actively coop-
erating in the schemes against Megawati. Through government engineering
and manipulation, Sukarno managed to have the PDI's National Executive
board "reshuffled" later that year and ordered the newly installed executives
"to replace Megawati's national board with people loyal to the dissident PDI
and Soeharto." The mere existence of this "rival executive" gave the government an excuse to turn around and blame Megawati for her inability to unite
the different factions of her party (Hefner 2000, 181). A "concerted campaign
of destabilization conducted by party rebels backed by the influential forces in
the government" had Megawati and her party supporters besieged, and on
the verge of disintegration (Patrick Walters in McIntyre 2005, 161).
Government-instigated attacks on Megawati and her supporters continued
throughout 1995 and into 1996. But the government's attempt to manipulate
the party election and install a pro-Suharto member as chair backfired. While
the government was able to manipulate some ambitious party leaders to run
against Megawati, ultimately it was unable to dilute the growing popular
support for their leader. She had scored a victory and her moral authority
grew in the face of the government's unscrupulous political manipulation.
Some scholars explain her popularity as a pent-up "enthusiasm for Sukarno,"
while others attribute it to her gender and the fact that like other South Asian
female leaders, such as Benazir Bhutto of Pakistan and Shaikh Hasina of
Bangladesh, she represented a "nemesis" come to avenge her father
(McIntyre 2005, 155; Bennett 2010). It is, however, also the case that
Megawati's noncombative and fresh political style, her motherly image –
the *ibu* (mother) factor – appealed to a large segment of the public, if not to
many male leaders on the political spectrum, and gave her the air of an
authentic and caring leader.

Then the unthinkable happened. In 1995 the PDI persuaded Megawati
to stand for the presidency – an unprecedented political act; no one had
dared to publicly challenge President Suharto's right to be president for

life. But by then Megawati had emerged as a serious political contender and popular rival. She did not openly accept the party's invitation, but nor did she reject it outright. She left it to the political elite and pundits to divine her intentions. And divine they did! Her silence signaled her acceptance, which infuriated Suharto. He let it be known to the party stalwarts that he wanted Megawati to disavow the idea publicly. Megawati was not intimidated; she remained impervious. She continued to play the "serious game" of political rivalry by not taking any overt action – a personal gesture that had become her political trademark. But in the face of Suharto's outright threats, intimidation, and reprisals, some party leaders caved in, and sought to persuade Megawati to change her mind. A few of Megawati's own friends, including Abdurrahman Wahid, vacillated. Wahid expressed fear that a confrontation with Suharto would be her downfall, and so advised her to quietly back out (McIntyre 2005, 163). In fact, Suharto had already reached out to Wahid and threatened to split his association, Nahdlatul Ulama (NU), by fomenting rivalry within the organization. Suharto put pressure on Wahid to force Megawati to drop out of the race. Wahid obliged. In turn, Wahid endorsed Suharto for a seventh term and courted his daughter, Mbak Tutut, who was groomed to follow her father to the presidency (McIntyre 2005, 172; Hefner 2000). Megawati's stoic and steely determination to withstand pressure gladdened the hearts of others who appreciated her challenge to the man who had ruthlessly toppled her father and brutalized the public for so long. Megawati herself was not unaware of the risks facing her. Acknowledging the fear that many shared in the wake of her audacious decision, Megawati summed up the public mood:

The feeling of fear is everywhere in the territory of the unitary state of the Republic of Indonesia, and its presence does not mature but rather stunts the autonomy of the people. We have been independent for fifty years, and have just now celebrated that anniversary with great joy. But, and I say this apologetically and with respectful feelings for this Republic, how come the feelings of its people and citizens are still blanketed in fear? Please ask yourselves, each of you, do you feel that fear? (quoted by McIntyre 2005, 164)

So much for silence!

Banishing Megawati from Party Leadership: "The Grey Day"

This is a critical situation not only for Mrs. Megawati but for Mr. Suharto. This is happening because the government thinks she is a threat. Mrs. Megawati is the first popularly elected political leader in the history of the New Order and she won't compromise.

Walters in McIntyre (2005, 165)

Megawati's determination to run for the presidency and the prospect of her winning became too much for Suharto and his supporters to tolerate. He went to "extraordinary length[s] to meet the electoral challenge posed by the PDI under Megawati's leadership" (McIntyre 2005, 162). Suharto now moved to oust Megawati, split the party, and once again play the "Islam card" (Hefner 2000). The realization had dawned on him, as it had on many others, that if a fair and democratic election were to be held, Megawati would win. And so Suharto, along with his supporters and his daughter, decided to force Megawati from the party, thus "legally" preventing her from standing. She had to be disqualified once and for all, they decided. Presumably that would stop Suharto's electoral train wreck in its tracks.

Early in 1996 Suharto ordered the press to stop using Megawati's last name, Sukarnoputri, to prevent her association with the former president (Eklof 1999, 36). Under Suharto's vast engineering machinery, some dissident PDI party members were swayed to raise objections to Megawati's leadership and demand her removal. Suharto then instructed the PDI to convene a congress in Medan (the capital of North Sumatra province) and packed it with state-supported anti-Megawati members:

> They then portrayed the consequent call for a congress as the democratic expression of opinion within the party, to which they as a government were obliged to respond – provided that the petitioners had acted in keeping with the party's constitution. Nobody was fooled by this performance, certainly not Megawati's supporters. (McIntyre 2005, 165; Hefner 2000, 181; Eklof 1999, 35–38)

As the government went on to execute its extraordinary plans to disrupt Megawati's party platform and expel her from the political domain, the public became more and more sympathetic toward her and her popular fortune rose dramatically, transforming this "modest Javanese woman" into a "hero of the pro-reform movement" (Hefner 2000, 182). Decades of political oppression and fear of Suharto's militarized regime had for the most part kept the public silent and compliant. With Megawati's rapid rise and the serious threat she posed to Suharto's regime, the long-stifled, pent-up political energy was released and millions of Indonesians, particularly the youth, saw their dreams of political agency and meaningful citizenship about to materialize; her silence and suffering gave voice and visibility to the dissident public. It was then that Suharto's regime unleashed extra-military thugs on Megawati's supporters; she had to be stopped physically.

By early June 1996, political events had taken a more ominous turn; the entire country was on edge. Megawati's supporters feared the worst and so "took up guard" at various party headquarters and displayed banners, saying, among other things, "Mega Yes, Congress No" and "I am willing to die for Mbak Megawati." Disregarding the government's order, over five thousand people marched through central Jakarta in support of Megawati's right to lead the PDI (McIntyre 2005, 165). Representatives from thirty nongovernmental organizations and other institutions issued statements, declaring their support for Megawati while condemning the government's strong-arm tactics. Not only did this not dissuade Suharto, it convinced him to forge on. Tension and antagonism between the government-supported provocateurs and Megawati's supporters showed no sign of letting up. On June 20, as the state-supported rival faction of the PDI convened in Medan, Megawati's supporters staged a rally in the streets of Jakarta. The security forces, "backed up by armored vehicles," attacked Megawati's supporters even though the demonstration had started peacefully. In the heat of the violence, one protester was killed and many others were injured. Later, at a peaceful rally, Megawati sought to calm her supporters, urging them to remain orderly. She reminded them of her father's legacy: "show that we can be as democratic as our father when he proclaimed independence" (McIntyre 2005, 166; see also Eklof 1999, 35–36).

Back in Medan, the government-orchestrated PDI faction swiftly voted to remove Megawati from her position as party chair.[19] However, this intrepid leader refused to be intimidated and rejected her ousting by the government-led "opposition" faction. Arriving at the PDI offices in the afternoon of June 23, dressed in the party's colors of black and red, Megawati addressed a crowd that overflowed from the grounds of the office and stood outside twenty deep. She said to "roars of approval":

I am the lawful, legal and constitutional chairperson of the PDI for the 1993–98 period. That which called itself a "congress" in Medan is in violation of the party's rules and the constitution ... Remember that what we are fighting for now is defending the sovereignty that is in the hands of people and to redress the democracy given to us under the 1945 constitution. (McIntyre 2005, 166; Hefner 2000, 182; Eklof 1999, 38)

The government, in the meantime, intensified its offensive to uproot Megawati and suppress her supporters. Suharto finally ordered his security forces and agents to actually take over PDI headquarters. Hefner argues that although Megawati had some support among the Marine Corps, who had kept her informed of the government's plan for a hostile takeover, ultimately she was unable to prevent government agents from forcibly seizing control of the PDI offices and driving out

---

[19] See Hefner (2000, 180–189; McIntyre 2005, part III) for details regarding the government's extraordinary effort to "demolish" Megawati.

her supporters (2000, 184). Countering the government's thuggish tactics, Megawati's supporters began an orchestrated campaign of civil disobedience and kept vigils at the PDI headquarters. Hefner describes it vividly:

> As the crowds grew larger and larger, Megawati and her supporters grew bolder. They proclaimed the grounds in front of the headquarters a free speech forum (*mimbar bebas*) open to all who wished to speak. They criticized not only Soeryadi[20] but the cronyism and violence of the Soeharto regime as a whole. Soon the forum had a momentum greater than the PDI cause itself. (2000, 184)

The entire nation was galvanized and focused on the political struggle between the forces loyal to the old regime of the New Order and the people demanding freedom, rule of law, and adherence to the 1945 constitution; the ranks of the latter grew bigger and bigger. Support for Megawati and expressions of solidarity came from all corners of the country, including the youth, the reformists, and the *abangan* secularists. A growing number of the religious elite, including Abdurrahman Wahid, voiced their support for Megawati (Hefner 2000, 184; Eklof 1999, 40). Far from remaining silent, Megawati arranged a press conference. Accompanied by Abdurrahman Wahid, who by then had abandoned his support of Suharto's daughter, Megawati declared that she could bring millions into the streets and disrupt the routine activities of the government, but that because she respected the constitution she would refrain from doing so (Eklof 1999, 37). Feeling the heat of popular anger and threatened by its rise, on July 22, 1996, the government called the free speech forum unconstitutional, claiming that it intended to overthrow the government. It proclaimed the forum's rhetoric seditious, similar to that of the outlawed Indonesian Communist Party. But the standoff continued. On July 24, Jakarta's chief of police finally banned the free speech forum, and the military threatened further action against Megawati's supporters (Eklof 1999, 41). The moment of reckoning was finally at hand. On July 27, government-supported thugs invaded the PDI headquarters at dawn and continued their attack into the wee hours of the following morning.[21] By then the military was in full control of the city (Eklof 1999, 41–44):

---

[20] Soerjadi (also spelled Soeryadi) was one of Megawati's main rivals for the chair of the PDI in 1993. He was a popular and outspoken man whose criticism of Suharto's government cost him his place in the party that year. But he was wooed back by Suharto, who found him useful for his long-term purpose of defeating Megawati and winning the upcoming presidential election (Hefner 2000, 180).

[21] Eklof (1999, 46) argues that it was initially believed that the thugs were "soldiers in mufti," but it was learned later that a number of the attackers were criminals recruited for

Thus, it was that on July 27, some of her loyalists who had taken up guard duty there, having declared their willingness to die for Mbak Megawati, proved as good as their words as they sought unsuccessfully to fend off an attack on the party building by thugs dressed as Soerjadi supporters and reinforced by police and army personnel. (McIntyre 2005, 167)

July 27, 1996 is memorialized in the annals of Indonesian politics as "The Grey Saturday." Suharto had won the battle, but the war was still ahead. Megawati managed her biggest achievement yet, helped her party survive the repression of that year, and solidified the source of her support (McCarthy 1999). She was not cowed by the forces of the dictatorship and stood up for the democratic rights of her people. This day also marked the rapid decline and fall of the Suharto regime.

By the time the violent government takeover of PDI headquarters was over, five of Megawati's supporters had been killed and 146 injured – though the Indonesian Commission on Human Rights put the number of missing and killed much higher (McIntyre 2005, 167; Eklof 1999, 44; Hefner 2000, 186–187). At a ceremony marking 100 days after the event, McIntyre reports, Megawati "wept and stopped speaking for almost three minutes" (2005, 167). But the daughter of Sukarno did not take her illegal ousting lightly. With her party solidly behind her, she resumed her struggle. She sued the government in courts all around the country and laid out the illegality and unconstitutionality of Suharto's action.[22] However, neither her supporters' continued protest nor her court appeals helped to reinstate Megawati as leader of her party in time for the May 1997 presidential election. She refused to participate in the electoral process, saying to her supporters: "What is the use of a victory if the virtues of honesty, sincerity, feeling of security, peace, and the light beaming the aspirations of the people do not shine like the morning sun over the sky of the nation" (Sumarno in Wibisono 2009, 88). What they did, however, was to thoroughly discredit Soeryadi's group – the splinter PDI backed by Suharto (Hefner 2000, 186).

Suharto's government had gone to violent lengths to ensure his presidential victory in 1998 and to reinscribe fear in his opponents to discourage them from any attempt to challenge his sovereignty. "His pride would settle for nothing less; certainly, it could not brook an electoral

---

the purpose. This, Eklof says, is a "long-standing tactic in Indonesian politics" that was particularly practiced under Suharto's New Order.

[22] Altogether, Megawati filed some 230 cases challenging her ousting from the PDI leadership, and only "seven verdicts went in her favor." But each case "gave her a political stage, and no one could stop her supporters from attending the court hearings. It was a case of 'even if I lose, I win.' She won people's hearts, if not the verdicts" (McCarthy 1999).

contest with the daughter of the man he had deposed in 1966–1967" (McIntyre 2005, 167; see also Eklof 1999, 33). Benedict Anderson attributes Suharto's obsession with Megawati to his traditional Javanese thinking, according to which, power "may easily pass on from a power holder to someone else, especially someone coming from a formerly powerful family" (in Eklof 1999, 34). I suggest the "servant clown" Limbuk, farcical though her voice and visibility might have traditionally appeared in *wayang*s, had in modern Indonesia upended the patriarchal palace hierarchy. Her challenge to the master of the house, though intolerable, was no longer a joking matter. Megawati/Limbuk had become visible, mobile, and active. There was no going back. Megawati's legitimacy was ironically authenticated by Suharto's violent policies that not only polarized the nation and dragged it into crisis but ultimately discredited his own legitimacy.

Suharto won his seventh term by a "landslide" and received the unanimous endorsement of the members of the MPR. But his victory was short-lived; his time was up! Just two months after he massively rigged the election and arranged to have himself elected to a seventh five-year term, he was forced to step down in May 1998 (Berger 2008). A month later, a lavish "thanksgiving" *wayang* – was organized to celebrate Suharto's downfall and forced resignation. Suharto departed with a whimper of an apology to the nation. "I am sorry for my mistakes," he said. But as Berger writes, "his quiet statement came only after the deaths of 500 student protesters, an event that shocked the people into a consensus that the president must go" (Pausacker 2002, 291). Suharto handed over the government to his vice president, B. J. Habibie (d. 2019), leaving the country in one of the worst economic crises it has seen.

Before discussing the events leading to Megawati's election in the post-Suharto era and the religious/political controversy surrounding the gender of the Indonesian president, I briefly discuss another unique aspect of the Indonesian battle of succession, that of the dynastic competition between the two first daughters of Indonesian's first two presidents.

Like Fathers, Like Daughters: The Battle of Dynastic Heirs

President Suharto was not the only one who felt vulnerable after Megawati's rise to power and was anxious to get rid of her. His eldest daughter, Siti Hardiyanti Rukmana (a.k.a. Mbak Tutut), also felt threatened, fearing that her chances of succeeding her father to the presidency were rapidly vanishing. By a twist of fate, the two women share the same birthday, though Mbak Tutut is two years younger than Megawati; she was born on January 23, 1949. While Megawati was raising her family away from politics – whether by choice or by force under Suharto's punitive regime – Mbak Tutut was being groomed to wear the crown after her father, as it were. At the time, no one would have given the idea of a president Megawati a second thought. Mbak Tutut became the deputy chair of the Golkar Party at almost the same time that Megawati became the president of the PDI in 1993, and held the position until 1998.

Little attention seems to have been given to the dynastic competition between the two first daughters of the first two presidents of Indonesia, or how the political rivalry between them may have evolved. Characteristically, Megawati showed little or no overt interest in Mbak Tutut's fortunes. But it is no secret that the latter did her utmost to "demolish" Megawati and to oust her from her party's leadership (Hefner 2000, 180–189). History provides ample evidence of politically ambitious women who, just as determinedly as powerful men, have sought to eliminate their actual or potential rivals. As part of her father's political machinery, Mbak Tutut quickly realized the danger of Megawati's popularity and embarked on a multi-pronged effort to eliminate the growing political threat to her father, and subsequently herself. Mbak Tutut was part of the political elite and was supported in the highest echelons of the government by no less a person than her father President Suharto himself.

Leaving nothing to chance, yet aware of some army leaders' dissatisfaction with his close ties to hardline Islamist parties, Suharto fortified his own power and that of his daughter in February 1995 by appointing General Hartono as the new army chief of staff. He was a "palace general," according to McIntyre, enjoying close ties with Mbak Tutut. The general and Mbak Tutut worked hard to undermine Megawati and to prove their loyalty to President Suharto yet again. Soon after his promotion, General Hartono committed the army to unwavering support for Suharto, and declared his devotion to "Golkar's board chair, Mbak Tutut," whom he accompanied to political rallies, and from whom he sought "advice and guidance" (McIntyre 2005, 162). Mbak Tutut and Hartono together "supported the regime's outreach to Muslims, but they wanted to make sure that the Muslims who were mobilized were of a sufficiently regimist stripe" (Hefner 2000, 172). Mindful of his daughter's political enemies, and despite his declining health – or maybe because of it – Suharto made sure "that he and not the military, would choose his successor" for the 2003 election cycle (Hefner 2000, 170). He thus reshuffled the party hierarchy and installed his daughter as "a vice chairperson of its new executive board" (McIntyre 2005, 162). When in 1998 Suharto had secured his seventh term, he appointed his daughter the minister of social affairs in his new government (Bennett 2010, 178). The message to the public was clear: Mbak Tutut would be the next president, following Suharto's seventh term in office.

General Hartono was not the only high-level official who threw his support behind Mbak Tutut. Faced with both overt and covert pressure from Suharto, in a surprise move Abdurrahman Wahid had switched course and announced his support for Suharto's re-election for a seventh term. Wahid was the leader of a Muslim reformist party, and an old friend of Megawati and her family. The move had signified the inevitability of Suharto's continued presidency. Wahid too accompanied Mbak Tutut to various campaign locations and pledged that his organization, the NU, would not oppose Mbak Tutut's quest for the office of the presidency (Van Doorn-Harder 2002, 169). At the time, as a progressive religious leader, he had clearly seemed to have no objection to a female president. Later, when he found himself in tight political competition with Megawati for the office of the presidency, however, Mr. Wahid conveniently turned his coat once again. Asked whether his action smacked of duplicity, he said, "Well, politics is dirty!"[23] More than three decades of Suharto's authoritarian and corrupt regime had left his children rich, including Mbak Tutut.[24] Megawati, on the other hand, was generally perceived to be free of financial corruption (Ziv 2001, 76). With their bank accounts swelling and property portfolios expanding, Suharto's government had become a powerful familial nexus wielding inordinate influence, while relying on pliant and self-serving members of the political elite and the army to maintain Suharto's brood and serve their interests (Ziv 2001, 76).

Both Mbak Tutut and Megawati had dynastic claims, were equally familiar with Indonesian's complex power structure, and could play the political games accordingly – each in her own individual style. Over time, as Mbak Tutut became less and less popular, Megawati's political star shined brighter.

Lamenting Mbak Tutut's falling popularity in 2015, Arief Firhanusa stated that, unlike Sukarno's children, Suharto's children had a bad rap. But he expressed hope that in time Mbak Tutut would receive more favorable attention and publicity in the press – attention that with any luck would surpass even that given to Megawati (Firhanusa 2014). It would be "naïve," however, "to expect a rise in Mbak Tutut's popularity," said Sekar Krisnauli, an Indonesian student of mine, "for compared with Megawati's role then and now, Tutut's contribution is

---

[23] Robert Hefner, personal communication, Boston University, September 2017.
[24] See fn. 14, above.

insignificant."[25] In the meantime, Megawati Sukarnoputri lavishly celebrated her seventieth birthday in Java, in the company of many dignitaries, most notably the current president Jokowi Widodo (Wira 2017).

Gender of the President: Winning the Election, Losing the Presidency

> In a political comedy, an adaptation of *wayang* performed in May 2001,
> the King of Ngamarta, Yudhistira, is portrayed – unlike his traditionally
> wise and just portrayal – as weak and his regime has become rife with
> corruption and collusion and is on the verge of collapse. Following his
> fall there is a general election, which is monitored by foreign observers to
> ensure that the poll is conducted fairly ... The party leader who wins the
> majority of the votes is unable to rule Ngamarta, because she is
> Srikandhi.[26] Arjuna's wife, Srikandhi thus represents Megawati, who
> was opposed by the Muslim faction because she is a woman.[27]
>
> Headlines of major newspapers in Indonesia such as *The Jakarta Post*,
> *Kompas*, *Republika*, *Jawa Post* and others were flooded with the issue of
> whether a woman could or could not be the president of Indonesia.
>
> (Diah Ariani Arimbi 2009, 27)

With Suharto at long last forced out of the Indonesian political landscape, the new president, B. J. Habibie, set out to democratize political
processes.[28] He removed the state's strangle hold over freedom of the
press and political parties, upholding the latter's rights to directly contest
elections. Some 148 parties mushroomed in the aftermath of Suharto's
resignation, but only forty-eight qualified to participate in the election of
1999 (Dagg 2007, 50). Habibie's liberalization policies also saw a quick
resurgence of Islamist parties, some of which demanded implementation
of *shari'a*, and moved swiftly to oppose Megawati's bid for the presidency
based on the alleged Prophetic hadith, cited earlier (Yulianti-Farid

---

[25] I wish to thank Sekar for translating Firhanusa's article for me.

[26] "Srikandhi" refers to almost any woman active outside the home – a fighter, career
woman, or politician (Pausacker 2004, 203). Reportedly Sukarno was fond of the
Srikandhi character.

[27] "Within the *wayang* world, there are few, if any, women who even attempt to become
queens in their own right. The depiction of Arjuna's wife Srikandhi contending for the
throne is therefore as anachronistic (and humorous) as a *punakawan*, a clown/servant,
striving to be king, because it disrupts the natural order of the *wayang* world" (Pausacker
2004, 229, 231).

[28] "B. J. Habibie, the New Order *wunderkind*, brilliant in everything except his choice of
mentor," writes McIntyre, "learned of Soeharto's contempt for him on the eve of his
appointment as president. This awful discovery appeared to encourage him to embrace
democracy rather than attempt to perpetuate the old dispensation and serve out the
remainder of his predecessor's term" (2005, 192). See also Aspinall and Fealy
(2010, 119).

2015, 4). A general election was held on June 7, 1999, but it was not declared valid until early August, and it was not until October that the MPR announced the winner. Tainted – some say cursed – by his long association with Suharto, Habibie was ultimately forced to withdraw his bid for the presidency.[29] Still reeling from the sociopolitical trauma of Suharto's violent and autocratic era, the country was deeply divided as to who had the proper democratic qualifications to lead the country. With Megawati's popularity at its peak, the issue that received greatest media coverage throughout the election period was gender.[30] The question was whether being female automatically disqualifies women for leadership of the country – based on the Prophetic hadith, "Never will succeed such a nation as makes a woman their ruler." The country was divided on the issue, and the national debate continued. Nelly Van Doorn-Harder (2002) and Lily Yulianti-Farid (2015) have dealt with the issue comprehensively, and I have incorporated their arguments in the following pages.

The possibility of Megawati actually winning the presidency of the world's largest Muslim-majority state confounded many on both sides of the Indonesian political spectrum. She would be the first Muslim woman in modern history to serve as a head of state. Several Muslim women had already been elected to lead government in contemporary Muslim-majority states, including Pakistan (Chapter 5), Bangladesh, and Turkey,[31] but none as head of state. Megawati's situation was particularly troublesome for some religious parties, many of which had become noticeably more vocal and intolerant in the last decade of Suharto's regime, and for the political elites, some of whom were in competition with Megawati. Van Doorn-Harder (2002) reports that a year before the election of 1999, several Muslim organizations brought together some

---

[29] After the fall of Suharto and his New Order, a special ritual was performed "to purify the Sultanate of the moral taints of Suharto's sin. In this ritual a *wayang* puppet of evil Ravana, representing Suharto, was thrown into the sea. However, when the tidal waves washed ashore the puppet's hand, this was perceived as an omen signifying that although Suharto was no longer publicly on the scene he continued to exercise his power in this sinister and secretive way" (Fic 2003, 183). The curse was not the only thing that drove Habibie out; the dissatisfaction with his annual state of the union report at the MPR proved consequential.

[30] For a comprehensive look at the media's role in the Indonesian election cycles of 1999, 2004, and 2009, see Yulianti Farid (2015).

[31] Tansu Çiller was prime minister of Turkey 1993–1996. In Bangladesh, Sheikh Hasina and Khalida Zia (daughter and widow of the founder and former presidents of Bangladesh, respectively) have dominated the political scene since the 1980s, alternately serving as prime minister and leader of the opposition, thus earning the label of the "battling Begums" (Bennet 2010). Both are leaders of their respective political parties, the Awami League and the Nationalist Party. Presently, Sheikh Hasina is serving her third term as the prime minister of Bangladesh.

2,000 participants, with only 132 women in attendance. The objective was to propose a plan for a community based on *shari'a*. The Congress of the Indonesian Muslim Community (CIMC) among them, found the moment opportune to lead the debate against female presidency – and vice presidency – in order to more firmly ensconce itself in the country's changing political landscape (Van Doorn-Harder 2002). Also present were members of the NGO Muhammadiya (headed by Amien Rais) and the NU (headed by Abdulrahman Wahid), two popular religious organizations with relatively progressive agendas and views on Muslim women's roles and status. Some hastily retrieved the alleged Prophetic hadith to legitimize their opposition to Megawati's bid for the presidency. The religious opposition came as a surprise to many Indonesian women. Had Mr. Wahid not supported Mbak Tutut for president? Back in 1997, the NU had expressed no known opposition to women holding high political office, provided that they had the right qualifications. This meant that no limits were placed on what women could do, including becoming the president (Andrée Feillard in Van Doorn-Harder 2002, 175). It was shocking now to realize that just as a woman's presidency seemed within reach, their compatriots revealed their conservative traditionalism (Van Doorn-Harder 2002, 186).

In the meantime, having discarded the straightjacket of Suharto-era censorship, the media rapidly expanded and operated more freely. The fierce competition among the profit-driven media outlets led to the issue of female leadership in Islam becoming a "news commodity" and to the simplifying of diverse and often contested views into the sensational conclusion of Islam's "rejection" of a female president (Yulianti-Farid 2015, 8). In the words of Siti Nurjanah, "gender paranoia" had set in and was repeatedly invoked to discredit Megawati's right to stand (2013). Helped by the media hype, the CIMC issued a terse statement that "The President and Vice-President have to be males" (Yulianti-Farid 2015, 6). More surprisingly, however, was the ambivalence manifested by progressive and reformist Indonesian leaders, such as Abdurrahman Wahid of the NU and Amien Rais of Muhammadiyah, who, as noted above, had long touted Muslim women's right to high office and advocated gender equity.

When all its efforts failed to dampen popular support for Megawati, the opposition played the ethnic card, says Van Doorn-Harder: Megawati was accused of not being a "true Muslim" because "One of her grandmothers was Balinese and her father was more comfortable with Javanese beliefs and rituals than with Islamic faith" (2002, 184). Media headlines would read: "She sometimes worships at a Hindu temple, she might be a Hindu," "She is arrogant," "She does not care about the voices of women," and so on. And to minimize her support among the more conservative Muslim populations, the media would state, "The majority of the members of her party are non-Muslims" and "she is more sympathetic to Christians" and so her support comes primarily from Christians (Van Doorn-Harder 2002, 184; Yulianti-Farid, 2015).

Despite her popular support, and the diversity of opinions among religious scholars, secular and reformist leaders, and the public in general, a majority of Indonesians still believed that the political leadership was a man's job (Chakrabarty 2001, 3440), though that is not exclusive to Indonesia (Eagly and Carli 2012). Indeed, by the 2004 election cycle the public had fallen back on tradition and elected Susilo Bambang Yudhoyono, a former army general and a minister of Megawati's cabinet, as president. Such a mindset had been reinforced under Suharto, who propagated the idea that women's place was not at the head of the political table,[32] but at home where they were to be mothers, housewives, and companions to their husband – but maybe with the exception of Suharto's own daughters.[33] Suharto would often sponsor *wayang* performances to drive his gender policy messages home and to indoctrinate the public (Pausacker 2002, 287–288; Haryogurinto 2002, 362–365).

The debate over the gender of the president reached fever pitch when, under the watchful eyes of foreign observers, including President Jimmy Carter of the United States, the much-anticipated election was finally held on June 7, 1999. By the time the election results were validated in early August, lo and behold, Megawati Sukarnoputri's party, the PDI-P, had won the biggest percentage of the votes, some 34 to 35 percent, despite religious objections. The next closest to her party was that of Suharto's Golkar with 22 percent, with Abdurrahman Wahid's party of National Awakening (PKB) lagging far behind in third place with 10 to 12 percent of the popular vote. More disappointing, however, was the abysmal showing of Amien Rais's National Mandate Party, which hardly mustered 7 percent. Believing that "everybody would love to vote for Amien Rais," his supporters were hugely disappointed (Van Doorn-Harder 2002, 173). Despite the wave of ideological propaganda, it is also important to note that only three of the nineteen religious/Islamist parties that participated in the parliamentary election gained a significant

---

[32] Likewise, President Richard Nixon explained his objection to appointing a woman to the US Supreme Court by saying, "I don't think a woman should be in any government job whatsoever ... mainly because they are erratic. And emotional. Men are erratic and emotional, too, but the point is a woman is more likely to be" (Eagly and Carli 2012, 148).

[33] For a brief discussion of Sukarno's and Suharto's gender policies see Bennett (2010, 177–178). On women's reaction to Suharto's New Order gender policies, see Robinson (2009).

number of votes, most notably the PPP, which won 10.7 percent.[34] This was a consequential moment in the history of Indonesia. *The first demo-cratically held election had resulted in the popular election of a female candidate.* The ball was now in the court of MPR members and its speaker Amien Rais to determine who was the winner of the election and would be the president of Indonesia, as the MPR was then constitutionally mandated to do. All eyes were now on Megawati, whose party had garnered the most seats in the parliament. Her presidency was almost assured. But it was not to be. What happened?

Disbelieving his glaring loss to Megawati, Amien Rais, once a chairman of the powerful and progressive Muhammadiyah organization and leader of the National Mandate Party, had second thoughts about women's qualifications for political leadership, and so he declared rather condes-cendingly: "a Muslim woman could only become a president in the absence of qualified men" (Van Doorn-Harder 2002, 179). Evidently, he considered himself more qualified – he had a Ph.D., and Megawati hadn't even finished college. Ultimately, it became obvious to many women – and some good men – that their leaders and many of their colleagues were indeed against Megawati's presidency because she was a woman (Van Doorn-Harder 2002, 176; Yulianti-Farid 2015) – despite their progressive and reformist rhetoric.

With her presidency hanging in the balance, thanks to the patriarchal double standard of her former reformist political friends and colleagues, Megawati gave a speech in which she heavily criticized the political and religious attacks against her. She stressed her intention to stay in the race and become the president of Indonesia. Many of Muhammadiyah's male members, including the chair, Syafi'i Ma'arif, considered her speech too brash for a woman (Van Doorn-Harder 2002, 179). The chair flatly stated that if Megawati were chosen as Indonesia's president, he would resign. He did not want "to have official meetings" with a woman "as president." Noting the patriarchal hypocrisy of this individual, Van Doorn-Harder highlights how the chair changed his mind once Wahid's presidency was assured and he was saved from having to work with a female president. Syafi'i Ma'arif then went on to say that the gender of the president did not matter, as long as the candidate had a "clear vision" (Van Doorn-Harder 2002, 179). Clearly, political motivation under only a thin layer of piety drove the male elite's opposition to Megawati's presidency. Not having sufficient votes himself, Amien Rais promoted Abdurrahman Wahid's bid, who was only too happy to oblige.

---

[34] For a fuller review of the voting figures and number of seats won by various parties, see Fic (2003, 185–188).

Having rejected the religious justification for ruling out a woman president at the onset of the gender debate, when he himself became a viable candidate for the job, Wahid could not resist and changed his position swiftly. He displaced his opposition to Megawati's presidency onto the party membership, lamely claiming that it was they who objected to a female president on religious grounds and were unwilling to vote for Megawati (Kees Van Dijk in Van Doorn-Harder 2002, 183). Wahid's "power grab exposed his trampling of his own long-term ideals of gender equality" (Soesastro, Smith, and Han, 2003).

As the contestation over the presidential gender became an all-consuming news item, far from staying silent and acquiescing to the male political intrigues, Megawati weighed in on the debate. She objected to the patriarchal politicization of gender as a way to undermine her credibility:

I am concerned because there are people who undermine women, particularly if it is related to national leadership. God created men and women as equals. So why do these people think that women are not capable to lead the nation? A national leader should not be judged from his or her gender, man or woman, but whether she or he is loved by people. That is why I, Megawati Sukarnoputri, who happens to be a woman and mother, will be running as a presidential candidate as I am receiving the mandate from the party's congress. (Yulianti-Farid 2015, 4)

Conscious of the rising anger of Megawati's supporters, once Abdurrahman Wahid secured his position as the fourth president of Indonesia, he proposed that Megawati serve as his vice president. But some hardline members of the parliament challenged her again, knowing that, constitutionally, a vice president would replace the president if the latter were to become incapacitated. Hamzah Haz, leader of the PPP, challenged Megawati's right to the vice presidency. He had "lobbied for the introduction of the Islamic law (*shari'a*) in Indonesia," and was firm in his opinion that a woman was unfit to be the president of Indonesia. Once the votes were counted by the MPR, however, it became clear that Megawati had won by a large margin (Van Doorn-Harder 2002, 186).

Opinions were divided as to why, despite having won the highest popular vote, Megawati was demoted to the second post. Her party had won the largest share of the vote and the most parliamentary seats but her win was not sufficient to put her over the top; she needed other parties' support. Some believe that it was Megawati's own fault for not being proactive and participating in the male games of backdoor negotiating and political bargaining. Others argue that as Sukarno's daughter, she expected the presidency to be handed to her and so "sat back passively waiting to be anointed in the role she believed was hers by right and destiny" (Mydans 2001, 3). But others have attributed her defeat to her Javanese temperament and grounding in a culture where "silence is golden" and "Power is seen as a mysterious mantle that cannot be seized but envelops a leader of its own accord" (Mydans 2001, 3). In the final analysis, Thompson argues, it was not her gender that lost her the presidency, but her reluctance to cut political deals (2002, 551). She was not unaware, I submit, of her competitors' politicking, but was reluctant to forge alliances with these turncoat politicians. I suggest it was the intersectionality of gender and authority that confounded the aspiring male elite. To begin with, the lure of the office of the presidency was too strong to be conceded to a woman – and a "housewife" at that. Second, they did their best to avoid negotiating with her. Wahid and Amien Rais both displayed reluctance to concede their losses to her and to relinquish the coveted office of the presidency to Megawati.

Be that as it may, as vice president, Megawati continued her uneasy and distant relationship with President Wahid, often absenting herself from cabinet meetings and other state functions. Some pundits have argued – again – that she "did not shine" as vice president, that in public "she was mostly silent," and that she was not fully engaged with the duties and responsibilities that Wahid delegated to her. McIntyre (2005) identifies Wahid's dismissive attitude toward Megawati as one reason for her reluctance to cooperate with him. Anthony Smith locates the difficulty in their relations in Wahid's general failure to share power, which Smith believes was his ultimate undoing. No sooner did he delegate some duties to Megawati than he would disable her by taking them back, claiming that he had "delegated tasks and not authority" (Smith 2003, 98). I believe there is logic in Megawati's apathy toward Wahid. She was being subversive. She had rightly resented Wahid's self-serving power grab and found it strategically convenient to silently sabotage his policies by doing little. Wahid's capricious behavior reinforced her instincts. His increasingly authoritarian approach to governance became damaging to him, and Megawati was certainly not unaware of the parliament's and the public's frustration with him. She was there to silently witness Wahid's slide from the zenith of political authority. She just waited her turn. Once the process of his impeachment got underway, Megawati again acted astutely by remaining disengaged from the clamor to oust Wahid. That made her politically strong by the time she was to replace Wahid and assume the presidency (Soesastro, Smith, and Han 2003, 5). "Compared to the verbal grenades, vindictive maneuvers, and divisive interventions of Mr. Wahid," writes Mark Thompson, "Mrs. Megawati's reticence" was a "healing relief" (2002, 548).

Despite his initial successes, Abdurrahman Wahid became embroiled in financial scandals and by the end of his first year in office, "the president stood alone, isolated, the hope for national reconciliation in tatters" (Fic 2003, 202). It was then, Fic believes, that "*wahju*, the divine inspiration to rule" left Gus Dur, as Wahid is popularly known (2003, 201). When the calls for his resignation intensified, Wahid almost reverted back to the days of Suharto's New Order and seriously contemplated imposing a civil emergency. As the tension between the MPR and Wahid deepened and the threat of his impeachment became all too real, Megawati remained aloof, watching the president's downfall impassively. Abdurrahman Wahid had burned his bridges with Megawati, and so in desperation he reached out to Rachmawati, her younger sister. Rachmawati did not disappoint him and joined Wahid in the presidential palace. Never a fan of her sister, Rachmawati chastised Megawati for not standing by the president and called upon her to resign. She urged President Wahid to go ahead with dismissing the MPR and declaring a civil emergency. The military, however, communicated its reluctance to intervene against the MPR on the president's behalf, mindful of repeating the bloody violence of the Suharto era. Megawati, coolly insensible to her sister's fiery demand, continued to observe the unfolding political drama impassively.

As President Wahid impulsively decided to drag the country into the quagmire of another civil emergency, the MPR acted quickly and decisively. On the morning of July 22, Amien Rais, the speaker of the MPR and the colleague who had orchestrated Wahid's election, sought to undermine the president's plan by calling on the MPR's members to vote for the impeachment and removal of Wahid. He also appealed to the army to safeguard the security of the parliamentarians. Procedures were quickly set in place to remove the president from his post, while at the same time several high-ranking officials went to Megawati's residence to inform her of the impending transition of power. Learning of this meeting and the rapid turn of the events, Wahid pushed ahead with his original plan. At one o'clock in the morning of July 23, he ordered the imposition of a national emergency and the dissolution of both houses of the parliament. But it was too late. His luck had run out and his army and the police had deserted him. Within hours President Wahid was deposed and Megawati was swiftly sworn in as the fifth president of Indonesia (Fic 2003, 209–217; McIntyre 2005, 201–251).

President Megawati Sukarnoputri: Limbuk Becomes Queen

Democracy demands gracefulness, sincerity and obedience to the games. I am calling on all parties to accept this democratic process gracefully.   Megawati in Mydans (2001, A9)

[Limbuk] has stepped out of the *kadhatona* and engaged in dialogue on her own ... She is no longer a daughter, but is herself a mother ... The audience ... both male and female, received all aspects of the Limbuken positively.   Pausacker (2002, 292)

During Megawati Sukarnoputri's swearing in, a "Muslim clergyman held a copy of the Koran above her head as she promised to uphold the Constitution" (Figure 6.2). In the assembly hall, one "speaker after another lavished praise on Mrs. Megawati," while a few delegates expressed their dissatisfaction (Mydans 2001, A9). Leaving the assembly hall in her presidential motorcade, her red license plate read "Indonesia 1," reflecting the transition of power and her new exalted status. With that, Megawati triumphantly "returned to the palace as a president where she had lived as a little girl" (Mydans 2001, A9).

Figure 6.2 President Megawati Sukarnoputri Taking the Oath of Office with the Qur'an Held Over Her Head

The deposed Wahid refused to publicly acknowledge the transfer of power and turned down a meeting with President Megawati before leaving for medical treatment in the USA. But it really did not matter much whether he endorsed her presidency (Fic 2003, 218). She was now the queen of her palace.

By the time Megawati's swearing-in ceremony as the fifth president of Indonesia was over, the debate over women's fitness for the presidency had become constitutionally moot. The gender of the president became irrelevant, not to be raised again during her administration. The conservative Islamic camp suddenly discovered that Megawati was "a true Muslim," and religious arguments were overlooked, muted, or brushed over. Megawati even received the backing of some of the most conservative Muslim parties in Indonesia, which wanted to be part of the new power structure:

It was ... embarrassing to witness the male players highlighting certain principles circumscribing women's rights when their own political power was at stake, and reverse them again when the concept of Megawati's presidency suited their interests. Some of her strongest opponents [became] part of her cabinet. (Van Doorn-Harder 2002, 185)

For her part, Megawati astutely sought to ameliorate any lingering religious unease by choosing Hamzah Haz as her vice president – the same man who had earlier opposed her bid for the vice presidency. Haz, leader of the Islamist United Development Party, had once lobbied for the introduction of *shari'a* in Indonesia and firmly believed that women were not suited for the office of the presidency. Once his position as the vice president was secured, Hamzah Haz seems to have discovered that a female president was preferable to an incompetent and corrupt man (Thompson 2002, 551; Van Doorn-Harder 2002, 186).

Some Reflections: Limbuk Is Subversive

It appears that I am considered to be a housewife ... I say to those people who belittle housewives: What's wrong with that? It does not mean a housewife does not understand politics.

Megawati in Mydans (2001)[35]

Megawati Sukarnoputri's steep climb unsettled powerful men such as Suharto, who belittled her as a mere "housewife," and perceived her active presence in politics and the public domain as disruptive and

---

[35] The same point was raised by Iranian women presidential contenders whom I interviewed for my video documentary, *Mrs. President: Women and Political Leadership in Iran* (2002).

subversive. Never loath to inflict violence, Suharto had sought to nip in the bud her challenge to his authority. He failed spectacularly. Next, a segment of the religious leadership and political elite who felt threatened by the possibility of a female president had raised the banner of "Islam-is-in-danger." Their sound and fury was over-hyped by the media and upheld by a limited number of Muslim leaders. They fell back on "tradition" and the Prophetic hadith to discredit and disqualify Megawati. Imagine a reverse situation in which a male politician could be disqualified based on the following hadith, the "leader of a Muslim country should be from the tribe of Quraish." This would effectively disqualify every Indonesian male candidate (Qodir in Van Doorn-Harder 2002, 166–167).[36] Ultimately, the opposition failed to stop Megawati or to discourage her public support. She was neither a "stupid housewife," as Suharto and some others would have it, nor did her leadership doom Indonesia. She turned out to be a canny politician: calm and unpretentious, the likes of whom Indonesia had not seen for five decades. As president, she faced as many challenges as any ambitious politician. But she faced an additional hurdle unique to her. She was a mature woman, a mother, and a housewife whose gender threatened male politicians and confounded the religious elite. They were unaccustomed to obeying a woman. In the end, the untenability of the religious elite's opposition to Megawati's gender became palpably obvious. It also became obvious to many, particularly to women, that it was not necessarily the gender of the Indonesian president that was problematic. The objection to female leadership was, rather, the male elite's excuse, opportunistically conjured up in order to prevent competition for political leadership that had for millennia been monopolized by male political and religious leaders.[37]

Megawati's decision to brave Suharto's intimidating machinery and stand for the presidential election challenges the assumption – held primarily by political elites and pundits – that she was a "reluctant" politician, and just a "housewife." She was a politician of a different order; she played the democratic games of succession astutely and manifested her charisma, not through dramatic speeches but through strategic silence and cautious remarks. Her public speeches were not bombastic, but measured and substantive. Interestingly, many people "praised"

---

[36] Indeed, the Islamic State of Iraq and Syria (ISIS) chose Abu Bakr al-Baghdadi as its first caliph/leader because he was considered to be a Qureishi descendent (Brown 2018, 211).

[37] It is worth noting, however, that in the 2004 and 2009 presidential cycles Megawati banked on her gender to appeal to voters: as a mother/housewife, as one who understood better than her male competitors issues regarding family, rising commodity prices, and the like. But she lost both elections. Thanks to Lily Yulianti Farid for making this point in an email to me on May 28, 2018.

Megawati for her silence while lambasting Amien Rais for "his loquaciousness." In the end, voters preferred a political novice to politicians such as Amien Rais; they admired Megawati for her honesty, her fighting spirit, and her resistance of Suharto's three-decade dictatorship (Thompson 2002, 548). That was her real appeal to the people, who found her authentic, genuine, and not fooled by her own importance as some male politicians are. Megawati's political style was also subversive, and that, too, appealed to a large segment of the population who had long felt stifled by Suharto's oppressive and corrupt regime. Although Habibie had initiated the democratization of the country and Abdulrahman Wahid continued to democratize Indonesian institutions, it was through Megawati's longer and relatively stable, corruption- and scandal-free administration that Indonesia's transition from autocratic to democratic governance was delivered.

Megawati came to power at a time when her country was going through severe political and economic crises and people were traumatized by the three decades of Suharto's arbitrary regime, and then Wahid's capricious and rudderless presidency. Some expected her to fail (including Wahid), while many others expected her to achieve miracles. The political structure and rampant corruption she inherited had already created a context that would doom many a politician's best efforts. Her strategy of remaining above the messy and degrading (as they are regarded in Javanese tradition) details of politicking and lobbying boosted her popularity – but also a perception of her political "weakness." She alleviated the political crisis, improved the country's economy, and allowed democratic reforms to continue (Bennett 2010, 188–191). These included a constitutional change, after which presidents would be elected directly by the people rather than by the MPR, a move away from personal power and toward constitutional rule (McIntyre 2005).

Growing up in the presidential palace, Megawati had experienced firsthand a sudden turn of fortune and closely watched the violent removal of her father, the charismatic hero of Indonesian independence. She was not unfamiliar with the popular pull of charismatic male politicians. She had seen it up close, but either by choice or by the force of her temperament, she did not follow that cultural model. The traumatic experiences in her early life had endowed her with a great emotional maturity and a strong sense of self, which in combination allowed her to forge her own style of political authority, one that was closer to an Indonesian cultural ideal of leadership and peaceful coexistence. "Her maternal, if not to say feudal approach to politics" was what Indonesia needed then (Chakrabarty, 2001, 3440). Her style of leadership was inspired by the concept of the traditional Javanese ruler, who is endowed with *halus* (denoting calmness, refined manners, asceticism, and purity and harmony). "Megawati, who has never outwardly displayed any signs of disturbance, has never harangued, abused, or spoken out of turn or has even behaved 'badly,'" epitomizes *halus* (Chakrabarty 2001, 3440). Embodying the traditional ruler, Megawati appealed to a vast majority of Indonesians of different backgrounds and beliefs.

Megawati Sukarnoputri's presidency was unique on multiple levels. To begin with, as a woman she had turned upside down the all-male hierarchy of the Indonesian power structure, though paradoxically what was once considered to be the main impediment to her presidency turned out to be her asset. Her presidency came about after four male presidents, two of whom had between them ruled Indonesia for fifty-three of the fifty-six years since its independence in 1945, and two of whom governed for less than two years each. The stumbling transition of power from one-man authoritarian rule to constitutional democracy had unsettled the political elite and the public alike. With *ibu* Megawati, "mother earth," in charge, her presidency and administration had a healing and calming effect on the public. Her leadership style, however, continued to baffle male political veterans, who equated her understated expressions of authority with inertia and an inability to govern. She was not unaware of what it took to make democracy possible in a country as diverse and hierarchical as Indonesia, and long habituated to a dictatorial arbitrary rule. She sought to establish a corruption-free administration, a set of tolerant rules for political games that had been so poorly played for so long by male politicians in her country. She consciously chose to change the "cultural logic" of the patriarchal power game in Indonesia. The longevity of her popularity – despite the fact that she lost her subsequent bids for presidency – attests to her unique approach to politics. Siti Nurjanah puts it succinctly:

Today [2013], the media seems to have forgotten those days. Since Megawati decided to approve Jokow to run for DKI [Jakarta] Governor, the media seemingly even forgot that Megawati is a female politician. There is almost not a line of newsprint suggesting that her silence over Jokow's potential presidential candidacy for 2014 is a typical show of weakness of her leadership. With mounting media pressure on Jokow's candidacy for 2014, Jokow has shown complete political obedience to the leader of his party [i.e. Megawati]. He has replied consistently to questions about his intentions with, "As it's up to the Madam Chair, you should ask her." Remarkably, the media has overlooked the fact that a man is waiting for a woman to decide whether he will run for president or not . . . Yet Megawati's decision could be one of the most politically momentous in the country since 1998. (2013)

On January 2017, President Jokowi Widodo attended a cultural event and public celebration commemorating Megawati's seventieth birthday.

Having inherited a country demoralized by policies put in place by capricious and authoritarian male leaders, what Megawati achieved during her presidency was anything but negligible. Her achievements in office challenge the characterization of her as a "do nothing" president.[38] In her first address to the nation she laid out a six-point agenda, stressing the nation's unity, the necessity of democratizing all aspects of national life, improving human rights, restoring the economy, enhancing security, restoring sound foreign policy, and eradicating rampant corruption (Fic 2003, 219). In 2004, under her leadership, the MPR finally institutionalized the democratic transition by approving direct presidential elections and limiting the presidency to two terms (McIntyre 2005; Bennett 2010, 188). She delivered democracy to her country. Megawati governed by consensus and created a "rainbow cabinet," to which she appointed ministers belonging to different parties. She called it a "Gotang Royong cabinet," meaning "a workhorse to pull the country out of the present crisis and guide it to a better future" (Fic 2003, 219). Characteristically, her government was corruption-free, she made no political enemies, owed nobody for her presidency, and so did not have to repay any favors when appointing those she wanted for her cabinet (Soesastro, Smith, and Han 2003, 55).

Megawati's conduct and speeches were under constant cultural scrutiny and media surveillance by those who threw every gender stereotype at her (Yulianti-Farid 2015). Once she was in power, some activists and political dissidents sought every opportunity to criticize her, arguing that Megawati did not represent change because her route to power was assured by her dynastic ties and the popularity of her father. Would a similar objection be raised against sons succeeding their fathers to power? Megawati's dynastic ties did initially give her the visibility and popularity she needed. But her challenge to Suharto was unparalleled; male politicians had quickly bent to Suharto's threat, and compromised. To then accuse her of expecting the presidency to be handed to her sounds disingenuous. She did not just sit back, expecting people to see the light. She campaigned actively for her political office in her own understated style. When necessary, she encouraged her supporters to participate in campaigning, and comforted them when they were brutalized by Suharto's thugs. She had siblings, brothers and sisters, none of whom carried the mantle of Sukarno with the finesse Megawati did. She was not charismatic in the way that her father was. She was as calm and

---

[38] For a discussion of her administrative accomplishments, see Bennett (2010, 188–191).

quiet in her public appearances as her father was vociferous and dramatic. But Megawati was charismatic in her own elegant, low-key way, in tune with the Javanese culture of leadership and feminine conduct, and that is what seems to have appealed to a large number of people. Megawati negotiated her path to presidential power carefully, peacefully, and intelligently – in her own unique way.

Some – many? – politicians did not appreciate the differences in gender leadership performance, but some – many? – creative artists reflected on the symbolic parallelism between Limbuk and Megawati: Limbuk was no longer willing to live quietly as an obedient – silent – daughter living in the inner sanctum of the palace in the women's section, the harem. She had moved out of *kadhatona*, the female domain, and stepped into the public sphere. She was determined to be visible and vocal. Megawati had finally settled as the president in the palace, out in front and public – where men had lived and ruled for so long, and not always successfully.[39] She was received positively by both men and women, the silent majority who were no longer willing to stay quiet and compliant. The Voice of Concerned Mothers movement provides a powerful example. These were women whose so-called "milk demonstration" drew on the "central trope of womanhood in the state ideology of Suharto's regime."[40] Challenging the ethos of Suharto's authoritarian government, they attracted national and international attention with their demonstrations (Robinson 2009, 1).

Both Benazir Bhutto and Megawati Sukarnoputri came to power in the aftermath of military coups that turned their respective societies into militarized authoritarian regimes – governments ruled by single men who, relying on their cronies and networks of power and patronage, did not relinquish power until finally were toppled by forces larger than themselves, one through a plane explosion and the other by popular uprising inspired by a woman, a "housewife." Both General Zia in Pakistan and General Suharto in Indonesia trampled the postcolonial constitutions drafted after their respective countries attained their independence – from the British in 1947 and the Dutch in 1945, respectively. Both women unseated men who had treacherously toppled their fathers and then sought to redeem their fathers' legacies. But while paying

---

[39] Perhaps for the same reason (i.e. where men have failed how can a woman succeed?), some Indonesians deride Megawati by associating her with Limbuk (Nurjanah, personal communication, May 27, 2018).

[40] The Voice of Concerned Mothers movement staged a highly successful public demonstration in Jakarta in February of 1998, objecting to the rising costs of basic commodities and the hardship it created for mothers and women to meet the needs of their families (Robinson 2009).

filial homage to their fathers, each was aware of her father's authoritarian tendencies and moved astutely to restore democracy – however haltingly, in the case of Benazir – and strengthen her country's founding constitutions, with Megawati having better success than Benazir.[41] Megawati and Benazir took on the leadership when the ongoing sociopolitical conflicts in their countries had left the public bruised and battered, dispirited and traumatized. Their long suffering at the hands of generals who had overthrown their fathers and abused their authority resonated with the public's own political and socioeconomic deprivations. In their symbolic roles as "mother" and "sister," they had a nurturing effect and widespread appeal among the public, who found them not dictatorial and distant, but caring, like members of their own families.[42] It was in fact their gender that appealed to their publics. Still, both Megawati and Benazir had to contend with deep-seated cultural and gender stereotyping, structural obstacles, popular skepticism, and military suspicions of their ability as women to lead densely populated modern countries; and both women struggled – perhaps unsuccessfully in the case of Benazir – to manage an uneasy relationship with the army. Both women had supportive husbands, but they could not escape being stereotyped in relation to the latter, who were perceived to control their wives. Both men acknowledged their wives' intelligence and admitted that no one could push them around. Both Asif Zardari and Taufiq Kiemas were accused of financial corruption, and Zardari suffered isolation in jail for several years. Both women were confronted with opposition from a segment of the religious elite and their followers, who claimed that women are by nature unsuited to lead a Muslim country, based on the authority of the alleged Prophetic hadith. But in neither case were the religious leaders unanimous or able to legitimately disqualify either woman, or to convince an overwhelming majority of the public of the "doom" awaiting them. Unlike Benazir Bhutto, Megawati Sukarnoputri did not cover her hair to placate religious oppositions – though both reached out to religious parties and leaders. By the time she arrived at the presidential palace, Megawati's right to occupy the highest temporal position in Indonesia was no longer questioned. By all accounts Benazir Bhutto would have won a third term as prime minister, and perhaps that is one major reason she was eliminated.

---

[41] Megawati has stated that her father once told her "the Assembly wanted to declare him president for life." She advised him against it: "Had he not trained cadres for just that purpose?" (Bennett 2010, 180). Nonetheless, in July 1963 the MPR did declare Sukarno president for life (Bennett 2010, 174).

[42] It is not only women leaders who may be symbolically categorized as a member of the larger "kinship." Men have also been identified as representing members of the family. The most notable is Ataturk, father of the Turks.

Megawati has emerged from the political turmoil in Indonesia with her power bases intact; her continuous leadership of the PDI-P attests to this. That she did not win a second term had less to do with gender and the alleged hadith than with changing international political relationships post-9/11 that affected Indonesia's internal dynamics. Her leadership and political visibility are no longer unthinkable, or out of the patriarchal order or farcical, as once was the case for the mythological character Limbuk, whose uncharacteristic mobility and visibility might have initially appeared comical to the viewing public. Megawati/Limbuk moved out of the private female domain and assumed their long-empty place at the center of the public palace, finally atop the hierarchy of an Indonesian "power play," and at the political table. Megawati/Limbuk have gendered authority by giving it voice and visibility; all stuff of a brand new *wayang*.

Some Concluding Remarks

> The anthropology of "agency" is not only about how social subjects, as empowered or disempowered actors, play the games of their culture, but about laying bare what those cultural games are, about their ideological underpinnings, and about how the play of games reproduces or transforms those underpinnings.   Ortner (2006, 152)

Looking back at the lives and legacies of the remarkable women rulers I have highlighted in the preceding pages, it seems to me that my fascination with them and my desire to tell their stories, connecting the historical dots between medieval and modern times, may have had deeper roots in my own thoughts and memory, a sensibility cultivated in the soil of my childhood and upbringing.

I grew up in a highly educated and intellectual family, surrounded by capable, socially active, and professionally accomplished women. My paternal grandmother, wife of an ayatollah and mother of six sons and four daughters, was foremost among them. She was the undisputed queen of her huge household and enjoyed the unwavering affection of my grandfather. Like her namesake, Khadija (incidentally, my religious name too), she was the quintessential powerful person in my mind. She had an independent disposition; she was caring yet resolute, nourishing yet authoritative. She observed veiling, but was not obsessively covered – not in black. For us she was, above all, a delightful storyteller – our own Shahrzad. Religion was an important part of our lives yet we, women and men alike, lived a secular life and maintained modern professions and appearances. The other women of the family did not wear a veil or headscarf in public – and my grandfather made no objection. Yet we were steeped in a cultural tradition that had deep respect for religion – the tolerant, intellectual, and spiritual Islam practiced by my grandparents and parents, which was passed onto us. Growing up in an Iranian middle-class family in the 1960s and 1970s, we lived our lives in a social milieu that seemed to effortlessly incorporate "tradition" and "modernity," religion and secularity. My family was not unique; we shared the prevailing cultural attitude of the educated and professional urban Iranian middle class. We did not live our lives in contradictions.

The "contradictions," if there were any, were in outsiders' bifurcated perception, engendered by the dominant Orientalist/Western gaze and reinforced by colonial narratives of "Muslim women," "Islam," and Iranian ayatollahs (Haeri 2010). Ironically, however, the Islamic Republic's policy of forced veiling and gender segregation has, in fact, led to "contradictions" in the lives of many middle-class Iranians, who are obliged to lead a double life, one in public and the other in private.

But the dominant perception runs deep. I remember the shocked reaction of an American colleague upon seeing the framed photograph of my parents in my office. It was taken when they were both in their early twenties (c. 1940s); my mother is unveiled and sporting a small white flower in her hair, and my father has a dark suit. "How modern!" my colleague exclaimed. The shock and surprise of my friend was repeated over and over again every time I told someone I was writing about Muslim women rulers. I would almost always get an incredulous reaction: "Muslim women rulers?!" Those more willing to entertain the possibility would say something like, "They must be modern." This skepticism is not totally unfounded. How, indeed, was it possible for a thirty-five-year-old woman to be democratically elected to the office of prime minister in Pakistan in 1989? Her ascendancy, and that of Megawati Sukarnoputri in Indonesia, or of Sheikh Hasina and Khaleda Zia in Bangladesh, is all the more astonishing in view of the fact that in much of the Western world only a few women had occupied such an exalted position in the late twentieth century. The image of women rulers from medieval or modern times did not match the disdainful narrative of "Muslim women" in the West. Ironically, it does not match the narrative of obedient "Muslim women" in some highly conservative Muslim societies either.

Muslim women's sovereignty and paths to power become even more remarkable when viewed against the background of the patriarchal invocation of the alleged Prophetic hadith, "Never will succeed such a nation as makes a woman their ruler." How did women rulers overcome such a serious obstacle? Did they disregard religious orders? Did riots break out in the streets of cities large and small? While Muslim women's political leadership is no longer as extraordinary as it once was, neither the religious establishment's response to, nor people's support for, women's political authority have been uniform or unanimously negative.

By bringing together the life stories of charismatic Muslim women rulers from medieval to modern times, I have mapped out their paths to power through kinship relations and their society's sociopolitical terrain. Counterintuitive though it may sound, it is in fact in modern times that institutional religious objections have been raised to women's political authority. The question is, what prompted opposition in one era and silent acceptance in the other?

In the following pages, I revisit the dynamic interaction between politics and religion, tradition and revelation, and discuss the pragmatics of dynastic support and father-daughter relations.

Medieval Era: Autocratic Sovereignty

The eleventh-century Yemenite Queen Arwa and the thirteenth-century Razia Sultan of India, as discussed in Chapters 3 and 4, both rose to power through the solid support of their father or husband, though neither queen was wanting in political ambition and charisma. And neither queen faced organized opposition from the religious elite – or from the public. Queen Arwa's long reign coincided with three successive Fatimid imam-caliphs in Cairo, none of whom is recorded to have raised any objection to the queen's authority, even if they might have personally felt threatened or politically uneasy about her gender or popularity and wished to curtail it. In fact, the all-powerful imam-caliph al-Mustansir (d. 1094), who was perceived as infallible by his followers, not only did not object to the queen's leadership, but in fact helped consolidate her political authority by elevating her status to that of *hujja*, the highest religious authority after that of the imam-caliph himself. As the highest temporal and religious authority, imam-caliph al-Mustansir pre-empted potential religious discontent by stating his full confidence in the wisdom of the queen – wisdom of religious knowledge. Likewise, *da'i* al-Khattab, one of the leading religious figures at the time, floated the mystical idea of a body "envelope" to legitimize the queen's spiritual authority. Al-Khattab's reasoning was that when a woman had reached such a certain level of religious knowledge and wisdom, she was no longer a woman but a man, even if her body "envelope" was female (Traboulsi 2003). The point here is that not only did the imam-caliph and the *da'i* not oppose the queen's religious authority, they did their utmost to justify her religious elevation.

A politically savvy ruler, Queen Arwa exercised power judiciously and seized the moment to create the position of *da'i mutlaq*, the supreme missionary, at a time when the Isma'ilis faced a violent and divisive battle of succession. Her timely and decisive intervention insured the survival of the Tayyibi branch of Isma'ilism, that split again along the way but has survived to the present day – a branch of Islam that owes its existence to a woman. Notwithstanding religious hand-wringing and political opposition, then or later, Queen Arwa continued to rule effectively for seventy-one years, and to provide for her people, who gratefully called her "our Mistress."

In India under the Delhi Sultanate, likewise, we hear of no institutional religious opposition to Razia Sultan's rise to power or to her occupation of the throne – not until three hundred years later, as noted by Kumar (2010). Most conspicuous is the silence of the court historian and biographer Minhaj al-Din Siraj Juzjani (b. 1193), who also happened to be a judge and a religious leader. He registered no objections, personal or institutional, to Razia Sultan's ascension to power in 1236. His silence may be explained by the fact that he was in the service of the queen. The religious establishment, likewise, must have felt beholden to the queen, who as the commander-in-chief successfully squashed religious minorities' rebellions, rescuing the former from the latter's sustained harassments. Razia Sultan was eventually toppled, not by religious opposition or popular uprising, but by a racially motivated political-military elite, who felt threatened by her independent spirit and solid public support, and accused her of immodesty in appearance and immorality in her relationship with her Ethiopian slave-*amir* advisor.

We may entertain at least two interrelated reasons for the absence of overt religious objections to women's political authority at the time. First is the issue of dynastic succession and the role of the political-military elite in supporting or opposing a ruler. So long as dynastic rivalries were restricted to the ruling dynasty or the "professional rulers," as Barfield (2012) puts it, the people – including religious leaders – were neither in a position to object nor particularly keen to intervene. Although women's political leadership was a rarity, when it did occur, as I discuss in Chapters 3 and 4, it depended primarily on the pragmatics of political authority on the ground, on the moral authority and support of an influential dynastic patriarch and the dynamics of his patronage of the religious clerics and institutions. Religious institutions and personnel, though commanding popular authority, functioned under the authority and sponsorship of the sultan or the caliph. Thus, in the face of the latter's support for his daughter (or wife), little or no organized and institutional religious objections were raised in medieval Yemen or in India. Challenges to women's political authority came primarily from other loci of political power, namely the political or military elite, or other dynastic contenders.

Second, in the absence of a mass women's movement and organized political agitation for gender equality and fair political representation, women rulers did not seem to pose any long-term political threat to the male elite – they were few and far between. The basis of the legitimacy of the few women who did come to power was often a combination of dynastic ties, ethnicity, personal ambition and charisma, and the absence – or incompetence – of a male ruler. In both modern and medieval Muslim societies, politics and religion are mutually constitutive, though in medieval Yemen and India politics trumped religion. It was the commanding power of an autocratic sultan or caliph in favor of his daughter that silenced opposition to her.

Neither Queen Arwa nor Razia Sultan had a female mentor or role model – though Arwa seems to have been a keen observer of her formidable aunt/mother-in-law, herself a queen consort and power behind the throne. Both women are immortalized in their association with the Quranic Queen of Sheba. Queen Arwa became "the little Queen of Sheba" and Razia Sultan is celebrated as "Bilqis-i Jihan," Queen of the World. Coins were minted in their names and *khutba*s recited in their honor. Both queens had strong public power bases and were supported by their people, the faithful masses, which confounded the political elite, and might have earned them the latter's envy and wrath.

Modern Era: Constitutional Basis of Political Authority

Modern times brought about significant shifts in women's knowledge and sensibilities regarding legal equality, gender justice, and political leadership. Modernity also triggered religious revivalism and an ideological reversion to an idealized past and an "immutable" tradition. It involved the resurrection of contentious religious discourse against women's autonomy and authority – hence the invocation of the alleged Prophetic hadith against Benazir Bhutto and Megawati Sukarnoputri. "Modern conservative scholars," writes Fadel, "have managed to put forth revisionist interpretation of this hadith despite the fact that the weight of the tradition is against them" (2011, 35). Prior to the modern era and Muslim women's clamor for social and gender justice, in other words, the religious elite had little reason to invoke the hadith, "especially when nothing practical seemed to turn on that interpretation" (Fadel 2011, 35).

Muslim women's global mobilization and their demand for gender equality and political representation have threatened the foundations of the belief in the "divinely" ordained patriarchal hierarchy, in the "natural" differences between male and female, and the "inherent" intellectual inferiority of women. Presently, women's competition for power and political sway is all too real, infringing on the "sacral" monopoly of male traditional domination and privileges – hence the greater political/religious push for the application of the Prophetic hadith to deny women political representation. Further, as more and more women from all over the world, including the Muslim world, demand inclusion of their political rights in their constitutions, many once secular and presumably democratic male political elites have joined forces with religious elites to prevent women from assuming political leadership. Both Benazir Bhutto and Megawati faced opposition from secular and religious leaders who raised the banner of "Islam-in-danger" in their bids to become prime minister and president of their respective countries. Pointing to "woman's nature," they upheld women's unsuitability for leadership, presumably based on the immutable "divine law," which in their understanding favors men over women. As prime minister, Benazir Bhutto was challenged by Jamaat-e-Islami, a well-established religious party who invoked the alleged Prophetic hadith and objected to her leadership on the basis of her gender. The Pakistani political elite, meanwhile, found it expedient to remain silent. But Jamaat-e-Islami's suit was dismissed by the Pakistan's supreme court. The fact that such organized opposition was ultimately ineffectual – momentarily – in barring Benazir Bhutto in Pakistan and Megawati Sukarnoputri in Indonesia is not only indicative of the enduring power of dynastic ties, but also of the relative efficacy of both the law and the constitution *and* the power of the popular vote in these countries. Like their medieval sisters, Benazir and Megawati enjoyed huge popular support, and their gender was no barrier to achieving political authority.

What is noteworthy, however, is that the two democratically elected women leaders themselves and their followers did not make any overt references to Quranic revelations or to their legendary predecessor the Queen of Sheba to further buttress their political legitimacy, or to counter male opposition with their own political games. But perhaps they had fewer reasons than their predecessors, for they had the support of the constitution – at least theoretically – as well as the people and the popular vote.

Popular Support, People's Power

As I have already mentioned, history is written by men and more often than not women's accomplishments and activities, until very recently, were either not recorded or treated subjectively. But women are not the only forgotten or overlooked category. Ordinary people, the "commoners," have also been systematically overlooked, because the recorded history has recounted the life and legacy of the "higher classes" and of the success and failures of the political elite (MacFarlane 1977, 4). However, as we learned in the preceding chapters, all the women leaders mentioned in this book enjoyed the support of their people, at least a good number of them – and that also includes the Queen of Sheba. This is not wishful thinking or historically anachronistic. I want to underscore the biases of chroniclers and biographers who have overwhelmingly represented the perspective of the male political – and religious – elite, while systematically ignoring or downplaying the people and the followers. Benazir Bhutto and Megawati Sukarnoputri enjoyed overwhelming popular support, as did Queen Arwa of Yemen and Razia Sultan of India. Razia Sultan was helped to power by Muslim and Hindu supporters, and Megawati's honesty and unpretentious political campaigning – even her enigmatic silences – brought her enthusiastic supporters together at huge and unprecedented rallies. In the case of the military leadership of ʿAʾisha, the beloved wife of the Prophet Muhammad, although many opposed the civil war in the first Muslim community, she had the backing of the rank and file, in addition to that of many of the political elite.

The irony of the history is that the Persian Queen Purandokht, Queen Arwa, Razia Sultan, and Prime Minister Benazir Bhutto all proved to be generally more effective and far more popular leaders than their brothers or other male relatives who overthrew them and succeeded them to power.

Succession: Patriarchal Paradox?

One thing on which both Hindu and Muslim kings seem to have been in singular agreement was a general distrust of their sons ... Princes, like crabs, have a notorious tendency of eating up their begetters.

Brijbhushan (1990, 120)

Where princes did not necessarily vanquish their begetters, or where the orderly transition of power did not, as a rule, devolve through primogeniture, royal succession was often won through what has been called the "Law of Fratricide." In patrilineal, feudal, and tribal societies, male children are strongly desired, and South Asia provides a notorious example. Descent is traced through the male line, and power, prestige, and privilege automatically pass on to male descendants. Yet the father-son axis is potentially, and sometimes actually, a nexus of tension and rivalry, as the two men may in fact fear, resent, and seek to eliminate each other. History provides ample examples of fatal rivalries between imperial fathers and covetous sons who are in a structural position to dislodge the patriarch. The seventeenth-century Mughal emperor Aurangzeb provides a telling – and painful – example. He imprisoned his father, Shah Jahan – the patron saint of the Taj Mahal – in Agra Fort and killed all his brothers to claim the throne in Delhi. The Safavid Shah Tahmasp exiled his son Ismail II and kept him in a fortress far away from the capital city of Qazvin until his own death, whereupon Ismail returned and slaughtered all his brothers but one. Such filial rivalry is of course not unique to South Asia and the Muslim world. From the Greek tragedies to the Japanese visual representation of Shakespeare's *King Lear* by Akira Kurosawa in his movie *Ran*, to the tenth-century Iranian poet Ferdowsi's epic of Rostam and Sohrab, deadly filial rivalries abound (Haeri 2002, 38–39).

But where do women fit into this contentious patriarchal dynastic scheme? Whether on the throne or more often behind it, women have shown their ambition and determination to become involved in palace intrigues. Unlike their brothers, however, women's relations with their fathers seem to have been based on more solid emotional foundations and mutual affection – as demonstrated in the preceding chapters. The emotional bonds between a ruling patriarch and his daughter may not only be psychologically satisfying and unthreatening to the father but also politically advantageous to the daughter.[1] With fathers bestowing land and property on their daughters and lavishing them with enormous wealth, feudal royal princesses are potentially placed in positions to exercise authority and patronage. Benazir Bhutto of Pakistan and Sitt al-Mulk, the eleventh-century Fatimid princess who had the "ability and the means to change dynastic history," provide perfect examples. The patriarch's support bestows power and prestige on the daughter, facilitates her presence in the public domain, and legitimizes her political authority and activities. Further, his authority helps to silence her detractors – at least for a while – thus expediting her assent to the apex of the political hierarchy. At this juncture, a father's political popularity is symbolically transferred to the daughter, whose own charisma appeals strongly to the people, making her gender irrelevant – or even an asset – to the adoring public.

Succession, as I have argued, works through dynastic lines – whether orderly or contentious – and women are just as structurally situated to benefit from this connection as men, though usually not as frequently. Dynastic ties account for an important measure of the visibility and popularity of contenders to the "throne," be they male or female. The difference is that the devolution of power to a male descendant is expected, it is considered "normal" and "natural," while that to daughters is not. In Muslim-majority societies, domination is associated with masculinity and authority is culturally assumed to be a man's birthright. But where a son fails, a charismatic daughter or sister may gain the attention of the patriarch and quickly rise to power. The royal women whose lives I highlight in this book, did not just benefit from their dynastic ties. They also exhibited political talent and charisma, which distinguished them in the eye of their fathers – or husbands – who then favored them over their sons.

---

[1] See *Journal of Persianate Studies* 4 (2011), edited by Julia Clancy-Smith, for a series of articles on the father-daughter relationship.

Although hailing from different cultural traditions and historical periods, almost all the women in this book possess a distinguished genealogical pedigree and enjoyed the support of their powerful fathers or, less frequently, husbands. The Queen of Sheba also had divine support. Besides, the medieval biographers conjured up a royal father for her from whom she presumably inherited her throne. This cross-gender filial relationship, I have argued elsewhere (Haeri 2002), is one of the prevailing paradoxes of patriarchal authority. In light of the discussion in the previous chapters, I now think that a dynastic patriarch's support for his daughter's leadership is not so much paradoxical as practical, even logical, indicative of the fluidity of patriarchy and its pragmatic malleability.

Further, because of the changes in political structures and social landscapes in modern times, both Benazir Bhutto and Megawati had to stand for election, and both won by a large margin. Both had male and female siblings, none of whom possessed the same charisma or interest in politics. In Benazir Bhutto's case, some contend that we may never know how Mr. Bhutto would have treated his sons, particularly Murtaza, had he not been incarcerated and forced to send his sons away. Sanam Bhutto, however, hints at the emotional distance between her father and her elder brother, which she attributes to the patriarchal feudal culture of Sindh: "somehow the fathers are a little shy of their eldest son, a little formal. But with the girls, the relationship is very loving … My father adored my sister." Sanam Bhutto herself was not interested in politics, nor was Megawati's older brother. Megawati's younger sisters were just as concerned to preserve their father's legacy, but they seemed to be lacking in the political finesse and acumen that Megawati exhibited in her interactions and negotiations with the people and the political elite (McIntyre 2005).

Patterns of Women's Political Leadership

Elucidating form and patterns in the historical and ethnographic data presented in the preceding chapters, we may ask what patterns emerge from this focus on Muslim women rulers. Is their political authority different from that of men? Does it make any difference in the lives of their followers? To begin with, my sample of Muslim queens is too small to make any meaningful cross-gender comparison. Nonetheless, a few general observations are in order. The very fact that few women have become rulers and sovereigns in highly patriarchal Muslim societies makes them appear "exceptional." But we may yet learn how many women in reality did rule independently, or as regents or in conjunction with their husbands. More often than not, women rulers occupy a liminal space in the political structure and social hierarchy of their society: their leadership is contested, transitory, and ensconced between two male leaders.[2] Nonetheless, women rulers, like their male counterparts, are first and foremost ambitious politicians interested in the preservation of their authority and expansion of their power base, though their hold on power is more tenuous. Like their male counterparts, they occupy a contested position and their policies and activities are scrutinized from many vantage points. Seldom, if ever, have sovereign leaders had universal support or unanimous approval ratings, be they male or female, in medieval or modern times.

What also makes women's exalted positions stand out is not just their dynastic heritages but also their individual charisma and political acumen that enable them to ascend to power at times of social unrest and political crisis. Charisma, as argued by Lindholm (1990, 7) is above all a relationship, and in that sense people relate to women leaders as a primordial member of their family, a "mother," a "sister." Interestingly, though, it may be that situating Muslim women rulers as a member of the family is more a modern phenomenon, for neither Queen Arwa nor Razia Sultan were categorized in terms of kinship in relation to their followers. But then they did not need to campaign for the people's vote; they primarily drew their legitimacy from their dynastic partriarch. Women leaders appear less threatening than male rulers, who may have a propensity to exhibit autocratic tendencies. At the same time, women may strategically highlight or downplay aspects of their gender while trying to project images of power and authority.

Women rulers' exceptionality puts them in a precarious position *vis-à-vis* their governing authority. Unlike male leaders, women have fewer or no networks of female experts, nor do they generally have experienced mentors who can lend their advice and support. As more and more women are elected into political institutions, however, the pattern may be changing. We hear little about women leaders' relations with their mothers, maybe with the exception of Benazir Bhutto, who collaborated with her mother initially only to split from her when she threw her support behind Benazir's brother. Queen Arwa of Yemen perhaps provides a unique case, in the sense that she was in a position to observe her aunt/mother-in-law before taking the helm herself. All we know about Razia Sultan's mother is that she was a pious woman who lived in seclusion in the royal palace. Megawati's mother left the palace when her daughter was very young, thus thrusting her into the position of being a "mother" to her younger siblings, though in time she came to be distinguished as "ibu," the mother of the nation. In such situations,

---

[2] Perhaps with the exception of Sheikh Hasina and Khaleda Zia in Bangladesh, who succeed each other to the Premiership alternately.

women rulers were bound to rely on men, usually their husbands, who were either intellectually not on par with them, or might have coveted their positions, or assumed that they could rule from the shadows.

Tolerant of diversity and ethnicity, by and large the women rulers mentioned in this book tended to be more inclusive and generally more caring, partly perhaps due to their own political marginality. They connected more easily with people, often presenting themselves as members of the larger national community or "family." In the face of political oppression and upheaval in the aftermath of their fathers' forced removal from office, Benazir Bhutto and Megawati both emerged to revive the transition to democracy. Both women paid tribute to their fathers, yet shrewdly avoided their fathers' autocratic policies and discourse to adopt instead inclusivity and tolerance. All the women rulers mentioned in this book had to face disgruntled military personnel – one of the most fiercely masculine and conservative institutions of the patriarchy – who found it difficult to obey or yield to a female-led civilian government. Feeling threatened by the possibility of greater democratization and loosening of the total control of patriarchal institutions, the political, military, and religious elites closed ranks (Mernissi 1991, 140), aiming to intimidate, dominate, and limit women's opportunities to participate in political games of succession, be it dynastic or electoral. Presently, militarism and "fundamentalism" form the most formidable barriers to the institutionalization of women's political participation and leadership in the Muslim world.

Aware of the dangerous games of succession they have engaged in, modern women leaders follow a pattern of governance that is, in short, more democratic, more inclusive, and less violent (Bennett 2010). They pay greater attention to women's issues and do not suffer bouts of male chauvinism (Thompson 2003, 536), and they may in time usher in a "revolution of values," to quote Martin Luther King. Lest we forget, however, Queen Arwa did not hesitate to exact revenge, be it from her tribal rivals or members of her family.

By bringing together the life stories of Muslim women rulers from medieval to modern times and situating their ascent to power within their society's kinship, religious/legal, and sociopolitical contexts, I have aimed to highlight on-the-ground patterns of gender politics, alliances and rivalries, tensions and dynamics between different sources of authority from sacred to profane. Religion, as it may have become clear in the preceding pages, is not necessarily the main obstacle to Muslim women's political authority, contrary to the dominant assumptions, be it Orientalist or Islamist. It is rather the entrenched political power structure and patriarchal domination that in modern times has sought ever-closer cooperation with the increasingly puritanical religious leaders and institutions. Their appeal to the purported Prophetic hadith has historically depended on the presence or absence of women's mass movements, which pose a serious threat to male political elites' monopoly of power and authority. It is not only women's attempt to develop a feminist theology that concerns the religious leader; it is more the power of women's demand for gender equality and the collective power of their political agency that poses a real threat to traditional male domination and privileges. As pointed out in the Introduction, Muslim women scholars have brilliantly engaged with religious texts and offered novel reinterpretations.[3] Women's political authority, however, has been historically contested and violently resisted by the powers that be and by religious institutions. Gendering Islamic political history, this book points to a different horizon in search of women's leadership and political authority in Islamic societies – not only in religious dictums, but also in the pragmatics of existing and functioning political structures.

The trajectories of the lives, triumphs, travails, and governance of the unforgettable queens of Islam vary greatly, given the historical distance between them, as well as their individuality, authority, charisma, and the nature of their relationships to their fathers and followers – and the particularities of the society in which they lived. The brief ethnohistory of their lives and legacy highlights the indelible marks they have left on their societies and on the history of Muslim cultures. Their biographies – and those of powerful women behind the throne – also lay bare the politically motivated religious narrative of doom foretold should women gain political authority. As for Bilqis, the Queen of Sheba, God gave her a Mighty Throne – the seat of her authority – and medieval Muslim sources and the local imagination endowed the legendary queen with a powerful father whose mantle of political authority and leadership she assumed after his death. May God continue to empower women with mighty thrones!

[3] See fn. 3 in the Preface.

Bibliography

Abbas, Hassan. (2005). *Pakistan's Drift into Extremism: Allah, the Army, and America's War on Terror*. New York: Routledge.

Abbott, Nabia. (1941a). "Pre-Islamic Arab Queens." *The American Journal of Semitic Languages and Literatures*, 58 (1) (January): 1–22.

(1941b). "Women and the State on the Eve of Islam." *The American Journal of Semitic Languages and Literatures*, 58 (3) (July): 259–284.

(1942). *Aishah the Beloved of Mohammed*. Chicago: Chicago University Press; reprint, London: Al-Saqi Books, 1985.

(1946). *The Two Queens of Baghdad*. Illustrated. Chicago: Chicago University Press; reprint, London: Al Saqi Books, 1986.

Abou El Fadl, Khaled. (2001). *Speaking in God's Name: Islamic Law, Authority and Women*. Oxford: Oneworld.

Abu-Lughod, Lila. (2013). *Do Muslim Women Need Saving?* Cambridge, MA: Harvard University Press.

Afsaruddin, Asma. (2010a). "Early Women Exemplars and the Construction of Gendered Space." *Harem Histories: Envisioning Places and Living Spaces*, ed. Marilyn Booth. Durham, NC and London: Duke University Press, pp. 23–48.

(2010b). "Literature, Scholarship, and Piety: Negotiating Gender and Authority in the Medieval Muslim World." *Religion & Literature*, 42 (1): 111–131.

(2011). "'Ā'isha bt. Abī Bakr." *Encyclopaedia of Islam, THREE*, ed. Kate Fleet, Gudrun Krämer, Denis Matringe, John Nawas, and Everett Rowson, http://dx.doi.org/10.1163/1573-3912_ei3_COM_23459.

Ahmad, Akbar, and Gustaaf Houtman. (2008). "Benazir Bhutto (1953–2007): A Conversation with Akbar Ahmed." *Anthropology Today*, 24 (1) (February): 4–5.

Ahmad, Eqbal. (1998). "I Am the Destiny." *London Review of Books*, June 18, www.lrb.co.uk/v20/n12/eqbal-ahmad/i-am-the-destiny.

Ahmed, Leila. (1992). *Women and Gender in Islam: Historical Roots of a Modern Debate*. New Haven: Yale University Press.

Ahsan, Aitzaz. (2013). *The Indus Saga and the Making of Pakistan*, 23rd ed. Lahore: Jumhoori Publications.

Ali, Daud. (2014). "The Idea of Medieval in the Writing of South Asian History: Contexts, Methods and Politics." *Social History*, 39 (3): 382–407.

Ali, Kecia. (2014). *The Lives of Muhammad*. Cambridge, MA: Harvard University Press.

Allen, Brooke. (2016). *Benazir Bhutto: Favored Daughter*. New York: New Harvest.

Altorki, Soraya (ed.). (2015). *A Companion to the Anthropology of the Middle East*. Malden: John Wiley & Sons.

Amaria, Kainaz. (2011). "The 'Girl in the Blue Bra.'" *NPR*, December 21, www .npr.org/sections/pictureshow/2011/12/21/144098384/the-girl-in-the-blue-bra.

Amirell, Stefan. (2011). "The Blessings and Perils of Female Rule: New Perspectives on the Reigning Queens of Patani, c. 1584–1718." *Journal of Southeast Asian Studies*, 42 (2): 303–323.

Amirrezvani, Anita. (2012). *Equal of the Sun: A Novel*. New York: Scribner.

Amjad Ali, Charles. (1989). "Women and Leadership in Islam." *Al-Mushir (The Counselor)*, 31 (4): 123–139.

Anderson, Benedict. ([1965] 2009). *Mythology and the Tolerance of the Javanese*. Ithaca: Cornell University Press; reprint, Singapore: Equinox Publishing.

Anwar, Raja. (1997). *The Terrorist Prince: The Life and Death of Murtaza Bhutto*, tr. Khalid Hasan. New York: Verso.

Arberry, Arthur J. (1991). *The Koran Interpreted: A Translation*. Oxford: Oxford University Press.

Arimbi, Diah Ariani. (2009). *Reading Contemporary Indonesian Muslim Women Writers: Representation, Identity and Religion of Muslim Women in Indonesian Fiction*. Amsterdam: Amsterdam University Press.

Aspinall, Edward, and Greg Fealy. (2010). *Soeharto's New Order and its Legacy: Essays in Honour of Harold Crouch*. Canberra: The Australian National University.

Athar Ali, M. (2012). "Raḍiyya." *Encyclopedia of Islam, Second Edition*, ed. P. Bearman, Th. Bianquis, C. E. Bosworth, E. van Donzel, and W. P. Heinrichs, http://dx.doi.org/10.1163/1573-3912_islam_SIM_6172.

Auer, Blain Howard. (2009). "Symbols of Authority: Religion, Islamic Legitimacy, and Historiography of the Sultans of Delhi." Unpublished Ph.D. thesis, Harvard University, Cambridge, MA.

Ayalon, D. (2012). "Amīr Akhūr." *Encyclopaedia of Islam, Second Edition*, ed. P. Bearman, Th. Bianquis, C. E. Bosworth, E. van Donzel, and W. P. Heinrichs, http://dx.doi.org/10.1163/1573-3912_islam_SIM_0610.

Ayyad, Essam S. (2013). "The House of the Prophet or the Mosque of the Prophet?" *Journal of Islamic Studies*, 24 (3): 273–334.

Barfield, Thomas. (2012). *Afghanistan: A Cultural and Political History*. Princeton: Princeton University Press.

Barlas, Asma. (2006). "Women's Reading of the Quran." *The Cambridge Companion to the Quran*, ed. Jane McAuliffe. Cambridge, Cambridge University Press, 255–271.

Bashir, Tariq. (2014). "The Story of Al-Zulfiqar." *The Friday Times*, October 31, www.thefridaytimes.com/tft/the-story-of-al-zulfiqar.

Bazmee Ansari, A. S. (2012). "Iltutmish." *Encyclopedia of Islam, Second Edition*, ed. P. Bearman, Th. Bianquis, C. E. Bosworth, E. van Donzel, and W. P. Heinrichs, http://dx.doi.org/10.1163/1573-3912_islam_SIM_3542.

Beard, Mary. (2017). *Women and Power: A Manifesto*. New York: Liveright.

Bennett, Clinton. (2010). *Muslim Women of Power: Gender, Politics and Culture in Islam*. New York: Continuum.

Bennett Jones, Owen. (2017). "Benazir Bhutto Assassination: How Pakistan Covered up Killing." *BBC News*, www.bbc.com/news/world-asia-42409374.

Berger, Marilyn. (2008). "Suharto Dies at 86; Indonesian Dictator Brought Order and Bloodshed." *The New York Times*, January 28, www.nytimes.co m/2008/01/28/world/asia/28suharto.html.

Bevin, Mark. (1999). "Foucault and Critique: Deploying Agency against Autonomy." *Political Theory*, 27 (1): 65–84.

Bhatia, Shyam. (2008). *Goodbye Shahzadi: A Political Biography of Benazir Bhutto*. New Delhi: Lotus Roli Collection.

Bhutto, Benazir. (1989). *Daughter of the East*. London: Mandarin Paperbacks
   (2008). *Reconciliation: Islam, Democracy, and the West*. New York: Harper Perennial.

Bhutto, Fatima. (2010). *Songs of Blood and Sword: A Daughter's Memoir*. New York: Nation Books.

Blois, de François. (1983–84). "Proceedings of the Seventeenth Seminar for Arabian Studies Held in London on 13th–15th July." *Arabian Studies*, 14: 1–7.

Booth, Marilyn. (2001). *May Her Likes Be Multiplied: Biography and Gender in Egypt*. Berkeley: University of California Press.
   (2010). *Harem Histories: Envisioning Places and Living Spaces*. Durham, NC and London: Duke University Press.
   (2015). *Classes of Ladies of Cloistered Spaces: Writing Feminist History through Biography in Fin-de-Siècle Egypt*. Edinburgh: Edinburgh University Press.

Bowley, Graham, and Salman Masood. (2007). "Date for Bhutto's Return Is Set." *The New York Times*, September 14, www.nytimes.com/2007/09/14/w orld/asia/14cnd-bhutto.html.

Brijbhushan, Jamila. (1990). *Sultan Razia, Her Life and Times: A Reappraisal*. New Delhi: Manohar Publications.

Britannica Academic, S. V. (2015). "Malik-Shāh." *Encyclopaedia Britannica*, www .britannica.com/biography/Malik-Shah.

Bromberger, Christian. (2007). "Hair: From the West to the Middle East through the Mediterranean." *The Journal of American Folklore*, 121 (482) (Fall): 379–399.

Brown, Jonathan A. C. (2018). *Hadith: Muhammad's Legacy in the Medieval and Modern World*. Rev. ed. Oxford: Oneworld.

Bukhari, Muhammad. *Sahih al-Bukhari*, https://sunnah.com/bukhari/92.

Bulliet, Richard. (2003). "Women and the Urban Religious Elite in the Pre-Mongol Period." *Women in Iran from the Rise of Islam to 1800*, ed. Guiti Nashat and Lois Beck. Urbana and Chicago: University of Illinois Press, pp. 68–79.

Burns, John F. (2007). "Benazir Bhutto, 54, Who Weathered Pakistan's Political Storm for 3 Decades, Dies." *The New York Times*,

December 28, www.nytimes.com/2007/12/28/world/asia/28bhutto.html?
    module=ConversationPiecesregion=Body&action=click&pgtype=article.
Calderini, Simonetta. (1993). " ʿĀlam al-din in Ismāʿīlism: World of Obedience or
    World of Immobility?" *Bulletin of the School of Oriental and African Studies*,
    56 (3): 459–469.
Calkins, Philip B. (1968). Review. *The Journal of Asian Studies*, 27 (4):
    906–908.
Campbell, Sandra. (2009). "Abdallah b. al-Zubayer." *Encyclopaedia of Islam*,
    THREE, ed. Kate Fleet, Gudrun Krämer, Denis Matringe, John Nawas, and
    Everett Rowson, http://dx.doi.org/10.1163/1573-3912_ei3_COM_22164.
Chakrabarty, Aditi. (2001). "Challenges before Megawati Sukarnoputri."
    Economic and Political Weekly, 36 (36): 3439–3441.
Chaumont, Louise. (1989). "Bōrān." *Encyclopaedia Iranica*, *Vol. 4, Fasc. 4*,
    p. 366, www.iranicaonline.org/articles/boran-pers.
Chittick, William C. (1995). "The Divine Roots of Human Love." *Journal of the
    Muhyiddin Ibn ʿArabi Society*, 17: 55–78, www.ibnarabisociety.org/articles/
    divinerootsoflove.html.
Clancy-Smith, Julia. (2011). "Introduction." *Journal of Persianate Studies*,
    4: 4–11.
Colmey, John, and David Liebhold. (1999). "The Family Firm." *Time Asia*,
    May 24, http://edition.cnn.com/ASIANOW/time/asia/magazine/1999/9905
    24/cover1.html.
Conrad, Peter. (2002). "I Am Not a Woman but a World." *Observer*, May 26,
    www.theguardian.com/theobserver/2002/may/26/features.review7.
Cortese, Delia. (2019). "A Patron of Men: Sitt al-Mulk and the Military at the
    Fatimid Court." *Guerre et paix dans le Proche-Orient médiéval (xe–xve siècle)*,
    ed. Mathieu Eychenne, Stéphane Pradines, and Abbès Zouache. Cairo:
    Institut français d'archéologie orientale, pp. 217–234.
Cortese, Delia, and Simonetta Calderini. (2007). *Women and the Fatimids in the
    World of Islam*. Edinburgh: Edinburgh University Press.
Coulter-Harris, Deborah M. (2013). *The Queen of Sheba: Legend, Literature and
    Lore*. Jefferson: McFarland & Company.
Daftary, Farhad. (1993). "A Major Schism in the Early Ismāʿīlī Movement."
    Studia Islamica, 77: 123–139
    (1999). "Sayyida Hurra: The Ismaʿili Sulayhid Queen of Yemen." *Becoming
    Visible: Medieval Islamic Women in Historiography and History*, ed. Gavin
    R. G. Hambly. New York: St. Martin's Press, pp. 117–130.
    (2006). *Ismailis in Medieval Muslim Societies: A Historical Introduction to an
    Islamic Community*. New York: I. B. Tauris.
Dagg, Christopher J. (2007). "The 2004 Elections in Indonesia: Political Reform
    and Democratization." *Asia Pacific Viewpoint*, 48 (1) (April): 47–59.
Dalkesen, Nilgun. (2007). "Gender Roles and Women's Status in Central Asia and
    Anatolia between the Thirteenth and Sixteenth Centuries." Unpublished
    Ph.D. thesis, Middle East Technical University, Ankara, Turkey.
Darke, Hubert (tr.). (1978). *The Book of Government or Rules for Kings: The Siyar
    al-Muluk or Siyasat-Nama of Nizam al-Mulk*. London and New York:
    Routledge, 2006.

Daryaee, Touraj. (1999). "The Coinage of Queen Boran and Its Significance for Late Sasanian Imperial Ideology." *Bulletin of Asia Institute*, 13: 77–81.

Davis, Dick (tr.). (1984). *The Conference of the Birds*. London: Penguin Books.
  (tr.). (2004). *Sunset of Empire: Stories from the Shahnameh of Ferdowsi*, 3 Vols. Washington, DC: Mage.

Dawn. (2013). "Kayani Doubted Taliban Killed Benazir, Recounts UN Investigator," August 21, www.dawn.com/news/1037227.

Delaney, Carol. (1994). "Untangling the Meanings of Hair in Turkish Society." *Anthropological Quarterly*, 67 (4) (October): 159–172.

Donner, Fred. (1981). *The Early Islamic Conquests*. Princeton: Princeton University Press.

Duindam, Jeroen. (2016). *Dynasties: A Global History of Power, 1300–1800*. Cambridge: Cambridge University Press.

Duncan, David J. (2000). "Scholarly Views of Shajarat al-Durr: A Need for Consensus." *Arab Studies Quarterly*, 22 (Winter): 51–69, https://hbr.org/20 07/09/women-and-the-labyrinth-of-leadership.

Eagly, Alice H., and Linda L. Carli. (2012). "Women and the Labyrinth of Leadership." *Contemporary Issues in Leadership*, ed. William E. Rosenbach, Robert L. Taylor, and Mark A. Youndt, 7th ed. New York: Routledge, pp. 147–162.

Eisenstadt, S. N. (2000). "Multiple Modernities." *Daedalus*, 129 (Winter): 1–29.

Eklof, Stefan. (1999). *Indonesian Politics in Crisis: The Long Fall of Suharto 1996–98*. Nordic Institute of Asian Studies (NIAS). Copenhagen: NIAS Press.

Elias, Jamal J. (2009). "Prophecy, Power and Propriety: The Encounter of Solomon and the Queen of Sheba." *Journal of Qur'anic Studies*, 11 (1): 57–74.
  (2014). *Encyclopaedia of the Qur'ān*, ed. Jane Dammen McAuliffe, http://dx.doi .org/10.1163/1875-3922_q3_EQSIM_00420.

Elkin, Benjamin. (1968). *The Wisest Man in the World*. New York: Parents' Magazine Press.

Elsadda, Hoda. (2001). "Discourses on Women's Biographies and Cultural Identity: Twentieth-Century Representations of the Life of ʿAʾisha bint Abi Bakr." *Feminist Studies*, 27 (1): 37–64.

El-Zain, Amira. (2009). *Islam, Arabs, and Intelligent World of the Jinn*. Syracuse: Syracuse University Press.

Emrani, Haleh. (2009). "Like Father, Like Daughter: Late Sasanian Imperial Ideology and the Rise of Boron to Power." *e-Sasanika*, www.academia.edu/ 3428780/Like_Father_Like_Daughter_Late_Sasanian_Imperial_Ideology_ and_the_Rise_of_B%C5%8Dr%C4%81n_to_Power.

Fadel, Mohammad. (2011). "Is Historicism a Viable Strategy for Islamic Law Reform? The Case of 'Never Shall a Folk Prosper Who Have Appointed a Woman to Rule Them.'" *Islamic Law and Society*, 18 (2): 131–176.

Fic, Victor M. (2003), *From Majapahit and Sukuh to Megawati Sukarnoputri: Continuity and Change in Pluralism of Religion, Culture, Politics of Indonesia from the XV to the XXI Century*. New Delhi: Abhinav Publications.

Firhanusa, Arief. (2014). "Mbak Tutut versus Mbak Mega." January 4, www.kompasiana.com/firhanusa/mbak-tutut-versus-mbak-mega_55283a17f17e61612a8b45cf.

Fletcher, Joseph. (1979–80). "Turco-Mongolian Monarchic Tradition in the Ottoman Empire," *Harvard Ukrainian Studies*, 3 (4), Part 1: Eucharisterion, Essays Presented to Omeljan Pritsak on his Sixtieth Birthday by his Colleagues and Students, pp. 236–251.

Foucault, Michele. (1982). "The Subject and Power." *Critical Inquiry*, 8 (4): 777–795.

Frank, Stewart H. (1994). *Honor*. Chicago: University of Chicago Press.

Gabbay, Alyssa. (2011). "In Reality a Man: Sultan Iltutmish, his Daughter, Raziya, and Gender Ambiguity in Thirteenth Century Northern India." *Journal of Persianate Studies*, 4, pp. 45–63.

(2014). "Fatima's Khutba: An Early Case of Female Religious Authority in Islam." Paper presented at ʿAlimahs, Muhadditha, and Mujtahids: The Past and Present of Female Religious Authority in Shiʿi Islam, Princeton University, March 6–8.

Ghirshman, R. (1954). *Iran*. New York: Penguin.

Gholsorkhi, Shohreh. (1995). "Pari Khan Khanum: A Masterful Safavid Princess." *Iranian Studies*, 28 (3–4) (Summer–Autumn): 143–56.

Gibb, H. A. R. (tr.) (1971). *The Travels of Ibn Battuta, A. D. 1325–1354*. Vol. 3. Cambridge: Cambridge University Press.

Gibb, H. A. R., and P. Kraus. (2015). "Al-Mustansir." *Encyclopedia of Islam, Second Edition*, ed. P. Bearman, Th. Bianquis, C. E. Bosworth, E. van Donzel, and W. P. Heinrichs, http://dx.doi.org/10.1163/9789004206106_eifo_COM_0817.

Gignoux, Ph. (1987). "Āzarmīgduxt." *Iranica Online*, Vol. 3, fasc. 2, p. 190, http://iranicaonline.org/articles/azarmigduxt

Gleave, Robert M. (2008). "Ali b. Abi Talib." *Encyclopaedia of Islam, THREE*, ed. Kate Fleet, Gudrun Krämer, Denis Matringe, John Nawas, and Everett Rowson, https://referenceworks.brillonline.com/entries/encyclopaedia-of-islam-3/ali-b-abi-talib-COM_26324.

Goody, Jack. (1966). *Succession to High Office*. Cambridge: Cambridge University Press.

Goody, Jack, and Tambiah, S. J. (1973). *Bridewealth and Dowry*. London: Cambridge University Press.

Habibullah, A. B. M. (1976). *The Foundation of Muslim Rule in India*, 3rd rev. ed. Allahabad: Central Book Depot.

Haeri, Shahla. (1995). "Politics of Dishonor: Rape and Power in Pakistan," *Faith & Freedom: Women's Human Rights in the Muslim World*, ed. M. Afkhami. London: I. B. Tauris, pp. 161–174.

(2002). *No Shame for the Sun: Lives of Professional Pakistani Women*. Syracuse: Syracuse University Press.

(2010). "Challenging Marriage Laws in Contemporary Shi'i Iran." *Contending Modernities*, December 14, https://sites.nd.edu/contendingmodernities/2010/12/14/challenging-the-shii-concept-of-marriage-in-todays-iran/.

(2014). *Law of Desire: Temporary Marriage in Shi'i Iran.* Rev. ed. Syracuse: Syracuse University Press.

(2015). "In the Garden of the Sexes: Of Men, Women, Gaze and Hair," *A Companion to the Anthropology of the Middle East*, ed. Soraya Altorki. Malden: John Wiley & Sons, pp. 151–171.

Haider, Najam. (2008). "On Lunatics and Loving Sons: A Textual Study of the Mamlūk Treatment of al-Hākim." *Journal of the Royal Asiatic Society*, 18 (2) (April): 109–139.

(2014). "Camel, Battle of the." *Encyclopedia of Islam, THREE*, ed. Kate Fleet, Gudrun Krämer, Denis Matringe, John Nawas, and Everett Rowson, http://dx.doi.org/10.1163/1573-3912_ei3_COM_25465.

Haleem, M. A. S. Abdel. (2004). *The Qur'an.* Oxford: Oxford University Press.

Hallpike, C. R. (1969). "Social Hair." *Man*, 4 (2) (June): 256–264.

Halm, Heinz. (2014). "Fāṭimids." *Encyclopedia of Islam, THREE*, ed. Kate Fleet, Gudrun Krämer, Denis Matringe, John Nawas, and Everett Rowson, http://dx.doi.org/10.1163/1573-3912_ei3_COM_27045.

Hambly, Gavin R. G. (1972). "Who Were the *Chihalgani*, the Forty Slaves of Sultan Shams al-Din Iltutmish of Delhi?" *Iran*, (10): 57–62.

(ed.). (1999). *Women in the Medieval Islamic World (The New Middle Ages).* New York: St. Martin's Press.

Hamdani, Abbas. (1950). "The Sira of al-Mu'ayyad fi'd-Din ash-Shirazi." PhD thesis, University of London.

(1974). "The *Dā'ī* Hātim ibn Ibrāhīm al-Hāmidī (d. 596 H./1199 A. D.)." *Oriens*, 23/24: 258–300.

Hamdani, Husain F. (1931). *The Life and Times of Queen Saiyidah Arwā the Sulaihid of the Yemen: A Lecture Given to the Royal Central Asian Society on Wednesday, April 29, 1931.* London: Royal Central Asian Society.

(1932). "The History of the Ismā'īlī Da'wat and its Literature during the Last Phase of the Fāṭimid Empire." *The Journal of the Royal Asiatic Society of Great Britain and Ireland*, 1: 126–136.

(1934). "The Letters of al-Mustanṣir Bi'llāh." *Bulletin of the School of Oriental Studies*, 7 (2): 307–324.

Haqqani, Husain. (2005). *Pakistan: Between Mosque and Military.* Washington, DC: Carnegie Endowment of International Peace.

Haryoguritno, Haryono. (2002). "Why Watch *Wayang?*" *Puppet Theater in Contemporary Indonesia: New Approaches to Performance Events*, ed. Jan Mrazek. Ann Arbor: University of Michigan Press, pp. 362–365.

Hassan, Riffat. (1985). "Made from Adam's Rib: The Woman's Creation Question." *Al-Mushir Theological Journal of the Christian Study Centre, Rawalpindi, Pakistan*, 124–156.

Hefner, Robert W. (2000). *Civil Islam: Muslims and Democratization in Indonesia.* Princeton University Press.

Hegland, Mary Elaine. (2014). *Days of Revolution: Political Unrest in an Iranian Village.* Stanford: Stanford University Press

Hinds, Martin. (1972). "The Murder of the Caliph 'Uthman." *International Journal of Middle East Studies*, 3: 150–469.

Hodgson, Marshal G. S. (1977). *The Venture of Islam: Conscience and History in a World Civilization the Classical Age of Islam*. Vol. 1. Chicago and London: The University of Chicago Press.

Hughes, Libby. (2000). *Benazir Bhutto: From Prison to Prime Minister*. Minneapolis: Dillon Press.

Husain, Agha Mahdi (tr. and ed.) (1938?). *Futuhus Salatin or Shah Namah-i Hind of Islami*, Vol. 2. New York: Asia Publishing House.

Ibrahim, Zakyi. (2016). "Reinstating the Queens: Reassessing the Hadith on Women's Political Leadership." *The American Journal of Islamic Social Sciences*, 33 (2): v–x.

Ishwari Prasad, M. A. (1931). *A Short History of Muslim Rule in India: From the Conquest of Islam to the Death of Aurangzeb*, 2nd ed. Allahabad: The Indian Press.

Jackson, Peter. (1999). "Sultan Radiyya Bint Iltutmish." *Becoming Visible: Medieval Islamic Women in Historiography and History*, ed. Gavin R. G. Hambly. New York: St. Martin's Press, pp. 180–197.

Jalalzai, Farida. (2008). "Women Rule: Shattering the Executive Glass Ceiling." *Politics and Gender*, (4): 205–231.

Jeenah, Na'eem. (2006). "Bilqis – a Qur'anic Model for Leadership and for Islamic Feminists" *Journal for Semitics*, 13 (1): 47–58.

Joseph, Suad, and Susan Slyomovics (eds.) (2001). *Women and Power in the Middle East*. Philadelphia: University of Pennsylvania Press.

Juzjani, Minhaj-al-Din Siraj. (1963). *Tabaqat-i Nasiri*, ed. A. Habibi, 2 vols. Kabul: Kabul University.

Kadivar, Mohsen. (2011). "Revisiting Women's Rights in Islam." *Gender and Equality in Muslim Family Law: Justice and Ethics in the Islamic Legal Tradition*, eds. Mir-Hosseini, Ziba, Kari Vogt, Lena Larsen, and Christian Moe. London: I. B. Tauris, pp. 213–236.

Kaplan, Robert D. (1989). "How Zia's Death Helped the U.S." *The New York Times*, August 23, www.nytimes.com/1989/08/23/opinion/how-zia-s-death-helped-the-us.html.

Katuzian, Homa. (2013). *Iran: A Beginner's Guide*. London: Oneworld.

Kay, Henry Cassels (tr.) (1892). *Yaman: Its Early Medieval History*. London: Edward Arnold Publisher to the India Office.

Keshavarz, Fatemeh. (2003). "Taming the Unruly King: Nizami's Shirin as Lover and Educator." *Women in Iran from the Rise of Islam to 1800*, eds. Guity Nashat, Lois Beck. Champaign: Illinois University Press. pp. 186–205.

Keyes, Charles F. (2002). "Weber and Anthropology." *Annual Review of Anthropology*, 31: 233–255.

Khan, Sher Banu A. L. (2009). Rule behind the Silk Curtain: The Sultanahs of Aceh 1641–1699. PhD thesis, Queen Mary, University of London.

Khan, Hussain. (1983). "The Institution of Iqṭāʿ and Its Impact on Muslim Rule in India." *Islamic Studies*, 22 (1) (Spring): 1–9.

Khan, Shaharyar M. (2000). *The Begums of Bhopal: A Dynasty of Women Rulers in Raj India*. London and New York: I. B. Tauris.

Kipling, Rudyard. (1907). "The Butterfly that Stamped." *Just So Stories*. New York: Doubleday, pp. 225–248.

Koltuv, Barbara Black. (1993). *Solomon and Sheba: Inner Marriage and Individuation*. York Beach: Nicolas-Hayes.

Krismantari, Ika. (2016). "Ken Setiawan: Moving Forward While Honoring the Past." *The Jakarta Post*, April 21, www.thejakartapost.com/news/2016/04/2 1/ken-setiawan-moving-forward-while-honoring-past.html.

Kumar, Sunil. (2007). "Raziyya Sultan." *Encyclopedia of Women in World History*, ed. Bonnie C. Wade. New York: Oxford University Press, pp. 585–586.

(2010). *Emergence of the Delhi Sultanate: AD 1192–1286*. New Delhi: Permanent Black.

Lal, Chaman. (2018). "The Only Empress of India Was a Muslim." *National Herald*, January 20, www.nationalheraldindia.com/people/the-only-empres s-of-india-was-a-muslim.

Lal, Ruby. (2018). *Empress: The Astonishing Reign of Nur Jahan*. New York: W. W. Norton & Company.

Lambert-Hurley, Siobhan. (2008). *A Princess's Pilgrimage: Nawab Sikandar Begum's A Pilgrimage to Mecca*. Bloomington and Indianapolis: Indiana University Press.

Lambton, Ann S. K. (1984). "The Dilemma of Government in Islamic Persia: The *Siyāsat-nāma* of Niẓām al-Mulk." *Iran*, 22: 55–66.

(1987). "Mongol Fiscal Administration in Persia (Part II)." *Studia Islamica*, 65: 97–123.

Lane-Poole, Stanley. (1903). *Medieval India under Mohammedan Rule, 712–1764*. New York: G. P. Putnam's Sons.

Lanti, Irman G. (2002). "Indonesia: The Year of Continuing Turbulence." *Southeast Asian Affairs*: 111–129.

Lassner, Jacob. (1993). *Demonizing the Queen of Sheba: Boundaries of Gender and Culture, in Postbiblical Judaism and Medieval Islam*. Chicago: University of Chicago Press.

Lawrence, Bruce. (2006). *The Qur'an: A Biography*. New York: Grove Press.

Leach, Edmund. (1958). "Magical Hair." *The Journal of the Royal Anthropological Institute of Great Britain and Ireland*, 82 (2) (July–December): 147–164.

Lewis, Franklin D. (2007). *Rumi – Past and Present, East and West: The Life, Teachings, and Poetry of Jalâl al-Din Rumi*. Oxford: A Oneworld Book.

Lieven, Anatol. (2011). *Pakistan: A Hard Country*. New York: Public Affairs.

Lindholm, Charles. (1990). *Charisma*. Boston: Blackwell.

Lone, Maliha. (2016). "Memorable Romance: Zulfiqar Ali Bhutto & Husna Sheikh." *Good Times*, March 17, www.goodtimes.com.pk/memorable-roma nce-zulfiqar-ali-bhutto-husna-sheikh/.

MacFarlane, Alan. (1977). "Historical Anthropology (Frazer lecture)." *Cambridge Anthropology*, 3 (3): 1–16.

Madelung, Wilferd. (2014). "Ṭalḥa b. ʿUbaydallāh." *Encyclopaedia of Islam, THREE*, ed. Kate Fleet, Gudrun Krämer, Denis Matringe, John Nawas, and Everett Rowson, http://dx.doi.org/10.1163/1573-3912_ei3_COM_24765.

Masood, Salman. (2012). "Top Pakistani Generals and Judges Trade Barbs." *The New York Times*, November 5, www.nytimes.com/2012/11/06/world/asia/pakistan-generals-and-judges-trade-barbs.html.

Mayer, Farhana. (2000). "Book Review: *The Women of Madina* by Muhammad ibn Sa'd (trans. Aisha Bewley)." *Journal of Qur'anic Studies*, 2 (1): 139–141.

McCarthy, Terry. (1999). "What Makes Megawati Run," Monday, June 21, http://content.time.com/time/world/article/0,8599,2054237,00.html.

McIntyre, Agnus. (2005). *The Indonesian Presidency: The Shift from Personal toward Constitutional Rule*. Oxford: Rowman and Littlefield.

Mernissi, Fatima. (1991). *The Veil and the Male Elite: A Feminist Interpretation of Women's Rights in Islam*, tr. Mary Jo Lakeland. Abingdon: Perseus Books.

  (1994). *Hidden from History: Forgotten Queens of Islam*, tr. Mary Jo Lakeland. Lahore: ASR.

Mobasher, Anilla. (2013). "Revisiting the Delhi Sultans in the Light of their Patronage Towards Learning and Education." *Journal of Research Society of Pakistan*, 50 (2) (December): 103–137

Moddares Sadiqi, Ja'far. (1994). *Tafsir-i Tabari: Qisseha*. Tehran: Nashr-e Markazi.

Monter, William. (2012). *The Rise of Female Kings in Europe, 1300–1800*. New Haven: Yale University Press.

Morony, Michael. (1986). "'ARAB ii. Arab Conquest of Iran." *Encyclopaedia Iranica*, Vol. 2, fasc. 2, ed. Ehsan Yarshater. New York: Columbia University Press, pp. 203–210, www.iranicaonline.org/articles/arab-ii.

  (2012). "Kisrā." *Encyclopaedia of Islam, Second Edition*, ed. P. Bearman, Th. Bianquis, C. E. Bosworth, E. van Donzel, and W. P. Heinrichs, http://dx.doi.org/10.1163/1573-3912_islam_SIM_4407.

Mottahedeh, Roy P. (1980). *Loyalty and Leadership in an Early Islamic Society*. London: I. B. Tauris.

  (2013). "The Eastern Travels of Solomon: Reimagining Persepolis and the Iranian Past." *Law and Tradition in Classical Islamic Thought: Studies in Honor of Professor Hossein Modarressi*, eds. Michael Cook, Najam Haider, Intisar Rabb, and Asma Sayeed. New York: Palgrave Macmillan. pp. 247–267.

Mrazek, Jan (ed.). (2002). *Puppet Theater in Contemporary Indonesia: New Approaches to Performance Events*. Ann Arbor: University of Michigan, Centers for South and Southeast Asian Studies.

Munoz, Heraldo. (2014). *Getting Away with Murder: Benazir Bhutto's Assassination and the Politics of Pakistan*. New York: W. W. Norton & Company.

Nadvi, Muhammad Akram. (2013). *Al-Muhaddithat: The Women Scholars in Islam*, 2nd rev. ed. Oxford: Interface Publications.

Nanda, Serena. (1999). *Neither Man nor Woman: The Hijras of India*, 2nd ed. Belmont: Wadsworth.

Nashat, Guity, and Lois Beck (eds.). (2003). *Women in Iran from the Rise of Islam to 1800*. Urbana and Chicago: University of Illinois Press.

Nasir, Abbas. (2015). "The Legacy of Pakistan's Loved and Loathed Hamid Gul." *Al Jazeera*, August 17, www.aljazeera.com/indepth/opinion/2015/08/legacy-pakistan-loved-loathed-hamid-gul-150817114006616.html.

Nasri, Musa. (1947). *Nasr va sharh-i Masnavi, Maulana Jalal ud-Din Muhammad Balkhi Rumi.* Vol. 1 & 4. Tehran: Kalale Khavar.

Newman, Saul. (2004). "The Place of Power in Political Discourse." *International Political Science Review/Revue internationale de science politique*, 25 (2) (April): 139–157.

Niaz, Anjum. (2018). "A Tale without an End." *Tribune*, July 1, https://tribune.com.pk/story/1746732/6-tale-without-end/.

Noorani, Muhammad Ahmad. (2005). "Mehsud Had Told Benazir: 'I Am Not Your Enemy,'" www.pakpassion.net/ppforum/showthread.php?51283-Mehsud-had-told-Benazir-%91I-am-not-your-enemy%92#4hB6mxf0mLXJQ1Mw.99.

Nurjanah, Siti. (2013). "Finally, Megawati's Silence Truly Is Golden," *iKNOW Politics*, http://iknowpolitics.org/en/knowledge-library/editorial-opinion-piece-blog-post/finally-megawati%E2%80%99s-silence-truly-golden.

Omidsalar, Mahmoud. (2003). "Waters and Women, Maidens and Might: The Passage of Royal Authority in the Shahnama." *Women in Iran from the Rise of Islam to 1800*. eds. Guity Nashat and Lois Beck. Urbana and Chicago: University of Illinois Press, pp. 170–185.

Ortner, Sherry. (2006). *Anthropology and Social Theory: Culture, Power, and the Acting Subject*. Durham, NC and London: Duke University Press.

Paracha, Nadeem F. (2010). "Al-Zulfikar: The Unsaid Story." *Dawn*, April 9, www.dawn.com/news/813223.

(2017). "The Tragic Life & Death of Shahnawaz Bhutto." *Dawn*, July 23, https://dailytimes.com.pk/735/the-tragic-life-death-of-shahnawaz-bhutto/.

Parsadust, Manučehr. (2009). "Parikān Kānom." *Encyclopaedia Iranica*, http://iranicaonline.org/articles/parikan-kanom-1548-1578.

Parvizi, Rasoul. (1969). "Malakeh Saba and Her Beauty" [Malakeh Saba va zibaihayash]. *Wahid*, 62–63: 162–168.

Pausacker, Helen, (2002). "Limbuk Breaks Out: Changes in the Portrayal of Women Clown Servants and the Inner Court Scene over the Twentieth Century." *Puppet Theater in Contemporary Indonesia: New Approaches to Performance Events*, ed. Jan Mrazek. Ann Arbor: University of Michigan, Centers for South and Southeast Asian Studies. pp. 284–295.

(2004). "Presidents as *Punakawan*: Portrayal of National Leaders as Clown-Servants in Central Javanese *Wayang*." *Journal of Southeast Asian Studies*, 35 (2) (June): 213–233.

Paydarfard, Arezou. (2011). "The Hoopoe's Symbolic Image in Islamic/Iranian Arts and Literature" [Naqsh-I namadin-i hudhud dar adabiyyat va honar-i islami-i Iran]. *Ketab-i Mah-i Honar*, 160: 58–65.

Peirce, Leslie P. (1993). *The Imperial Harem: Women and Sovereignty in the Ottoman Empire*. New York and Oxford: Oxford University Press.

(2017). *Empress of the East: How a European Slave Girl Became Queen of the Ottoman Empire*. New York: Basic Books.

Pickthal, Mohammad Marmaduke (tr.) (n.d.) *The Meaning of the Glorious Quran*. New York: Mentor Book.

Poonawala, Ismail K. (1977). *Bibliography of Ismāʿīlī Literature*. Malibu: Undena Publications.

Pourshariati, Parvaneh. (2008). *The Decline and Fall of the Sasanian Empire*. London: I. B. Tauris.

Preckel, Claudia. (2011). "Bhopāl." *Encyclopaedia of Islam, THREE*, ed. Kate Fleet, Gudrun Krämer, Denis Matringe, John Nawas, and Everett Rowson, http://dx.doi.org/10.1163/1573-3912_ei3_COM_23872.

Rahnema, Zainalabedin (tr.). (1974). *Quran-i Majid*, Vol. 3. Tehran: Oqaf Foundation.

Rashid, Ahmad. (2001). *Taliban: Militant Islam, Oil, and Fundamentalism in Central Asia*. New Haven: Yale Nota Bene.

Raverty, H. G. (tr.) (1970). *Tabakat-i Nasiri: A General History of the Muhammad and Dynasties of Asia, Including Hindustan; from A. H. 194 (810 A. D.) to A. H. 658 (1260 A. D.)*, Vol. 1. New Delhi: Oriental Books Reprint Corporation.

Rentse, Anker. (1947). "The Origin of the *Wayang* Theatre (Shadow Play)." *Journal of the Malayan Branch of the Royal Asiatic Society*, 20 (1) (June): 12–15.

Ricklefs, M. C. (2006). "The Birth of the *Abangan*." *Bijdragen Tot De Taal, Land-En Volkenkunde*, 162 (1): 35–55.

Robinson, Kathryn. (2009). *Gender, Islam and Democracy in Indonesia*. London and New York: Routledge.

Rose, Jenny. (1999). "Three Queens, Two Wives, and a Goddess: Roles and Images of Women in Sasanian Iran." *Women in the Medieval Islamic World*, ed. Gavin R. G. Hambly. New York: St. Martin's Press, pp. 29–54.

Rowson, E. K. (1991). "The Effeminates of Early Medina." *Journal of the American Oriental Society*, 3 (4) (October–December): 671–693.

Rumi, Maulana Jalal ud-Din Muhammad Balkhi. *Masnavi*. See Nasri Saleh, Alodwan Khalil. (2004). *Early Islamic Coinage in North India (800 A. D. to 1500 A.D. and its Impact in Tourism ISLA University*. Gujarat: The Maharaja Sayajirao University of Baroda.

Sattari, Jalal. (2002). *Rereading the Story of Solomon and Bilqis* [Pazhuhishi dar Qissih Sulaiman va Bilqis]. Tehran: Markaz.

Saunders, John Joseph. (1978). *A History of Medieval Islam*. New York: Routledge.

Sayyid, Ayman Fuad. (2002). *The Fatimids and Their Successors in Yaman: The History of an Islamic Community*. London: I. B. Tauris.

Schimmel, Annemari. (1992). *Islam: An Introduction*. New York: State University of New York Press.

(1997). *My Soul Is a Woman: The Feminine in Islam*, tr. Susan H. Ray. New York: Continuum.

Sethi, Najam. (1993). "Murtaza Bhutto's Dilemma." Editorial, *The Friday Times*, August 26.

Shafqat, Saeed. (2009). "Pakistan: Militancy, the Transition to Democracy and Future Relations with the United States." *Journal of International Affairs*, 63 (1): Pakistan and Afghanistan: Domestic Pressures and Regional Threats (Fall/Winter): 89–109.

Shahbazi, Shapur A. (1990). "Sasanian Dynasty." *Encyclopaedia Iranica, Vol. 4, Fasc. 6*, http://iranicaonline.org/articles/byzantine-iranian-relations.

Shakir, Mohammed. (1999). Sirat al-Mulik al-Mukarram: An Edition and Study. PhD thesis, School of Oriental and African Studies, University of London.

Shyrock, Andrew. (1997). *Nationalism and the Genealogical Imagination: Oral History and Textual Authority in Tribal Jordan.* Berkeley: University of California Press.

Siddique, Kaukab. (1986). *The Struggle of Muslim Women.* Delhi: Amer Society for Education.

Silberman, Lou H. (1974). "The Queen of Sheba in Judaic Tradition." *Solomon and Sheba*, ed. James B. Pritchard. London: Phaidon Press, pp. 65–84.

Singh, Surinder. (2010). "Sunil Kumar, The Emergence of the Delhi Sultanate, 1192–1286." *The Medieval History Journal*, 13 (1): 131–151.

Sirmed, Mirvi. (2011). "Remembering Benazir Bhutto, Personally!" *Daily Times*, December 25, https://dailytimes.com.pk/110697/remembering-benazir-bhutto-personally/.

Smith, Anthony L. (2003). "Indonesia in 2002: Megawati's Way." *Southeast Asian Affairs*, 54 (5): 97–116.

Smith, G. R. (2015). "Ṣulayḥids." *Encyclopaedia of Islam, Second Edition*, ed. P. Bearman, Th. Bianquis, C. E. Bosworth, E. van Donzel, and W. P. Heinrichs, https://referenceworks.brillonline.com/entries/encyclopaedia-of-islam-2/*-COM_1112.

Soesastro, Hadi, Anthony L. Smith, and Mui Ling Han. (2002). *Governance in Indonesia: Challenges Facing the Megawati Presidency*, muse.jhu.edu/chapter/698292.

Soleimani, Muhammad Husain. (2010). "Pari Khan Khanum: A Powerful Safavid Politician" [Pari Khan Khanum: zan-i siasatmadar va qodratmand-i Safavi], http://khiaraji.blogfa.com/post-492.aspx.

Southern, Pat. (2008). *Empress Zenobia Palmyra's Rebel Queen.* London: Hambledon Continuum.

Spellberg, D. A. (1994). *Politics, Gender, and the Islamic Past: The Legacy of Aisha Bint Abi Bakr.* New York: Columbia University Press.

Spuler, B. (2011). "Ābeš Kātūn." *Encyclopaedia Iranica*, Vol. 1, fasc. 2, ed. Ehsan Yarshater. New York: Columbia University Press, p. 210, www.iranicaonline.org/articles/abes-katun-salghurid-ruler-of-fars-1263-84-daughter-of-atabeg-sad-ii.

Stern, S. M. (1950). "The Epistle of the Fatimid Caliph al-Āmir (al-Hidāya al-Āmiriyya): Its Date and Its Purpose." *The Journal of the Royal Asiatic Society of Great Britain and Ireland*, 1 (2) (April): 20–31.

  (1951). "The Succession to the Fatimid Imam al-Āmir, the Claims of the Later Fatimids to the Imamate, and the Rise of Ṭayyibī Ismailism." *Oriens*, 4 (2) (December 31): 193–255.

Stowasser, Barbara F. (1994). *Women in the Quran, Tradition, Interpretation.* New York: Oxford University Press.

Strothmann, R., and G. R., Smith. (2012). "Nadjāḥids." *Encyclopaedia of Islam, Second Edition*, ed. P. Bearman, Th. Bianquis, C. E. Bosworth,

E. van Donzel, and W. P. Heinrichs, http://dx.doi.org/10.1163/1573-3912_islam_SIM_5717.

Suvorova, Anna. (2015). *Benazir Bhutto: A Multidimensional Portrait*. Karachi: Oxford University Press.

Szuppe, Maria. (1999). "'The Jewels of Wonder': Learned Ladies and Princess Politicians in the Provinces of Early Safavid Iran." *Becoming Visible: Medieval Islamic Women in Historiography and History*, ed. Gavin R. G. Hambly. New York: St. Martin's Press, pp. 325–345.

(2003). "Status, Knowledge, and Politics: Women in Sixteenth Century Safavid Iran." *Women in Iran from the Rise of Islam to 1800*, eds. Guity Nashat and Lois Beck. Chicago: University of Illinois Press, pp. 140–169.

Tabari, Abu Ja'far Muhammad ibn Jarir. (1989). *The History of al-Tabari*. Vol. 30: *The Abbasid Caliphate in Equilibrium*, tr. Clifford Edmund Bosworth. Albany: State University of New York Press.

(1990). *The History of al-Tabari*. Vol. 15: *The Crisis of the Early Caliphate*, tr. Stephen Humphreys. Albany: State University of New York Press.

(1991). *The History of al-Tabari*, Vol. 3: *The Children of Israel*, tr. by William M. Brinner. Albany: State University of New York Press.

(1997). *The History of al-Tabari*. Vol. 16: *The Community Divided*, tr. Adrian Brockett. Albany: State University of New York Press.

(1999). *The History of al-Tabari*. Vol. 5: *The Sasanids, the Byzantines, the Lakhmids, and Yemen*, tr Clifford Edmund Bosworth. Albany: State University of New York Press.

Tabataba'i, Sayyid Muhammad Husayn. (1977). *Shi'ite Islam*, tr. Seyyed Hossein Nasr. Albany: State University of New York Press.

Tambiah, S. J. (1973). "Dowry and Bridewealth, and the Property Rights of Women in South Asia." *Bridewealth and Dowry*, ed. Jack Goody and S. J. Tambiah. London: Cambridge University Press, pp. 59–169.

Tayob, Abdelkader I. (1999). "Ṭabarī on the Companions of the Prophet: Moral and Political Contours in Islamic Historical Writing." *Journal of the American Oriental Society*, 119 (2) (April–June): 203–210.

Tha'labi, Abu Ishaq Ahmad Ibn Muhammed Ibn Ibrahim. (2002). *'Arā'is al-majālis fi qiṣaṣ al-anbiyā' (Lives of the Prophets)*, tr. William M. Brinner. Brill: Leiden.

Thompson, Eric C. (1999). "Indonesia in Transition: The 1999 Presidential Elections." *National Bureau of Asian Research (NBR), Policy Report*, 9 (December): 1–17.

Thompson, Mark R. (2002–2003). "Female Leadership of Democratic Transitions in Asia." *Pacific Affairs*, 75 (Winter): 535–555.

Tottoli, Roberto. (2009). "Āṣaf b. Barakhyā." in *Encyclopaedia of Islam, THREE*, ed. Kate Fleet, Gudrun Krämer, Denis Matringe, John Nawas, and Everett Rowson, https://referenceworks.brillonline.com/entries/encyclopae dia-of-islam-3/asaf-b-barakhya-COM_22814.

Traboulsi, Samer. (2003). "The Queen Was Actually a Man: Arwā Bint Aḥmad and the Politics of Religion." *Arabica*, 50 (1) (January): 96–108.

Ullendorff, Edward. (1974). "The Queen of Sheba in Ethiopian Tradition." *Solomon and Sheba*, ed. James B. Pritchard. London: Phaidon Press, pp. 104–114.

Usha, A. S. (ed.) (1948). *Isami's Futuhus-Salatin*. Madras: University of Madras.

Van Beek, Gus W. (1974). "The Land of Sheba." *Solomon and Sheba*, ed. James B. Pritchard. London: Phaidon Press, pp. 40–64.

Van Doorn-Harder, Nelly. (2002). "The Indonesian Islamic Debate on a Woman President." *Sojourn*, 17 (2): 164–190.

Van Gelder, Geert Jan. (2013). "How the Queen of Sheba Became Queen." *Classical Arabic Literature: A Library of Arabic Literature Anthology*. New York: New York University Press, pp. 117–118.

Varisco, Daniel. M. (2018). *Culture Still Matters: Notes from the Field*. Leiden: Brill.

Wadud, Amina. (1999). *Qur'an and Women: Rereading the Sacred Text from a Woman's Perspective*. New York: Oxford University Press.

(2006). *Inside the Gender Jihad: Women's Reform in Islam*. London: Oneworld.

Walker, Ashley Manjarrez, and Michael A. Sells. (1999). "The Wiles of Women and Performative Intertextuality: ʿAʾisha, the Hadith of the Slander, and the Sura of Yusuf." *Journal of Arabic Literature*, 30 (1): 55–77.

Walker, Paul. (1993). "The Ismaili Daʿwa in the Reign of the Fatimid Caliph Al-Ḥākim." *Journal of the American Research Center in Egypt*, 30: 161–182.

(1995). "Succession to Rule in the Shiʿite Caliphate." *Journal of the American Research Center in Egypt*, 32: 239–264.

(2002). *Exploring an Islamic Empire: Fatimid History and Its Sources*. London: I. B. Tauris.

(2011a). "The Responsibilities of Political Office in a Shiʿi Caliphate and the Delineation of Public Duties under the Fatimids." *Islam, the State, and Political Authority: Medieval Issues and Modern Concerns*, ed. Asma Afsaruddin. New York: Palgrave Macmillan, pp. 93–110.

(2011b). "The Fatimid Caliph al-ʿAziz and his Daughter Sitt al-Mulk: A Case of Delayed but Eventual Succession to Rule by a Woman." *Journal of Persianate Studies*, 4: 30–44.

(2016). "Al-Āmir bi-Aḥkām Allāh." *Encyclopaedia of Islam, THREE*, ed. Kate Fleet, Gudrun Krämer, Denis Matringe, John Nawas, and Everett Rowson, https://referenceworks.brillonline.com/entries/encyclopaedia-of-islam-3/al-amir-bi-ahkam-allah-COM_23060.

(2017). "Al-Afḍal b. Badr al-Jamālī." *Encyclopaedia of Islam, THREE*, ed. Kate Fleet, Gudrun Krämer, Denis Matringe, John Nawas, and Everett Rowson, http://dx.doi.org/10.1163/1573-3912_ei3_SIM_0189.

Wallis Budge, E. A. (tr.). (1932). *The Kebra Nagast: The Queen of Sheba and Her Only Son Menyelek*. London: Forgotten Books.

Walthall, Anne (ed.) (2008). *Servants of the Dynasty: Place of Women in World History*. Berkeley: University of California Press.

Warburton, David. (1993). "A Campaign Rally in Sanʿa." *Middle East Report*, 185 (November December): 12.

Watt, Montgomery W. (1974). "The Queen of Sheba in Islamic Tradition." *Solomon and Sheba*, ed. James B. Pritchard. London: Phaidon Press, pp. 85–103.

Weintraub, Andrew N. (2004). *Power Plays: Wayang Golek Puppet Theater of West Java*. Center for International Studies, Ohio University. ProQuest Ebook Central. http://ebookcentral.proquest.com/lib/bu/detail.action?docID=3026832.

Wibisono, A. T. Mahendra. (2009). Political Elites and Foreign Policy: Democratization in Indonesia. PhD thesis, Graduate School of Legal Studies, Faculty of Law, Leiden University.

Wira, Ni Nyoman. (2017). "Megawati Hosts Play to Mark 70th Birthday." *The Jakarta Post*, January 24, www.thejakartapost.com/life/2017/01/24/mega wati-hosts-play-to-mark-70th-birthday.html.

Wolfe, Eric R. (2001). *Pathways of Power: Building an Anthropology of the Modern World*. Berkeley: University of California Press.

Yazigi, Maya. (2005). "Some Accounts of Women Delegates to Caliph Muʿāwiya: Political Significance." *Arabica*, 52 (3) (July): 437–449.

Yousafzai, Malala, and Christina Lamb. (2013). *The Girl Who Stood up for Education and Was Shot by the Taliban*. London: Orion Books.

Yulianti-Farid, Lily. (2015). Representations of Gender in the Indonesian Media: A Case Study of the Coverage of Megawati Sukarnoputri's Presidential Campaigns in 1999, 2004 and 2009 Elections. PhD thesis, University of Melbourne, Parkville, Victoria.

Yusofi, Golam-Hosayn. (1989). "Belqīs." *Encyclopaedia Iranica*, Vol. 4, fasc. 2, pp. 129–130, http://iranicaonline.org/articles/belqis-the-queen-of-sheba-sa ba-whose-meetings-with-solomon-solayman-are-a-favorite-theme-in-per sian-and-arabic-literat.

Yusuf Ali, Abdallah. (1946). *The Holy Quran: Translation and Commentary*. Birmingham: Islamic Propagation Centre International.

Zafarullah Khan, Mohammad. (1981). *The Quran*. Richmond: Curzon Press.

Zakaria, Rafiq. (1989). *The Trial of Benazir: Insight into the Status of Woman in Islam*. Bombay: Popular Prakashan.

(1966). *Razia: Queen of India*. Delhi: Oxford University Press.

Zarrinkoub, Abdolhossein. (1957). *Two Centuries of Silence* [Do Qarn Sokūt]. Tehran: Amirkabir.

Ziv, Daniel. (2001). "Populist Perceptions and Perceptions of Populism in Indonesia: The Case of Megawati Soekarnoputri." *South East Asia Research*, 9 (1) (Special issue, March): 73–88.

Index